To Kimlan

To Andrew and Elena

Contents at a Glance

Contents

About the Authors

 **SING LI** is a systems consultant, avid open source developer, and active freelance writer. With over two decades of industry experience, Sing is a regular contributor to printed magazines and e-zines. His book credits include *Beginning JavaServer Pages*; *Professional Apache Tomcat 5*; *Pro JSP, Third Edition*; *Early Adopter JXTA*; *Professional Jini*; and numerous others. He is an active evangelist of the mobile Java, VON, and P2P evolutions.

 **JONATHAN KNUDSEN** is the author of several other Java books, including *Learning Java*, *Java 2D Graphics*, and *Java Cryptography*. He is also the author of *The Unofficial Guide to LEGO® MINDSTORMS™ Robots*, but, sadly, was unable to parlay that success into a full-time career. Jonathan has written numerous articles about Java and a few about LEGO robots as well. He is the father of four children and enjoys bicycling and playing the piano. For more information, see http://jonathanknudsen.com/.

About the Technical Reviewer

CHRIS HARRIS is from Dublin, Ireland, and received his BS in mathematics and computer science from the Dublin Institute of Technology. He has worked in the wireless software industry for over five years, and has been involved in the Java Community Process as both Specification Lead and Expert Group member. He currently works in Bordeaux, France, for a mobile games company called IN-FUSIO.

Acknowledgments

Thanks to everyone at Apress for putting this book together on such a tight schedule. Thanks to Gary Cornell for the initial vision for such a title. To Steve Anglin, for putting the two of us together on this fascinating project. To Laura Cheu, our "sleepless in New York" project manager, without whom this book would have never wrapped in time. To Ami Knox, our tireless copy editor, for transforming the techno-babble we churn out into understandable material. Last but not least, a hearty thanks to Chris Harris, for keeping us honest with his excellent technical review.

Preface

This book describes how to program mobile telephones, pagers, PDAs, and other small devices using Java technology. It is about the Mobile Information Device Profile (MIDP), which is part of the Java 2 Platform, Micro Edition (J2ME). It is concise and complete, describing all of MIDP as well as moving into several exciting advanced concepts such as 3D graphics and cryptography.

This third edition covers MIDP 2.0, and has been updated to track the Java Technology for the Wireless Industry (JTWI 1.0) de facto standard. Every chapter has been revised and meticulously updated, and four completely new chapters have been added.

Who Are You?

You're probably reading this book because you're excited about building wireless applications with Java. This book is aimed at people who already have experience programming in Java. At a minimum, you should understand the Java programming language and the fundamentals of object-oriented programming. Some chapters delve into subjects that in themselves could occupy entire books. These chapters include suggested reading if you want to get up to speed on a particular subject.

If you are unfamiliar with Java, we suggest you read an introductory book or take a course. *Learning Java, Second Edition* (O'Reilly 2002) is a good introduction to Java for programmers who are already experienced in another language such as C or C++.

The Structure of This Book

This book is organized into 18 chapters and one appendix. There are basically three sections. The first two chapters are introductory material. Chapters 3 through 16 provide complete coverage of the MIDP 2.0 and JTWI 1.0 APIs, together with some of the most frequently used optional APIs available. Chapters 17 and 18 cover advanced topics. The complete breakdown of chapters is listed here:

- Chapter 1, "Introduction," provides context and motivation for the rest of the book. J2ME is explained in detail, gradually zooming in to MIDP and JTWI.

- Chapter 2, "Building MIDlets," is intended to be a teaser. It includes an example application that allows you to look up the definitions of words over the Internet using any MIDP device. Along the way you'll learn a lot about developing applications for the MIDP platform.

- Chapter 3, "All About MIDlets," goes into detail about the life cycle and packaging of MIDP applications. It includes coverage of the MIDP 2.0 security architecture.

- Chapter 4, "Almost the Same Old Stuff," describes the pieces of the MIDP API that will be familiar to Java programmers.

- Chapter 5, "Creating a User Interface," is the first of a handful of chapters devoted to MIDP's user interface packages. It provides an overview of MIDP's user interface package and goes into detail about the simple visual components.

- Chapter 6, "Lists and Forms," picks up where Chapter 5 left off, describing MIDP's advanced user interface components.

- Chapter 7, "Custom Items," shows how to create your own form items in MIDP.

- Chapter 8, "Persistent Storage I: MIDP Record Store," describes MIDP's mechanism for storing data.

- Chapter 9, "Persistent Storage II: File Connection and PIM API," covers popular optional APIs for accessing a device's file system, memory cards, and PIM features.

- Chapter 10, "Connecting to the World," contains all the juicy details about how MIDP applications can send and receive data over the Internet.

- Chapter 11, "Wireless Messaging API," describes WMA, a standard component of JTWI 1.0 that can be used to access the rich Short Message Service (SMS) and Cell Broadcast Service (CBS) available on modern wireless networks. This chapter also covers the new WMA 2.0 for working with audio and video messages via Multimedia Messaging Service (MMS).

- Chapter 12, "Bluetooth and OBEX," provides coverage of the optional API that enables communications of devices through Bluetooth radio Personal Area Networks (PANs) and infrared links.

- Chapter 13, "Programming a Custom User Interface," describes the low-level API that can be used for specialized application user interfaces.

- Chapter 14, "The Game API," describes MIDP 2.0 features for creating games, including sprites and tiled layers.

- Chapter 15, "3D Graphics," includes a hands-on, easy-to-understand introduction to the Mobile 3D Graphics optional API (M3G), providing you with a springboard into the fascinating world of 3D graphics programming on mobile devices.

- Chapter 16, "Sound, Music, and Video: MMAPI," is about MIDP 2.0 new multimedia capabilities and the Mobile Media API (MMAPI). You'll learn how to produce simple tones, play sampled audio data, play MP3 music, play video clips, and even take snapshots with your camera-phone.

- Chapter 17, "Performance Tuning," describes techniques for coping with the limited resources that are available on small devices.

- Chapter 18, "Protecting Network Data," discusses how to protect valuable data on the insecure Internet. It includes two sample applications that demonstrate cryptographic techniques for protecting data.

- Finally, the appendix, "MIDP API Reference," contains an API reference for the classes and interfaces that make up MIDP. The method signatures for the public API of each class and interface are listed for handy quick reference.

CHAPTER 1

■ ■ ■

Introduction

Java 2 Platform, Micro Edition (J2ME) is the second revolution in Java's short history. When Java was introduced in 1995, it looked like the future of computing was in *applets*, small programs that could be downloaded and run on demand. A slow Internet and a restrictive all-or-nothing sandbox security model accounted for the initially slow adoption of applets. Java, as a platform, really took off with the advent of *servlets*, Java programs that run on a server (offering a modular and efficient replacement for the vulnerable CGI). Java further expanded into the server side of things, eventually picking up the moniker of Java 2 Platform, Enterprise Edition (J2EE). This was the first revolution, the blitz of server-side Java.

The second revolution is the explosion of small-device Java, and it's happening now. The market for small devices is expanding rapidly, and Java is important for two reasons. First, developers can write code and have it run on dozens of small devices, without change. Second, Java has important safety features for downloadable code.

Understanding J2ME

J2ME isn't a specific piece of software or specification. All it means is Java for small devices. Small devices range in size from pagers, mobile phones, and personal digital assistants (PDAs) all the way up to things like set-top boxes that are just shy of being desktop PCs.

J2ME is divided into *configurations*, *profiles*, and *optional APIs*, which provide specific information about APIs and different families of devices. A configuration is designed for a specific kind of device based on memory constraints and processor power. It specifies a Java Virtual Machine (JVM) that can be easily ported to devices supporting the configuration. It also specifies a strict subset of the Java 2 Platform, Standard Edition (J2SE) APIs that will be used on the platform, as well as additional APIs that may be necessary. Device manufacturers are responsible for porting a specific configuration to their devices.

Profiles are more specific than configurations. A profile is based on a configuration and provides additional APIs, such as user interface, persistent storage, and whatever else is necessary to develop running applications for the device.

Optional APIs define specific additional functionality that may be included in a particular configuration (or profile). The whole caboodle—configuration, profile, and optional APIs—that is implemented on a device is called a *stack*. For example, a possible future device stack might be CLDC/MIDP + Mobile Media API. See the section "Platform Standardization" later in this chapter for information on JSR 185, which defines a standard J2ME stack.

Currently, there are a handful of configurations and profiles; the most relevant ones for J2ME developers are illustrated in Figure 1-1.

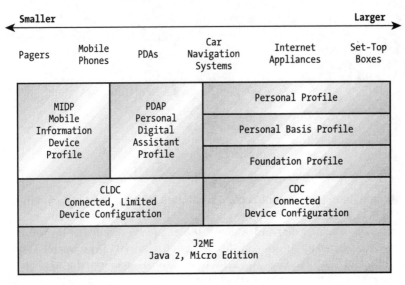

Figure 1-1. *Common J2ME profiles and configurations*

To give you a flavor of what's happening in the J2ME world, Table 1-1 shows some of the configurations, profiles, and optional APIs that are available and under development. This is not a comprehensive list; for more information, check out the JCP web site at http://jcp.org/.

Table 1-1. *J2ME Configurations, Profiles, and Optional APIs*

Configurations

JSR	Name	URL
30	Connected, Limited Device Configuration (CLDC) 1.0	http://jcp.org/jsr/detail/30.jsp
139	Connected, Limited Device Configuration (CLDC) 1.1	http://jcp.org/jsr/detail/139.jsp
36	Connected Device Configuration 1.0.1	http://jcp.org/jsr/detail/36.jsp
218	Connected Device Configuration 1.1	http://jcp.org/jsr/detail/218.jsp

Table 1-1. *J2ME Configurations, Profiles, and Optional APIs (Continued)*

Configurations

JSR	Name	URL

Profiles

JSR	Name	URL
37	Mobile Information Device Profile 1.0	http://jcp.org/jsr/detail/37.jsp
118	Mobile Information Device Profile 2.0	http://jcp.org/jsr/detail/118.jsp
75	PDA Profile 1.0	http://jcp.org/jsr/detail/75.jsp
46	Foundation Profile 1.0	http://jcp.org/jsr/detail/46.jsp
129	Personal Basis Profile 1.0	http://jcp.org/jsr/detail/129.jsp
62	Personal Profile 1.0	http://jcp.org/jsr/detail/62.jsp
219	Foundation Profile 1.1	http://jcp.org/jsr/detail/219.jsp
217	Personal Basis Profile 1.1	http://jcp.org/jsr/detail/217.jsp

Optional APIs

JSR	Name	URL
75	PDA Optional Packages for J2ME	http://jcp.org/jsr/detail/75.jsp
82	Java APIs for Bluetooth	http://jcp.org/jsr/detail/82.jsp
135	Mobile Media API 1.1	http://jcp.org/jsr/detail/135.jsp
184	Mobile 3D Graphics	http://jsp.org/jsr/detail/184.jsp
179	Location API for J2ME	http://jcp.org/jsr/detail/179.jsp
120	Wireless Messaging API 1.0	http://jcp.org/jsr/detail/120.jsp
205	Wireless Messaging API 2.0	http://jcp.org/jsr/detail/205.jsp
172	J2ME Web Services APIs	http://jsp.org/jsr/detail/172.jsp
66	RMI Optional Package	http://jcp.org/jsr/detail/66.jsp

Configurations

A configuration specifies a JVM and some set of core APIs for a specific family of devices. Currently there are two: the Connected Device Configuration (CDC) and the Connected, Limited Device Configuration (CLDC).

The configurations and profiles of J2ME are generally described in terms of their memory capacity. Usually a minimum amount of ROM and RAM is specified. For small devices, it makes sense to think in terms of volatile and nonvolatile memory. The nonvolatile memory is capable of keeping its contents intact as the device is turned on and off. ROM is one type, but nonvolatile memory could also be flash memory or battery-backed RAM. Volatile memory is essentially workspace and does not maintain its contents when the device is turned off.

Connected Device Configuration

A connected device has, at a minimum, 512KB of read-only memory (ROM), 256KB of random access memory (RAM), and some kind of network connection. The CDC is designed for devices like television set-top boxes, car navigation systems, and high-end PDAs. The CDC specifies that a full JVM (as defined in the Java Virtual Machine Specification, 2nd edition) must be supported.

CDC is developed under the Java Community Process. For more information on the CDC, see http://java.sun.com/products/cdc/. A Linux reference of CDC 1.0.1 implementation is available now.

CDC 1.0.1 is the basis of the Personal Profile 1.0 stack. The Personal Profile 1.0 increases the minimum memory requirement to 2.5MB of ROM and 1MB of RAM, and requires a robust network plus a GUI display on a device that can support applet display.

CDC 1.1 is currently a work in progress. It will support Personal Profile 1.1 and will introduce APIs to match the level of JDK 1.4.

Connected, Limited Device Configuration

CLDC is the configuration that interests us, because it encompasses mobile phones, pagers, PDAs, and other devices of similar size. CLDC is aimed at smaller devices than those targeted by the CDC. The name CLDC appropriately describes these devices, having limited display, limited memory, limited CPU power, limited display size, limited input, limited battery life, and limited network connection.

The CLDC is designed for devices with 160KB to 512KB of total memory, including a minimum of 160KB of ROM and 32KB of RAM available for the Java platform. If you've ever watched J2SE gobble up tens of megabytes of memory on your desktop computer, you'll appreciate the challenge of J2ME. The "Connected" simply refers to a network connection that tends to be intermittent and probably not very fast. (Most mobile telephones, for example, typically achieve data rates of 9.6Kbps.) These connections also tend to be costly, typically billed by the data packets exchanged. Between the high cost and intermittent slow network connection, applications designed in the CLDC space should be very sparing with the use of the network connection.

The reference implementation of the CLDC is based around a small JVM called the KVM (J2ME licensees may use this KVM or implement their own as long as it conforms to the CLDC). Its name comes from the fact that it is a JVM whose size is measured in kilobytes rather than megabytes. While the CLDC is a specifications document, the KVM refers to a specific piece of software.[1] Because of its small size, the KVM can't do everything a JVM does in the J2SE world.

- Native methods cannot be added at runtime. All native functionality is built into the KVM.

- The KVM only includes a subset of the standard bytecode verifier. This means that the task of verifying classes is split between the CLDC device and some external mechanism. This has serious security implications, as we'll discuss later.

---

1. The KVM was originally part of the Spotless system, a Sun research project. See http://www.sun.com/research/spotless/.

You can find more information at the CLDC home page, `http://java.sun.com/products/cldc/`. Most deployed devices implement CLDC 1.0, but CLDC 1.1 devices are making their way onto the market as this is written. CLDC 1.1 includes enhancements to CLDC 1.0, including support for floating-point data types.

Profiles

A profile is layered on top of a configuration, adding the APIs and specifications necessary to develop applications for a specific family of devices.

Current Profiles

Several different profiles are being developed under the Java Community Process. Table 1-1 (shown earlier) provides a bird's-eye view.

The Foundation Profile is a specification for devices that can support a rich networked J2ME environment. It does not support a user interface; other profiles can be layered on top of the Foundation Profile to add user interface support and other functionality.

Layered on top of the Foundation Profile are the Personal Basis Profile and the Personal Profile. The combination of CDC + Foundation Profile + Personal Basis Profile + Personal Profile is designed as the next generation of the PersonalJava application runtime environment (see `http://java.sun.com/products/personaljava/`). As such, the Personal Profile has the specific goal of backward compatibility with previous versions of PersonalJava.

The PDA Profile (PDAP), which is built on CLDC, is designed for palmtop devices with a minimum of 512KB combined ROM and RAM (and a maximum of 16MB). It sits midway between the Mobile Information Device Profile (MIDP) and the Personal Profile. It includes an application model based on MIDlets but uses a subset of the J2SE Abstract Windowing Toolkit (AWT) for graphic user interface. Although the PDAP specification is nearly finished, to our knowledge no hardware manufacturer has announced that it will be implementing PDAP. The J2ME world currently is covered by MIDP on the small end and Personal Profile on the higher end.

Mobile Information Device Profile

The focus of this book is the Mobile Information Device Profile (MIDP). According to the MIDP 2.0 specification (JSR-118), a Mobile Information Device has the following characteristics:

- A minimum of 256KB of ROM for the MIDP implementation (this is in addition to the requirements of the CLDC)

- A minimum of 128KB of RAM for the Java runtime heap

- A minimum of 8KB of nonvolatile writable memory for persistent data

- A screen of at least 96×54 pixels

- Some capacity for input, either by keypad, keyboard, or touch screen

- Two-way network connection, possibly intermittent

Try to imagine a device that might be a MIDP device: mobile telephones and advanced pagers are right in the groove, but entry-level PDAs could also fit this description.

More information about MIDP, including a link to the official specification document, is at `http://java.sun.com/products/midp/`. There are two versions of MIDP: MIDP 1.0 (JSR 37), and MIDP 2.0 (JSR 118). Many of the currently available devices do and all new devices will support MIDP 2.0. Compared to MIDP 1.0, MIDP 2.0 features a number of enhancements, including support for multimedia, a new game user interface API, support for HTTPS connection, and other features. Most importantly, MIDP 2.0 is fully backward compatible with MIDP 1.0.

JTWI standard compliance requires devices to implement MIDP 2.0 (see the next section on platform standardization). This book's focus will be on MIDP 2.0. We will mention MIDP 1.0 differences only in this introductory chapter as background information.

Platform Standardization

Given the profusion of configurations, profiles, and especially optional APIs, how do you know what APIs are likely to be available on typical devices? Sun's answer to this question is JSR 185 (`http://jcp.org/jsr/detail/185.jsp`), impressively titled *Java Technology for the Wireless Industry (JTWI)*. This specification attempts to standardize software stacks to bring coherence to the J2ME world. A reference implementation and a TCK (kit for compatibility testing) of the unified software stack is made available with JSR 185. As currently specified, a JTWI-compliant device must have MIDP 2.0 with CLDC 1.0 (or CLDC 1.1), and must support WMA (Wireless Messaging API 1.0—JSR 120). If a JTWI device exposes video or audio API to applications, they must also support Mobile Media API (MMAPI).

In the next generation of J2ME, a concept called Building Blocks is supposed to replace configurations and profiles. A *Building Block* is just some subset of a J2SE API. For example, one Building Block might be created from a subset of the J2SE `java.io` package. Conceptually, a Building Block represents a smaller chunk of information than a configuration. Profiles, then, will be built on top of a set of Building Blocks rather than a configuration.

The definition of Building Blocks is a JSR, which is briefly described here: `http://jcp.org/jsr/detail/68.jsp`. Progress on JSR 68 has been extremely slow since its creation in June 2000.

In the meantime, JSR 185 will better serve as a standardization platform. Recently, leveraging the success of the JTWI work, Nokia and Vodafone have submitted a new JSR, JSR-248: Mobile Service Architecture for CDC (`http://jcp.org/jsr/detail/248.jsp`), to define a new standard software stack for the next generation of mobile devices.

Anatomy of MIDP Applications

The APIs available to a MIDP application come from packages in both CLDC and MIDP, as shown in Figure 1-2. Packages marked with a + are new in CLDC 1.1 and MIDP 2.0.

CLDC defines a core of APIs, mostly taken from the J2SE world. These include fundamental language classes in `java.lang`, stream classes from `java.io`, and simple collections from `java.util`. CLDC also specifies a generalized network API in `javax.microedition.io`.

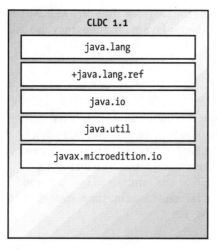
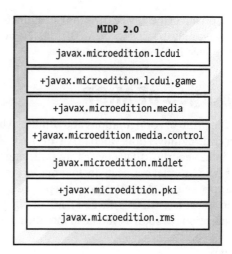

Figure 1-2. *MIDP packages*

Note While the MIDP 2.0 specification suggests that MIDP 2.0 will most likely be paired with CLDC 1.1, the JTWI compatibility platform only requires implementation atop CLDC 1.0. As a result, most current implementations of MIDP 2.0 are paired with CLDC 1.0. Historically, the MIDP 2.0 specification was moving faster through the Java Community Process than the CLDC 1.1 specification.

Optionally, device vendors may also supply Java APIs to access device-specific features. MIDP devices, then, will typically be able to run several different flavors of applications. Figure 1-3 shows a map of the possibilities.

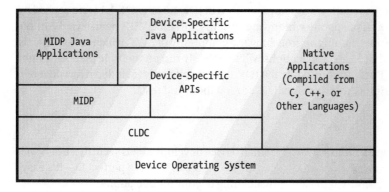

Figure 1-3. *MIDP software components*

Each device implements some kind of operating system (OS). Native applications run directly on this layer and represent the world before MIDP—many different kinds of devices, each with its own OS and native applications.

Layered on top of the device OS is the CLDC (including the JVM) and the MIDP APIs. MIDP applications use only the CLDC and MIDP APIs. Device-specific Java applications may also use Java APIs supplied by the device vendor.

Advantages of MIDP

Given the spectrum of configurations and profiles, why is this book about MIDP? First, MIDP comes at a critical time, a time when MIDP devices, like mobile phones, are an exploding market. Simultaneously, MIDP devices are achieving the kind of processing power, memory availability, and Internet connectivity that makes them an attractive platform for mobile networked applications. MIDP is already deployed on millions of handsets all over the world.

Second, of course, MIDP is the first J2ME profile that is ready for prime time. You will start writing applications as soon as you head into the next chapter!

Portability

The advantage of using Java over using other tools for small device application development is portability. You could write device applications with C or C++, but the result would be specific to a single platform. An application written using the MIDP APIs will be directly portable to any MIDP device.

If you've been following Java's development for any time, this should sound familiar. It's the same "Write Once, Run Anywhere" (WORA) mantra that Sun's been repeating since 1995. Unfortunately, WORA is a bit of a four-letter word for developers who struggled with cross-platform issues in JDK 1.0 and JDK 1.1 (particularly the browser implementations). While Java's cross-platform capabilities in Java 2 are generally successful, WORA still has the taint of an unfulfilled promise.

Does MIDP deliver painless cross-platform functionality? Yes. There will always be platform-specific bugs in MIDP implementations, but we believe MIDP works as advertised because it is so much smaller than desktop Java. Less code means fewer bugs when porting to multiple platforms. Most of the cross-platform incompatibilities of JDK 1.0 and JDK 1.1 were caused by the nightmare of trying to fit disparate windowing systems into the AWT's peer-based component architecture. MIDP has nothing approaching the complexity of AWT, which means there's an excellent possibility that MIDP applications will seamlessly run on multiple platforms right out of the starting gate. Furthermore, while the JDK 1.0 test suite only included a few dozen tests, the MIDP compatibility test suite includes several thousand tests.

Security

A second compelling reason for using Java for small device development is security. Java is well known for its ability to safely run downloaded code like applets. This is a perfect fit—it's easy to imagine nifty applications dynamically downloading to your mobile phone.

But it's not quite such a rosy picture. For one thing, the JVM used in the CLDC only implements a partial bytecode verifier, which means that part of the important task of bytecode verification must be performed off the MIDP device.

Second, the CLDC does not allow for application-defined classloaders. This means that most dynamic application delivery is dependent on device-specific mechanisms.

MIDP applications do offer one important security promise: they can never escape from the confines of the JVM. This means that, barring bugs, a MIDP application will never be able to write to device memory that doesn't belong to the JVM. A MIDP application will never mess up another application on the same device or the device OS itself.[2] This is the killer feature of MIDP. It allows manufacturers and carriers to open up application development to the world, more or less free from certification and verification programs, without the fear that rogue coders will write applications that crash phones.

In MIDP 2.0, MIDlet suites can be cryptographically signed, and then verified on the device, which gives users some security about executing downloaded code. A new permissions architecture also allows the user to deny untrusted code access to certain API features. For example, if you install a suspicious-looking MIDlet suite on your phone, it will only be able to make network connections if you explicitly allow it to do so.

MIDP Vendors

Several large players have thrown their weight behind MIDP. A quick browse of the JSR page for MIDP exposes the most important companies.

Two Asian companies led the charge to provide network services for Java-enabled mobile phones. In Korea, LG TeleCom deployed a service called ez-i in mid-2000. Later that same year, NTT DoCoMo deployed their wildly popular i-mode. The APIs developed for LG TeleCom (KittyHawk) and NTT DoCoMo (i-Appli) are similar to MIDP but were completed before the MIDP 1.0 specification.

In the United States, Motorola was the first manufacturer to produce a MIDP telephone. The i50sx and i85s were released on April 2, 2001, with service provided by Nextel. Motorola has since expanded its offerings with a handful of new devices.

Nokia has also made serious commitments to MIDP, and the expert group that created the MIDP specification includes an impressive list of manufacturers—Ericsson, Hitachi, Nokia, Sony, Symbian, and many more. You can go read the industry predictions if you wish—a gazillion MIDP phones sold in the next three years, and so on. It's a safe bet that your MIDP application will have a large market. For a comprehensive listing of MIDP devices, visit http://wireless.java.sun.com/device/.

Fragmentation

Platform fragmentation is a serious concern in the MIDP community. Many devices that implement MIDP 1.0 also include device-specific APIs. These APIs access device-specific features or provide functionality that wasn't addressed in MIDP 1.0's least-common-denominator specification. Current software vendors, particularly game developers, sometimes create and distribute multiple versions of an application, each tailored to a specific platform. Obviously this is a concern: part of the point of using MIDP in the first place is the ability to write one set of code and deploy it on multiple platforms.

---

2. A MIDP application could conceivably launch a denial-of-service attack (that is, sucking up all the processor's time or bringing the device OS to a standstill). It's widely acknowledged that there's not much defense against denial-of-service attacks. Applications and applets in J2SE suffer from the same vulnerability.

MIDP 2.0 addresses a long list of the shortcomings inherent with MIDP 1.0. Its timing is good, so the current adoption and deployment of MIDP 2.0 devices should provide a standard, unified platform for wireless development.

Another fragmentation issue is the confusion surrounding the assembly of configurations, profiles, and optional APIs into a software stack. As a developer, you want to understand exactly what set of APIs will be available or are likely to be available, but there seem to be so many choices and so many possibilities. The standardization on a software stack, via JTWI (JSR 185— http://jcp.org/jsr/detail/185.jsp), should bring clarity to this issue.

Summary

J2ME is the Java platform for small devices, a broad field that covers pretty much everything smaller than a breadbox. Because J2ME spans such a diverse selection of hardware, it is divided into configurations, profiles, and optional APIs. A configuration specifies a subset of J2SE functionality and the behavior of the JVM, while profiles are generally more specific to a family of devices with similar characteristics. Optional APIs offer added functionality in a flexible package. The Mobile Information Device Profile, which is the focus of this book, includes APIs for devices like mobile phones and two-way pagers.

CHAPTER 2

■■■

Building MIDlets

MIDP applications are piquantly called MIDlets, a continuation of the naming theme begun by applets and servlets. Writing MIDlets is relatively easy for a moderately experienced Java programmer. After all, the programming language is still Java. Furthermore, many of the fundamental APIs from `java.lang` and `java.io` are basically the same in the MIDP as they are in J2SE. Learning the new APIs (in the `javax.microedition` hierarchy) is not terribly difficult, as you'll see in the remainder of this book.

The actual development process, however, is a little more complicated for MIDlets than it is for J2SE applications. Beyond a basic compile-and-run cycle, MIDlets require some additional tweaking and packaging. The complete build cycle looks like this: Edit Source Code ➤ Compile ➤ Preverify ➤ Package ➤ Test or Deploy.

To show how things work, and to give you a taste of MIDlet development, this chapter is dedicated to building and running a simple MIDlet. In later chapters, we'll delve into the details of the MIDP APIs. In this chapter, you'll get a feel for the big picture of MIDlet development.

Tooling Up

MIDlets are developed on regular desktop computers, although the MIDlet itself is designed to run on a small device. To develop MIDlets, you'll need some kind of development kit, either from Sun or another vendor. Remember, MIDP is only a specification; vendors are free to develop their own implementations.

The world is full of MIDlet development tools if you know where to look. Furthermore, many of these tools are freely available.

The bare bones set of tools is Sun's MIDP reference implementation. This includes the `preverify` tool (more on this later), a MIDP device emulator, source code, and documentation. You can download the MIDP reference implementation by following the links from `http://java.sun.com/products/midp/`. However, we don't recommend using the reference implementation unless you really enjoy being in the middle of the gritty details of building and packaging MIDlets. (You should also investigate the reference implementation if you are interested in porting the MIDP runtime to a new device or platform.)

A much better tool for beginners is Sun's J2ME Wireless Toolkit, available from `http://java.sun.com/products/j2mewtoolkit/`. The J2ME Wireless Toolkit (or J2MEWTK, as it's affectionately known) includes a GUI tool that automates some of the tedious details of building and packaging MIDlets, providing a simple path from source code to running MIDlets. At the same time, the J2ME Wireless Toolkit is a relatively lightweight solution, almost a miniature IDE, not something that will choke your machine.

Larger IDEs are available in abundance, from device manufacturers, wireless carriers, IDE vendors, and open source communities including the following:

- Borland JBuilder X Mobile Edition:

  http://www.borland.com/mobile/jbuilder/index.html

- IBM WebSphere Studio Device Developer:

  http://www-306.ibm.com/software/wireless/wsdd/

- Research In Motion BlackBerry Java Development Environment:

  http://www.blackberry.com/developers/na/java/tools/jde/index.shtml

- Sun Java Studio Mobility:

  http://wwws.sun.com/software/products/jsmobility/index.html

- NetBeans IDE 4.x:

  http://www.netbeans.org/

- Eclipse J2ME Plugin:

  http://eclipseme.sourceforge.net/

- Nokia Developer's Suite for J2ME:

  http://www.forum.nokia.com/main/0,6566,034-2,00.html

You can use whatever development kit you wish. We suggest you start with the J2ME Wireless Toolkit, which is easy to use and authoritative. We'll be using the J2ME Wireless Toolkit (version 2.2, or WTK 2.2) throughout the rest of the book. Other development environments generally use the J2ME Wireless Toolkit as a plug-in anyhow, so your experiences are likely to be similar no matter what tool you use. You'll notice details about the development environment most in this chapter, where we'll go into detail about the build tools and the emulators. For much of the remainder of this book, we'll be describing the MIDP APIs, so it won't really matter which development kit you use.

Debugging Your MIDlets

If you are using any of the previously listed IDEs, you will have an integrated full-featured debugger for stepping through and debugging your MIDlets. If you are using the WTK standalone, and an external text editor, you can debug most of your MIDlets using the familiar System.out.println() call to output to console. The WTK maintains a console that will show all your debug and stack traces.

Creating Source Code

Writing Java source code is the same as it always was: use your favorite text editor to create a source file with a .java extension. The example we'll build and run is Jargoneer, a MIDlet that looks up words in the Jargon File. The Jargon File is a comprehensive lexicon of hacker slang (find out more by visiting http://www.catb.org/~esr/jargon/).

When you enter a word into Jargoneer, it connects to a server to find the definition. Running this MIDlet will allow you to appear cool in the company of your hacker friends. When someone uses an unfamiliar word, like "cruft" or "grok," you can surreptitiously key the word into your mobile phone and see a definition in a few seconds.

Jargoneer's source code is provided in Listing 2-1. If you don't want to type it in, you can download all of the code examples in this book from the Downloads page at http://www.apress.com.

Listing 2-1. *Jargoneer's Source Code*

```
import java.io.*;

import javax.microedition.io.*;
import javax.microedition.midlet.*;
import javax.microedition.lcdui.*;

public class Jargoneer extends MIDlet
    implements CommandListener, Runnable {
  private Display mDisplay;

  private Command mExitCommand, mFindCommand, mCancelCommand;

  private TextBox mSubmitBox;
  private Form mProgressForm;
  private StringItem mProgressString;

  public Jargoneer() {
    mExitCommand = new Command("Exit", Command.EXIT, 0);
    mFindCommand = new Command("Find", Command.SCREEN, 0);
    mCancelCommand = new Command("Cancel", Command.CANCEL, 0);

    mSubmitBox = new TextBox("Jargoneer", "", 32, 0);
    mSubmitBox.addCommand(mExitCommand);
    mSubmitBox.addCommand(mFindCommand);
    mSubmitBox.setCommandListener(this);

    mProgressForm = new Form("Lookup progress");
    mProgressString = new StringItem(null, null);
    mProgressForm.append(mProgressString);
  }

  public void startApp() {
    mDisplay = Display.getDisplay(this);

    mDisplay.setCurrent(mSubmitBox);
  }
```

```
public void pauseApp() {}

public void destroyApp(boolean unconditional) {}

public void commandAction(Command c, Displayable s) {
  if (c == mExitCommand) {
    destroyApp(false);
    notifyDestroyed();
  }
  else if (c == mFindCommand) {
    // Show the progress form.
    mDisplay.setCurrent(mProgressForm);
    // Kick off the thread to do the query.
    Thread t = new Thread(this);
    t.start();
  }
}

public void run() {
  String word = mSubmitBox.getString();
  String definition;

  try { definition = lookUp(word); }
  catch (IOException ioe) {
    Alert report = new Alert(
        "Sorry",
        "Something went wrong and that " +
        "definition could not be retrieved.",
        null, null);
    report.setTimeout(Alert.FOREVER);
    mDisplay.setCurrent(report, mSubmitBox);
    return;
  }

  Alert results = new Alert("Definition", definition,
      null, null);
  results.setTimeout(Alert.FOREVER);
  mDisplay.setCurrent(results, mSubmitBox);
}

private String lookUp(String word) throws IOException {
  HttpConnection hc = null;
  InputStream in = null;
  String definition = null;
```

```
    try {
      String baseURL = "http://65.215.221.148:8080/wj2/jargoneer?word=";
      String url = baseURL + word;
      mProgressString.setText("Connecting...");
      hc = (HttpConnection)Connector.open(url);
      hc.setRequestProperty("Connection", "close");
      in = hc.openInputStream();

      mProgressString.setText("Reading...");
      int contentLength = (int)hc.getLength();
      if (contentLength == -1) contentLength = 255;
      byte[] raw = new byte[contentLength];
      int length = in.read(raw);

      // Clean up.
      in.close();
      hc.close();

      definition = new String(raw, 0, length);
    }
    finally {
      try {
        if (in != null) in.close();
        if (hc != null) hc.close();
      }
      catch (IOException ignored) {}
    }

    return definition;
  }
}
```

Compiling a MIDlet

Writing MIDlets is an example of cross-compiling, where you compile code on one platform and run it on another. In this case, you'll be compiling a MIDlet using J2SE on your desktop computer. The MIDlet itself will run on a mobile phone, pager, or other mobile information device that supports MIDP.

The J2ME Wireless Toolkit takes care of the details as long as you put the source code in the right directory.

1. Start the toolkit, called KToolbar.

2. Choose New Project from the toolbar to create a new project.

3. When the J2ME Wireless Toolkit asks you for the name of the project and the MIDlet class name, use "Jargoneer" for both.

4. Click the Create Project button, and then the OK button to dismiss the project settings window.

Figure 2-1 shows the New Project dialog box.

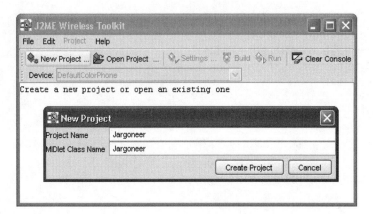

Figure 2-1. *Creating a new project with the J2ME Wireless Toolkit*

The J2ME Wireless Toolkit represents projects as subdirectories of its apps directory. The following shows the contents of the Jargoneer directory after the new project is created:

```
<J2ME Wireless Toolkit directory>
    apps
        Jargoneer
            bin
            lib
            res
            src
```

Save the source code as Jargoneer.java in the project's src directory. You can simply click the Build button in the J2ME Wireless Toolkit toolbar to compile the open project.

Behind the scenes, the J2ME Wireless Toolkit uses J2SE's compiler. Normally, when you're compiling J2SE source code, the CLASSPATH environment variable points to all the classes that your source code needs to know about. When you use javac to compile a file, there are some implied APIs that get included, like the classes in java.lang. With MIDlets, however, the situation is a little more complicated. Say that you use the java.lang.System class in your MIDlet. How do you (or how does the J2ME Wireless Toolkit) let the compiler know that you want to use the MIDP version of this class, not the J2SE version?

The answer is a command line option, -bootclasspath. This option lets you point to a classpath that describes the fundamental APIs against which you will be compiling your source code. In this case, this option should be used to specify the classes directory in the MIDP reference implementation installation. If you install the MIDP reference implementation, the command line looks like this:

```
javac -bootclasspath \midp\classes Jargoneer.java
```

You will need to adjust the path to `classes` if you installed the MIDP reference implementation in a different location.

Preverifying Class Files

Now comes an entirely new step in building your program, *preverifying*. Because the memory on small devices is so scarce, MIDP (actually, CLDC) specifies that bytecode verification be split into two pieces. Somewhere off the device, a preverify step is performed. The device itself is only required to do a lightweight second verification step before loading classes.

If you are using the J2ME Wireless Toolkit, you don't have to worry about preverifying class files, and you may not even notice that it's happening when you click the Build button. If you'd like to understand more about preverifying, read the rest of this section. Otherwise, you can just skip ahead.

As you may recall, bytecode verification is one of the foundation stones of Java's runtime security model. Before a classloader dynamically loads a class, the bytecode verifier checks the class file to make sure it behaves well and won't do nasty things to the JVM. Unfortunately, the code that implements the bytecode verifier is bulky, too large to fit on a small device like a mobile phone. The CLDC dictates a two-step bytecode verification:

1. Off the device, class files are preverified. Certain checks are performed, and the class file is massaged into a format that the lightweight second-step verifier can easily handle. This format is really just a regular class file, with some additional data attached by the preverifier.

2. On the device, the second step of verification is performed as classes are loaded. If a class file has not been preverified, it is rejected.

The MIDP reference implementation and the J2ME Wireless Toolkit contain a tool called `preverify` that performs the first step.

The `preverify` tools takes, as input, a class file. It produces a preverified class file. You need to specify a classpath so that the tool can find the class you want to preverify as well as any referenced classes. Finally, you can specify an output directory using the `-d` option. To overwrite an existing class file with a preverified version, you could do something like this:

```
preverify -classpath .;\ midp\ classes -d . Jargoneer
```

In this example, the `-d` option tells `preverify` to write the preverified class file to the current directory. Don't forget about inner classes, which must also be preverified.

■**Note** Splitting bytecode verification into two pieces like this has important security ramifications. Devices should only download code from trusted sources, using a secure method because some bytecode verification is performed off the device. (See Chapter 3 for more information on MIDlet suite security.) An attacker could supply malicious code that appeared to be preverified, even if it violated the rules of the full J2SE bytecode verifier. To the MIDP second-step verifier, the code would look okay and it would be loaded and run.

Sun's J2ME Wireless Toolkit Emulators

The J2ME Wireless Toolkit includes several different emulators that you can use to test your applications. When you click the Run button in the J2ME Wireless Toolkit, your application is launched in the currently selected emulator.

The Wireless Toolkit Devices

The J2ME Wireless Toolkit 2.2 contains four main device emulators:

- DefaultColorPhone is a device with a 240×320-pixel color screen. This is the device shown later in Figure 2-2 and is used for most of the screen shots in the remainder of this book.

- DefaultGrayPhone has a 108×208 pixel grayscale screen.

- MediaControlSkin is similar to the default phone emulator and has a color screen of 108×208 pixels, but its buttons are labeled with controls like a music player: a square for stop, a triangle for play, volume control buttons, etc.

- QwertyDevice is a smartphone with a 636×235-color screen and a miniature QWERTY keyboard.

Running MIDlets

Sun's MIDP reference implementation includes an emulator named midp. It emulates an imaginary MID, a mobile telephone with some standard keys and a 182×210-pixel screen. The J2ME Wireless Toolkit includes a similar emulator, as well as several others.

Once you've got a preverified class file, you can use the midp emulator to run it. The emulator is an application that runs under J2SE and acts just like a MIDP device. It shows itself on your screen as a representative device, a generic mobile phone. You can run your MIDlet by typing the following at the command line, assuming you added \midp\bin to your PATH:

```
midp Jargoneer
```

If you're using the J2ME Wireless Toolkit, you can simply choose an emulator from the Device combo box and click the Run button to fire up your application.

If all goes well, you'll see something like the window shown in Figure 2-2 in the next section. Congratulations! You've just built and run your first MIDlet.

Using the Emulator Controls

The J2ME Wireless Toolkit emulator appears as a generic mobile phone, as shown in Figure 2-2.

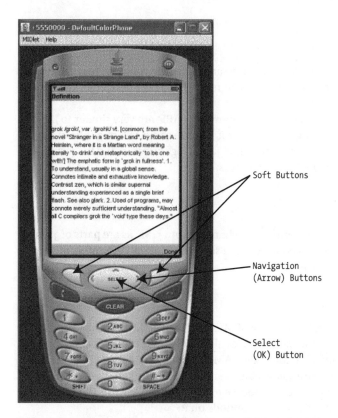

Figure 2-2. *Buttons on the J2ME Wireless Toolkit emulator*

SUN's J2ME Wireless Toolkit emulator exhibits several qualities that you are likely to find in real devices:

- The device has a small screen size and limited input capabilities. (It's not as small as the earlier J2ME Wireless Toolkit 1.x emulators, which included emulated devices with 96×128 and 96×54-pixel screens.)

- Two *soft buttons* are available. A soft button does not have a fixed function. Generally, the function of the button at any given time is shown on the screen near the button. In MIDlets, the soft buttons are used for commands.

- *Navigation buttons* are provided to allow the user to browse through lists or other sets of choices.

- A *select button* allows the user to make a choice after moving to it with the navigation buttons. (Think "Yes, that's my final answer.")

Tour of MIDP Features

Now that you have run your first MIDlet, take a moment to admire it. There are several salient features, even in such a small example.

It's Java

First of all, Jargoneer is written in the Java language, the same language you'd use to code servlets, Enterprise JavaBeans, or J2SE client applications. If you're already a J2SE developer, you should be quite comfortable developing MIDlets.

Not only is the Java language familiar, but also many core APIs are very similar to J2SE. Notice, for example, that multithreading in Jargoneer is just the same as it might be in any other Java code. The MIDlet class Jargoneer implements java.lang.Runnable, and the technique for kicking off a new thread is the same as it always was:

```
Thread t = new Thread(this);
t.start();
```

Significant parts of java.lang are essentially unchanged from J2SE, as are parts of java.io and java.util. The code that reads the result from the server in lookUp() is familiar stream handling, just like what you might see in J2SE.

MIDlet Life Cycle

Jargoneer also demonstrates the basic structure of MIDlets. Like all MIDlets, it extends javax.microedition.midlet.MIDlet, the base class for all MIDP applications. Special software on the device, called the Java Application Manager (JAM), Application Management Software (AMS), or MIDlet management software, allows the user to control the process of installing, running, and removing MIDlets. When a user chooses to run your MIDlet, it is the JAM that creates an instance of the MIDlet class and runs methods on it.

The sequence of methods that will be called in your MIDlet subclass is defined by the MIDlet life cycle. MIDlets, like applets and servlets, have a small set of well-defined states. The JAM will call methods in the MIDlet to signify transitions from one state to another. You can see these methods in Jargoneer—startApp(), pauseApp(), destroyApp(), and Jargoneer's constructor are all part of the MIDlet life cycle.

Generalized User Interface

Jargoneer's user-interface code may take you by surprise. Later on, we'll spend several chapters on user interface. For now, the important thing to notice is how Jargoneer's user interface is flexible enough to run on devices with different screen sizes and different input capabilities. A big part of MIDP's appeal, after all, is the concept of writing one set of source code that runs on multiple devices.

One example of MIDP's generalized user interface is the TextBox that is initially shown when Jargoneer is launched. Figure 2-3 shows this TextBox.

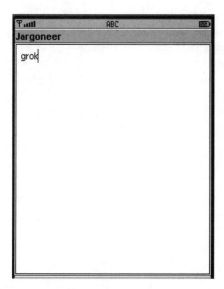

Figure 2-3. *Jargoneer's TextBox*

TextBox is a text input field. It has a title and an area for entering text. It has a simple design and can easily be shown on screens of different sizes. Even more interesting are the commands that appear at the bottom of the TextBox. These are Exit and Find. The code that creates the TextBox and its commands is in Jargoneer's constructor:

```
mExitCommand = new Command("Exit", Command.EXIT, 0);
mFindCommand = new Command("Find", Command.SCREEN, 0);
// ...
mSubmitBox = new TextBox("Jargoneer", "", 32, 0);
mSubmitBox.addCommand(mExitCommand);
mSubmitBox.addCommand(mFindCommand);
mSubmitBox.setCommandListener(this);
```

Notice how the commands are created. You specify only a label and a type, and you register an event listener to find out when the commands are invoked. This is purposely vague—it leaves the implementation considerable latitude in deciding how commands should be displayed and invoked. In Sun's J2ME Wireless Toolkit emulator, for example, TextBox shows its commands at the bottom of the screen and allows the user to invoke them using soft buttons. Another device might put both commands in a menu and allow the user to invoke them using a selector wheel or some other mechanism. This is an example of the typical tradeoff between portability (the ability to run the application across multiple MIDP implementation) and precise control.

The Likelihood of Server-Side Components

The Jargoneer example connects to a web server, sends a request, and receives a response. The web server is actually an intermediary—it connects to the real Jargon File server, makes a request, parses the result, and sends the stripped-down definition back to the MIDP device.

In the first edition of this book, Jargoneer connected directly to the Jargon File server. In response to its query, it received a lot of information it didn't need. The original Jargoneer went to considerable trouble to parse through the HTML response to extract the definition it wanted. Architecturally, the old Jargoneer looked like Figure 2-4.

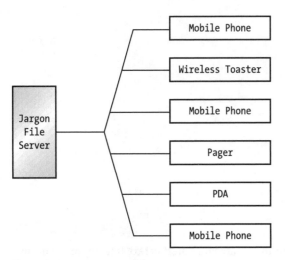

Figure 2-4. *Jargoneer architecture*

The new architecture is shown in Figure 2-5.

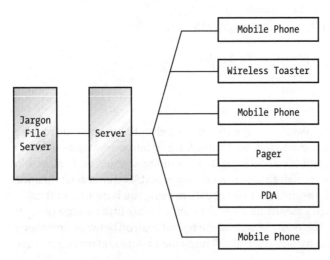

Figure 2-5. *A cleaner architecture for Jargoneer*

Instead of hitting the web server directly, Jargoneer goes through a different server hosted by Apress. This server queries the Jargon File, parses the result, and returns the definition to the device. This is advantageous from several standpoints:

- Bandwidth is expensive in terms of both time and money. Today's wireless networks are relatively slow, so less data passing through the air means less waiting time for your users. Also, wireless service tends to be pricey, so less data passing through the air means smaller bills for your users.

- Small devices have limited memory and processing power. It is unwise to spend these limited resources on tasks like parsing HTML. In general, you will be able to place most of the processing burden of your application on a server component, making your client MIDlet's life very easy.

- In this particular application, the HTML parsing is not very stable. Suppose the server we are using decides to return its Jargon File definitions in a different format; if four million users are running Jargoneer, then four million copies of our code have just broken. Performing this task on a server gives it a single point of failure and a single point of update. If we fix the parsing code on the server, the interface between the server and the client devices can remain unchanged. This makes it easy to upgrade or fix Jargoneer.

Network MIDP applications are likely to need a server component. If you're planning to do much MIDP development, you might like to study up on Java servlets.

Packaging Your Application

You won't pass class files directly to a MIDP to deploy an application. Instead, you'll package them in a Java Archive (JAR) using a packager such as the jar tool that comes with the Java 2 SDK.

If you're using the J2ME Wireless Toolkit, you won't ever have to perform these steps manually; the toolkit automatically packages your MIDlets when you choose Project ➤ Package ➤ Create Package from the menu. (You don't have to do this if you just want to test your application in the emulator, but you need to create a package if you're going to distribute the MIDlet suite.) Even if you use the J2ME Wireless Toolkit, you might want to read through this section so that you understand exactly what's going on.

If you're using the MIDP reference implementation, you should follow these steps to package your MIDlets. We'll only sketch the steps here; in the next chapter, you'll learn all the gory details of MIDlets and MIDlet suites.

Manifest Information

Every JAR includes a manifest file, META-INF\MANIFEST.MF, that describes the contents of the archive. For MIDlet JARs, the manifest file must contain extra information. The extra information is stuff that's important to the MIDP runtime environment, like the MIDlet's class name and the versions of CLDC and MIDP that the MIDlet expects.

You can specify extra manifest information in a simple text file and tell the jar utility to include that information in the manifest when the JAR is created. To package Jargoneer, for example, save the following text in a file named extra.mf:

```
MIDlet-1: Jargoneer, , Jargoneer
MIDlet-Name: Jargoneer
MIDlet-Vendor: Jonathan Knudsen
MIDlet-Version: 1.0
MicroEdition-Configuration: CLDC-1.0
MicroEdition-Profile: MIDP-2.0
```

Now assemble the MIDlet classes and the extra manifest information into a JAR with the following command:

```
jar cvmf extra.mf Jargoneer.jar Jargoneer.class
```

With the J2ME Wireless Toolkit, the toolkit automatically assembles your application into a MIDlet suite JAR when you click the Build button. It's very convenient, and it saves you from the effort of learning the jar tool.

Creating a MIDlet Descriptor

One additional file is needed before your MIDlet is ready to go out the door. An *application descriptor* file must be created. This file contains a lot of the same information that's in the MIDlet JAR manifest file. However, it lives outside the JAR and enables application management software to learn about a MIDlet JAR without installing it.

The application descriptor is a text file with a .jad extension. Type in the following and save it as Jargoneer.jad:

```
MIDlet-1: Jargoneer, , Jargoneer
MIDlet-Jar-Size: 2347
MIDlet-Jar-URL: Jargoneer.jar
MIDlet-Name: Jargoneer
MIDlet-Vendor: Jonathan Knudsen
MIDlet-Version: 1.0
MicroEdition-Configuration: CLDC-1.0
MicroEdition-Profile: MIDP-2.0
```

If your MIDlet suite JAR is a different size, enter the actual size for the MIDlet-Jar-Size entry. The MIDlet descriptor is automatically generated when you click the Build button in the J2ME Wireless Toolkit. If you're using the J2ME Wireless Toolkit, you won't need to create the application descriptor yourself.

Using an Obfuscator

Because MIDP devices have so little memory, MIDlet suites should be as compact as possible. An *obfuscator* is a useful tool for minimizing the size of MIDlet suite JARs. Obfuscators, originally designed to foil attempts to reverse engineer compiled bytecode, perform any combination of the following functions:

- Renaming classes, member variables, and methods to more compact names

- Removing unused classes, methods, and member variables

- Inserting illegal or questionable data to confuse decompilers

Except for the last point, obfuscators can significantly reduce the size of compiled classes in a MIDlet suite JAR.

There's a wide spectrum of obfuscators, with a variety of licenses, costs, and features. For a comprehensive list, see `http://proguard.sourceforge.net/alternatives.html`.

Using an obfuscator requires some finesse. The trick is to obfuscate the classes before they are preverified. The J2ME Wireless Toolkit includes support for inserting an obfuscator into the build cycle. Support for ProGuard is built in with version 2.2, and you can write adapter code to use other obfuscators. If you're using the 2.2 version of the toolkit, you just need to download ProGuard and copy the `proguard.jar` file into the toolkit's bin directory. Then choose Project ➤ Package ➤ Create Obfuscated Package and the toolkit handles all the details.

There is an article that describes how to use the ProGuard obfuscator with the J2ME Wireless Toolkit at `http://developers.sun.com/techtopics/mobility/midp/ttips/proguard/`.

The documentation that comes with the J2ME Wireless Toolkit includes a document called "J2ME Wireless Toolkit Basic Customization Guide." This guide describes how to add support for any obfuscator to the toolkit.

Obfuscators tend to be a little finicky, but once you get them configured correctly, they can provide significant size savings.

▓**Tip** You should not use the obfuscator during the regular coding/debug cycle, but just before packaging and deployment. This is because the obfuscator can often make debugging difficult.

Using Ant

Ant is a powerful build tool that is useful for automating MIDlet suite builds. It's similar in concept to `make`, but it is cleaner and easier to use. Ant is open source software, part of the Apache Jakarta project, at `http://ant.apache.org/`.

Ant is a tool for serious developers. If you believe you've exhausted the possibilities of the J2ME Wireless Toolkit, Ant is probably the next tool you should learn. Ant provides considerable flexibility in structuring your build cycle and lets you easily automate tasks like generating documentation or packaging source code. For an introduction to Ant and MIDP, see `http://developers.sun.com/techtopics/mobility/midp/articles/ant/`.

The code download for this book includes an Ant build script. A simplified version of the build script is shown in Listing 2-2.

Listing 2-2. *An Example Ant Build Script*

```
<project name="wj2" default="dist" basedir="..">
  <property name="project" value="wj2"/>

  <property name="midp" value="/WTK20"/>
  <property name="midp_lib" value="${midp}/lib/midpapi.zip"/>
```

```xml
  <target name="run">
    <exec executable="${midp}/bin/emulator">
      <arg line="-classpath build/bin/${project}.jar"/>
      <arg line="-Xdescriptor build/bin/${project}.jad"/>
    </exec>
  </target>

  <target name="dist" depends="preverify">
    <mkdir dir="build/bin"/>
    <jar basedir="build/preverified"
        jarfile="build/bin/${project}.jar"
        manifest="bin/MANIFEST.MF">
      <fileset dir="res"/>
    </jar>
    <copy file="bin/${project}.jad"
        tofile="build/bin/${project}.jad"/>
  </target>

  <target name="preverify" depends="obfuscate_null">
    <mkdir dir="build/preverified"/>
    <exec executable="${midp}/bin/preverify">
      <arg line="-classpath ${midp_lib}"/>
      <arg line="-d build/preverified"/>
      <arg line="build/obfuscated"/>
    </exec>
  </target>

  <target name="obfuscate_null" depends="compile">
    <mkdir dir="build/obfuscated"/>
    <copy todir="build/obfuscated">
      <fileset dir="build/classes"/>
    </copy>
  </target>

  <target name="compile" depends="init">
    <mkdir dir="build/classes"/>
    <javac destdir="build/classes" srcdir="src"
        bootclasspath="${midp_lib}" target="2.0"/>
  </target>

  <target name="init">
    <tstamp/>
  </target>
</project>
```

This build script contains targets that correspond to the steps of MIDlet suite development: `compile`, `preverify`, and `dist` (which packages the application). An `obfuscate_null` target is also included; it serves as a placeholder for inserting obfuscation in the build cycle. (The actual build script in the source download includes a target for obfuscating using ProGuard.)

Several developers have created specialized Ant tasks to help with MIDlet suite builds. One such project is here: `http://antenna.sourceforge.net/`.

Running on a Real Device

As of this writing, millions of MIDP-enabled phones are deployed worldwide. A comprehensive list of MIDP devices is available at `http://wireless.java.sun.com/device/`. How do you actually put MIDlets on a device? There are two possibilities: either you'll transfer MIDlet suites to the phone from your computer via an external connection (can be serial cable, USB cable, IRDA, Bluetooth, etc.—depending on the device manufacturer) , or you'll transfer MIDlet suites over the wireless network. This second possibility is called *over the air (OTA) provisioning*. There's a standard protocol for OTA, included with MIDP 2.0 specification. This protocol is available to MIDP 1.0 as an addendum to the specification.

Installing MIDlets via serial cable or OTA provisioning is specific to whatever device you're using. You'll have to check the documentation for your device to see exactly how to install MIDlet suites.

Summary

This chapter took you on a tour of MIDP development. Creating source code is much the same as in J2SE development, but the build process is different. First, the source code must be compiled against the MIDP classes using `javac`'s `-bootclasspath` option. Second, the class files must be preverified using the `preverify` command-line tool. With the J2ME Wireless Toolkit, these steps are conveniently automated. Just click the Build button to build and preverify. Applications can be easily tested in emulators using the J2ME Wireless Toolkit.

■ ■ ■

CHAPTER 3

All About MIDlets

In Chapter 2, you got a quick introduction to the process of building and running MIDlets. In this chapter, you'll explore the details. We'll cover the subjects that we skimmed in the last chapter, starting with the MIDlet life cycle and continuing through to a full discussion of MIDlet packaging. The chapter concludes with a look at the MIDlet security architecture.

The MIDlet Life Cycle

MIDP applications are represented by instances of the `javax.microedition.midlet.MIDlet` class. MIDlets have a specific life cycle, which is reflected in the methods and behavior of the `MIDlet` class.

A piece of device-specific software, the *application manager*, controls the installation, execution, and life cycle of MIDlets. MIDlets have no access to the application manager. A MIDlet is installed by moving its class files to a device. The class files will be packaged in a Java Archive (JAR), while an accompanying descriptor file (with a `.jad` extension) describes the contents of the JAR.

A MIDlet goes through the following states:

1. When the MIDlet is about to be run, an instance is created. The MIDlet's constructor is run, and the MIDlet is in the *Paused* state.

2. Next, the MIDlet enters the *Active* state after the application manager calls `startApp()`.

3. While the MIDlet is Active, the application manager can suspend its execution by calling `pauseApp()`. This puts the MIDlet back in the Paused state. A MIDlet can place itself in the Paused state by calling `notifyPaused()`.

4. While the MIDlet is in the Paused state, the application manager can call `startApp()` to put it back into the Active state.

5. The application manager can terminate the execution of the MIDlet by calling `destroyApp()`, at which point the MIDlet is *destroyed* and patiently awaits garbage collection. A MIDlet can destroy itself by calling `notifyDestroyed()`.

Figure 3-1 shows the states of a MIDlet and the transitions between them.

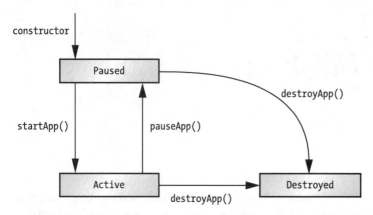

Figure 3-1. MIDlet life cycle

There is one additional method in the MIDlet class and it is related to the MIDlet life cycle: resumeRequest(). A MIDlet in the Paused state can call this method to signal to the application manager that it wants to become Active. It might seem weird to think about a MIDlet in the Paused state running any code at all. However, Paused MIDlets are still able to handle timer events or other types of callbacks and thus have some chances to call resumeRequest(). If the application manager does decide to move a MIDlet from the Paused to the Active state, it will do so through the normal mechanism of calling startApp().

Requesting a Wakeup Call

MIDlets can request to be launched at a later time, in essence requesting a wakeup call from the implementation. The method is defined in javax.microedition.io.PushRegistry, which is kind of a weird place for it. All of PushRegistry's other methods have to do with launching MIDlets in response to incoming network connections; the class is fully described in Chapter 10. The following method in PushRegistry requests that a named MIDlet be woken up at a specific time:

```
public static long registerAlarm(String midlet, long time)
    throws ClassNotFoundException, ConnectionNotFoundException
```

You need to supply the class name of a MIDlet in the MIDlet suite, and time specifies exactly when you want the MIDlet to be launched, in the standard form as the number of milli-seconds since January 1, 1970. (Chapter 4 contains a discussion of MIDP's classes and methods pertaining to time.)

If you supply a class name that is not found in the current MIDlet suite, a ClassNotFoundException is thrown. If the implementation is unable to launch MIDlets at specified times, a ConnectionNotFoundException is thrown.

If the MIDlet for which you are requesting a timed launch was previously registered for timed launch, this method returns the previous wakeup time.

A Bridge to the Outside World

Many MIDP devices, especially mobile phones, have web browsers, using either the WAP or HTTP protocol. The MIDlet class supplies a bridge to these browsers and other capabilities:

```
public final boolean platformRequest(String URL)
    throws ConnectionNotFoundException
```

On a sophisticated device, the browser and the MIDlet suite may be able to run at the same time, in which case the browser will be launched and pointed to the specified URL. In this case, the method returns true.

On smaller devices, the browser may not be able to run until the MIDlet is destroyed. In this case, platformRequest() returns false, and it's the MIDlet's responsibility to terminate. After the MIDlet terminates, it's the implementation's responsibility to launch the browser and point it at the specified URL.

In either case, platformRequest() is a nonblocking method.

There are two special possibilities for the supplied URL. If you supply a telephone number URL of the form tel:<number> as specified in RFC 2806 (http://ietf.org/rfc/rfc2806.txt), the implementation should initiate a voice call.

If you supply the URL of a MIDlet suite descriptor or JAR, the implementation should eventually start the application manager and attempt to install the given MIDlet suite (after asking for your permission, of course).

Packaging MIDlets

MIDlets are deployed in *MIDlet suites*. A MIDlet suite is a collection of MIDlets with some extra information. There are two files involved. One is an *application descriptor*, which is a simple text file. The other is a JAR file that contains the class files and resource files that make up your MIDlet suite. Like any JAR file, a MIDlet suite's JAR file has a manifest file. Figure 3-2 shows a diagram of a MIDlet suite.

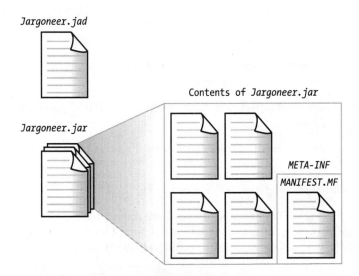

Jargoneer.jad

Jargoneer.jar

Contents of *Jargoneer.jar*

META-INF

MANIFEST.MF

Figure 3-2. Antatomy of a MIDlet suite

If you are using a tool like the J2ME Wireless Toolkit, you don't need to worry much about MIDlet suite packaging because most of the details are handled automatically. If you want to understand things at a lower level, or if you're just curious, keep reading for a complete description of MIDlet suite packaging.

Packaging a MIDlet suite consists of three steps:

1. The class files and resource files that make up the MIDlets are packaged into a JAR file. Usually, you'll use the jar command-line tool to accomplish this.

2. Additional information that's needed at runtime is placed in the JAR's manifest file. All JARs include a manifest; a MIDlet suite JAR contains some extra information needed by application management software.

3. An application descriptor file should also be generated. This is a file with a .jad extension that describes the MIDlet suite JAR. It can be used by the application management software to decide whether a MIDlet suite JAR should be downloaded to the device.

MIDlet Manifest Information

The information stored in a MIDlet's manifest file consists of name and value pairs, like a properties file. For example, an unadorned JAR manifest might look like this:

```
Manifest-Version: 1.0
Created-By: 1.4.2_04 (Sun Microsystems Inc.)
```

A MIDlet JAR manifest for Jargoneer looks like this:

```
Manifest-Version: 1.0
MIDlet-1: Jargoneer, Jargoneer.png, Jargoneer
MIDlet-Name: Jargoneer
MIDlet-Version: 2.0
MIDlet-Vendor: Sun Microsystems
Created-By: 1.4.2_04 (Sun Microsystems Inc.)
MicroEdition-Configuration: CLDC-1.0
MicroEdition-Profile: MIDP-2.0
```

The extra attributes describe software versions, class names, and other information about the MIDlet suite. The following attributes must be included:

- MIDlet-Name: Despite the moniker, this attribute actually refers to the name of the entire MIDlet suite, not just one MIDlet.

- MIDlet-Version: This describes the version of the MIDlet suite. It's a number you pick yourself in the form major.minor.micro.

- MIDlet-Vendor: This is your name or the name of your company.

- MIDlet-n: For each MIDlet in the MIDlet suite, the displayable name, icon file name, and class name are listed. The MIDlets must be numbered starting from 1 and counting up. For example, several MIDlets in a single MIDlet suite could be listed like this:

```
MIDlet-1: Sokoban, /icons/Sokoban.png, example.sokoban.Sokoban
MIDlet-2: Tickets, /icons/Auction.png, example.lcdui.TicketAuction
MIDlet-3: Colors, /icons/ColorChooser.png, example.chooser.Color
MIDlet-4: Stock, /icons/Stock.png, example.stock.StockMIDlet
```

- `MicroEdition-Configuration`: This attribute describes the J2ME configurations upon which this MIDlet suite can run. Multiple configuration names should be separated by spaces.

- `MicroEdition-Profile`: This describes the set of profiles upon which this MIDlet suite can run. For MIDP 2.0 applications, this is `MIDP-20`. For applications that can also run on the older MIDP 1.0 profile, use "MIDP-2.0 MIDP-1.0".

In addition to the required manifest attributes, the following attributes may be defined:

- `MIDlet-Description`: The description of the MIDlet suite goes in this attribute.

- `MIDlet-Icon`: Icons for individual MIDlets are described in the `MIDlet-n` attributes. This attribute specifies an icon to represent the entire MIDlet suite.

- `MIDlet-Info-URL`: If additional information about the MIDlet suite is available online, use this attribute to list the URL.

- `MIDlet-Data-Size`: If you know how many bytes of persistent data are required by the MIDlet suite, you can specify the number with this attribute.

■**Tip** Don't get tripped up by the attribute names. Many of them appear to refer to a single MIDlet, like `MIDlet-Name` and `MIDlet-Description`. In fact, these attributes describe an entire MIDlet suite. The only attribute that applies to a specific MIDlet is the `MIDlet-n` attribute, which is used to list each MIDlet in the suite.

Several additional attributes may be included. Network APIs can be protected from unauthorized access using a permission scheme, which will be fully discussed later in this chapter. MIDlets can list necessary permissions and optional permissions in the MIDlet JAR manifest as follows:

- `MIDlet-Permissions`: Use this attribute to list permissions that are critical to the operation of the MIDlet suite. Multiple permissions are separated by commas.

- `MIDlet-Permissions-Opt`: This attribute lists permissions that may be used but are not critical for this MIDlet suite.

Finally, there is also a way for MIDlet suites to signal their dependence on optional APIs:

- `MIDlet-Extensions`: List the required Optional APIs used by this MIDlet suite in this attribute. The exact names are determined by the individual optional API specifications.

Application Descriptor

The attributes in a MIDlet suite JAR are used by the application management software to run MIDlets within a suite. The application descriptor, by contrast, contains information that helps a device and/or the user decide whether or not to load a MIDlet suite. Because an application descriptor is a file separate from the MIDlet suite JAR, it is easy for a device to load and examine the file before downloading the MIDlet suite.

As it happens, a lot of the information in the application descriptor has to be the same as the information that's in the MIDlet suite JAR. For example, the application descriptor must contain the `MIDlet-Name`, `MIDlet-Version`, and `MIDlet-Vendor` attributes. In addition, it must include the following:

- `MIDlet-Jar-URL`: This is the URL where the MIDlet suite JAR can be found.

- `MIDlet-Jar-Size`: This is the size, in bytes, of the MIDlet suite JAR.

The application descriptor can optionally contain the `MIDlet-Description`, `MIDlet-Icon`, `MIDlet-Info-URL`, and `MIDlet-Data-Size` attributes.

Devices and emulators vary widely in their handling of MIDlet suite descriptors. Some will fail installation if any fields in the descriptor are incorrect, while others are more lenient. A tool like the J2ME Wireless Toolkit is extremely useful in creating well-formed descriptors.

The application descriptor is useful in over the air (OTA) deployment. A device (and the user) can download and inspect the descriptor, a relatively short file, before deciding whether the entire MIDlet suite JAR should be downloaded and installed. For OTA provisioning, the server's returned MIME type for the application descriptor should be `text/vnd.sun.j2me.app-descriptor`. This and more (a whole protocol) is described in the "Over the Air User Initiated Provisioning Specification" section of the MIDP 2.0 specification.

MIDlet Properties

There's one other possibility for attributes in the manifest or application descriptor. You can add attributes that have meaning to your MIDlets. MIDlets can retrieve the values of these attributes using the `getAppProperty()` method in the `javax.microedition.midlet.MIDlet` class. An attribute can be listed in the application descriptor, JAR manifest, or both; if it is listed in both, the value from the application descriptor will be used. In general, it makes sense to store application properties in the application descriptor file. Because it's distinct from the MIDlet suite JAR, the application descriptor can easily be changed to modify the behavior of your MIDlets. You might, for example, store a URL or other configuration information in the application descriptor.

For example, suppose you put an application-specific attribute in the application descriptor, like this:

```
Jargoneer.url: http://www.dict.org/bin/Dict
```

Inside the MIDlet, you can retrieve the value of the attribute like this:

```
String url = getAppProperty("Jargoneer.url");
```

Changing the URL is as easy as changing the application descriptor, a simple text file. None of your code needs to be recompiled. This could be useful if you were expecting to distribute many copies of a MIDlet and wanted to share the server load among a group of servers. You could distribute the same MIDlet suite JAR with a group of different application descriptors, each one using a MIDlet attribute to point to a different server.

MIDlet Suite Security

Wireless application security is important to almost everyone involved in the wireless industry:

- Carriers want to be sure that viruses do not bring down their customers' devices or their networks.

- Device manufacturers don't want customer-installed software crashing their devices.

- Users want to be able to run downloaded code without threatening the stability of their device or the safety of their personal information. Additionally, they may want control over the network usage of their applications, as network usage often costs money.

- Application developers do not want their applications to be compromised by other applications.

Permissions

Permissions provide MIDlets with an explicit security architecture. In a nutshell, MIDlets must have *permission* to perform sensitive operations. The only parts of the API that are protected by permissions are the network connections. Optional APIs are free to define additional permissions to protect sensitive data or functionality.

Permission names use the same prefix and class or interface name as the API that they protect. In Chapter 10, we'll explain the names of the network permissions in detail. For the moment, suppose that you write a MIDlet that needs to make a socket connection. This MIDlet would need the permission of `javax.microedition.io.Connector.socket`. The MIDlet itself needs no knowledge of permissions. It simply attempts the connection, which either succeeds or throws a `java.lang.SecurityException`.

There is a method in the `MIDlet` class that programmers can use to check if a permission will be granted or denied:

```
public final int checkPermission(String permission)
```

This method returns 1 if the permission is granted and 0 if the permission is denied. A special return value, -1, indicates that the implementation cannot determine whether the permission will be granted or denied, which might be the case if the user will be asked about the given permission.

Protection Domains

MIDlet suites belong to *protection domains* that determine which permissions are granted, which are denied, and which ones must be deferred to the user's judgment. A protection domain is kind of like a secret club and comprises two parts:

1. The set of permissions that are allowed and those for which the user must be consulted

2. The rules for how a MIDlet suite can get into this protection domain

A very simple protection domain, "SimplePD," might contain the permission `javax.microedition.io.Connector.http`. The rules for membership in SimplePD could be something as simple as verifying the origin IP address of the MIDlet suite. For example, if the MIDlet suite is downloaded from `www.bigcarrier.com`, then the application management software on the device would know to place the MIDlet suite in the SimplePD protection domain. At runtime, any MIDlet that tries to make an HTTP connection will be granted the permission. Attempts to make other connection types will be denied.

The simple IP-origin criterion for SimplePD is pretty weak. MIDlet suites in SimplePD are susceptible to many attacks, including data modification, data replacement, man-in-the-middle attacks, and DNS spoofing. More robust rules are based on cryptographic solutions for data integrity and authentication. In the MIDP 2.0 specification, the section "Trusted MIDlet Suites Using X.509 PKI" describes one such scheme, including additional manifest attributes.

MIDlet suites whose contents and origin cannot be verified are placed in a kind of default protection domain, the *untrusted* domain. The only restriction placed on the untrusted domain is that, given explicit confirmation from the user, it must allow MIDlets access to HTTP and HTTPS connections.

The concept of protection domains is deliberately vague, leaving MIDP vendors with considerable latitude in their implementation. Our guess is that many implementations will choose to have a single untrusted domain and a single trusted domain, with entry to the trusted domain limited to cryptographically signed (and verified) MIDlet suites.

Permission Types

The protection domain contains the permissions that will be granted to MIDlets (*allowed* permissions) as well as the permissions for which the user must be consulted (*user* permissions). There are several varieties of user permissions. *Blanket* means that the user is only required to grant or deny the permission once for a MIDlet suite. *Session* means that the user must grant or deny permission once per invocation of a MIDlet suite. Finally, *oneshot* indicates that the user must be consulted each time the necessary permission is needed.

Permissions in MIDlet Suite Descriptors

There are additional attributes for MIDlet suite descriptors. If your MIDlet suite absolutely, positively needs certain permissions, use the `MIDlet-Permissions` attribute. For example, if your MIDlet suite needs to make HTTP connections to function correctly, you would have a line in your descriptor file like this:

```
MIDlet-Permissions: javax.microedition.io.Connector.http
```

Multiple permission types are placed on the same line, separated by commas.

If your MIDlet suite does not need certain permissions to function, but it may use them for enhanced functionality, these permissions can be placed in the `MIDlet-Permissions-Opt` attribute.

At installation time, the application management software will compare the permissions requested in the descriptor with the permissions in the destination protection domain. If there are irreconcilable differences, the MIDlet suite will not be installed.

Summary

MIDP applications are called MIDlets. Like applets or servlets, MIDlets have a specific life cycle; they are managed by device software. This chapter detailed the entries that must and may be in the MIDlet suite manifest file and the application descriptor. Application properties can be used as a way to store information in the application descriptor instead of hard-coding values into the MIDlet source code. A tool like the J2ME Wireless Toolkit automatically handles many of the details of MIDlet attributes packaging. MIDlets enjoy a comprehensive security architecture based on protection domains.

■ ■ ■

CHAPTER 4

Almost the Same Old Stuff

As we discussed in Chapter 1, one of the reasons you might be interested in MIDP as a platform is that it's based on the Java programming language and the Java APIs. You'll also recall that MIDP is built on top of the Connected, Limited Device Configuration (CLDC). The CLDC contains most of the APIs that will look familiar to experienced Java programmers. As of this writing, CLDC 1.0 is the most widely available version, but many newer devices are beginning to support the CLDC 1.1 specification. We'll mention the differences between CLDC 1.0 and CLDC 1.1 throughout this chapter.

In this chapter, we'll explore the java.lang, java.io, and java.util packages as defined in the CLDC. We'll assume you're already familiar with the basic APIs of J2SE; we'll walk through what's the same and what's different.

At the time of this writing (first quarter 2005), CLDC 1.1 and MIDP 2.0 have been implemented on real devices from several manufacturers (Nokia, Siemens, Sony Ericsson, just to name a few). The industry-wide endorsement of the JTWI (JSR 185) has prompted the rapid adoption of MIDP 2.0. Although some JTWI devices only implement MIDP 2.0 over CLDC 1.0, it is anticipated most new devices will be implemented on top of CLDC 1.1.

No Floating Point in CLDC 1.0

CLDC 1.0 does not support floating-point types at all. That means there are no float or double primitive types. The corresponding wrapper types, java.lang.Float and java.lang.Double, have also been eliminated.

Floating-point support is absent in CLDC 1.0. On CLDC 1.0 devices, if calculations involving fractional numbers are important to your application, you can perform them in software. One implementation (using fixed-point integers) can be found at http://home.rochester.rr.com/ohommes/MathFP/.

CLDC 1.1 includes floating-point support, the primitive types double and float, and the wrapper types Double and Float. Various other classes have been modified for floating-point support in CLDC 1.1, but the changes are minor.

java.lang

Table 4-1 and Table 4-2 list the classes and interfaces of java.lang and java.lang.ref in both J2SE (SDK version 1.4.2) and CLDC. The CLDC columns indicate whether the class is identical to its J2SE counterpart, is present with API differences, or is not present at all.

Table 4-1. *The java.lang Package*

J2SE SDK 1.4.2	CLDC 1.0	CLDC 1.1
Interfaces		
CharSequence	–	–
Cloneable	–	–
Comparable	–	–
Runnable	Same	Same
Classes		
J2SE SDK 1.4.2	**CLDC 1.0**	**CLDC 1.1**
Boolean	Different	Different
Byte	Different	Same as CLDC 1.0
Character	Different	Same as CLDC 1.0
Character.Subset	–	–
Character.UnicodeBlock	–	–
Class	Different	Same as CLDC 1.0
ClassLoader	–	–
Compiler	–	–
Double	–	Different
Float	–	Different
InheritableThreadLocal	–	–
Integer	Different	Different
Long	Different	Different
Math	Different	Different
Number	–	–
Object	Different	Same as CLDC 1.0
Package	–	–
Process	–	–
Runtime	Different	Same as CLDC 1.0
RuntimePermission	–	–
SecurityManager	–	–
Short	Different	Same as CLDC 1.0
StackTraceElement	–	–
StrictMath	–	–

Table 4-1. *The java.lang Package (Continued)*

J2SE SDK 1.4.2	CLDC 1.0	CLDC 1.1
String	Different	Different
StringBuffer	Different	Different
System	Different	Same as CLDC 1.0
Thread	Different	Different
ThreadGroup	–	–
ThreadLocal	–	–
Throwable	Different	Same as CLDC 1.0
Void	–	–

Table 4-2. *The java.lang.ref Package*

J2SE SDK 1.4.2	CLDC 1.0	CLDC 1.1
Classes		
PhantomReference	–	–
Reference	–	Different
ReferenceQueue	–	–
SoftReference	–	–
WeakReference	–	Different

java.lang.Object, as always, is the root of every Java class. It remains mostly unchanged from J2SE, but there are some important differences. These differences are detailed in the upcoming text.

No Object Finalization

Object finalization is not available in CLDC (and, by extension, MIDP). Finalization is a mechanism by which objects can clean up after themselves just before they are garbage collected. In J2SE, an Object's finalize() method is called before the object is reclaimed by the garbage collector. No such mechanism exists in CLDC. If you need to clean up resources, you will need to do it explicitly instead of placing cleanup code in finalize(). This is a good idea anyhow, particularly in a small device with limited resources. Explicitly cleaning up resources means that the memory and processing power they consume will be reclaimed sooner rather than later. Cleanup code in finalize() methods doesn't get executed until the garbage collector runs, and you never know exactly when that's going to happen.

■**Tip** On the topic of cleaning up after yourself, it is always a good idea when programming in a small platform such as MIDP to set any object references to null as soon as you finish using them. Doing so will help the garbage collector to perform its job.

No Reflection

CLDC does not support the Reflection API. The target devices of CLDC/MIDP are simply too small to allow it. Although most developers don't need to use reflection directly, this omission has important implications. Without reflection, no Remote Method Invocation (RMI) is possible. Without RMI, JINI is not possible. Therefore, bare-bones CLDC/MIDP implementations cannot run JINI. If you want to run JINI, you'll need to investigate one of the larger J2ME profiles, most likely the Personal Profile (see Chapter 1) and the RMI Optional API (JSR 66).

No Native Methods

Native methods are not supported in CLDC (and, by extension, MIDP). The specification does not support a way to access native device methods from Java. Although the MIDP implementation does, of course, include native methods, they are compiled into the implementation itself. Applications cannot define new native methods.

Don't worry about losing access to platform-specific features, however, because device vendors are likely to implement proprietary APIs in addition to MIDP. For details, check the developer web site of the manufacturer or network carrier of your device. Bear in mind that your use of vendor- or device-specific APIs will limit the audience of your application. In certain instances (games, for example), it makes sense to distribute multiple versions of an application targeted at specific devices.

No User Classloading

As we discussed in Chapter 1, one of the strengths of the Java platform is the ability to load classes at runtime. Unfortunately, because of resource constraints and security concerns, CLDC does not allow you to define your own classloaders. The application manager that runs MIDlets has a classloader, but you cannot access it or use it yourself in any way.

Multithreading

Using threads is much as you remember it from J2SE, as long as you keep things simple. Creating new threads, starting them, and using the handy java.lang.Runnable interface are the same as in J2SE. One important omission in CLDC 1.0 is the interrupt() method, which is not present in the java.lang.Thread class. In CLDC 1.1, the interrupt() method is available.

The pause(), resume(), and stop() methods (which are deprecated in the J2SE SDK) are also absent. Thread groups and daemon threads are not supported in CLDC/MIDP; thread naming is not supported in CLDC 1.0 but is available in CLDC 1.1.

String and StringBuffer

Both String and StringBuffer are present in the CLDC java.lang package. They are largely unchanged from their J2SE counterparts.

The largest change in the String class in CLDC 1.0 is the elimination of valueOf() static methods that convert between floating-point primitives and Strings, although these are present in CLDC 1.1. A few other obscure methods are absent from CLDC's String class, but you probably won't miss them. For example, although CLDC's String includes the compareTo(String str) method, it doesn't have either the compareTo(Object o) or compareToIgnoreCase(String str) methods that are found in the J2SE SDK. (CLDC 1.1 does include an equalsIgnoreCase() method in the String class.) There are simple workarounds for these limitations. You can, for example, call the toString() method on an object and pass it to compareTo(String str).

StringBuffer's append() and insert() methods do not include overrides for floating-point types in the CLDC 1.0 version of the class, but these are available in CDLC 1.1. Also, the substring() method has been pruned. Other than that, however, StringBuffer should be very familiar for seasoned J2SE programmers.

Math

The Math class contains static methods for performing mathematical calculations. In J2SE, many of these methods involve trigonometric functions on floating-point numbers. In CLDC 1.0, these are all gone, leaving only a handful of methods. CLDC 1.1, because it supports floating-point types, includes several more methods in java.lang.Math, but CLDC's java.lang.Math is still a subset of the J2SE version of the class. In the API listing that follows, the plus signs (+) indicate new variables or methods in CLDC 1.1.

```
   public final class Math
       extends java.lang.Object {
       // Constants
+      public static final double E;
+      public static final double PI;
          // Static methods
       public static int abs(int a);
       public static long abs(long a);
+      public static float abs(float a);
+      public static double abs(double a);
+      public static native double ceil(double a);
+      public static native double cos(double a);
+      public static native double floor(double a);
       public static int max(int a, int b);
       public static long max(long a, long b);
+      public static float max(float a, float b);
+      public static double max(double a, double b);
       public static int min(int a, int b);
       public static long min(long a, long b);
+      public static float min(float a, float b);
+      public static double min(double a, double b);
+      public static native double sin(double a);
```

```
+    public static native double sqrt(double a);
+    public static native double tan(double a);
+    public static double toDegrees(double angrad);
+    public static double toRadians(double angdeg);
}
```

Runtime and System

Runtime and System provide access to the Java Virtual Machine (JVM) and system-wide resources.
These two classes are greatly reduced from their J2SE counterparts, so much so that it makes
sense to reproduce their entire public API here. First, let's take a look at Runtime:

```
public class Runtime
    extends java.lang.Object {
  // Static methods
  public static Runtime getRuntime();


  // Methods
  public void exit(int status);
  public  long freeMemory();
  public  void gc();
  public  long totalMemory();
}
```

To get the single Runtime instance, call getRuntime(). You can tell the JVM to run its garbage
collector by calling gc(). On MIDP, if you try to call exit(), a SecurityException will be thrown;
the application life cycle is managed entirely through the methods of the MIDlet class. The
other two methods, totalMemory() and freeMemory(), allow you to examine the amount of
memory that is available for your application's data.

Note that Runtime does not support running external processes with the exec() method.
MIDlets cannot step outside the bounds of the JVM.

System provides static methods for performing various common tasks:

```
public final class System
    extends java.lang.Object {
  // Constants
  public static final PrintStream err;
  public static final PrintStream out;

  // Static methods
  public static  void arraycopy(Object src, int src_position,
      Object dst, int dst_position, int length);
  public static  long currentTimeMillis();
  public static void exit(int status);
  public static void gc();
  public static String getProperty(String key);
  public static  int identityHashCode(Object x);
}
```

The first thing you might notice is that while the err and out PrintStreams are defined, there is no System.in. This makes sense—System.in represents the console input; on a MIDP device, there really isn't any console. In fact, it may seem weird to have System.out and System.err defined. If you print information to System.out, it may not come out anywhere on a device; however, on a device emulator, you may be able to view System.out in a console window. Of course, any code that contains output to System.out and System.err should be removed from production code.

The gc() and exit() methods are shortcuts for calling the corresponding methods in the Runtime class.

All of System's methods are static. The arraycopy() method provides a fast implementation of array copying.

Finally, identityHashCode() is a default used by Object's hashCode() method.

The getProperty() method returns system properties, which are different from the MIDlet properties returned by MIDlet's getAppProperty() method. The following standard system properties are supported and their values can be retrieved at runtime:

- microedition.platform: This property contains the name of the device or host platform. If the implementation does not supply a value, the default is null.

- microedition.encoding: This property contains the default character encoding, which specifies how Unicode characters are represented in a byte stream, for example, "ISO-8859-1".

- microedition.configuration: This property contains the name of the implemented configuration, for example, "CLDC-1.1".

- microedition.profiles: Implemented profiles are contained in this system property, for example, "MIDP-2.0".

Streams in java.io

The java.io package in the CLDC/MIDP world is a stripped-down version of java.io in J2SE. Table 4-3 summarizes the classes of java.io in both J2SE and CLDC/MIDP. As you can see, many of the java.io classes you normally find in J2SE are missing from CLDC/MIDP.

Table 4-3. *The java.io Package*

J2SE SDK 1.4.2	CLDC 1.0	CLDC 1.1
Interfaces		
DataInput	Different	Different
DataOutput	Different	Different
Externalizable	–	–
FileFilter	–	–
FilenameFilter	–	–
ObjectInput	–	–
ObjectInputValidation	–	–

Table 4-3. *The java.io Package (Continued)*

J2SE SDK 1.4.2	CLDC 1.0	CLDC 1.1
ObjectOutput	–	–
ObjectStreamConstants	–	–
Serializable	–	–
Classes		
J2SE SDK 1.4.2	**CLDC 1.0**	**CLDC 1.1**
BufferedInputStream	–	–
BufferedOutputStream	–	–
BufferedReader	–	–
BufferedWriter	–	–
ByteArrayInputStream	Same	Same
ByteArrayOutputStream	Different	Same as CLDC 1.0
CharArrayReader	–	–
CharArrayWriter	–	–
DataInputStream	Different	Different
DataOutputStream	Different	Different
File	–	–
FileDescriptor	–	–
FileInputStream	–	–
FileOutputStream	–	–
FilePermission	–	–
FileReader	–	–
FileWriter	–	–
FilterInputStream	–	–
FilterOutputStream	–	–
FilterReader	–	–
FilterWriter	–	–
InputStream	Same	Same
InputStreamReader	Different	Same as CLDC 1.0

Table 4-3. *The java.io Package (Continued)*

J2SE SDK 1.4.2	CLDC 1.0	CLDC 1.1
LineNumberInputStream	–	–
LineNumberReader	–	–
ObjectInputStream	–	–
ObjectInputStream.GetField	–	–
ObjectOutputStream	–	–
ObjectOutputStream.PutField	–	–
ObjectStreamClass	–	–
ObjectStreamField	–	–
OutputStream	Same	Same
OutputStreamWriter	Different	Same as CLDC 1.0
PipedInputStream	–	–
PipedOutputStream	–	–
PipedReader	–	–
PipedWriter	–	–
PrintStream	Different	Different
PrintWriter	–	–
PushbackInputStream	–	–
PushbackReader	–	–
RandomAccessFile	–	–
Reader	Same	Same
SequenceInputStream	–	–
SerializablePermission	–	–
StreamTokenizer	–	–
StringBufferInputStream	–	–
StringReader	–	–
StringWriter	–	–
Writer	Same	Same

Although the differences between the J2SE and CLDC classes appear large, they can be easily grouped into three categories:

1. Because CLDC/MIDP by itself has no concept of a local file system, all the classes having to do with files have been pruned from the java.io package. This includes File, FileInputStream, FileOutputStream, the corresponding Reader and Writer classes, RandomAccessFile, and various supporting classes. If you need to store data persistently on a device, you'll need to use the javax.microedition.rms package API, described in Chapter 8. Some devices may expose a file system through an optional API: the File Connection Optional Package (JSR 75). In addition, devices that act as a Personal Information Manager (PIM) can also provide access to its persistent data through the optional PIM APIs (also part of JSR 75). These optional APIs are described in Chapter 9.

2. Object serialization is not supported in CLDC. This means that the Serializable interface and various object stream classes are not present.

3. Finally, J2SE includes a handful of utility stream classes—things you might want someday but shouldn't include on a device with a small amount of memory. These classes include piped streams, pushback streams, sequence streams, line numbering streams, and a few other gems like StreamTokenizer. If you really need one of these in your MIDlet, you may be able to package it with your application.[1] Bear in mind that there are licensing restrictions and technical problems with using classes directly from J2SE; be sure you understand the legal implications before you start copying files.

Character Encodings

MIDP includes the Reader and Writer character streams for working with Unicode characters. InputStreamReader and OutputStreamWriter handle the conversion between byte streams and character streams, just as in J2SE. An encoding determines how translation occurs between byte streams and character streams. A default encoding is used if you don't specify one. You can pass an encoding name to the constructors for InputStreamReader and OutputStreamWriter, if you wish. So far, this is all the same as in J2SE. In MIDP, though, you will likely find many fewer available encodings than in J2SE.

The default encoding for a MIDP implementation can be obtained by calling System.getProperty("microedition.encoding")—for example, ISO8859-1.

Resource Files

As described in Chapter 8, you can retrieve resource files from your MIDlet suite's JAR file. Use the getResourceAsStream() method in Class; it returns an InputStream that you can use as you please.

---

1. A better idea would be to redesign your application so that complicated stream processing isn't necessary on the device. In general, you should make your server do as much work as possible and your MIDlet do as little as possible.

java.util

CLDC includes only a dozen classes from J2SE's java.util package. Many of the missing classes are part of the Collections API, which is too bulky for small devices. Table 4-4 lists the classes and interfaces of java.util in both J2SE and CLDC/MIDP.

Table 4-4. *The java.util Package*

J2SE SDK 1.4.2	CLDC 1.0	CLDC 1.1
Interfaces		
Collection	–	–
Comparator	–	–
Enumeration	Same	Same
EventListener	–	–
Iterator	–	–
List	–	–
ListIterator	–	–
Map	–	–
Map.Entry	–	–
Observer	–	–
RandomAccess	–	–
Set	–	–
SortedMap	–	–
SortedSet	–	–
Classes		
J2SE SDK 1.4.2	**CLDC 1.0**	**CLDC 1.1**
AbstractCollection	–	–
AbstractList	–	–
AbstractMap	–	–
AbstractSequentialList	–	–
AbstractSet	–	–
ArrayList	–	–
Arrays	–	–
BitSet	–	–
Calendar	–	–
Collections	–	–

Table 4-4. *The java.util Package (Continued)*

J2SE SDK 1.4.2	CLDC 1.0	CLDC 1.1
Currency	–	–
Date	Different	Same as CLDC 1.0
Dictionary	–	–
EventListenerProxy	–	–
EventObject	–	–
GregorianCalendar	–	–
HashMap	–	–
HashSet	–	–
Hashtable	Different	Same as CLDC 1.0
IdentityHashMap	–	–
LinkedHashMap	–	–
LinkedHashSet	–	–
LinkedList	–	–
ListResourceBundle	–	–
Locale	–	–
Observable	–	–
Properties	–	–
PropertyPermission	–	–
PropertyResourceBundle	–	–
Random	Different	Different
ResourceBundle	–	–
SimpleTimeZone	–	–
Stack	Same	Same
StringTokenizer	–	–
Timer	Same (MIDP)	Same (MIDP)
TimerTask	Same (MIDP)	Same (MIDP)
TimeZone	Different	Same as CLDC 1.0
TreeMap	–	–
TreeSet	–	–
Vector	Different	Same as CLDC 1.0
WeakHashMap	–	–

Collections

Although the full J2SE Collections API is not supported by CLDC, the old familiar Vector and Hashtable classes remain, as well as the lesser-known Stack. If you are familiar with the J2SE SDK Vector and Hashtable classes, you should have no trouble with them in MIDP.

Timers

MIDP includes the Timer and TimerTask classes that were introduced into J2SE in the 1.3 version of the SDK. These are the only J2SE classes that are not included in the CLDC but are included in MIDP.

Timer's API is identical to the J2SE version with one exception. The constructor that specifies whether the thread is a daemon is missing, as daemon threads are not supported in MIDP. The TimerTask API is exactly the same in the J2SE SDK and MIDP.

Telling Time

J2SE has an impressive array of classes that can be used for specifying dates and times and translating to and from human-readable representations of dates and times. The J2SE time classes have four distinct responsibilities:

- *Points in time* are represented by instances of java.util.Date. If you think of time as a line graph, then an instance of Date is just a point on the line.

- *Calendars* are used for representing points in time with calendar fields like year, month, and day. If you're using a Gregorian calendar, for example, then you can translate from a single point in time to a set of calendar values like month, day, and hours, minutes, and seconds. In J2SE, java.util.Calendar is a parent class for calendars, while the java.util.GregorianCalendar class represents the Gregorian calendar system that is familiar to most of the world.

- *Formatting* classes translate between points in time and human-readable strings. In J2SE, java.text.DateFormat is the parent for classes that can both generate and parse human-readable strings representing points in time. Formatting classes are very likely to make use of a calendar. For example, a typical DateFormat implementation might use a GregorianCalendar to translate a point in time to a set of calendar values, which it would then format in a string.

- *Time zone* classes represent the time zones of the world. The calendar and format classes use a time zone to create a localized representation of a particular point in time. In J2SE, java.util.TimeZone is the parent class of all time zones, with java.util.SimpleTimeZone as a concrete implementation.

Understanding these classes and their interactions is a little tricky, and it's complicated by the fact that the APIs changed considerably between JDK 1.0 and JDK 1.1. The java.util.Date class used to have extra functionality in it; although the methods are deprecated, they're still present and may be confusing. Fortunately, you don't have to deal with this in the CLDC/MIDP world.

The situation is somewhat simpler in CLDC/MIDP. There are fewer classes, for one thing, and the Date class API has been cleaned up. In MIDP, the four responsibilities we just discussed are assigned to classes as follows:

- *Points in time* are represented by instances of java.util.Date, just like before. The Date class, in essence, is just a wrapper for a long value that indicates the number of milliseconds since midnight on January 1, 1970. (This is a standard way of representing time. It will work for about another 290 million years, so don't worry about another millennium bug.)

- *Calendars* are still represented by instances of java.util.Calendar. However, the GregorianCalendar class is no longer part of the public API. To get a Calendar instance, you can use the getInstance() factory method. Chances are you won't need to do this.

- *Formatting* classes are hidden from view in MIDP. One of the user interface classes, javax.microedition.lcdui.DateField, can convert a Date to a human-readable display, eliminating the need for you to mess around with date formatters yourself. Essentially DateField is a graphic wrapper around a Date instance. It also allows the user to edit calendar and clock fields to produce a new Date value. See Chapter 6 for a full discussion of DateField.

- *Time zones* are still represented by instances of java.util.TimeZone. TimeZone offers several static methods for examining the available time zones and getting an instance representing a particular time zone.

Summary

Developers are bombarded with information, and the best developers are the ones who can learn new material fast. Every once in a while, though, something you already know can be used again. This is one of those cases—something you already know about, the J2SE APIs, comes in very handy as you learn MIDP programming. MIDP's java.lang, java.io, and java.util packages contain classes that look and act a lot like the corresponding classes in J2SE.

CHAPTER 5

Creating a User Interface

Many MIDP applications are built to run on many different devices without modification. This is particularly difficult in the area of the user interface because devices have screens of all sizes, in grayscale and in color. Furthermore, devices vary widely in their input capabilities, from numeric keypads to alphabetic keyboards, soft keys, and even touch screens. The minimum screen size mandated by MIDP is 96×54 pixels, with at least one bit of color depth.[1] As for input, MIDP is fairly open ended: devices are expected to have some type of keyboard, or a touch screen, or possibly both.

Given the wide variety of devices that are compliant with MIDP, there are two ways to create applications that work well on all devices:

- *Abstraction*: Specify a user interface in abstract terms, relying on the MIDP implementation to create something concrete. Instead of saying something like, "Display the word 'Next' on the screen above the soft button," you say, "Give me a Next command somewhere in this interface."

- *Discovery*: The application learns about the device at runtime and tailors the user interface programmatically. You might, for example, find out how big the device's screen was in order to scale your user interface appropriately.

The MIDP APIs support both methods. Abstraction is the preferred method because it involves less code in your application and more work by the MIDP implementation. In some cases, like games, you need to be more specific about the user interface; these types of applications will discover the capabilities of a device and attempt to tailor their behavior appropriately. MIDP's user interface APIs are designed so that it's easy to mix the two techniques in the same application.

The View from the Top

MIDP contains user interface classes in the javax.microedition.lcdui and javax.microedition.lcdui.game packages. The device's display, as seen by the MIDlet, is represented by an instance of the Display class, accessed from a factory method, getDisplay(). Display's main purpose in life is to keep track of what is currently shown, which is an instance

---

1. Color depth is the number of bits that determine the color of a pixel on the screen. One bit allows for two colors (usually black and white). Four bits allows for 16 colors, which could be different levels of gray or a palette of other colors. In general, N bits allow 2 to the power of N colors or levels of gray.

of Displayable. If you think of Display as an easel, a Displayable instance is akin to a canvas on that easel.

MIDlets can change the contents of the display by passing Displayable instances to Display's setCurrent() method. This is the basic function of a typical MIDlet:

1. Show a Displayable.

2. Wait for input.

3. Decide what Displayable should be next.

4. Repeat.

Displayable has a small family of subclasses that represent various types of user interfaces. Figure 5-1 shows the lineage.

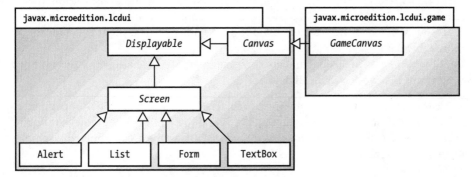

Figure 5-1. *Displayables in the javax.microedition.lcdui and javax.microedition.lcdui.game package*

Displayable's progeny are split between two branches that correspond to the two methods for creating generalized user interfaces, abstraction and discovery. The Screen class represents displays that are specified in abstract terms.

These screens contain standard user interface items like combo boxes, lists, menus, and buttons. Four subclasses provide a wide range of functionality, as illustrated in Figure 5-2.

The remainder of this chapter is devoted to explaining the simplest of these four classes: TextBox and Alert. The next chapter explores the more flexible List and Form.

For particularly demanding or idiosyncratic displays, you'll have to create a subclass of Canvas. Your MIDlet will assume responsibility for most of the drawing, but you get much finer control over what is shown and how user input is handled. Canvas supplies methods that allow your MIDlet to learn about its environment—the size of the display, for example, and which kinds of events are supported by the device. User interfaces built on Canvas discover the attributes of a device and attempt to create something that looks reasonable. Chapter 13 explains Canvas-based user interfaces in detail. GameCanvas provides user interface functionality specifically for game displays. This API is explained in Chapter 14.

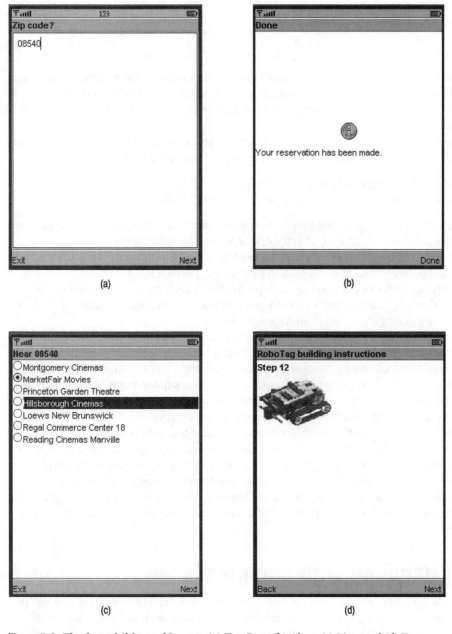

Figure 5-2. *The four children of Screen: (a) TextBox, (b) Alert, (c) List, and (d) Form*

Using Display

Display manages a device's screen. You can get a reference to the device's display by supplying a MIDlet reference to the static getDisplay() method. Typically, you'll do this in the startApp() method of a MIDlet:

```
public void startApp() {
  Display d = Display.getDisplay(this);
  // ...
}
```

You may be tempted to call getDisplay() in a MIDlet's constructor, but according to the specification, getDisplay() can only be called after the beginning of the MIDlet's startApp() method. If you try to call it before startApp() is called, your MIDlet may throw an exception and terminate before starting!

Once you've got a reference to a device's Display, you'll just need to create something to show (an instance of Displayable) and pass it to one of Display's setCurrent() methods:

```
public void setCurrent(Displayable next)
public void setCurrent(Alert alert, Displayable nextDisplayable)
```

The second version is used when you want to show a temporary message (an Alert) followed by something else. We'll talk more about Alerts at the end of this chapter.

Display's getCurrent() method returns a reference to what's currently being shown. Note that a MIDlet may return a valid object from getCurrent() even if it is not visible to the user. This could happen on a device running multiple MIDlets simultaneously, for example. Note that the Displayable interface has a method called isShown() that indicates whether the given object is actually being shown on the device screen.

You can also query a Display to determine its capabilities, which is helpful for applications that need to adapt themselves to different types of displays. The numColors() method returns the number of distinct colors supported by this device, while the isColor() method tells whether the device supports color or grayscale. A Display for a device supporting 16 levels of gray, for example, would return false from isColor() and 16 from numColors(). You can also find out whether the device supports transparency by calling numAlphaLevels(), which returns the number of transparency levels. The minimum return value is 2, indicating that image pixels with full transparency and full opacity are supported. Return values greater than 2 indicate that alpha blending is supported. The getColor() and getBorderStyle() methods are used for finding out colors and line styles from the system user interface scheme. These are useful for drawing custom items, a topic that is covered in Chapter 7. The flashBacklight() and vibrate() methods invoke the corresponding features of the device. These are more fully discussed in Chapter 14.

Event Handling with Commands

Displayable, the parent of all screen displays, supports a very flexible user interface concept, the command. A *command* is something the user can invoke—you can think of it as a GUI button. Like a button, it has a title, like OK or Cancel, and your application can respond appropriately when the user invokes the command. The premise is that you want a command to be available to the user, but you don't really care how it is shown on the screen or exactly how the user invokes it—keypad button, soft button, touch screen, voice recognition, whatever.

Every Displayable keeps a list of its Commands. You can add and remove Commands using the following methods:

```
public void addCommand(Command cmd)
public void removeCommand(Command cmd)
```

Creating Commands

In MIDP, commands are represented by instances of the Command class. To create a Command, just supply a name, a type, and a priority. The name is usually shown on the screen. The type can be used to signify a commonly used command. It must be one of the values defined in the Command class. Table 5-1 shows the type values and their meanings.

Table 5-1. *Command Types*

Name	Meaning
OK	Confirms a selection
CANCEL	Cancels pending changes
BACK	Moves the user back to a previous screen
STOP	Stops a running operation
HELP	Shows application instructions
SCREEN	Indicates generic type for specific application commands

To create a standard OK command, for example, you would do this:

```
Command c = new Command("OK", Command.OK, 0);
```

To create a command specific to your application, you might do this:

```
Command c = new Command("Launch", Command.SCREEN, 0);
```

It's up to the MIDP implementation to figure out how to show the commands. In the Sun J2ME Wireless Toolkit emulator, commands are assigned to the two soft buttons. A *soft button* is a button on the device keypad with no predefined function. A soft button can serve a different purpose at different times. If there are more commands than there are soft buttons, the commands that don't fit will be grouped into a menu that is assigned to one of the soft buttons.

A simple priority scheme determines who wins when there are more commands than available screen space. Every command has a priority that indicates how hard the display system should try to show the command. Lower numbers indicate a higher priority. If you add a command with priority 0, then several more with priority 1, the priority 0 command will show up on the screen directly. The other commands will most likely end up in a secondary menu.

Long labels are supported on commands. The actual MIDP implementation decides which label it will use based on the available screen space and the size of the labels. You can create a command with a short and long label like this:

```
Command c = new Command("Run", "Run simulation", Command.SCREEN, 0);
```

The Command class provides getLabel(), getLongLabel(), and getCommandType() methods for retrieving information about commands.

Responding to Commands

By themselves, Commands aren't very exciting. They'll show up on the screen, but nothing happens automatically when a user invokes a command. An object called a *listener* is notified when the user invokes any command in a Displayable. This follows the basic form of the JavaBeans event model; a Displayable is a *unicast event source*. A Displayable fires off an event every time the user invokes one of its Commands.

The listener is an object that implements the CommandListener interface. To register the listener with a Displayable, use the following method:

```
public void setListener(CommandListener l)
```

Displayable is a unicast event source because it can only have one listener object. (Multicast event sources can have multiple listeners and use an add... method for adding listeners rather than a set... method.)

Implementing a CommandListener is a matter of defining a single method:

```
public void commandAction(Command c, Displayable s)
```

When a command is invoked, the Displayable that contains it calls the commandAction() method of the registered listener.

■Tip Event listeners should not perform lengthy processing inside the event-handling thread. The system uses its own thread to call commandAction() in response to user input. If your implementation of commandAction() does any heavy thinking, it will tie up the system's event-handling thread. If you have anything complicated to do, use your own thread. Some JVM implementations may protect itself from what is effectively a denial-of-service attack and terminate threads or applications that abuse system thread.

A Simple Example

By way of illustration, consider the following class:

```
import javax.microedition.midlet.*;
import javax.microedition.lcdui.*;

public class Commander extends MIDlet {
  public void startApp() {
    Displayable d = new TextBox("TextBox", "Commander", 20, TextField.ANY);
    Command c = new Command("Exit", Command.EXIT, 0);
    d.addCommand(c);
    d.setCommandListener(new CommandListener() {
      public void commandAction(Command c, Displayable s) {
        notifyDestroyed();
      }
    } );
```

```
    Display.getDisplay(this).setCurrent(d);
  }

  public void pauseApp() { }

  public void destroyApp(boolean unconditional) { }
}
```

This MIDlet creates a `TextBox`, which is a kind of `Displayable`, and adds a single command to it. The listener is created as an anonymous inner subclass. In Sun's toolkit, this MIDlet appears as shown in Figure 5-3.

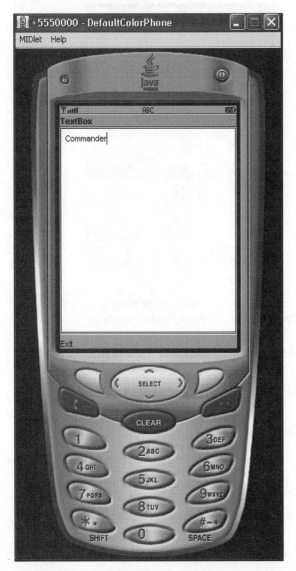

Figure 5-3. *A simple MIDlet with a single command, Exit*

Figure 5-3 shows the Exit command being mapped to one of the MIDP simulator's soft buttons. If you add another command to this MIDlet, it will be mapped to the other soft button. If you continue adding commands, the ones that don't fit on the screen will be put into an off-screen menu. For example, a screen with four commands shows up in the MIDP simulator as illustrated in Figure 5-4a.

If you press the soft button for Menu, you'll see the remainder of the commands as shown in Figure 5-4b. Menu items can now be selected by pressing a number or using the arrow keys for navigation. In the example shown in Figure 5-4, the Exit command is given a higher priority (lower number) than the other commands, which ensures that it appears directly on the screen. The other commands, with a lower priority, are relegated to the command menu.

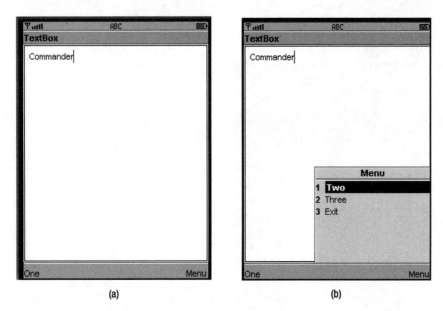

(a)   (b)

Figure 5-4. *This MIDlet has more commands than the device has soft buttons. Invoking the (a) system-generated Menu command brings up the (b) remaining commands.*

All Displayables have a title and an optional ticker. The title is just what you expect: a string that appears at the top of a Displayable. As you saw in Figure 5-3, the title of the screen is TextBox. Subclasses of Screen have constructors that set the title, but the title may also be accessed using the following methods:

```
public void setTitle(String newTitle)
public String getTitle()
```

Tickers

A ticker is simply a bit of text that scrolls across the top of a Displayable; it is named after old-fashioned stock tickers.

The Ticker class is a simple wrapper for a string. To add a ticker to a screen, you would do something like this:

```
// Displayable d = ...
Ticker ticker = new Ticker("This is the ticker message!");
d.setTicker(ticker);
```

Figure 5-5 shows a ticker in action.

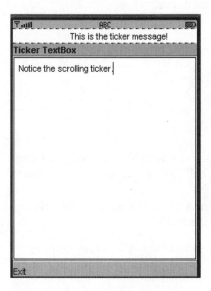

Figure 5-5. *A ticker scrolls across the top of a screen.*

Screens

The remainder of this chapter and all of Chapter 6 are devoted to Screen and its subclasses, which is the left branch of the hierarchy shown in Figure 5-1. Screen is the base class for all classes that represent generalized user interfaces. This class has no methods of its own, but inherits all from Displayable.

Canvas, by contrast, is a base class for specialized interfaces, such as those for games. Canvas will be fully covered later, in Chapter 13.

In the coming sections, we'll explore each of Screen's child classes.

TextBox, the Simplest Screen

The simplest type of screen is the TextBox, which you've already seen in action. TextBox allows the user to enter a string. Keep in mind that on a garden-variety MIDP device, text input is a tedious process. Many devices only have a numeric keypad, so entering a single character is a matter of one, two, three, or even more button presses. A good MIDlet requires minimal user input.

That said, your MIDlet may need some kind of input—perhaps a zip code, or a short name, or some kind of password. In these cases, you'll probably want to use a TextBox.

A TextBox is created by specifying four parameters:

```
public TextBox(String title, String text, int maxSize, int constraints)
```

The title is used as the screen title, while `text` and `maxSize` determine the initial text and maximum size of the text box. Finally, `constraints` can be used to restrict the user's input. Constants from the `TextField` class are used to specify the type of input required:

- `ANY` allows any type of input that is supported by the device.

- `NUMERIC` restricts the input to integers.

- `DECIMAL` allows numbers with fractional parts.

- `PHONENUMBER` requires a telephone number.

- `EMAILADDR` input must be an e-mail address.

- `URL` input must be a web address.

It's up to the implementation to determine how these constraints are enforced. The toolkit emulators simply don't allow invalid input; for example, a `NUMERIC TextBox` doesn't allow you to enter alphabetic characters.

The preceding constraints may be combined with the flags listed next. Constraints limit the behavior of users, while flags define the behavior of the `TextBox`.

- `PASSWORD` characters are not shown when entered; generally, they are represented by asterisks.

- `UNEDITABLE` indicates text that cannot be edited.

- `SENSITIVE` is used to flag text that the implementation should not store. Some input schemes store input from the user for later use in autocompletion. This flag indicates that the text is off limits and should not be saved or cached.

- `NON_PREDICTIVE` indicates that you are expecting the user to enter text that any text-predicting input scheme will probably not be able to guess. For example, if you're expecting the user to enter an order number like Z51002S, you would use this flag to tell the input scheme to not bother trying to predict the input.

- `INITIAL_CAPS_WORD` is used for input where each word should be capitalized.

- `INITIAL_CAPS_SENTENCE` indicates input where the first character of each sentence should be capitalized.

If you don't want the `TextBox` to perform any validation, use `ANY` or its numerical equivalent, 0, for the `constraints` parameter in the constructor.

The flags may be combined with any of the other constraints using the `OR` operator. For example, to create a `TextBox` that constrains input to an e-mail address but keeps the entered data hidden, you would do something like this:

```
Displayable d = new TextBox("Email", "", 64,
        TextField.EMAILADDR | TextField.PASSWORD);
```

If you think about it, though, `PASSWORD` is probably more trouble than it's worth. The point of `PASSWORD` fields, at least on desktop machines, is to keep someone walking past your computer screen from seeing your secret password. For every character you enter, the password field shows an asterisk or some other symbol. As you type your secret password, all that shows up on the screen is a line of asterisks. On mobile phones and other small devices, this is less of a concern because the screens are smaller and much more difficult to read than a typical desktop monitor.

Furthermore, the difficulty of entering data on a small device means that it will be hard to correctly enter passwords if you are typing blind. Mobile phones, for example, typically require you to press keys several times to enter a single letter. On Sun's toolkit emulator, pressing the 7 key twice enters the letter "Q." On a real device, you would have to enter a password "gandalf" with the following sequence of key presses: 4, 2, 6, 6, 3, 2, 5, 5, 5, 3, 3, 3. Without visual feedback, it would be extremely easy to make a mistake when entering a password. ("Did I press the 5 key two times or three times?") The J2ME Wireless Toolkit emulator shows the current character, but previously typed characters are shown as asterisks. Good passwords typically have mixed case, numbers, and possibly punctuation; these would be hard to enter correctly.

Password fields (whether or not they use the PASSWORD flag) should be protected with the SENSITIVE flag so that the password doesn't show up in any system dictionaries or pop up unexpectedly when the user is entering other text.

A method in the TextBox class called setInitialInputMode(String characterSubset) is used to suggest to the implementation what input mode would be best suited to the expected text. You can only suggest the input mode, and you have no way of knowing whether the implementation has honored the request. The string passed to the method can be one of the constants from the J2SE java.lang.Character.UnicodeBlock class, prepended with "UCB_". For example, you might pass "UCB_BASIC_LATIN" or "UCB_KATAKANA" to this method. You can also use input subsets defined by java.awt.im.InputSubset by prepending them with "IS_". For example, "IS_LATIN" or "IS_KANJI" would be valid. Finally, the character subsets "MIDP_UPPERCASE_LATIN" and "MIDP_LOWERCASE_LATIN" are also defined.

The input mode is complementary to the text constraints and flags. You might specify ANY for the constraints, then call setInitialInputMode("MIDP_LOWERCASE_LATIN") to request that the implementation begin by allowing lowercase input. This doesn't prevent the user from changing the input mode, it just starts things off on the right foot.

Using Alerts

An alert is an informative message shown to the user. In the MIDP universe, there are two flavors of alert:

- A timed alert is shown for a certain amount of time, typically just a few seconds. It displays an informative message that does not need to be acknowledged, like "Your transaction is complete," or "I can't do that right now, Dave."

- A modal alert stays up until the user dismisses it. Modal alerts are useful when you need to offer the user a choice of actions. You might display a message like "Are you ready to book these tickets?" and offer Yes and No commands as options.

MIDP alerts can have an associated icon, like a stop sign or question mark. Alerts may even have an associated sound, although this depends on the implementation. MIDP alerts are very much the same concept as modal dialog boxes in windowing systems like MacOS and Windows. Figure 5-6 shows a typical Alert.

Figure 5-6. *Alerts are similar to modal dialog boxes in a desktop windowing system.*

Alerts are represented by instances of the javax.microedition.lcdui.Alert class, which offers the following constructors:

```
public Alert()
public Alert(String title, String alertText, Image alertImage, AlertType alertType)
```

Any or all of the parameters in the second constructor may be null. (Don't worry about the Image class right now; we'll discuss it in the next chapter in the section on Lists.)

By default, timed Alerts are created using a default timeout value; you can find out the default value by calling getDefaultTimeout(). To change the Alert's timeout, call setTimeout() with the timeout value in milliseconds. A special value, FOREVER, may be used to indicate that the Alert is modal.

You could create a simple timed Alert with the following code:

```
Alert alert = new Alert("Sorry", "I'm sorry, Dave...", null, null);
```

To explicitly set the timeout value to five seconds, you could do this:

```
alert.setTimeout(5000);
```

If, instead, you wanted a modal alert, you would use the special value FOREVER:

```
alert.setTimeout(Alert.FOREVER);
```

The MIDP implementation will automatically supply a way to dismiss a modal alert. Sun's reference implementation, for example, provides a Done command mapped to a soft button. This command is exposed as the static member DISMISS_COMMAND, allowing you to register your own command listener and explicitly recognize this command. You can add your own commands to an Alert using the usual addCommand() method. The first time you call addCommand(), the system's Done command is removed.

The default behavior for Alerts automatically advances to the next screen when the Alert is dismissed or times out. You can specify the next screen by passing it and the Alert to the two-argument setCurrent() method in Display. If you call the regular one-argument setCurrent() method, the previous screen is restored when the Alert is dismissed. Alert types serve as hints to the underlying MIDP implementation. The implementation may use the alert type to decide what kind of sound to play when the alert is shown. The AlertType class provides five types, accessed as static member variables: ALARM, CONFIRMATION, ERROR, INFO, and WARNING.

There is an optional indicator to an Alert. By default, no indicator is present, but you can add one by passing a Gauge to Alert's setIndicator() method. (Gauge is presented in the next chapter in the section on Forms.) The indicator is handy for showing progress in a network connection or a long computation.

The following example, TwoAlerts, shows both types of alert. It features a main TextBox that is displayed when the MIDlet begins. Two commands, Go and About, provide access to the alerts. The Go command shows a timed alert that contains a message about a fictitious network error. The About command displays a modal alert that could contain copyright information. A third command, Exit, provides a way to exit the MIDlet. Keep in mind that all three commands may not fit on the screen; some of them may be accessible from a secondary menu.

```java
import javax.microedition.midlet.*;
import javax.microedition.lcdui.*;

public class TwoAlerts
    extends MIDlet
    implements CommandListener {
  private Display mDisplay;

  private TextBox mTextBox;
  private Alert mTimedAlert;
  private Alert mModalAlert;

  private Command mAboutCommand, mGoCommand, mExitCommand;

  public TwoAlerts() {
    mAboutCommand = new Command("About", Command.SCREEN, 1);
    mGoCommand = new Command("Go", Command.SCREEN, 1);
    mExitCommand = new Command("Exit", Command.EXIT, 2);

    mTextBox = new TextBox("TwoAlerts", "", 32, TextField.ANY);
    mTextBox.addCommand(mAboutCommand);
    mTextBox.addCommand(mGoCommand);
    mTextBox.addCommand(mExitCommand);
    mTextBox.setCommandListener(this);

    mTimedAlert = new Alert("Network error",
        "A network error occurred. Please try again.",
        null,
        AlertType.INFO);
```

```
    mModalAlert = new Alert("About TwoAlerts",
        "TwoAlerts is a simple MIDlet that demonstrates the use of Alerts.",
        null,
        AlertType.INFO);
      mModalAlert.setTimeout(Alert.FOREVER);
    }

    public void startApp() {
      mDisplay = Display.getDisplay(this);

      mDisplay.setCurrent(mTextBox);
    }

    public void pauseApp() {
    }

    public void destroyApp(boolean unconditional) {}

    public void commandAction(Command c, Displayable s) {
      if (c == mAboutCommand)
        mDisplay.setCurrent(mModalAlert);
      else if (c == mGoCommand)
        mDisplay.setCurrent(mTimedAlert, mTextBox);
      else if (c == mExitCommand)
        notifyDestroyed();
    }
}
```

Summary

MIDP's main user interface classes are based on abstractions that can be adapted to devices that have different display and input capabilities. Several varieties of prepackaged screen classes make it easy to create a user interface. Screens have a title and an optional ticker. Most importantly, screens can contain Commands, which the implementation makes available to the user. Your application can respond to commands by acting as a listener object. This chapter described TextBox, a screen for accepting user input, and Alert, a simple screen for displaying information. In the next chapter, we'll get into the more complex List and Form classes.

CHAPTER 6

■ ■ ■

Lists and Forms

In the last chapter, you learned about MIDP's simpler screen classes. Now we're getting into deeper waters, with screens that show lists and screens with mixed types of controls.

Using Lists

After TextBox and Alert, the next simplest Screen is List, which allows the user to select items (called *elements*) from a list of choices. A text string or an image is used to represent each element in the list. List supports the selection of a single element or of multiple elements.

There are two main types of List, denoted by constants in the Choice interface:

- MULTIPLE designates a list where multiple elements may be selected simultaneously.

- EXCLUSIVE specifies a list where only one element may be selected. It is akin to a group of radio buttons.

Understanding List Types

For both MULTIPLE and EXCLUSIVE lists, selection and confirmation are separate steps. In fact, List does not handle confirmation for these types of lists—your MIDlet will need to provide some other mechanism (probably a Command) that allows users to confirm their choices. MULTIPLE lists allow users to select and deselect various elements before confirming the selection. EXCLUSIVE lists also permit users to change their minds several times before confirming the selection.

Figure 6-1a shows one implementation of an EXCLUSIVE list. With this list, the user navigates through the list using the arrow up and down keys. An element can selected by pressing the select button on the device. Figure 6-1b shows a MULTIPLE list. It works basically the same way as an EXCLUSIVE list, but multiple elements can be selected simultaneously. As before, the user moves through the list with the up and down arrow buttons. The select button toggles the selection of a particular element.

A further refinement of EXCLUSIVE also exists: IMPLICIT lists combine the steps of selection and confirmation. The IMPLICIT list acts just like a menu. Figure 6-2 shows an IMPLICIT list with images and text for each element. When the user hits the select button, the list immediately fires off an event, just like a Command. An IMPLICIT list is just like an EXCLUSIVE list in that the user can only select one of the list elements. But with IMPLICIT lists, there's no opportunity for the user to change his or her mind before confirming the selection.

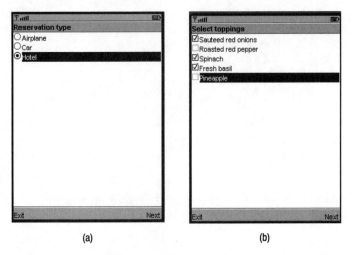

(a)   (b)

Figure 6-1. *List types: (a) EXCLUSIVE and (b) MULTIPLE*

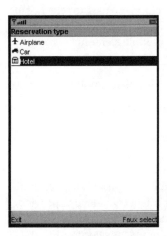

Figure 6-2. *IMPLICIT lists combine selection and confirmation.*

Event Handling for IMPLICIT Lists

When the user makes a selection in an IMPLICIT list, the commandAction() method of the list's CommandListener is invoked. A special value is passed to commandAction() as the Command parameter:

```
public static final Command SELECT_COMMAND
```

For example, you can test the source of command events like this:

```
public void commandAction(Command c, Displayable s) {
  if (c == nextCommand)
    // ...
  else if (c == List.SELECT_COMMAND)
    // ...
}
```

The example at the end of this section, in Listing 6-1, demonstrates an IMPLICIT list.

You can also use the setSelectCommand() method to specify your own Command to be used for selections instead of having to use the SELECT_COMMAND.

Creating Lists

To create a List, specify a title and a list type. If you have the element names and images available ahead of time, you can pass them in the constructor:

```
public List(String title, int type)
public List(String title, int type,
    String[] stringElements, Image[] imageElements)
```

The stringElements parameter cannot be null but can be empty; however, imageElements may contain null array elements. If the image associated with a list element is null, the element is displayed using just the string. If both the string and the image are defined, the element will display using the image and the string.

Some Lists will have more elements than can be displayed on the screen. Indeed, the actual number of elements that will fit varies from device to device. But don't worry: List implementations automatically handle scrolling up and down to show the full contents of the List. MIDlet developers have no control over how the implementation handles this scrolling.

About Images

Our romp through the List class yields a first look at images. Instances of the javax.microedition.lcdui.Image class represent images in MIDP. The specification dictates implementations be able to load images files in PNG format.[1] This format supports both a transparent color and lossless compression.

Image has no constructors, but the Image class offers a handful of createImage() factory methods for obtaining Image instances. The first are for loading images from PNG data.

```
public static Image createImage(String name)
public static Image createImage(byte[] imagedata, int imageoffset,
    int imagelength)
public static Image createImage(InputStream stream)
```

The first method attempts to create an Image from the named file, which should be packaged inside the JAR that contains your MIDlet. You must use an absolute pathname or the image file will not be found. The second method creates an Image using data in the supplied array. The data starts at the given array offset, imageoffset, and is imagelength bytes long. The third method creates an Image from an InputStream.

Images may be *mutable* or *immutable*. Mutable Images can be modified by calling getGraphics() and using the returned Graphics object to draw on the image. (For full details on Graphics, see Chapter 13.) If you try to call getGraphics() on an immutable Image, an IllegalStateException will be thrown.

---

1. MIDP implementations are not required to recognize all varieties of PNG files. The documentation for the Image class has the specifics.

The createImage() methods described previously return immutable Images. To create a mutable Image, use the following method:

```
public static Image createImage(int width, int height)
```

Typically you would create a mutable Image for off-screen drawing, perhaps for an animation or to reduce flicker if the device's display is not double buffered.

Any Image you pass to Alert, ChoiceGroup, ImageItem, or List should be immutable. To create an immutable Image from a mutable one, use the following method:

```
public static Image createImage(Image image)
```

You can also create an Image from a portion of another Image using the following method:

```
public static Image createImage(Image image,
    int x, int y, int width, int height, int transform)
```

This method takes the part of the original image described by x, y, width, and height; applies the specified transformation; and returns the result as an immutable Image. The possible transformations are described by constants in the javax.microedition.lcdui.game.Sprite class and include things like mirroring and 90-degree rotation.

Image also includes methods that handle image data as an int array. We'll talk about these methods later in Chapter 13.

How do you figure out what size Images you need? Actually, Display provides methods that return information about the optimal width and height for various types of images:

```
public int getBestImageHeight(int imageType);
public int getBestImageWidth(int imageType);
```

The imageType parameter should be one of Display's constants: LIST_ELEMENT, ALERT, or CHOICE_GROUP_ELEMENT. (You'll learn all about ChoiceGroup later in this chapter.) If you were building a List, you could query Display to find the best size for element images. Assuming you had packaged icons of various sizes in your application, you could select the best-sized images at runtime.

Editing a List

List provides methods for adding items, removing elements, and examining elements. Each element in the List has an index. The first element is at index 0, the next at index 1, and so forth. You can replace an element with set() or add an element to the end of the list with append(). The insert() method adds a new element to the list at the given index; this bumps all elements at that position and higher up by one.

```
public void set(int elementNum, String stringPart, Image imagePart)
public void insert(int elementNum, String stringPart, Image imagePart)
public int append(String stringPart, Image imagePart)
```

You can examine the string or image for a given element by supplying its index. Similarly, you can use delete() to remove an element from the List.

```
public String getString(int elementNum)
public Image getImage(int elementNum)
public void delete(int elementNum)
public void deleteAll()
```

The deleteAll() method removes every element from the List.

Finally, the size() method returns the number of elements in the List.

Although you usually give the MIDP implementation the responsibility of displaying your List, methods in List give you some control over the appearance of a List. The first method, setFitPolicy(), tells the List how it should handle elements whose text is wider than the screen. The possible values (from the Choice interface) are the following:

- TEXT_WRAP_ON denotes that long elements will be wrapped to multiple lines.

- TEXT_WRAP_OFF denotes that long elements will be truncated at the edge of the screen.

- TEXT_WRAP_DEFAULT indicates that the implementation should use its default fit policy.

Another new method is setFont(), which allows you to specify the font that will be used for a specific List element. (Fonts will be fully discussed in Chapter 13.) The current Font for an element can be retrieved by calling getFont(). Calls to setFitPolicy() and setFont() only serve as hints; it's up to the implementation to decide how to display the List and whether the requested fit policy or font can be honored.

Working with List Selections

You can find out whether a particular element in a List is selected by supplying the element's index to the following method:

```
public boolean isSelected(int index)
```

For EXCLUSIVE and IMPLICIT lists, the index of the single selected element is returned from the following method:

```
public int getSelectedIndex()
```

If you call getSelectedIndex() on a MULTIPLE list, it will return -1.

To change the current selection programmatically, use setSelectedIndex().

```
public void setSelectedIndex(int index, boolean selected)
```

Finally, List allows you to set or get the selection state en masse with the following methods. The supplied arrays must have as many array elements as there are list elements.

```
public int getSelectedFlags(boolean[] selectedArray_return)
public void setSelectedFlags(boolean[] selectedArray)
```

An Example

The example in Listing 6-1 shows a simple MIDlet that could be part of a travel reservation application. The user chooses what type of reservation to make. This example uses an IMPLICIT list, which is essentially a menu.

Listing 6-1. *The TravelList Source Code*

```java
import java.io.*;
import javax.microedition.midlet.*;
import javax.microedition.lcdui.*;

public class TravelList
    extends MIDlet
    implements CommandListener {
  private List mList;
  private Command mExitCommand, mNextCommand;

  public TravelList() {
    String[] stringElements = { "Airplane", "Car", "Hotel" };
    Image[] imageElements = { loadImage("/airplane.png"),
        loadImage("/car.png"), loadImage("/hotel.png") };
    mList = new List("Reservation type", List.IMPLICIT,
        stringElements, imageElements);
    mNextCommand = new Command("Next", Command.SCREEN, 0);
    mExitCommand = new Command("Exit", Command.EXIT, 0);
    mList.addCommand(mNextCommand);
    mList.addCommand(mExitCommand);
    mList.setCommandListener(this);
  }

  public void startApp() {
    Display.getDisplay(this).setCurrent(mList);
  }

  public void commandAction(Command c, Displayable s) {
    if (c == mNextCommand || c == List.SELECT_COMMAND) {
      int index = mList.getSelectedIndex();
      Alert alert = new Alert("Your selection",
          "You chose " + mList.getString(index) + ".",
          null, AlertType.INFO);
      Display.getDisplay(this).setCurrent(alert, mList);
    }
    else if (c == mExitCommand)
      notifyDestroyed();
  }

  public void pauseApp() {}

  public void destroyApp(boolean unconditional) {}
```

```
private Image loadImage(String name) {
  Image image = null;
  try {
    image = Image.createImage(name);
  }
  catch (IOException ioe) {
    System.out.println(ioe);
  }

  return image;
}
}
```

To see images in this example, you'll need to either download the examples from the book's web site or supply your own images. With the J2ME Wireless Toolkit, image files should go in the res directory of your toolkit project directory. TravelList expects to find three images named airplane.png, car.png, and hotel.png.

Construction of the List itself is very straightforward. This application also includes a Next command and an Exit command, which are both added to the List. The TravelList instance is registered as the CommandListener for the List. If the Next command or the List's IMPLICIT command is fired off, you simply retrieve the selected item from the List and show it in an Alert.

The Next command, in fact, is not strictly necessary in this example since you can achieve the same result by clicking the select button on one of the elements in the List. Nevertheless, it might be a good idea to leave it there. Maybe all of the other screens in your application have a Next command, so you could keep it for user interface consistency. It never hurts to provide the user with more than one consistent way of doing things.

The difference between EXCLUSIVE and IMPLICIT lists can be subtle. Try changing the List in this example to EXCLUSIVE to see how the user experience is different.

Creating Advanced Interfaces with Forms

A Form is a screen that can include an arbitrary collection of user-interface controls, called *items*. In a movie ticket reservation MIDlet, you might use a form to allow the user to enter a date and a Zip code on one screen.

Keep in mind that the minimum screen size for a MID is 96×54 pixels. You can't fit a whole lot on a screen this size, nor should you try to. Forms that don't fit on the screen will automatically be made scrollable if needed, so your MIDlet will be able to show forms, regardless of the screen size. Scrolling forms tend to be confusing to users, however, so you should keep your forms as small as possible.

The javax.microedition.ldcui.Form class itself is fairly simple. One way to create a Form is by specifying a title:

```
public Form(String title)
```

In essence, a Form is a collection of items. Each item is represented by an instance of the Item class. If you have all the items ahead of time, you can pass them to Form's other constructor:

```
public Form(String title, Item[] items)
```

As a subclass of Screen and Displayable, Form inherits both a title and a ticker. Given the small screen size of a typical MIDP device, however, you may want to avoid using a ticker with your forms.

■**Caution** The use of a ticker may also affect battery life on a small device, due to the need to constantly update the ticker's display area.

Form's grandparent class, Displayable, gives Form the capabilities of displaying commands and firing command events. Again, you should probably keep commands simple with forms; in many cases a Next and a Back will probably be sufficient.

As with any Displayable, the basic strategy for showing a Form is to create one and pass it to Display's setCurrent() method. If you have a form that is larger than the Display, you may want to use the setCurrentItem() method in Display. This method makes the form containing the item visible, then it scrolls the form so the item is visible and has input focus.

Managing Items

Items may be added and removed, even while the Form is showing. The order of items is important as well; most MIDP implementations will display a form's items top to bottom and possibly left to right, scrolling the form vertically as needed if there are more items than available screen space.

To add an Item to the bottom of a form, use one of the append() methods. The first one can be used to add any Item implementation. The second two append() methods are strictly for convenience; behind the scenes, a StringItem or an ImageItem will be created for you.

```
public int append(Item item)
public int append(String str)
public int append(Image image)
```

Every item in a form has an index. You can place an item at a specific index (replacing the previous item at that index) using the method:

```
public void set(int index, Item item)
```

Alternately, if you'd like to add an item somewhere in the middle of the form, just supply the desired index for the new item to the insert() method. Subsequent items will move up by one index.

```
public void insert(int index, Item item)
```

To remove an item from a form, use delete().

```
public void delete(int index)
```

To remove all items with one call, use deleteAll().

```
public void deleteAll()
```

If you forget what you put in a form, you can find out the number of items and retrieve them with the following methods:

```
public int size()
public Item get(int index)
```

Understanding Form Layout

MIDs can have very different screen size and shapes. Forms have support for very specific layout. There's an exhaustive description of the layout algorithm in the documentation for javax.microedition.lcdui.Form, in the section titled "Layout." Stated briefly, Form attempts to lay out items left-to-right in rows, stacking rows top-to-bottom, just like English text on a page. The Item class includes plumbing that allows some control over the layout of individual items.

The Item Pantry

The MIDP specification includes a handy toolbox of items that can be used to build forms. We'll cover each of them briefly in the following sections and show how some of them look in Sun's MIDP reference implementation.

The Item Class

All of the items that can be added to forms descend from the class javax.microedition.lcdui.Item. This class has a getLabel() and setLabel() method. All Items have a string label, although it may or may not be shown by the specific subclass.

Items can also have commands, just like Displayables. When an Item is selected in a form, the Item's commands are shown along with the commands in the form. Figure 6-3 shows a form with four string items, cunningly named "one," "two," "three," and "four." The form itself has one command, "Exit." None of the string items has commands, except for "three," which has one command named "Details."

Figure 6-3. *Item "three" has a command.*

Note how the toolkit emulator indicates the presence of one or more commands on the item with a light underline. When you navigate through the form to the item with the additional command, it shows up just like any other command, as shown in Figure 6-4.

Figure 6-4. *When an item is selected, its commands are shown.*

The semantics for managing item commands are nearly identical to the semantics for managing form commands. You can manage the commands on an Item using addCommand() and removeCommand(). Note that the command type should be ITEM for commands added to Item, although no exception will be thrown if this is not true. A command listener may be assigned using the setItemCommandListener() method. The ItemCommandListener interface contains a single method, similar to CommandListener's single method:

```
public void commandAction(Command c, Item item)
```

It's up to the implementation to figure out how to show commands for an item. All you do in a MIDlet is add commands, set a listener, and wait for command events.

Items also support a *default command*. This command may be invoked if the runtime device has a button or knob or other user interface control that is appropriate for a default command. You can set an Item's default command by calling setDefaultCommand().

Item has fields that are related to layout control. Items have a *minimum size* and a *preferred size* that can be used to control how large an item appears in a form. The minimum size is computed by the implementation and can be retrieved using getMinimumWidth() and getMinimumHeight(). The minimum size depends on the contents of the Item and can be changed by the implementation every time the contents change. There's no way to change an item's minimum size, but examining the minimum size may be useful to your application in deciding how to lay out a form.

The preferred size, by contrast, can either be computed by the implementation or specified by you. The default values for preferred width and height are -1, a special value that tells the implementation, "I don't care, you go ahead and figure out the best size for this item." If you pass a specific positive value for the width or height in setPreferredSize(), that dimension is said to be *locked* and the implementation will attempt to use it during layout.

The getPreferredWidth() and getPreferredHeight() methods don't always return the values you've passed to setPreferredSize(). For example, if you've unlocked the width and height by calling setPreferredSize(-1, -1), the values returned from getPreferredWidth() and getPreferredHeight() are the preferred sizes that the implementation has computed.

Finally, the Item class includes a layout directive, accessed using getLayout() and setLayout(). Represented by an integer, the layout value is usually a combination of LAYOUT_2 with a horizontal value and a vertical value. LAYOUT_2 is a flag to the implementation that the item should be laid out using MIDP 2 rules. The previous MIDP version (1.0) had very limited layout control capabilities. The horizontal values are

- LAYOUT_LEFT

- LAYOUT_RIGHT

- LAYOUT_CENTER

The vertical values are

- LAYOUT_TOP

- LAYOUT_BOTTOM

- LAYOUT_VCENTER

In addition, a layout value may include *shrinking* or *expanding*. Shrinking means that an item's minimum width or height is used, while expanding means that an item's size is stretched to fill the available width or row height. The constants for shrinking and expanding are

- LAYOUT_SHRINK (for width)

- LAYOUT_EXPAND (for width)

- LAYOUT_VSHRINK (for height)

- LAYOUT_VEXPAND (for height)

Finally, an Item's layout may include a request for a new line before or after the item using the LAYOUT_NEWLINE_BEFORE or LAYOUT_NEWLINE_AFTER constants. Items are laid out in Forms much like text flows on a page, so these constants allow you to request a new row before or after an item.

Figure 6-5 shows a simple example, three components with the following layouts:

- LAYOUT_2 | LAYOUT_LEFT | LAYOUT_NEWLINE_AFTER

- LAYOUT_2 | LAYOUT_CENTER | LAYOUT_NEWLINE_AFTER

- LAYOUT_2 | LAYOUT_RIGHT | LAYOUT_NEWLINE_AFTER

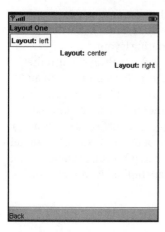

Figure 6-5. *Form layout example*

StringItem

`StringItem` represents a simple text label. For example, consider the following code:

```
Form form = new Form("Form Title");
StringItem stringItem = new StringItem("Label: ", "Value");
form.append(stringItem);
```

■**Caution** You need to be careful when using a ":" in your `StringItem` labels. Some MIDP implementation may append its own ":" for a label, resulting in double colons. The MIDP implementation of the WTK emulator does not append colons automatically for `StringItem` labels.

The form produced by this code (plus a `Back` command) is shown in Figure 6-6.

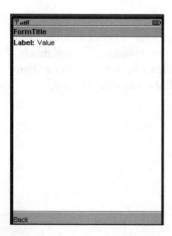

Figure 6-6. *A form with a single StringItem and a Back command*

You can use null for the StringItem's label or value to indicate that it should not be shown on the screen. (Better yet, you could just use Form's append(String) method.) StringItem inherits setLabel() and getLabel() methods from Item. It also includes getText() and setText() methods for accessing and adjusting the string value.

The appearance of both StringItem and ImageItem can be controlled using *appearance mode*. The appearance mode allows the item to look like a URL link or a button, although in all other respects the item behaves the same as a regular StringItem or ImageItem. The three appearance modes (which are defined in the Item class) are as follows:

- PLAIN shows the item in its normal state.

- HYPERLINK shows the item as a URL. A typical action would be to attempt to open the link using MIDlet's platformRequest() method.

- BUTTON shows the item as a button. Note that this may be clumsy, especially on devices without pointer events, and you should generally use a Command where you feel tempted to use an item with a BUTTON appearance mode.

As with almost everything else in the javax.microedition.lcdui package, it's the implementation's responsibility to show different appearance modes, and your application may look different on different devices. Furthermore, it is your application's responsibility to implement appropriate behavior. For example, you might want to add a command to a HYPERLINK StringItem that calls MIDlet's platformRequest() method to open the link.

■**Note** The J2ME Wireless Toolkit emulators don't show HYPERLINK or BUTTON StringItems any differently from PLAIN ones, except for one special case. If the StringItem has a BUTTON type and it has an associated item command, it is shown with a beveled border.

Finally, there are also getFont() and setFont() methods in the StringItem class. We'll describe the Font class in Chapter 13.

Spacer

Spacer represents empty space in a Form. Unlike other Items, Spacer cannot gain focus and cannot have commands. It may be used for layout purposes. All you need to do is specify a minimum width and height:

```
public Spacer(minWidth, minHeight)
```

TextField

TextField represents an editable string. Figure 6-7 shows a TextField with a label of "TextFieldTitle" and a value of "text".

In Sun's MIDP emulator, text can be entered directly into a TextField either by clicking the number buttons in the emulator or by typing on the keyboard. Of course, it's up to the implementation to decide exactly how to allow editing. Some implementations may even show a separate screen for editing.

Figure 6-7. *A form with a single TextField and a Back command*

TextFields can limit input. The following constants are defined:

- ANY allows any type of input.

- NUMERIC restricts the input to numbers.

- DECIMAL allows numbers with fractional parts.

- PHONENUMBER requires a telephone number.

- EMAILADDR input must be an e-mail address.

- URL input must be a URL.

These input constraints might look familiar; they're the same ones used by TextBox, which we covered in the previous chapter. As with TextBox, the flags PASSWORD, SENSITIVE, UNEDITABLE, NON_PREDICTIVE, INITIAL_CAPS_WORD, and INITIAL_CAPS_SENTENCE can be combined with constraints using the OR operator.

To create a TextField, you need to supply the label, text value, maximum length, and input constraints.

```
public TextField(String label, String text, int maxSize, int constraints)
```

For an initially empty TextField, pass null for the text parameter.

As with TextBox, the TextField class includes a setInitialInputMode() method for suggesting to the implementation an appropriate input mode.

ImageItem

Forms can also contain images, which are represented by instances of ImageItem. ImageItems have several pieces of associated data:

- A *label* may be displayed with the image.

- The *layout* determines the placement of the image.

- *Alternate text* is displayed if the image cannot be shown.

To create an ImageItem, just supply the Image that is to be displayed, the label, layout, and alternate text.

Layout is controlled with the layout constants in the Item class. ImageItem also defines constants for the layout parameter. One way to control the layout is to specify the default value, LAYOUT_DEFAULT. If you need more control, combine a horizontal value with a vertical value. The horizontal values are LAYOUT_LEFT, _LAYOUT_CENTER, and LAYOUT_RIGHT. The vertical values are LAYOUT_NEWLINE_BEFORE and LAYOUT_NEWLINE_AFTER. The constants in the ImageItem class are present mainly for backward compatibility with older MIDP versions.

ImageItem supports appearance modes just like StringItem. ItemItem includes a constructor that allows you to set the appearance mode.

Figure 6-8 shows a form containing a single ImageItem.

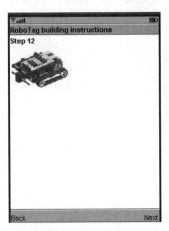

Figure 6-8. *An ImageItem*

DateField

DateField is an extremely handy mechanism by which users can enter dates, times, or both. It's up to the implementation to determine some reasonable way for users to enter dates and times; you, as the MIDlet programmer, simply use DateField and not worry about the implementation.

To create a DateField, specify a label and a type. Three constants in the DateField class describe the different types:

- DATE displays an editable date.

- TIME displays an editable time.

- DATE_TIME displays both a date and a time.

DateField provides two constructors. The first uses the default time zone, while the second allows you to specify a TimeZone explicitly:

```
public DateField(String label, int mode)
public DateField(String label, int mode, TimeZone timeZone)
```

In essence, a DateField is an editor for a java.util.Date. As you saw in Chapter 4, Dates represent points in time. DateField takes the role of translating between a Date and strings that humans can read, much like the Calendar class. You can set or get the Date represented by the DateField using the following methods:

```
public Date getDate()
public void setDate(Date date)
```

In the J2ME Wireless Toolkit emulator, a DateField appears as shown in Figure 6-9a. Note that if you do not supply a Date to setDate() before showing the DateField, it will appear uninitialized, as shown in Figure 6-9b.

When the user selects either the date or time portion of the DateField for editing, the MIDP implementation provides some kind of appropriate editor. Sun's emulator provides the editors shown in Figure 6-9c and Figure 6-9d.

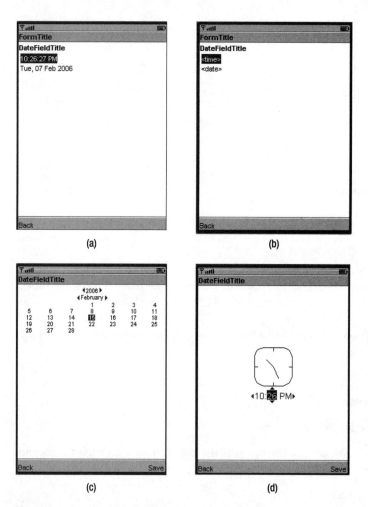

Figure 6-9. *DateField in Sun's MIDP 2.0 emulator*

Gauge

Gauge represents an integer value. It's up to the implementation of the Gauge class to decide how to display it. In Sun's MIDP implementation, Gauge appears as shown in Figure 6-10.

Figure 6-10. *A gauge*

The value of a Gauge instance can be retrieved and modified with the getValue() and setValue() methods. This value runs from 0 to a variable maximum value. The maximum for the gauge can be retrieved and modified with the getMaxValue() and setMaxValue() methods.

The visual appearance of the Gauge is an approximation of the gauge's value. The gauge shown in Figure 6-10 could, for example, have a value of 7 and a maximum of 10, or perhaps a value of 42 and a maximum of 61.

In an *interactive* gauge, the user can modify the value. Again, it's up to the implementation to decide exactly how this works. In Sun's reference implementation, the left and right navigation buttons can be used to modify a gauge's value.

Gauge's constructor is straightforward:

```
public Gauge(String label, boolean interactive,
    int maxValue, int initialValue)
```

For example, the following code creates an interactive Gauge with a maximum value of 24 and an initial value of 2:

```
Gauge g = new Gauge("Power", true, 24, 2);
```

There are three varieties of noninteractive gauges that can be useful as progress indicators. You can use a regular noninteractive gauge with a known maximum value to show the progress of a download or a calculation. For example, if you were going to run through a loop 20 times, you could create a gauge with a maximum of 20 and update its value each time through the loop.

There are two kinds of noninteractive gauges with no maximum value. In this case, you use the special value INDEFINITE for the maximum. Such gauges can be either *incremental* or *continuous*. An incremental gauge shows an operation with measurable steps; your application will update the gauge every time it does something significant. For example, if you were downloading a file, but you didn't know how big it was, you could use an incremental gauge and update the gauge whenever you read some data. A continuous gauge shows progress, probably using an animation, with no prodding needed from the application. This type of gauge is useful for operations where you can't measure the progress.

The gauge value itself can be set to one of the following:

- INCREMENTAL_UPDATING indicates that you have just accomplished something and the gauge should be updated to reflect it.

- INCREMENTAL_IDLE means that you want the gauge to be incremental but nothing is currently happening.

- CONTINUOUS_RUNNING indicates a continuous gauge in its running mode.

- CONTINUOUS_IDLE is used for a continuous gauge, indicating that no progress is currently being made.

The following example shows interactive, continuous, and incremental gauges. Commands (Update and Idle) set the appropriate values on the continuous and incremental gauges. Normally you would set these from separate threads, but using commands makes it easy to understand what's going on in this example.

In Sun's MIDP emulator, the continuous and idle gauges use simple Duke animations to show progress. See Figure 6-11 for a screen shot. Listing 6-2 contains the source code for a MIDlet that demonstrates different kinds of Gauges.

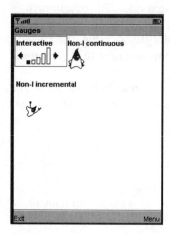

Figure 6-11. *Three kinds of Gauges in MIDP 2.0*

Listing 6-2. *GaugeMIDlet Source Code*

```
import javax.microedition.midlet.*;
import javax.microedition.lcdui.*;

public class GaugeMIDlet
    extends MIDlet
    implements CommandListener {
  private Display mDisplay;
```

```
private Form mGaugeForm;
private Command mUpdateCommand, mIdleCommand;

private Gauge mInteractiveGauge;
private Gauge mIncrementalGauge;
private Gauge mContinuousGauge;

public GaugeMIDlet() {
  mGaugeForm = new Form("Gauges");
  mInteractiveGauge = new Gauge("Interactive", true, 5, 2);
  mInteractiveGauge.setLayout(Item.LAYOUT_2);
  mGaugeForm.append(mInteractiveGauge);
  mContinuousGauge = new Gauge("Non-I continuous", false,
      Gauge.INDEFINITE, Gauge.CONTINUOUS_RUNNING);
  mContinuousGauge.setLayout(Item.LAYOUT_2);
  mGaugeForm.append(mContinuousGauge);
  mIncrementalGauge = new Gauge("Non-I incremental", false,
      Gauge.INDEFINITE, Gauge.INCREMENTAL_UPDATING);
  mIncrementalGauge.setLayout(Item.LAYOUT_2);
  mGaugeForm.append(mIncrementalGauge);

  mUpdateCommand = new Command("Update", Command.SCREEN, 0);
  mIdleCommand = new Command("Idle", Command.SCREEN, 0);
  Command exitCommand = new Command("Exit", Command.EXIT, 0);
  mGaugeForm.addCommand(mUpdateCommand);
  mGaugeForm.addCommand(mIdleCommand);
  mGaugeForm.addCommand(exitCommand);
  mGaugeForm.setCommandListener(this);
}

public void startApp() {
  if (mDisplay == null) mDisplay = Display.getDisplay(this);
  mDisplay.setCurrent(mGaugeForm);
}

public void pauseApp() {}

public void destroyApp(boolean unconditional) {}

public void commandAction(Command c, Displayable s) {
  if (c.getCommandType() == Command.EXIT)
    notifyDestroyed();
  else if (c == mUpdateCommand) {
    mContinuousGauge.setValue(Gauge.CONTINUOUS_RUNNING);
    mIncrementalGauge.setValue(Gauge.INCREMENTAL_UPDATING);
  }
```

```
        else if (c == mIdleCommand) {
          mContinuousGauge.setValue(Gauge.CONTINUOUS_IDLE);
          mIncrementalGauge.setValue(Gauge.INCREMENTAL_IDLE);
        }
      }
    }
```

ChoiceGroup

Another class in the Form arsenal of Items is ChoiceGroup. ChoiceGroup offers a list of choices. It is very similar to javax.microedition.lcdui.List, which was described at the beginning of this chapter. This similarity is more than coincidental; ChoiceGroup and List both implement the Choice interface, which is the wellspring of all of the instance methods in both classes.

If you read the section about List, you already know almost everything you need to know to use ChoiceGroup because the instance methods work exactly the same way.

ChoiceGroup features the following constructors:

```
public ChoiceGroup(String label, int choiceType)
public ChoiceGroup(String label, int choiceType, String[] stringElements,
    Image[] imageElements)
```

The choiceType should look familiar; it can be either EXCLUSIVE or MULTIPLE, the constants defined in the Choice interface. In fact, ChoiceGroup's constructors work exactly like List's constructors, except that IMPLICIT is not allowed. This makes sense, since a ChoiceGroup is one item in a form, not an entire screen. There is also a POPUP type for ChoiceGroup that makes it appear like a combo box or a drop-down menu. The ChoiceGroup appears like any other element in the Form; Figure 6-12 shows examples.

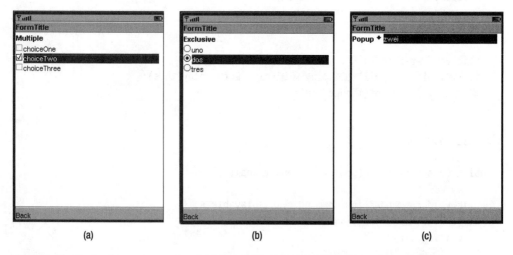

Figure 6-12. *ChoiceGroup examples: (a) MULTIPLE, (b) EXCLUSIVE, and (c) POPUP*

Responding to Item Changes

Most items in a Form fire events when the user changes them. Your application can listen for these events by registering an ItemStateListener with the Form using the following method:

```
public void setItemStateListener(ItemStateListener iListener)
```

ItemStateListener is an interface with a single method. This method is called every time an item in a Form is changed:

```
public void itemStateChanged(Item item)
```

Listing 6-3 creates a Form with two items, an interactive Gauge and a StringItem. As you adjust the Gauge, its value is reflected in the StringItem using the ItemStateListener mechanism.

Listing 6-3. *GaugeTracker Source Code*

```
import javax.microedition.midlet.*;
import javax.microedition.lcdui.*;

public class GaugeTracker
    extends MIDlet
    implements ItemStateListener, CommandListener {
  private Gauge mGauge;
  private StringItem mStringItem;

  public GaugeTracker() {
    int initialValue = 3;
    mGauge = new Gauge("GaugeTitle", true, 5, initialValue);
    mStringItem = new StringItem(null, "[value]");
    itemStateChanged(mGauge);
  }

  public void itemStateChanged(Item item) {
    if (item == mGauge)
      mStringItem.setText("Value = " + mGauge.getValue());
  }

  public void commandAction(Command c, Displayable s) {
    if (c.getCommandType() == Command.EXIT)
      notifyDestroyed();
  }
```

```
  public void startApp() {
    Form form = new Form("GaugeTracker");
    form.addCommand(new Command("Exit", Command.EXIT, 0));
    form.setCommandListener(this);
    // Now add the selected items.
    form.append(mGauge);
    form.append(mStringItem);
    form.setItemStateListener(this);

    Display.getDisplay(this).setCurrent(form);
  }

  public void pauseApp() {}

  public void destroyApp(boolean unconditional) {}
}
```

Summary

This chapter described MIDP's advanced user-interface screens, List and Form. A List is a list of elements that allows for single or multiple selections. You supply the items—it's up to the implementation to figure out how to show them, how the user navigates through them, and how the user selects items. Forms are generalized screens that are built up from a collection of Items. The MIDP API supplies a handy toolbox of Items—everything from simple string and image Items to the more complex DateField and ChoiceGroup classes.

Even though List and Form are very capable, you should use them sparingly, particularly Form. Small devices have small screens, so you don't want to put much information in each screen, especially if it's going to force the user to scroll up and down a lot. Furthermore, ease of use is crucial on consumer devices like mobile phones and pagers. Make sure your interface is clean, intuitive, and as simple as it can possibly be.

CHAPTER 7

■ ■ ■

Custom Items

In the last chapter, you learned about Forms, the most flexible and powerful descendents of javax.microedition.lcdui.Screen. Forms are essentially collections of Items. The MIDP APIs include a useful toolbox of Item subclasses, everything from text and image display to interactive date fields and gauges.

You can have even more power through the opportunity to define your own items. In this chapter, you'll learn how to create items that do their own drawing and respond to user input.

Introducing CustomItem

The class that makes custom items possible is appropriately named CustomItem. Like all items that live in a Form, it is a subclass of Item. To create your very own item, all you have to do is define a subclass of CustomItem by implementing five abstract methods. The first four, listed next, have to do with the size of the item's *content area*, which is the area for which your code has responsibility. The total area of the custom item includes a label and perhaps borders, but these are the responsibility of the implementation. Your CustomItem subclass is only responsible for the content area.

```
protected int getPrefContentWidth(int height)
protected int getPrefContentHeight(int width)
protected int getMinContentWidth()
protected int getMinContentHeight()
```

The first two methods should return values that define how big your item *wants* to be. When the MIDP implementation lays out a Form containing your item, it may not be able to honor your preferred size, but it will try. The implementation passes a proposed height and width into these methods to give your item class an idea of what its dimensions might eventually be. For example, the implementation might call your item's getPrefContentWidth() method and pass a value of 18 for the height parameter. This is the implementation asking your item, "What width would you like to be if I make your height 18?"

The second pair of methods should return information about the minimum size of the item. This is the smallest size that your item believes it can tolerate.

The fifth method that must be defined by a concrete CustomItem subclass is the paint() method, which the implementation calls to render the item.

```
protected void paint(Graphics g, int w, int h)
```

The Graphics object can be used to draw lines, shapes, text, and images on the content area of the item. The Graphics class is fully covered in Chapter 13; for now, we'll just use a few simple methods to demonstrate how to draw custom items. The w and h parameters indicate the current width and height of the content area.

Armed with this knowledge, you can create a simple CustomItem by implementing the five abstract methods described previously and providing a constructor. Listing 7-1 shows one such class, SimpleItem. This class returns hard-coded values for the minimum and preferred content dimensions and provides a paint() method that draws a simple pattern of triangles.

Listing 7-1. *A Simple Custom Item*

```java
import javax.microedition.lcdui.*;

public class SimpleItem
    extends CustomItem {
  public SimpleItem(String title) { super(title); }

  // CustomItem abstract methods.

  public int getMinContentWidth() { return 100; }
  public int getMinContentHeight() { return 60; }

  public int getPrefContentWidth(int width) {
    return getMinContentWidth();
  }

  public int getPrefContentHeight(int height) {
    return getMinContentHeight();
  }

  public void paint(Graphics g, int w, int h) {
    g.drawRect(0, 0, w - 1, h - 1);
    g.setColor(0x000000ff);
    int offset = 0;
    for (int y = 4; y < h; y += 12) {
      offset = (offset + 12) % 24;
      for (int x = 4; x < w; x += 24) {
        g.fillTriangle(x + offset,     y,
                       x + offset - 3, y + 6,
                       x + offset + 3, y + 6);
      }
    }
  }
}
```

We won't make you write your own MIDlet to see your new item. Listing 7-2 shows a MIDlet that uses SimpleItem.

Listing 7-2. *A MIDlet That Demonstrates SimpleItem*

```
import javax.microedition.midlet.*;
import javax.microedition.lcdui.*;

public class SimpleItemMIDlet
    extends MIDlet
    implements CommandListener {
  public void startApp() {
    Form form = new Form("SimpleItemMIDlet");
    form.append(new SimpleItem("SimpleItem"));

    Command c = new Command("Exit", Command.EXIT, 0);
    form.addCommand(c);
    form.setCommandListener(this);

    Display.getDisplay(this).setCurrent(form);
  }

  public void pauseApp() {}

  public void destroyApp(boolean unconditional) {}

  public void commandAction(Command c, Displayable s) {
    if (c.getCommandType() == Command.EXIT)
      notifyDestroyed();
  }
}
```

Figure 7-1 shows this MIDlet in action.

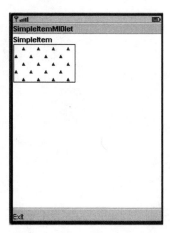

Figure 7-1. *A simple custom item*

CustomItem Painting

As you've seen, a CustomItem is drawn on the screen in its paint() method. This method is passed a Graphics object that serves two purposes. First, it represents the drawing surface of the CustomItem's content area. Second, it provides numerous methods for drawing shapes, images, and text. We won't cover all of these methods until Chapter 13, but you'll see a couple of them in the examples in this chapter: for instance, drawString() renders text, while drawLine() renders a straight line.

The paint() method is an example of a *callback*, a method in your code that is called by the MIDP implementation. The implementation calls paint() whenever it needs to show your custom item on the screen. It calls other methods to find out the minimum and preferred sizes of your component when its containing form is being laid out. It's the implementation's job to show the whole screen; it just calls your paint() method to show the part of the screen occupied by your custom item. You don't tell the implementation when to draw your item; you just tell it that your item is part of a form, and then it figures out how to show everything.

If something needs to change in your custom item's appearance, you can request a refresh by calling the repaint() method. This method signals to the implementation that your item needs to be drawn. In response, the implementation will soon call the paint() method again. For optimized drawing, you may only wish to redraw part of the item. In this case, use repaint(int x, int y, int width, int height) to describe a rectangular region of the item that needs to be drawn.

Two methods return information that can help you make your item's appearance consistent with the device's look and feel. The first is getColor() in the Display class. This method returns an int representing a color when you supply one of the following constants:

- COLOR_BACKGROUND

- COLOR_BORDER

- COLOR_FOREGROUND

- COLOR_HIGHLIGHTED_BACKGROUND

- COLOR_HIGHLIGHTED_BORDER

- COLOR_HIGHLIGHTED_FOREGROUND

For example, you could set the current drawing color to the system's highlighted foreground color with the following code:

```
public void paint(Graphics g) {
  // Display mDisplay = ...
  int fhc = mDisplay.getColor(
      Display.COLOR_HIGHLIGHTED_FOREGROUND);
  g.setColor(fhc);
  // Draw stuff ...
}
```

Similarly, if you want any text drawn by your custom item to harmonize with other items in a Form, you can retrieve an appropriate Font using the following method in the Font class:

```
public static Font getFont(int fontSpecifier)
```

Just pass either FONT_STATIC_TEXT or FONT_INPUT_TEXT and this method returns an appropriate Font object that you can use for drawing text. The following code shows how to use an appropriate font for drawing user-editable text:

```
public void paint(Graphics g) {
  Font f = Font.getFont(Font.FONT_INPUT_TEXT);
  g.setFont(f);
  // Draw text ...
}
```

We'll cover Font in detail in Chapter 13. In brief, a Font determines the appearance of text that is drawn on the screen.

Showing, Hiding, and Sizing

When a CustomItem is made visible, even partially visible, its showNotify() method is called by the MIDP implementation. You can expect subsequent calls to paint() to render the item. Similarly, hideNotify() is called when the item is no longer visible (if the user has scrolled the item off the screen, for example).

The size of your custom item may be changed by the implementation, perhaps if the containing Form gets laid out again in response to changing content. In this case, your item's sizeChanged() method is called with the new width and height of the content area.

Similarly, your custom item may decide that it needs to be a different size. In this case, your item should call the invalidate() method, which signals the implementation that it may need to lay out the containing Form again.

Handling Events

A CustomItem can respond to keyboard and pointer events by overriding any or all of the following methods:

```
protected void keyPressed(int keyCode)
protected void keyReleased(int keyCode)
protected void keyRepeated(int keyCode)
protected void pointerPressed(int x, int y)
protected void pointerReleased(int x, int y)
protected void pointerDragged(int x, int y)
```

These methods are called in response to the user's actions. The keyCode parameter will most likely be one of the constants defined in the Canvas class: KEY_NUM0 through KEY_NUM9, KEY_POUND, or KEY_STAR. The CustomItem class also supports a handy mechanism called *game actions*, which maps device-specific keys to device-independent actions. The getGameAction() method performs this mapping. For a full discussion of game actions, see Chapter 13.

The pointer callback methods supply the location of the pointer event as a pair of coordinates relative to the custom item's content area.

Devices have varying capabilities, and some may not be able to deliver certain types of events to CustomItems. Many phones, for example, will not support pointer events. To find out the capabilities of the device at runtime, custom items use the getInteractionModes() method. This method returns some combination of the following constants (defined in CustomItem):

- KEY_PRESS

- KEY_RELEASE

- KEY_REPEAT

- POINTER_PRESS

- POINTER_RELEASE

- POINTER_DRAG

- TRAVERSE_HORIZONTAL

- TRAVERSE_VERTICAL

Except for the traversal items (which are covered in the next section), the combination of values returned from getInteractionModes() corresponds directly to which callbacks are likely to be invoked in your custom item. You can use this information to build a CustomItem that will work under any circumstances. For example, in the unlikely event that a device was unable to deliver both key and pointer events to a custom item, you could supply a Command on the item to invoke a separate editing screen.

Item Traversal

Forms support a concept of *focus*, where one item in the form is currently selected. *Traversal* refers to the user being able to shift focus from one item to another. In most cases, the MIDP implementation handles the details of Form traversal. In the Sun emulator, for example, you can move the focus through the items in a form by pressing the up and down keys. Focus is indicated by a solid black border around an item. Figure 7-2 shows a form with several items; the third item, an ImageItem, has the focus.

Figure 7-2. *The focus is on the third item in this form.*

So far, so good—this is all pretty straightforward. As a matter of fact, the default implementation provided in CustomItem means you don't even have to think about traversal in many cases.

What makes things a little wonky is the concept of *internal* traversal. Some items support traversal of multiple choices *inside* the item. A good example is the ChoiceGroup item. The following sequence shows traversal through a form with three items in the MIDP reference implementation emulator. Figure 7-3 shows the traversal progressing from the text field through the gauge and into the ChoiceGroup.

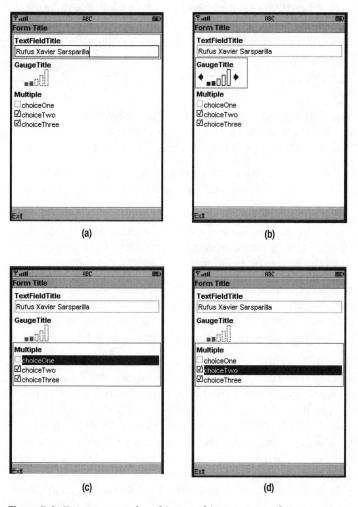

(a)   (b)

(c)   (d)

Figure 7-3. *Form traversal and internal item traversal*

Two methods signal traversal events. The first, traverse(), is called the first time the user traverses into the item. By default this method returns false, indicating that the item does not support internal traversal. The second method, traverseOut(), is called whenever the user leaves the item.

```
protected boolean traverse(int dir, int viewportWidth, int viewportHeight,
        int[] visRect_inout);
protected void traverseOut();
```

■**Note** At first glance, you might expect custom items to receive calls on both the traversal methods and the key event methods when keys are pressed on the device. For example, if the user presses the down arrow key to move into the item, you might expect both the `traverse()` and `keyPressed()` methods to be called. In reality, the implementation should keep key events and traversal events unambiguous. Bear in mind that some devices will have alternate traversal controls (wheels, for example), so the implementation (and your custom item) should treat the events distinctly.

If you do write a custom item that supports internal traversal, you need to pay attention to the arguments passed to `traverse()` and you need to return `true` to indicate that your item supports internal traversal. The information passed to the `traverse()` method is as follows:

- `dir` indicates the traversal direction requested by the user. It is one of the following: `Canvas.UP`, `Canvas.DOWN`, `Canvas.LEFT`, `Canvas.RIGHT`, or `CustomItem.NONE`.

- `viewportWidth` and `viewportHeight` indicate the size available for items in the `Form` containing this custom item. (In essence, `viewportWidth` and `viewportHeight` describe the content area of the `Form`.) These dimensions may be useful for determining the relationship between an item's choices and the amount of available screen area.

- `visRect_inout` is kind of weird. It is an integer array with four elements. When the `traverse()` method is called, `visRect_inout` describes the region of the custom item's visible content area. When the `traverse()` method returns, `visRect_inout` should contain the bounds of the currently selected choice in the item.

If this is starting to sound a little hairy, just wait. The traversal mechanism is flexible enough to support different kinds of traversal. Some devices may only be able to support vertical traversal, while others may only support horizontal, and still others may support both. You can find out the device's traversal capabilities with the `getInteractionModes()` method, which can return `CustomItem.TRAVERSE_HORIZONTAL`, `CustomItem.TRAVERSE_VERTICAL`, or both. Depending on the nature of the choices contained in your custom item, you may have to be flexible about the traversal directions you're receiving and the actual traversal inside the item.

Remember, the `traverse()` method is called when focus first comes to your item. If this method returns `true`, `traverse()` will be repeatedly called while traversal progresses through your item. When the user traverses out of your item, return `false` from the `traverse()` method. This lets the implementation know that internal traversal has ended. Most likely the implementation will call `traverseOut()`, although this only happens if focus actually moves away from the item. This may not be the case if the user has reached the end or beginning of the form.

All of this is discussed in meticulous detail in the API documentation for `CustomItem`'s `traverse()` method. If you're planning to implement a custom item with internal traversal, go read the documentation a few times until it all sinks in.

An Example

In this section, we'll show you StationSign, a CustomItem of medium complexity. StationSign has the following features:

- Implements a simple scrolling list of string choices. Pointer events and key events cause the current selection to move to the next choice. The scrolling is animated. StationSign is a Runnable—a separate thread is created in the constructor and used to call the run() method. If there's a difference between the current display state of the item and the current selection, run() reconciles the two by scrolling.

- Conforms to the device's look and feel by using the font for static text and colors returned from Display's getColor() method.

- Does not implement internal traversal.

- Uses the traverse() and traverseOut() methods to recognize focus and paint using highlight colors. When traverse() is called, StationSign sets a boolean member variable, mFocus, to indicate that the item has focus. In the paint() method, mFocus is used to determine what colors are used to draw the item. When traverseOut() is called, mFocus is set to false, indicating that focus has been lost.

The entire source code for StationSign is shown in Listing 7-3.

Listing 7-3. *The StationSign Custom Item*

```java
import java.util.Vector;

import javax.microedition.lcdui.*;

public class StationSign
    extends CustomItem
    implements Runnable {
  private Vector mValues;
  private int mSelection;
  private boolean mTrucking;

  private Display mDisplay;
  private Font mFont;
  private int mVisibleIndexTimesTen;
  private boolean mFocus;

  public StationSign(String title, Display display) {
    super(title);
    mDisplay = display;
    mValues = new Vector();
    mSelection = 0;
    mTrucking = true;
    mFont = Font.getFont(Font.FONT_STATIC_TEXT);
    mVisibleIndexTimesTen = mSelection * 10;
```

```
    Thread t = new Thread(this);
    t.start();
}

public void add(String value) {
  if (value == null) return;
  mValues.addElement(value);
}

public void remove(String value) {
  if (value == null) return;
  mValues.removeElement(value);
}

public String getSelection() {
  if (mValues.size() == 0) return "";
  return (String)mValues.elementAt(mSelection);
}

public void flip() {
  mSelection++;
  if (mSelection >= mValues.size()) mSelection = 0;
}

public void dispose() {
  mTrucking = false;
}

// Runnable interface.

public void run() {
  while (mTrucking) {
    int target = mSelection * 10;
    if (mVisibleIndexTimesTen != target) {
      mVisibleIndexTimesTen++;
      if (mVisibleIndexTimesTen >= mValues.size() * 10)
        mVisibleIndexTimesTen = 0;
      repaint();
    }
    try { Thread.sleep(50); }
    catch (InterruptedException ie) {}
  }
}

// CustomItem abstract methods.
```

```java
public int getMinContentWidth() {
  // Loop through the values. Find the maximum width.
  int maxWidth = 0;
  for (int i = 0; i < mValues.size(); i++) {
    String value = (String)mValues.elementAt(i);
    int width = mFont.stringWidth(value);
    maxWidth = Math.max(maxWidth, width);
  }
  // Don't forget about the title, although we don't
  // really know what font is used for that.
  int width = mFont.stringWidth(getLabel()) + 20;
  maxWidth = Math.max(maxWidth, width);
  return maxWidth;
}

public int getMinContentHeight() {
  return mFont.getHeight();
}

public int getPrefContentWidth(int width) {
  return getMinContentWidth();
}

public int getPrefContentHeight(int height) {
  return getMinContentHeight();
}

public void paint(Graphics g, int w, int h) {
  int fraction = mVisibleIndexTimesTen % 10;
  int visibleIndex = (mVisibleIndexTimesTen - fraction) / 10;
  String value = (String)mValues.elementAt(visibleIndex);

  g.setFont(mFont);
  int bc = mDisplay.getColor(Display.COLOR_BACKGROUND);
  int fc = mDisplay.getColor(Display.COLOR_FOREGROUND);
  if (mFocus == true) {
    bc = mDisplay.getColor(Display.COLOR_HIGHLIGHTED_BACKGROUND);
    fc = mDisplay.getColor(Display.COLOR_HIGHLIGHTED_FOREGROUND);
  }
  g.setColor(bc);
  g.fillRect(0, 0, w, h);
  g.setColor(fc);

  // Simple case: visibleIndex is aligned on a single item.
  if (fraction == 0) {
    g.drawString(value, 0, 0, Graphics.TOP | Graphics.LEFT);
    return;
  }
```

```
        // Complicated case: show two items and a line.
        int lineHeight = mFont.getHeight();
        int divider = lineHeight - lineHeight * fraction / 10;

        // Draw the piece of the visible value.
        g.drawString(value, 0, divider - lineHeight,
            Graphics.TOP | Graphics.LEFT);
        // Now get the next value.
        visibleIndex = (visibleIndex + 1) % mValues.size();
        value = (String)mValues.elementAt(visibleIndex);

        // Draw the line.
        g.setStrokeStyle(Graphics.DOTTED);
        g.drawLine(0, divider, w, divider);

        g.drawString(value, 0, divider,
            Graphics.TOP | Graphics.LEFT);
    }

    // CustomItem methods.

    protected void keyPressed(int keyCode) { flip (); }

    protected void pointerPressed(int x, int y) { flip(); }

    protected boolean traverse(int dir,
        int viewportWidth, int viewportHeight,
        int[] visRect_inout) {
      mFocus = true;
      repaint();
      return false;
    }

    protected void traverseOut() {
      mFocus = false;
      repaint();
    }
  }
```

The MIDlet in Listing 7-4 displays a form that contains a StationSign.

Listing 7-4. *A MIDlet That Demonstrates StationSign*

```
import javax.microedition.midlet.*;
import javax.microedition.lcdui.*;

public class StationSignMIDlet
    extends MIDlet
    implements CommandListener {
  public void startApp() {
    Display display = Display.getDisplay(this);


    Form form = new Form("StationSignMIDlet");
    form.append(new StringItem("StringItem: ", "this is the first item "));
    StationSign ss = new StationSign("Destination", display);
    ss.add("Albuquerque");
    ss.add("Savannah");
    ss.add("Pocatello");
    ss.add("Des Moines");
    form.append(ss);
    form.append(new StringItem("StringItem: ", "this is item two"));

    Command c = new Command("Exit", Command.EXIT, 0);
    form.addCommand(c);
    form.setCommandListener(this);

    display.setCurrent(form);
  }

  public void pauseApp() {}

  public void destroyApp(boolean unconditional) {}

  public void commandAction(Command c, Displayable s) {
    if (c.getCommandType() == Command.EXIT)
      notifyDestroyed();
  }
}
```

The MIDlet in action appears in Figure 7-4. The figure shows an instance of StationSign sandwiched between two StringItems. You can navigate through the form to see how the appearance of StationSign changes when it has input focus. If you click the select button on StationSign, you'll see the next choice scroll into view.

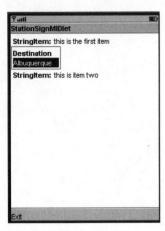

Figure 7-4. *StationSign in action in a Form*

Summary

This chapter described MIDP's support for custom items. The CustomItem class is the basis of items you can write to include in Forms. You can determine the custom item's appearance in the paint() method by drawing using a Graphics object. Callback methods throughout CustomItem let you know when the item is shown or hidden and deliver key, pointer, and traversal events. Two examples, SimpleItem and StationSign, provided a foundation of working code that you can adapt to build your own items.

A word of caution is appropriate here. While custom items allow almost unlimited flexibility for creating new Form items, it is quite difficult to create a CustomItem that has a consistent look and feel with the rest of the standard MIDP Form items. Testing can be intensive if the final application has to run across different devices with different MIDP implementations.

■ ■ ■

Persistent Storage I: MIDP Record Store

MIDP applications have to run seamlessly on many devices. You've already seen how this can be a challenge in the user interface arena. The trick there was to use abstract concepts that would be mapped to the screen by a device-specific implementation.

MIDP's approach to persistent storage is basically the same. Your application could run on a device with flash ROM or battery-backed RAM. MIDP applications don't really care; all they know about are small databases called record stores. It's up to the device's MIDP implementation to map record stores in some reasonable manner to whatever persistent storage is available.

These are *small* amounts of data we're talking about; the MIDP specification dictates that the minimum amount of persistent storage is only 8KB. The record store mechanism is highly effective for these small amounts of persistent storage.

Overview

In MIDP, persistent storage is centered around record stores. A *record store* is a small database that contains pieces of data called *records*. Record stores are represented by instances of javax.microedition.rms.RecordStore. The scope of a record store can either be limited to a single MIDlet suite or be shared between MIDlet suites. Said another way, you can either restrict a MIDlet to only access record stores that were created by a MIDlet in the same suite, or you can explicitly allow MIDlets from multiple suites to share a record store . Figure 8-1 shows the relationship between MIDlet suites and record stores.

Record stores are identified by a name. Within a MIDlet suite's record stores, the names must be unique.

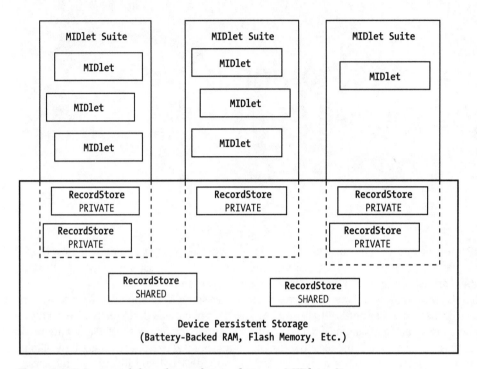

Figure 8-1. *Private and shared record stores between MIDlet suites*

Managing Record Stores

The RecordStore class serves two purposes. First, it defines an API for manipulating individual records. Second, it defines an API (mostly static methods) for managing record stores.

Opening, Closing, and Removing Record Stores

To open a record store, you simply need to name it.

```
public static RecordStore openRecordStore(String recordStoreName,
    boolean createIfNecessary) throws RecordStoreException,
    RecordStoreFullException, RecordStoreNotFoundException
```

If the record store does not exist, the createIfNecessary parameter determines whether a new record store will be created or not. If the record store does not exist, and the createIfNecessary parameter is false, then a RecordStoreNotFoundException will be thrown.

The following code opens a record store named "Address":

```
RecordStore rs = RecordStore.openRecordStore("Address", true);
```

The record store will be created if it does not already exist.

An open record store can be closed by calling the closeRecordStore() method. As with anything that can be opened and closed, it's a good idea to close record stores when you're finished with them. Memory and processing power are in short supply on a small device, so you should remember to clean up after yourself as much as possible. You probably shouldn't even keep a record store open over the lifetime of the MIDlet; after all, your MIDlet may be paused by the device's application manager, and it would be unwise to have open resources while the MIDlet is paused.

To find out all the record stores available to a particular MIDlet suite, call the listRecordStores() method:

```
public static String[] listRecordStores()
```

Finally, to remove a record store, call the static deleteRecordStore() method. The record store and its contained records will be deleted.

■Note Record store operations, particularly opening and closing, may be time-consuming on actual devices. You probably won't notice the delays using a desktop MIDP emulator, but on a real device, it may slow down applications noticeably. (See http://www.poqit.com/midp/bench/ for some sobering measurements from real devices.) For many applications, it may be appropriate to place record store access in its own thread, just as network access goes in its own thread.

An additional consideration is that frequent read/write operations to the RMS can cause quite a drain on the battery. A useful strategy for avoiding this problem is to cache records in memory and only write to the actual persistent storage when a record is modified.

Sharing Record Stores

Record stores also have an authorization mode. The default authorization mode is AUTHMODE_PRIVATE, which means that a record store is only accessible from MIDlets in the MIDlet suite that created the record store. This is exactly as described earlier.

Record stores can be shared by changing their authorization mode to AUTHMODE_ANY, which means that any other MIDlet on the device can access the record store. Be careful with this! Don't put any secrets in an AUTHMODE_ANY record store. In addition, you can decide if you want a shared record store to be writable or read-only.

You can create a shared record store using an alternate openRecordStore() method in the RecordStore class:

```
public static RecordStore openRecordStore(String recordStoreName,
    boolean createIfNecessary, byte authMode, boolean writable)
    throws RecordStoreException, RecordStoreFullException,
    RecordStoreNotFoundException
```

The authMode and writable parameters are only used if the record store is created, which implies that the record store doesn't exist and createIfNecessary is true. You can change the authorization mode and writable flag of an open record store using the following method:

```
public void setMode(byte authmode, boolean writable)
    throws RecordStoreException
```

Note that only a MIDlet belonging to the suite that created the record store can change its authorization mode and writable flag.

How do you access a shared record store? One final `openRecordStore()` method provides the answer:

```
public static RecordStore openRecordStore(String recordStoreName,
    String vendorName, String suiteName)
    throws RecordStoreException, RecordStoreNotFoundException
```

To access a shared record store, you need to know its name, the name of the MIDlet suite that created it, and the name of the MIDlet suite's vendor. These names must be the `MIDlet-Name` and `MIDlet-Vendor` attributes in the MIDlet suite JAR manifest or the application descriptor.

Record Store Size

Record stores consist of records; each record is simply an array of bytes. On space-constrained devices, you'll probably want to keep a close eye on the size of your record stores. To find out the number of bytes used by a record store, call the following method on a `RecordStore` instance:

```
public int getSize()
```

You can find out how much more space is available by calling the following method:

```
public int getSizeAvailable()
```

Note that this method returns the total space available in the record store, which is not the same as the amount of record data that is available. That is, there is some overhead associated with each record in the record store; the `getSizeAvailable()` method returns the amount of space available for both record data and overhead.

Version and Timestamp

Record stores maintain both a version number and a timestamp. The version number is updated every time the record store is modified. It is represented by an integer and can be retrieved by calling `getVersion()`.

The record store also remembers the last time it was modified. This moment in time is represented by a `long`, which can be retrieved with `getLastModified()`. The long represents the number of milliseconds since midnight on January 1, 1970. You may recall (from Chapter 4) that this is the same way that `Date` uses a `long` to represent a moment in time. If you need to examine the timestamp of a record store, you can create a `Date` from the `long` timestamp. Then you could use a `Calendar` to translate from a `Date` to calendar fields like month, day, hour, and minute.

Working with Records

A *record* is simply an array of bytes. Each record in a `RecordStore` has an integer identification number. Figure 8-2 shows a diagram of a `RecordStore` with four records.

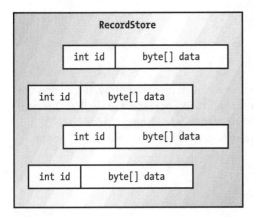

Figure 8-2. *Inside a RecordStore*

Adding Records

To add a new record, supply the byte array to the addRecord() method:

```
public int addRecord(byte[] data, int offset, int numBytes)
    throws RecordStoreNotOpenException,
           RecordStoreException,
           RecordStoreFullException
```

The added record will be numBytes long, taken from the data array starting at offset. The new record's ID is returned. Most other record operations need this ID to identify a particular record.

There's no explicit maximum record length, although, of course, there will be limits based on the amount of space that is available on the device for record stores.

The following code fragment illustrates adding a new record to a record store named rs. It creates a byte array from a String, and then writes the entire byte array into a new record.

```
String record = "This is a record";
byte[] data = record.getBytes();
int id = rs.addRecord(data, 0, data.length);
```

Retrieving Records

You can retrieve a record by supplying the record ID to the following method:

```
public byte[] getRecord(int recordId)
    throws RecordStoreNotOpenException,
           InvalidRecordIDException,
           RecordStoreException
```

This method returns a freshly created byte array containing the record with the requested ID. An alternate version of this method puts the record data into an array that you supply:

```
public int getRecord(int recordId, byte[] buffer, int offset)
    throws RecordStoreNotOpenException,
           InvalidRecordIDException,
           RecordStoreException
```

This method returns the number of bytes that were copied into your array. If the array you supply is not large enough to hold the record, an ArrayOutOfBoundsException will be thrown. You can find out the size of a particular record ahead of time by calling getRecordSize().

Given a RecordStore rs and a record ID id, here is one way to retrieve a record's data:

```
byte[] retrieved = new byte[rs.getRecordSize(id)];
rs.getRecord(id, retrieved, 0);
String retrievedString = new String(retrieved);
```

If you're going to be pulling many records out of the record store, you probably won't want to create a new byte array each time. For efficiency, you would create one array and use it over and over again to pull records out of the record store. One way to create the buffer is to make it as large as the largest record in the record store. If that's not practical, or if you don't know how large the largest record will be, you can simply check the size of each record before you retrieve it. If you come across a record that's larger than the buffer, you could create a larger buffer.

If you're not worried about memory usage or speed, then you might as well use the other form of getRecord(), which is essentially the same as the previous code example:

```
byte[] retrieved = rs.getRecord(id);
```

Deleting and Replacing Records

So far you've seen how to add new records and retrieve them. There are two more record operations supported by RecordStore. First, you can remove a record by passing its ID to deleteRecord(). Second, you can replace the data of an existing record by calling the following method:

```
public void setRecord(int recordId, byte[] newData, int offset, int numBytes)
    throws RecordStoreNotOpenException,
           InvalidRecordIDException,
           RecordStoreException,
           RecordStoreFullException
```

Getting RecordStore Record Information

The RecordStore keeps an internal counter that it uses to assign record IDs. You can find out what the next record ID will be by calling getNextRecordID(). And you can find out how many records exist in the RecordStore by calling getNumRecords().

Saving User Preferences

Let's put some of this knowledge to work. This section details a simple MIDlet that saves a user name and password in a RecordStore. Each time the MIDlet is used, it can load the user name and password from the RecordStore instead of requiring the user to enter the same information over and over.

The MIDlet itself is very simple. Its only screen is a Form that contains fields for entering the user name and password. It uses a helper class, Preferences, to do all the RecordStore work. Listing 8-1 shows the source code for the MIDlet.

Listing 8-1. *Source Code for RecordMIDlet*

```java
import javax.microedition.midlet.*;
import javax.microedition.lcdui.*;
import javax.microedition.rms.RecordStoreException;

public class RecordMIDlet
    extends MIDlet
    implements CommandListener {
  private static final String kUser = "user";
  private static final String kPassword = "password";

  private Preferences mPreferences;
  private Form mForm;
  private TextField mUserField, mPasswordField;

  public RecordMIDlet() {
    try {
      mPreferences = new Preferences("preferences");
    }
    catch (RecordStoreException rse) {
      mForm = new Form("Exception");
      mForm.append(new StringItem(null, rse.toString()));
      mForm.addCommand(new Command("Exit", Command.EXIT, 0));
      mForm.setCommandListener(this);
      return;
    }

    mForm = new Form("Login");
    mUserField = new TextField("Name",
        mPreferences.get(kUser), 32, 0);
    mPasswordField = new TextField("Password",
        mPreferences.get(kPassword), 32, 0);
    mForm.append(mUserField);
    mForm.append(mPasswordField);

    mForm.addCommand(new Command("Exit", Command.EXIT, 0));
    mForm.setCommandListener(this);
  }
```

```
public void startApp() {
  Display.getDisplay(this).setCurrent(mForm);
}

public void pauseApp() {}

public void destroyApp(boolean unconditional) {
  // Save the user name and password.
  mPreferences.put(kUser, mUserField.getString());
  mPreferences.put(kPassword, mPasswordField.getString());
  try { mPreferences.save(); }
  catch (RecordStoreException rse) {}
}

public void commandAction(Command c, Displayable s) {
  if (c.getCommandType() == Command.EXIT) {
    destroyApp(true);
    notifyDestroyed();
  }
}
}
```

All the RecordStore work is encapsulated in the Preferences class shown in Listing 8-2.
Preferences is a wrapper for a map of string keys and values, stored internally as mHashtable.
When a Preferences object is created, key and value pairs are loaded from the record store.
A key and value pair is stored in a single record using a pipe character separator (|).

Preferences uses a RecordEnumeration to walk through all the records in the record store.
We'll talk about RecordEnumeration soon; for now, just trust us when we tell you it gives you a
way to paw through the data in the record store.

Listing 8-2. *A Class That Encapsulates RecordStore Access*

```
import java.util.*;
import javax.microedition.lcdui.*;
import javax.microedition.rms.*;

public class Preferences {
  private String mRecordStoreName;

  private Hashtable mHashtable;

  public Preferences(String recordStoreName)
      throws RecordStoreException {
    mRecordStoreName = recordStoreName;
    mHashtable = new Hashtable();
    load();
  }
```

```java
public String get(String key) {
  return (String)mHashtable.get(key);
}

public void put(String key, String value) {
  if (value == null) value = "";
  mHashtable.put(key, value);
}

private void load() throws RecordStoreException {
  RecordStore rs = null;
  RecordEnumeration re = null;

  try {
    rs = RecordStore.openRecordStore(mRecordStoreName, true);
    re = rs.enumerateRecords(null, null, false);
    while (re.hasNextElement()) {
      byte[] raw = re.nextRecord();
      String pref = new String(raw);

      // Parse out the name.
      int index = pref.indexOf('|');
      String name = pref.substring(0, index);
      String value = pref.substring(index + 1);
      put(name, value);
    }
  }
  finally {
    if (re != null) re.destroy();
    if (rs != null) rs.closeRecordStore();
  }
}

public void save() throws RecordStoreException {
  RecordStore rs = null;
  RecordEnumeration re = null;
  try {
    rs = RecordStore.openRecordStore(mRecordStoreName, true);
    re = rs.enumerateRecords(null, null, false);

    // First remove all records, a little clumsy.
    while (re.hasNextElement()) {
      int id = re.nextRecordId();
      rs.deleteRecord(id);
    }
```

```
      // Now save the preferences records.
      Enumeration keys = mHashtable.keys();
      while (keys.hasMoreElements()) {
        String key = (String)keys.nextElement();
        String value = get(key);
        String pref = key + "|" + value;
        byte[] raw = pref.getBytes();
        rs.addRecord(raw, 0, raw.length);
      }
    }
    finally {
      if (re != null) re.destroy();
      if (rs != null) rs.closeRecordStore();
    }
  }
}
```

RecordMIDlet saves the updated values back to the RecordStore in its destroyApp() method. It saves the user name and password from the user interface in the Preferences object, then calls the save() method to write the new values out to the RecordStore. The save() method removes all records from the record store, and then adds each key and value pair.

To test out the MIDlet, enter some text into the user name and password fields. Then exit the MIDlet and restart it. You will see the same values loaded into the text fields.

Note that Preferences only deals with String values, but records can contain any data packed into a byte array. By using stream classes from the java.io package, it's possible to store complex data types in records. For example, you could use a DataOutputStream wrapped around a ByteArrayOutputStream to generate data to be written into the record store. To extract data values, you would use a DataInputStream wrapped around a ByteArrayInputStream based on the record data.

Listening for Record Changes

RecordStores support a JavaBeans-style listener mechanism. Interested objects can listen for changes to a record store by registering themselves as listeners.

The listener interface is javax.microedition.rms.RecordListener. You can manage a RecordStore's listeners with the following two methods:

```
public void addRecordListener(RecordListener listener)
public void removeRecordListener(RecordListener listener)
```

The RecordListener interface has three methods: recordAdded(), recordChanged(), and recordDeleted(). These are called whenever a record is added, changed, or deleted. Each method is passed the RecordStore involved and the ID of the record in question.

Performing RecordStore Queries

The real power of a database is being able to pull out just the record or records you want. In a larger database, this is called *performing a query*. In the RecordStore world, you use the enumerateRecords() method:

```
public RecordEnumeration enumerateRecords(RecordFilter filter,
    RecordComparator comparator, boolean keepUpdated)
    throws RecordStoreNotOpenException
```

This single method in RecordStore involves three different interfaces that you've never seen before. Let's start with the big picture first, and then drill down into the new interfaces.

The enumerateRecords() method returns a sorted subset of the records in a RecordStore. The RecordFilter determines which records will be included in the subset, while the RecordComparator is used to sort them. The returned RecordEnumeration allows you to navigate through the returned records.

RecordFilter

The simplest interface is RecordFilter. When you call enumerateRecords() on a RecordStore, each record's data is retrieved. RecordFilter has a single method, matches(), which is called for each record. A record filter should examine the record data and return true if the record should be included in the results returned from enumerateRecords().

Here's a simple RecordFilter implementation that will only select records whose first byte of data is 7:

```
public class SevenFilter
    implements javax.microedition.rms.RecordFilter {
  public boolean matches(byte[] candidate) {
    if (candidate.length == 0) return false;
    return (candidate[0] == 7);
  }
}
```

RecordComparator

The job of a RecordComparator implementation is to determine the order of two sets of record data. RecordComparator is similar to the java.util.Comparator interface in J2SE.

To implement the RecordComparator interface, you just need to define one method:

```
public int compare(byte[] rec1, byte[] rec2)
```

This method examines the data contained in rec1 and rec2 and determines which of them should come first in a sorted list. It should return one of the following constants defined in RecordComparator:

- PRECEDES indicates that rec1 should come before rec2.

- FOLLOWS indicates that rec1 should come after rec2.

- EQUIVALENT signals that rec1 and rec2 are the same, at least as far as sorting is concerned.

The following simple implementation compares each byte of the given records and sorts them numerically. If the two records have the same data, up to the length of the shorter one, then they are deemed EQUIVALENT.

```
public class SimpleComparator
    implements javax.microedition.rms.RecordComparator {
  public int compare(byte[] rec1, byte[] rec2) {
    int limit = Math.min(rec1.length, rec2.length);

    for (int index = 0; index < limit; index++) {
      if (rec1[index] < rec2[index])
        return PRECEDES;
      else if (rec1[index] > rec2[index])
        return FOLLOWS;
    }
    return EQUIVALENT;
  }
}
```

Working with RecordEnumeration

RecordStore's enumerateRecords() method returns an implementation of the RecordEnumeration interface. RecordEnumeration is surprisingly complicated. Its basic function is to allow you to iterate through the records retrieved from the RecordStore. Unlike a regular J2SE Enumeration or Iterator, however, RecordEnumeration allows you to scroll both forward and backward through its contents. In addition, you can peek at the next or previous record ID. Finally, RecordEnumeration offers the possibility of keeping its data synchronized with the actual RecordStore. Behind the scenes, this can be accomplished by registering the RecordEnumeration as a listener for RecordStore changes.

The basic operation of RecordEnumeration is to iterate through a set of records. You can find out if there's a next record by calling hasNextElement(). If the next record exists, you can retrieve its data by calling the following method:

```
public byte[] nextRecord()
    throws InvalidRecordIDException,
           RecordStoreNotOpenException,
           RecordStoreException
```

Alternately, you can retrieve the next record's ID by calling this method:

```
public int nextRecordId() throws InvalidRecordIDException
```

You can't really have your cake and eat it, though; both nextRecord() and nextRecordId() advance the RecordEnumeration to the next record. If you want to retrieve both the ID and the data for the next record, you'd need to call nextRecordId() and then retrieve the record data directly from the RecordStore.

A typical use of RecordEnumeration would be to walk straight through the selected records, like this:

```
// Open a RecordStore rs
// Create a RecordFilter rf
// Create a RecordComparator rc

RecordEnumeration re = rs.enumerateRecords(rf, rc, false);
while (re.hasNextElement()) {
  byte[] recordBytes = re.nextRecord();
  // Process the retrieved bytes.
}
```

The RecordFilter and RecordComparator can both be null, in which case the RecordEnumeration will iterate through every record in the record store. The Preferences class uses RecordEnumeration in this way.

■Note RecordEnumeration makes no guarantees about the order of the returned records if the RecordComparator is null.

As you're moving through the selected records, you can also move backward. RecordEnumeration includes hasPreviousElement(), previousRecord(), and previousRecordId() methods that work just like their next counterparts.

Four out of the five ways to move the current position in the RecordEnumeration are the nextRecord(), nextRecordId(), previousRecord(), and previousRecordId() methods. The fifth method is kind of like a rewind button: reset() moves the record pointer back to the very beginning of the selected records.

When you're finished using a RecordEnumeration, you should release its resources. You can do this by calling destroy(), after which the RecordEnumeration is no longer usable.

Keeping a RecordEnumeration Up-to-Date

In a multithreaded environment, it's entirely possible that a RecordStore will change at the same time you're iterating through a RecordEnumeration for the same RecordStore. There are two ways to deal with this.

The first thing you can do is call rebuild(), which explicitly rebuilds the RecordEnumeration based on the RecordFilter and RecordComparator you originally specified.

The other possibility is to request a RecordEnumeration that is automatically updated with any changes to the underlying RecordStore. You can do this by passing true for the keepUpdated parameter of RecordStore's enumerateRecords() method. You can find out if the RecordEnumeration is automatically updated by calling isKeptUpdated(). Furthermore, you can change its state by calling keepUpdated().

Automatically updated RecordEnumerations typically register themselves as RecordListeners with the underlying RecordStore. Each time the RecordStore is changed, the RecordEnumeration is rebuilt. Keep in mind that this is an expensive operation (in terms of time), so if there are many RecordStore changes, you'll be paying a price for it.

Using Resource Files

Resource files are another form of persistent storage. Accessing resource files is very simple, but they are important nevertheless. Resource files can be images, text, or other types of files that are stored in a MIDlet suite JAR. These files are read-only.

You can access a resource file as an InputStream by using the getResourceAsStream() method in Class. A typical usage looks like this:

```
InputStream in = this.getClass().getResourceAsStream("/Robotag-t.png");
```

Summary

The MIDP API for persistent storage is deliberately abstract in recognition that small devices will likely have many different methods for storing data. In MIDP, the central concept for persistent storage is the record store, which is a collection of bits of data called records. A record store is really a tiny database, but the details of exactly how records are stored is specific to a device implementation. The javax.microedition.rms.RecordStore class encapsulates all access to persistent storage. It provides methods for accessing and manipulating RecordStores, as well as methods for working with individual records. For more advanced RecordStore work, methods and interfaces exist to help keep track of changes to a RecordStore or to perform RecordStore queries.

CHAPTER 9

■ ■ ■

Persistent Storage II: File Connection and PIM API

Beyond the typically small persistent storage managed by MIDP's record store mechanism, devices may have additional persistent data storage mechanisms that can be made available to J2ME applications.

JSR 75 addresses two such mechanisms: file systems and Personal Information Management (PIM) databases.

Large file systems can be found on devices that accept plug-in flash memory cards. The File Connection Optional Package provides an API to access these file systems.

PIM databases, such as phone directories and to-do lists, are managed by some devices natively. The PIM Optional Package provides an API for J2ME applications to access these PIM databases.

File Connection Optional Package

Modern devices may have slots for optional flash memory cards (maybe even small hard disks) that can be added. Common flash memory card formats include Secure Data (SD) cards, Compact Flash, and Memory Stick. These memory cards can expand the available persistent storage to megabytes or even gigabytes of data. The record store mechanism of MIDP is inefficient for handling such large-capacity storage. The persistent storage on these cards is accessed as a file system, instead of a database, with directories and files.

A device may expose its file systems through the File Connection Optional Package. This optional API is contained in the javax.microedition.io.file package. Much like with a desktop PC, you can read or write files, and you can create or remove directories on the exposed file system. The file systems exposed by this API are usually fairly large in size, from megabytes to gigabytes large.

This optional package is implemented on top of CLDC. The API requires only CLDC 1.0, and works also with CLDC 1.1. The relationship between the File Connection Optional Package and CLDC is illustrated in Figure 9-1.

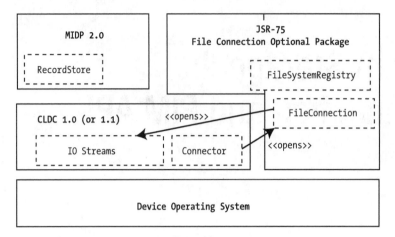

Figure 9-1. *Relationship between File Connection Optional Package and CLDC*

In Figure 9-1, note that the key interface in the API is the `FileConnection` interface. You need to use the `Connector` class from CLDC's Generic Connection Framework (GCF—a primary networking/communications framework covered in Chapter 10) to obtain an instance of a `FileConnection`. Once you have the `FileConnection`, you can start working with the file system, perhaps using the IO stream classes of CLDC to read and write data.

■**Note** Incidentally, for some implementations, it may be possible to read from (and even write to) specific files in an exposed file system without using the File Connection Optional Package. In these cases, you use `InputConnection` or `OutputConnection` from CLDC instead. However, you will not have the ability to work with directories and discover file names. Using `FileConnection` gives you full access to all that the underlying file system has to offer.

Determining If FileConnection API Is Available

It is always a good idea to make sure an optional API is available on a device before attempting to use it. If you want to confirm that the `FileConnection` optional API is available on a device, check for the system property called `microedition.io.file.FileConnection.version`. All JSR 75 implementations are required to support this property. You can obtain the available version using this code:

```
String currentVersion =
System.getProperty("microedition.io.file.FileConnection.version" )
```

You can also use the returned version to make sure your code is compatible. At this time, however, only version "1.0" has been defined. Null is returned if the API is not available.

Accessing File Systems

You perform read and write operations through the input and output stream classes from the java.io package. These streams are a standard part of the CLDC, as Chapter 4 shows.

To obtain a stream to a file in the file system, however, you first need to have an opened file connection. For this, you will need to use the File Connection optional API.

The main interface of this API is the FileConnection interface. You obtain an instance of a FileConnection by using a method of the javax.microedition.io.Connector class. This class is part of the Generic Connection Framework in CLDC. GCF is used primarily to make connections through a network or a communications port (see Chapter 10).

Obtaining FileConnections from GCF

At this time, the important thing you need to know about GCF is that the following static method of the Connector class can return a FileConnection instance:

```
 public static Connection open(String URL, int mode) throws IOException,
IllegalArgumentException,
  ConnectionNotFoundException, SecurityException
```

The URL to obtain a file connection will always start with "file:///", indicating that a file is accessed on the local host. The full syntax for the URL is actually "file://<hostname>/", but <hostname> is omitted when local. The mode indicates the type of access you want for the file connection. You can use Connector.READ, Connector.WRITE, or Connector.READ_WRITE. For example, you may get an input stream to an existing abc.txt file on an SD card using the following:

```
FileConnection fc = (FileConnection) Connector.open("file:///SDCard/abc.txt",
Connector.READ);
InputStream is = fc.openInputStream();
```

You can then use the InputStream for reading the file. The FileConnection interface has five methods for obtaining a stream:

```
DataInputStream openDataInputStream()
DataOutputStream openDataOutputStream()
InputStream openInputStream()
OutputStream openOutputStream()
OutputStream openOutputStream(long Offset)
```

The second variation of openOutputStream() allows you to specify a byte offset to start writing to the file.

■**Note** The top-level directory of a file system is called the root. Each file system on a device may correspond to a separate flash memory card or storage subsystem, and will have a different root name. The name of the root is arbitrary and totally device dependent. For example, a vendor may choose to name the root of an inserted SD memory card "SDCard1/", while the device's own internal flash file system may have a root name of "InternalFlash/". You can obtain an enumeration of all the available roots on a device using the FileSystemRegistry, described later in this chapter.

File or Directory

An open FileConnection can be referring to either a directory or a file. You can determine if the connection is associated with a directory via the following method:

```
public boolean isDirectory()
```

Some file systems, such as Win32, support hidden files. Hidden files do not appear on regular directory listings, and are often used for system files. You can determine whether a file or directory is hidden by calling the following method:

```
public isHidden()
```

On a file system that does not support hidden files, isHidden() always returns false. You can also control the hidden attribute of a file on file systems that support it, by using this method:

```
public void setHidden(boolean hiddenFlag)
```

Setting hiddenFlag to true will make the file hidden, while a false value will make it visible. This method has no effect on file systems that do not support hidden files nor on file systems where you must rename the file to make files hidden.

Modifying File Attributes

Some file attributes may prevent you from reading or writing to a file. You can determine whether a file can be read by using this method:

```
public boolean canRead()
```

Or find out if a file can be written to using the following:

```
public boolean canWrite()
```

To change the read or write attribute of a file on a file system that supports it, use this:

```
public void setReadable(boolean readable)
 throws IOException
```

```
public void setWriteable(boolean readable) throws IOException
```

Note Most of the input/output methods on the FileConnection interface will throw ConnectionClosedException if the call is made on a closed connection, IllegalModeException if a write is tried on a connection that is opened as read-only, and SecurityException if the operation would violate security policy. When a SecurityException is thrown, the operation is not actually performed. For methods that accept arguments, NullPointerException and IllegalArgumentException may also be thrown if an error occurs during argument processing.

Directory and File Size

Your application may need to determine the available space on a file system associated with a FileConnection instance. You can call the availableSize() method to find out the available size in bytes:

```
public long availableSize()
```

This returns the total available space in the entire file system. On plug-in memory cards, this can be up to gigabytes of data. There is another method to find out the size of the storage area already used up:

```
public long usedSize()
```

By adding up the value returned from availableSize() and usedSize(), you can figure out the total size of the file system.

If you only want to find out the size of the specific file associated with the current FileConnection instance, use the following method:

```
public long fileSize()
```

If the FileConnection instance refers to a directory, you can find out the total size of all the files in the directory by calling the following method:

```
public long directorySize()
```

Creating New Files or Directories

To create a new file, you first have to use Connector.open() with the new file name and Connector.WRITE mode. A FileConnection will be returned, but the file does not yet exist. You can confirm its nonexistence by calling

```
boolean exists() throws SecurityException, IllegalModeException,
   ConnectionClosedException
```

To create the file, you call

```
public void create() thows IOException
```

Creating a new directory is similar. Use Connector.open() with the new directory name. Then call the mkdir() method on the returned FileConnection:

```
public void mkdir() throws IOException
```

Note that it is not possible to create a directory using the create() call for a file using a URL such as "file:///mydir/". The trailing / will cause the create() call to throw an IOException. Use only the mkdir() call for directory creation.

Renaming and Deleting Files and Directories

To delete a file or directory, you need to first open it with Connector.WRITE mode enabled, then call the method:

```
public void delete() throws IOException
```

You should immediately call `close()` on the `FileConnection` after a `delete()`. The `FileConnection` is no longer valid once the underlying file has been deleted.

Similarly, to rename a file or directory, open it with `Connector.WRITE` mode enabled, and then call the `rename()` method of the `FileConnection` instance with the new name:

```
public void rename(String newName) throws IOException
```

Listing Directory Content

When you have a `FileConnection` to a directory, you can obtain an `Enumeration` of its content (files and subdirectory) using this method:

```
Enumeration list() throws IOException
Enumeration list(String filter, boolean includeHidden) throws IOException
```

The returned `Enumeration` contains objects of string type. Each object in the enumeration is the name of a file or directory. If the object is a directory, the name will end with /.

The second form of `list()` uses a filter that can contain the * (asterisk) wildcard character. For example, a filter value of "*.png" will select only the PNG graphics files in the directory. The `includeHidden` flag indicates whether the matching should be performed against files with the hidden flag set.

To make directory traversal more efficient, `FileConnection` does not force you to go back to GCF and use `Connector.open()` on every level of a new directory (although you can do so if you want to). Instead, a convenient method allows you to dive down a specific subdirectory (or move up) with the current `FileConnection`:

```
public void setFileConnection(String itemName) throws IOException
```

This will reset the `FileConnection` to the specified subdirectory, parent directory, or file. The `itemName` must be a string that is from a `list()`-returned `Enumeration`.

Path and URL Information

Note that the string from a `list()`-returned `Enumeration` does not contain full path information, or any of the "file:///" URL preamble. If you are only navigating subdirectories, you don't need the full URL. However, if you actually need the full URL, you can call this method to get the complete path and preamble:

```
public String getPath()
```

By appending the string from the `list()`-returned `Enumeration` to the string returned from the preceding method, you end up with a full URL. The full URL is useful if you ever need to open the file or directory again using the GCF `Connector.open()`.

If you already have a `FileConnection` open, you can always get the complete URL associated it by calling the following method:

```
public String getURL()
```

To get just the name of the file or directory, without the path and URL preamble, you can call

```
public String getName()
```

Similar to the strings from the list() enumeration, a directory name will have a trailing / character.

If you are constructing file paths manually, you should always obtain the file separator to use through the system property called file.separator. All FileConnection implementations must support this property. Use code like this:

```
String fileSep = System.getProperty("file.separator" )
```

Listening for Card Insertion and Removal

A user may insert or remove flash memory card at any time, which will affect the availability of file systems on a device. The File Connection API supports a JavaBeans-style listener mechanism. Interested objects can listen for addition and removal of file system roots (corresponding to insertion and removal of memory cards) by registering themselves as listeners.

The listener interface is javax.microedition.io.file.FileSystemListener. Because a device may have multiple file systems (for example, built-in flash memory and a slot for plug-in cards), a central registry class is used to manage the listeners. This central registry is the javax.microedition.io.file.FileSystemRegistry class.

You can add and remove file system listeners by using the two static methods of FileSystemRegistry:

```
public static boolean addFileSystemListener(FileSystemListener listener) throws
SecurityException,
    NullPointerException
public static boolean removeFileSystemListener(FileSystemListener listener) throws
NullPointerException
```

The returned boolean value on these two methods will indicate success of the operation.

The FileSystemListener interface has only a single method:

```
void rootChanged(int state, String rootName)
```

This method is called whenever there is a change in the set of file systems available. The state value is either FileSystemListener.ROOT_ADDED (for insertion of memory card) or FileSystemListener.ROOT_REMOVED (when memory card is removed). The rootName will provide the name of the root used to access the file system.

■**Tip** If you are using the default phone emulator of the J2ME Wireless Toolkit 2.x, the file systems are actually subdirectories under the appdb\DefaultColorPhone\filesystem directory. There should be a root1 default file system (subdirectory) there already. You can also simulate the addition and removal of new file system roots while a MIDlet is running. This can be done by selecting from the emulator's menu MIDlet ➤ External events. A dialog box will appear, allowing you to mount or unmount new file systems.

Discovering the Available File Systems

Another frequent use for the centralized `FileSystemRegistry` is for listing all the available file systems. Recall that each file system has a unique corresponding root name. The `static` method to call to discover all the root names is the following:

```
public static Enumeration listRoots() throws SecurityException
```

The returned value is an `Enumeration` of strings. Each element in the `Enumeration` is an available file system root. Typical code to iterate through the roots may be as follows:

```
Enumeration roots = FileSystemRegistry.listRoots();
String currentRoot = null;
while (roots.hasMoreElements()) {
    currentRoot = (String) roots.nextElement();
    ... do something with the discovered root...
}
```

FileConnection and Security

JSR 75 requires that all implementations of the File Connection Optional Package to isolate the MIDP RMS databases from the file system exposed through `FileConnection`. This means that there will be no way for you to accidentally overwrite any data that is accessed through `RecordStore`.

The specification recommends strongly that general file system access only be granted to designated public areas. It also recommends that file systems be protected based on users, applications, and system. However, enforcement is left up to the individual device implementation. Most CLDC devices are single user, and access restrictions based on user may not make sense.

When you make a call to `Connector.open()`, the MIDP protection domain-based security policy will kick in. For untrusted MIDlet suites, a user must explicitly allow access to the protected `FileConnection` API. This is identical to the behavior when untrusted MIDlet suites access the network through GCR.

For trusted MIDlet suites, a set of permissions is used to provide specific access to the `FileConnection` API. This set of permissions include the following:

```
javax.microedition.io.Connector.file.read
javax.microedition.io.Connector.file.write
```

Review Chapter 3 if you need a refresher on protection domains, permissions, or the MIDP security model in general.

An Example

Putting some of this to work, the example in Listing 9-1 stores preferences to the file system using the File Connection Optional Package. `FileBasedPreferences` is similar to the `RecordStore`-based `Preferences` class from Chapter 8. It maintains a preferences hash table that is persisted to the file system using the File Connection API.

Listing 9-1. *A Preferences Class That Encapsulates File System Access*

```java
import java.util.*;
import javax.microedition.io.*;
import javax.microedition.io.file.*;
import java.io.*;

public class FileBasedPreferences implements Runnable {
  private String mDirectoryName;
  private static final String fileURLRoot = "file:///";
  private static final String fileExt = ".pfs";
  private Hashtable mHashtable;
  private boolean mSaving = false;
  private String mFileRoot = null;

  public FileBasedPreferences(String dirName)
  throws IOException {
    mDirectoryName = dirName;
    mHashtable = new Hashtable();
    Enumeration em = FileSystemRegistry.listRoots();
    // Take the first root available for simplicity.
    if (em.hasMoreElements())
      mFileRoot = fileURLRoot + em.nextElement();
    if (mFileRoot != null)
      load();
    else
      throw new IOException("No file system available");
  }

  public String get(String key) {
    return (String)mHashtable.get(key);
  }

  public void put(String key, String value) {
    if (value == null) value = "";
    mHashtable.put(key, value);
  }

  private void load() throws IOException {
    FileConnection fc = null;
    DataInputStream dis = null;
```

```
    StringBuffer fileURL = new StringBuffer(mFileRoot);
    fileURL.append(mDirectoryName);
    fileURL.append(fileExt);
    try {
      fc = (FileConnection) Connector.open(
      fileURL.toString(), Connector.READ);
      if (fc == null)
        return;
      if (!fc.exists()) {
        return;
      }

      dis = fc.openDataInputStream();

      String curInput;
      while ( (curInput = dis.readUTF()) != null ) {
        int index = curInput.indexOf('|');
        String name = curInput.substring(0, index);
        String value = curInput.substring(index + 1);
        put(name, value);
      }
    } catch (Exception ex) {
      // End of file detected the hard way.
    }
    finally {
      if (dis != null) dis.close();
      if (fc != null) fc.close();
    }
  }

  public void save() {
    Thread t = new Thread(this);
    t.start();
  }
  public void run() {
    mSaving = true;
    try {
      savePref();
    } catch (IOException ex) {
    }
    mSaving = false;
  }
  public boolean isSaving() {
    return mSaving;
  }
```

```
  public void savePref() throws IOException {
    FileConnection fc = null;
    DataOutputStream dos = null;
    try {
      // If exists already, first delete file, a little clumsy.
      StringBuffer fileURL = new StringBuffer(mFileRoot);
      fileURL.append(mDirectoryName);
      fileURL.append(fileExt);
      fc = (FileConnection) Connector.open( fileURL.toString(),
Connector.READ_WRITE);
      if (fc.exists()) {
        fc.delete();
        fc.close();
        fc = (FileConnection) Connector.open( fileURL.toString(),
Connector.READ_WRITE);
      }
      fc.create();
      dos = new DataOutputStream(fc.openOutputStream());

      // Now save the preferences records.
      Enumeration keys = mHashtable.keys();
      while (keys.hasMoreElements()) {
        String key = (String)keys.nextElement();
        String value = get(key);
        String pref = key + "|" + value;
        dos.writeUTF(pref);
      }


    }
    finally {
      if (dos != null) {
        dos.flush();
        dos.close();
      }
      if (fc != null) fc.close();

    }
  }
}
```

Note the use of FileSystemRegistry to obtain the file system root in the constructor. The first returned file root is used (usually root1/ for the Wireless Toolkit).

Loading of data is done in the constructor, before the GUI becomes active. However, in the MIDlet, saving of data is performed when handling a Save command. Since this is done within the GUI event handling thread, you don't want it to hold it up. The save() method starts another thread to perform the actual persistence.

The run() method contains the code to write the HashTable to the file system. The mSaving flag is used to ensure that the user will not exit the application while an I/O thread is still saving data to the file system.

The GUI MIDlet that uses the FileBasedPreferences class is called FCMIDlet, which is shown in Listing 9-2. The user interface is identical to the one in RecordMIDlet from Chapter 8.

Listing 9-2. *Source Code of the FCMIDlet*

```
import javax.microedition.midlet.*;
import javax.microedition.lcdui.*;
import javax.microedition.rms.RecordStoreException;
import java.io.*;

public class FCMIDlet
extends MIDlet
implements CommandListener {
  private static final String kUser = "user";
  private static final String kPassword = "password";
  private FileBasedPreferences mPreferences;
  private Form mForm;
  private TextField mUserField, mPasswordField;
  private Command mExitCommand, mSaveCommand;

  public FCMIDlet() {
    try {
      verifyFileConnectionSupport();
      mPreferences = new FileBasedPreferences("preferences");
    }
    catch (IOException ex) {
      mForm = new Form("Exception");
      mForm.append(new StringItem(null, ex.toString()));
      mExitCommand = new Command("Exit", Command.EXIT, 0);
      mForm.addCommand(mExitCommand);
      mForm.setCommandListener(this);
      return;
    }

    mForm = new Form("Login");
    mUserField = new TextField("Name",
    mPreferences.get(kUser), 32, 0);
    mPasswordField = new TextField("Password",
    mPreferences.get(kPassword), 32, 0);
    mForm.append(mUserField);
    mForm.append(mPasswordField);
    mExitCommand =new Command("Exit", Command.EXIT, 0);
    mSaveCommand = new Command("Save", "Save Password", Command.SCREEN, 0);
    mForm.addCommand(mExitCommand);
```

```java
    mForm.addCommand(mSaveCommand);
    mForm.setCommandListener(this);
  }

  public void startApp() {
    Display.getDisplay(this).setCurrent(mForm);
  }

  public void pauseApp() {}

  public void savePrefs() {
    // Save the user name and password.
    mPreferences.put(kUser, mUserField.getString());
    mPreferences.put(kPassword, mPasswordField.getString());
    mPreferences.save();
  }
  public void destroyApp(boolean flg) {
  }
  public void commandAction(Command c, Displayable s) {
    if (c == mExitCommand) {
      if (mPreferences == null) {
        destroyApp(true);
        notifyDestroyed();
      }
      else if ( !mPreferences.isSaving()) {
        destroyApp(true);
        notifyDestroyed();
      }
    }
    else if (c == mSaveCommand)
      savePrefs();
  }
  public void verifyFileConnectionSupport() throws IOException {
    String version = "";
    version = System.getProperty("microedition.io.file.FileConnection.version");
    if (version != null) {
      if (!version.equals("1.0"))
        throw new IOException("Package is not version 1.0.");
    }
    else
      throw new IOException("File connection optional package is not available.");
  }
}
```

Note the use of the verifyFileConnectionSupport() method to assert the availability of the optional package in the constructor. When the Exit command is selected, the MIDlet will terminate only if the isSaving() method of the FileBasedPreferences instance returns false. Otherwise, the background thread is still saving data to the persistent storage.

You can try out the application. Enter in a user name and a password, and then click the Save button. You can then exit the MIDlet. When you start the MIDlet again, the persisted information should be redisplayed.

■**Tip** If you are using the default phone emulator of the J2ME Wireless Toolkit 2.x, the file systems are actually subdirectories under the appdb\DefaultColorPhone\filesystem directory. You should be able to find the preferences.pfs file storing the preference under the root1 subdirectory.

PIM Optional Package

Many devices, especially phones, have the ability to maintain lists of phone numbers and names. Some devices also store addresses, e-mails, events, to-do lists, and other personal information. This PIM data is stored in PIM databases. Most devices will have built-in applications that manage the PIM data. Until recently, there was no direct way of accessing this information from your MIDP application. A device vendor may now expose access to its PIM databases through the PIM Optional Package, specified in JSR 75.

Figure 9-2 shows the hierarchy of major classes and interfaces in the PIM API.

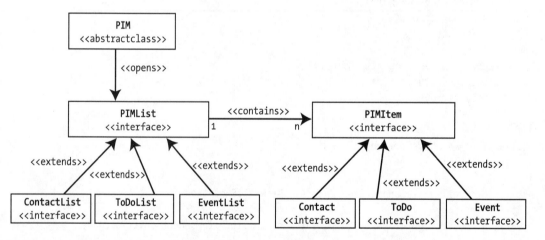

Figure 9-2. *The major classes and interfaces of the JSR 75 PIM API*

In Figure 9-2, PIM is a singleton object that is used to open lists of records. Think of PIM as representing the PIM database. Lists are accessed through the PIMList interface. Each list contains items. Each item represents a single record in the PIM database. Items are accessed through the PIMItem interface. Contact, Event, and ToDo all inherit from PIMItem, while ContactList, EventList, and ToDoList all inherit from PIMList.

Determining If PIM Optional Package Is Available

You should check to see if the PIM Optional Package is available on a device before attempting to use it. Check for the system property called microedition.pim.version. All PIM Optional Package implementations are required to support it. Use code similar to

```
String currentVersion = System.getProperty("microedition.pim.version " )
```

You should also use the returned version to make sure your code is version compatible. At this time, however, only version "1.0" is available. The call will return null if the optional package is not available.

Obtaining the Singleton PIM Instance

The API centers around the PIM abstract class. You cannot instantiate this class with the new operator. However, there is a class factory method to obtain the one and only instance:

```
public static PIM getInstance()
```

Opening the PIM Lists

You can access the PIM lists once you have the singleton instance. A PIM list can be obtained using one of these openPIMList() methods:

```
public PIMList openPIMList(int pimListType, int mode) throws PIMException
public PIMList openPIMList(int pimListType, int mode, String name) throws
PIMException
```

The pimListType can contain PIM.CONTACT_LIST, PIM.EVENT_LIST, or PIM.TODO_LIST. The JSR 75 specification requires at least one list to be available if the optional package is supported. The access mode can be PIM.READ_ONLY, PIM.READ_WRITE, or PIM.WRITE_ONLY.

JSR 75 allows a device to maintain multiple lists of the same type. Not all implementations will have this need. If you need to, the second form of the openPIMList() method enables you to select a list by name and type. The name of the lists available, if an implementation supports multiple lists of the same type, can be obtained via the following:

```
String [] listPIMLists( int pimListType);
```

pimListType is any one of PIM.CONTACT_LIST, PIM.EVENT_LIST, or PIM.TODO_LIST.

Obtaining Items from a PIM List

Once you have a list opened, you can start accessing its content. The openPIMList() call returns a PIMList. The javax.microedition.pim.PIMList interface is the superinterface of ContactList, EventList, and ToDoList. You need to cast it to the expected type before accessing the list, for example:

```
ContactList clist = (ContactList)
    pimInst.openPIMList( PIM.CONTACT_LIST, PIM.READ_WRITE);
```

All the records in a list can be accessed via an Enumeration (java.util.Enmeration) of PIMItems. You can obtain the Enumeration using one of the items() methods on the PIMList:

```
public Enumeration items() throws PIMException
public Enumeration items(PIMItem matchingItem) throws PIMException
public Enumeration items(String matchingValue) throws PIMException
```

The second and third form in the preceding list will both return a subset of the items in a list.

The second form matches based on a supplied PIMItem template (which is a contact, an event, or a to-do item). You need to set the fields on this template that you want to match (setting field values is covered later in this chapter; see the section "Modifying Field Values"). For a String typed field, you can specify a partial string. For example, specifying "hom" will match both "homing pigeon" and "HOMER".

The third form attempts to perform the partial string match across all string-typed fields of an item. For a ContactList, it is essentially saying, "Find me all the contacts that contain the string in any of its (string-typed) fields."

Manipulating Categories

Some PDAs support the notion of a category. You can classify a list of items by categories. A category is a just a string. For example, a "personal" category can be used to flag all the personal contacts in the content list, while a "business" category is used for business contacts. To obtain all the list items in a particular category, you can use the following:

```
public Enumeration itemsByCategory(String category) throws PIMException
```

To get a list of categories supported by the device, call

```
String [] getCategories() throws PIMException
```

If you get a zero-length array in return, you know that either the device does not support categories or the user hasn't defined any.

Once you've determined that the device supports categories, you can add new categories using the following:

```
public void addCategory(String category) throws PIMException
```

This method will never add the same category twice. It will return without throwing an exception if the specified category already exists. To delete a category, use this method:

```
public void deleteCategory(String category, boolean deleteUnassignedItems)
```

Note that some items may end up having no category assigned once a category is deleted. Set the deleteUnassignedItems flag to true if you want these items deleted from the list. The deleteCategory() method will return without throwing an exception even if the category specified does not exist. It will, however, throw a PIMException if categories are not supported on the device.

A category can be renamed using the following method:

```
public void renameCategory(String currentCategoryName, String newCategoryName)
throws PIMException
```

Four methods can be used to manipulate the categories associated with a contact:

```
public String [] getCategories()
public int maxCategories()
public void addToCategory(String category) throws PIMException
public void removeFromCategory(String category)
```

getCategories() gets a list of the categories associated with the contact. maxCategories() can be used to discover the maximum number of categories that can be assigned to a contact—this is highly implementation dependent. addToCategory() will add a category association to a contact. removeFromCategory() removes a category association from a contact.

Standard Fields on an Item

A PIMItem can hold a contact record, an event record from the event list, or a to-do item from the to-do list. Accordingly, the PIMItem interface is the superinterface to the Contact, Event, and ToDo interfaces.

The PIMItem interface contains many methods for working with fields within an item. The PIM functions of a device are typically accessed by native applications. This may be a phone directory application on a cell phone or an address book on a wireless PDA. The set of fields supported and their format can be quite different between devices. As a result, the PIM API must be able to deal with a completely flexible set of fields.

Each of the Contact, Event, and ToDo interfaces defines a set of constants that can be used to specify a set of "standard fields" in the record. The standard fields for Contact are based on the vCard 3.0 specifications from the Internet Mail Consortium (http://www.imc.org/pdi/). The vCard format is a cross-platform data interchange format that is widely used by contact management applications.

■**Note** The set of standard fields in the Event and ToDo items is based on the vCalendar 1.0 specification from the Internet Mail Consortium. You can work with these fields in the same way as the fields in Contact.

For example, Contact defines the standard fields and subfields detailed in Table 9-1. The Contact interface has constants defined for all of these fields and subfields.

Table 9-1. *Standard Fields of a Contact Record*

Field Name/Constant	Description	Data Type
ADDR	Field specifying address.	String []
ADDR_COUNTRY	Index into ADDR of the country portion of the address.	String
ADDR_EXTRA	Index into ADDR of extra information in the address.	String
ADDR_LOCALITY	Index into ADDR of locality information associated with an address. Typically used to hold city name.	String
ADDR_POBOX	Index into ADDR of the post office box associated with the address.	String

Table 9-1. *Standard Fields of a Contact Record (Continued)*

Field Name/Constant	Description	Data Type
ADDR_REGION	Index into ADDR of the region information associated with an address. Typically used to hold province or state name.	String
ADDR_POSTALCODE	Index into ADDR of the postal or zip code portion of an address.	String
BIRTHDAY	Field containing the birthday.	Date
CLASS	Field containing access class information. Can contain Contact.CLASS_CONFIDENTIAL, Contact.CLASS_PRIVATE, or Contact.CLASS_PUBLIC.	int
EMAIL	Field containing the e-mail address.	String
FORMATTED_ADDR	Field containing the complete preformatted address.	String
FORMATTED_NAME	Field containing the preformatted name.	String
NAME	Field containing the name.	String []
NAME_FAMILY	Index.	String
NAME_GIVEN	Index.	String
NAME_OTHER	Index.	String
NAME_PREFIX	Index.	String
NAME_SUFFIX	Index.	String
NICKNAME	Field containing the nickname.	String
NOTE	Field containing additional note.	String
ORG	Field containing the organization name.	String
PHOTO	Field including a photo.	byte []
PHOTO_URL	Field specifying a link to a photo.	String
PUBLIC_KEY	Field containing public encryption key in binary form.	byte []
PUBLIC_KEY_STRING	Field containing public encryption key in string form. May be tied together with PUBLIC_KEY field.	String
REVISION	Field containing date of last modification.	Date
TEL	Field containing a telephone number. No fixed format required.	String
TITLE	Field specifying the job title.	String
UID	Field containing a unique ID.	String
URL	Field containing a link.	String

There are two fields in Contact that are string arrays: NAME and ADDR. These are somewhat special because each member of the string array contains a different subfield. Constants such as NAME_FAMILY contain the corresponding index into the string array. For example, if pimName is the string array containing NAME, then you can access the last name using

```
String lastName = pimName[Contact.NAME_FAMILY];
```

JSR 75 does not require implementation of any of these standard fields. You should check to see whether the field is supported by the actual API implementation before using it. You need to use a method on the ContactList (actually PIMList, ContactList's superinterface) to check for field support:

```
public boolean isSupportedField(int field)
```

You can also get a list of all the supported fields using this method:

```
public int [] getSupportedFields()
```

Reading Field Values

To read the value in a field, you need to know its data type. Table 9-1 describes the data type of all standard Contact fields. You can look up the data type for Event and ToDo from the JSR 75 Javadocs.

There are accessor methods for each data type on the Contact (actually PIMItem) interface:

```
public byte [] getBinary(int field, int index)
public long getDate(int field, int index)
public int getInt(int field, int index)
public String getString(int field, int index)
public Boolean getBoolean(int field, int index)
public String [] getStringArray(int field, int index)
```

Each field instance can actually contain multiple values of the same type, which is why an index is needed for the preceding methods. For example, the Contact.TEL field may have three values—one for fax, one for work, and one for home. In this case, the three values are accessed on a different index of the Contact.TEL field and will each have a different attribute. Attributes are discussed in the next section.

In many cases, there is only one single field value, and using index 0 is adequate. For example, you can get the Contact.EMAIL field from a Contact instance (called myContact) using the following code:

```
String tmpEmail = null;
if ( myContList.isSupportedField(Contact.EMAIL))
  tmpEmail = myContact.getString(Contact.EMAIL, 0);
```

The Contact.NAME and Contact.ADDR fields are of string array types. The code to access a subfield requires one more level of indexing. For example, to obtain the value of the last name of a Contact, use the following:

```
String [] curName = myContact.getStringArray(Contact.NAME, 0);
String lastName = curName[Contacat.NAME_FAMILY];
```

Adding Attributes to Field Values

Attributes are bit flags used to qualify field values. Attributes defined in the Contact interface include ATTR_FAX, ATTR_HOME, ATTR_MOBILE, ATTR_OTHER, ATTR_PAGER, ATTR_SMS, ATTR_WORK, ATTR_AUTO, ATTR_ASST, and ATTR_PREFERRED. Attributes may be combined using the | (bitwise or) operator.

Attributes are useful for some fields that can have multiple values. For example, the Contact.TEL field may have a value of "402-323-1111" with ATTR_FAX, another value of "402-341-8888" with ATTR_WORK, and a value of "402-872-2001" with ATTR_HOME | ATTR_PREFERED.

Only one value can be marked with ATTR_PREFERRED. The index corresponding to the preferred attribute, if set, can be obtained using this method on the Contact interface:

```
public int getPreferredIndex(int field)
```

Attributes are specified when adding values to a field. A series of data type–dependent methods on Contact (actually PIMItem) are available for this purpose:

```
public void addBinary(int field, int attributes, byte[] value,
        int offset, int length)
public void addDate(int field, int attributes, long value)
public void addInt(int field, int attributes, int value)
public void addString(int field, int attributes, String value)
public void addBoolean(int field, int attributes, boolean value)
public void addStringArray(int field, int attributes, String [] value)
```

Most fields are single valued, and not all fields have attributes. You can use Contact.ATTR_NONE for an attribute when adding a value to a field.

Creating a New Contact

Creating a new Contact is a three-step process (for Event or ToDo, the procedure is similar):

1. Call the factory method, createContact(), on the ContactList, returning a new Contact for the list.

2. Use the add<data type>() methods of the Contact to set values for the fields of the Contact.

3. Call the commit() method on the Contact to save the new field values to persistent storage.

The createContact() method on the ContactList will create a new Contact item for the list, with no value set for any of the fields:

```
public Contact createContact()
```

The commit() method of Contact causes the underlying implementation to save all the new field values to persistent storage.

```
public void commit() throws PIMException
```

For example, the code to create a new Contact with only a Contact.NAME field may be as follows:

```
ContactList contList = (ContactList)
    PIM.getInstance().openPIMList(PIM.CONTACT_LIST, PIM.READ_WRITE);
Contact ct = list.createContact();
 String [] name = new String[contList.stringArraySize(Contact.NAME)];
 name[Contact.NAME_GIVEN] = "Joe";
 name[Contact.NAME_FAMILY] = "Tanner";
 ct.addStringArray(Contact.NAME,Contact.ATTR_NONE , name);
 ct.commit();
```

Note the use of the stringArraySize() method in the preceding code; this method is part of the ContactList interface that can be used to obtain the (fixed) array size of string array typed field. The method has the following signature:

```
public int stringArraySize(int stringArrayField)
```

Modifying Field Values

To change the value of the fields in an existing item, you can use any of the type-specific methods on a Contact:

```
public void setBinary(int field, int index, int attributes, byte[] value,
 int offset, int length)
public void setDate(int field, int index, int attributes, long value)
public void setInt(int field, int index, int attributes, int value)
public void setString(int field, int index, int attributes, String value)
public void setBoolean(int field, int index, int attributes, boolean value)
public void setStringArray(int field, int index, int attributes, String [] value)
```

Note that every method in the preceding list requires an index to specify the field value to set in the case of fields with multiple values. Most fields are single valued, and using 0 as an index will suffice.

You can determine if any fields in an item has been modified by calling

```
public boolean isModified()
```

Any change you make to the field values in the contact will be persisted to persistent storage when you call the commit() method.

Removing Contacts

To remove a Contact, you will need to get a reference to the Contact to be removed. This can be done by iterating through the Enumeration returned from an items() method call (see the earlier section "Obtaining Items from a PIM List"). Once you have a reference to the Contact to be removed, call the removeContact() method on the ContactList interface:

```
public void removeContact(Contact contact) throws PIMException
```

There is no method to remove all items from a list. You will need to iterate through the Enumeration and remove each one individually.

Working with the PIM API

Putting the API to use, the first MIDlet will write contact information to the PIM database. SeedMIDlet, shown in Listing 9-3, writes four contact records into the PIM database using the PIM optional APIs.

Listing 9-3. *Source Code for a MIDlet to Seed the PIM Database with Contacts*

```java
import java.io.*;
import javax.microedition.lcdui.*;
import javax.microedition.midlet.*;
import javax.microedition.pim.*;

public class SeedMIDlet
extends MIDlet implements CommandListener {
  private Form mForm;
  private Command mExitCommand;

  public SeedMIDlet() {
    try {
      verifyPIMSupport();
      seed();
    }
    catch (Exception ex) {
      mForm = new Form("Exception");
      mForm.append(new StringItem(null, ex.toString()));
      mExitCommand = new Command("Exit", Command.EXIT, 0);
      mForm.addCommand(mExitCommand);
      mForm.setCommandListener(this);
      return;
    }

    mForm = new Form("Data Seeded");
    mForm.append(new StringItem(null, "PIM data stored."));
    mExitCommand = new Command("Exit", Command.EXIT, 0);
    mForm.addCommand(mExitCommand);
    mForm.setCommandListener(this);
  }

  public void startApp() {
    Display.getDisplay(this).setCurrent(mForm);
  }

  public void pauseApp() {}
```

```java
public void destroyApp(boolean flg) {
}
public void commandAction(Command c, Displayable s) {
  if (c == mExitCommand) {
    destroyApp(true);
    notifyDestroyed();
  }
}


public void verifyPIMSupport() throws IOException {
  String version = "";
  version = System.getProperty("microedition.pim.version");
  if (version != null) {
    if (!version.equals("1.0"))
      throw new IOException("Package is not version 1.0.");
  }
  else
    throw new IOException("PIM optional package is not available.");
}

private ContactList contList = null;
private void seed() throws PIMException {
  try {
    PIM pimInst = PIM.getInstance();
    contList = (ContactList)
    pimInst.openPIMList(PIM.CONTACT_LIST, PIM.READ_WRITE);
  }
  catch (PIMException ex) {
    // Contact list is not supported.
  }
  addContact(contList, "Jack", "Goldburg", "2345 High Park Ave",
  "Orlando", "USA", "32817");
  addContact(contList, "Mary", "Johnson", "777 Lucky Road",
  "London", "UK", "SW10 0XE");
  addContact(contList, "Johnathan", "Knudsen", "234 Sunny Java Street",
  "Sausalito", "USA", "94965");
  addContact(contList, "Sing", "Li", "168 Technology Drive",
  "Edmonton", "Canada", "T6G 2E1");
  if (contList != null)
    contList.close();
  contList = null;

}
```

```
  private void addContact( ContactList list, String firstName, String lastName,
  String street, String city, String country, String postalcode)
  throws PIMException {
    Contact ct = list.createContact();
    String [] name = new String[contList.stringArraySize(Contact.NAME)];
    name[Contact.NAME_GIVEN] = firstName;
    name[Contact.NAME_FAMILY] = lastName;
    ct.addStringArray(Contact.NAME,Contact.ATTR_NONE , name);
    String [] addr = new String[contList.stringArraySize(Contact.ADDR)];
    addr[Contact.ADDR_STREET] = street;
    addr[Contact.ADDR_LOCALITY] = city;
    addr[Contact.ADDR_COUNTRY] = country;
    addr[Contact.ADDR_POSTALCODE] = street;
    ct.addStringArray(Contact.ADDR, Contact.ATTR_NONE , addr);
    ct.commit();
  }
}
```

Note the use of the verifyPIMSupport() method to check for PIM Optional Package before proceeding. The addContact() method is used to add a contact to the PIM list. Only the NAME and ADDR fields are set in this example.

Build and run this on the emulator before proceeding with the next MIDlet. This will seed the PIM database with the contact records.

The PIM MIDlet in Listing 9-4 reads the contact list using the PIM optional API and shows the names of all the contacts in the database.

Listing 9-4. *A MIDlet to Display Contact Names in the PIM Database*

```
import javax.microedition.midlet.*;
import javax.microedition.lcdui.*;
import javax.microedition.pim.*;
import java.io.*;
import java.util.*;
import javax.microedition.lcdui.List;

public class PIMMIDlet
extends MIDlet
implements CommandListener {
  private ContactList contList = null;
  private Enumeration contacts = null;
```

```
private Form mForm;
private List mNameList;
private Command mExitCommand;
public PIMMIDlet() {
  try {
    verifyPIMSupport();
    PIM pimInst = PIM.getInstance();
    contList = (ContactList)
    pimInst.openPIMList(PIM.CONTACT_LIST, PIM.READ_ONLY);
    contacts = contList.items();
  }
  catch (Exception ex) {
    mForm = new Form("Exception");
    mForm.append(new StringItem(null, ex.toString()));
    mExitCommand = new Command("Exit", Command.EXIT, 0);
    mForm.addCommand(mExitCommand);
    mForm.setCommandListener(this);
    return;
  }

  if (contacts == null)
    return;
  mNameList = new List("List of contacts", List.EXCLUSIVE);
  while (contacts.hasMoreElements()) {
    Contact tCont = (Contact) contacts.nextElement();
    int [] flds = tCont.getFields();
    String [] nameValues = tCont.getStringArray( Contact.NAME, 0);
    String firstName = nameValues[Contact.NAME_GIVEN];
    String lastName = nameValues[Contact.NAME_FAMILY];
    mNameList.append(lastName + ", " + firstName, null);
  }


  mExitCommand =new Command("Exit", Command.EXIT, 0);
  mNameList.addCommand(mExitCommand);
  mNameList.setCommandListener(this);
}

public void startApp() {
  Display.getDisplay(this).setCurrent(mNameList);
}
```

```
public void pauseApp() {}
public void destroyApp(boolean flg) {
}
public void commandAction(Command c, Displayable s) {
  if (c == mExitCommand) {
    destroyApp(true);
    notifyDestroyed();
  }
}
public void verifyPIMSupport() throws IOException {
  String version = null;
  version = System.getProperty("microedition.pim.version");
  if (version != null) {
    if (!version.equals("1.0"))
      throw new IOException("Package is not version 1.0.");
  }
  else
    throw new IOException("PIM optional package is not available.");
}
}
```

In the constructor, notice the use of the items() method of the ContactList to obtain an Enumeration of contacts. The Contact.NAME_GIVEN and Contact.NAME_FAMILY subfields of the Contact.NAME field are then extracted and displayed in a GUI list.

Summary

JSR 75 specifies two optional packages for persistent storage beyond the record store mechanism of MIDP.

The File Connection Optional Package exposes an API that can be used by applications to access a device's file systems. These file systems typically correspond to a flash memory card that can be added or removed at any time. A centralized file system registry that tracks the addition and removal of file systems is available to applications using the FileConnection API.

The PIM Optional Package enables applications to access PIM databases. These databases are typically created and maintained by native PIM applications. You can add, modify, or delete records contained in contacts, events, and to-do lists. PIM applications across different devices may maintain different data fields. The API handles these differences by mapping to a standard set of fields, selected from the vCard and vCalendar personal data interchange specifications from the Internet Email Consortium.

CHAPTER 10

∎∎∎

Connecting to the World

It's cool running Java on mobile phones and pagers, but the real kicker is getting your MIDlets connected to the Internet. With an Internet connection, you can write applications that allow you to access information and do work from your mobile telephone, from wherever you are in the world.

The Generic Connection Framework

The CLDC defines an extremely flexible API for network connections, the *generic connection framework*. The core GCF is contained in the `javax.microedition.io` package and based around the `Connection` interface. Figure 10-1 details the `Connection` interface and its various child interfaces.

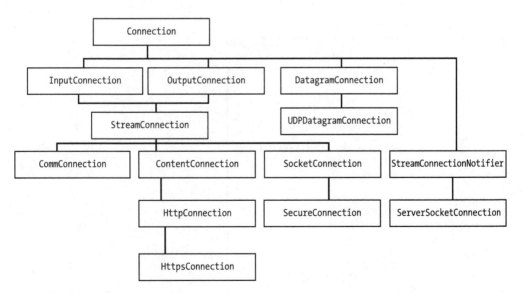

Figure 10-1. *The Connection family tree*

The link between the Connection interfaces and reality is a class called javax.microedition.io.Connector. The basic idea is that you pass a connection string to one of Connector's static methods and get back some Connection implementation. A *connection string* looks something like a URL, but there are various other possibilities. The connection string socket://apress.com:79 might open a TCP/IP connection to apress.com on port 79, then return a StreamConnection implementation. Chapter 9 used a FileConnnection from the JSR 75 optional package to access file systems.

MIDP 2.0 requires support of Hypertext Transfer Protocol (HTTP) connections. You pass an HTTP URL to Connector and get back an implementation of HttpConnection. Mandatory support for HTTPS connections (secure HTTP) is also required by MIDP 2.0. There are also standardized connection strings for several types of connections. We'll discuss these later in this chapter (see the sections following "Making a Connection with HTTP GET").

HttpConnection's methods are detailed in Figure 10-2. Most of the methods in HttpConnection have to do with details of HTTP, which we won't cover here. We'll cover everything you need to know to connect to a server here, including both GET and POST requests. If you need to dig deeper, you can read RFC 2616 (one of the Internet standards documents), available at http://ietf.org/rfc2616.html. Note that MIDP uses a subset of the full HTTP 1.1; only the GET, POST, and HEAD commands are required.

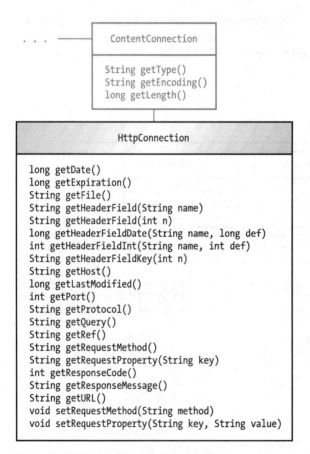

Figure 10-2. *The HttpConnection interface*

Review of HTTP

This section presents a brief review of the Hypertext Transfer Protocol. The whole story is in RFC 2616; this section covers the essentials.

Requests and Responses

HTTP is built around requests and responses. A client sends a request to a server—something like, "Please give me such-and-such HTML page." The server sends back a response—something like, "Here's the file," or, "I don't know what you're talking about."

Requests and responses have two parts: headers and content. If you type a URL into your browser, the browser creates an HTTP request (mostly headers) and sends it to a server. The server finds the requested file and sends it back in an HTTP response. The response headers describe things like the type of web server, the file type of the response, the length of the response, and other information. The response content is the data of the file itself.

Parameters

Browsers and other HTTP clients request specific named resources from HTTP servers. In addition, clients can pass parameters to the server. Parameters are simple name and value pairs. For example, a client might send a userid parameter with a value of "jonathan" to a server. HTTP also supports passing binary data to the server in the body of a request, and the Java stream classes make it easy to exchange a variety of data types.

When a browser is the HTTP client, parameters are generally collected from HTML forms. You've seen these forms, like the one in which you fill in your shipping address and your credit card number. Form values are sent as parameters to a web server when you click the Submit or Next button on the form.

The client encodes parameters before they are sent to the server. Parameters are passed as name and value pairs; multiple parameters are separated by ampersands. The exact way that parameters are encoded is documented in the J2SE documentation for java.net.URLEncoder. The rules are relatively simple.

1. The space character is converted to a plus (+) sign.

2. The following characters remain unchanged: lowercase letters a through z, uppercase letters A through Z, the numbers 0 through 9, the period (.), the hyphen (-), the asterisk (*), and the underscore (_).

3. All other characters are converted into "%xy", where "xy" is a hexadecimal number that represents the low 8 bits of the character.

GET, HEAD, and POST

The simplest HTTP operation is GET. This is what happens when you type a URL into your browser. The browser says, "GET me this URL," and the server responds with the headers and content of the response.

With a GET request, parameters are added to the end of the URL in encoded form. (Some servers have trouble with very long URLs; if you have a lot of parameters, or binary data, you may wish to pass data in the body of the HTTP request.) For example, suppose the following hypothetical URL maps to a servlet or some other server-side component of your application:

```
http://jonathanknudsen.com/simple
```

Adding a parameter is easy. If you want to pass a parameter with a name of user and a value of "jonathan", you would use the following URL:

```
http://jonathanknudsen.com/simple?user=jonathan
```

Additional name and value pairs can be added, separated by ampersands:

```
http://jonathanknudsen.com/simple?user=jonathan&zip=08540&day=saturday
```

The HEAD operation is identical to GET, but the server sends back only the headers of the response.

POST is basically the same as GET, but parameters are handled differently. Instead of being pasted on the end of the URL, as they are with GET, the parameters are passed as the body of the request. They are encoded in the same way.

Making a Connection with HTTP GET

Loading data from a server is startlingly simple, particularly if you're performing an HTTP GET. Simply pass a URL to Connector's static open() method. The returned Connection will probably be an implementation of HttpConnection, but you can just treat it as an InputConnection. Then get the corresponding InputStream and read data to your heart's content.

In code, it looks something like this:

```
String url = "http://jonathanknudsen.com/simple";
InputConnection ic = (InputConnection)Connector.open(url);
InputStream in = ic.openInputStream();
// Read stuff from the InputStream
ic.close();
```

Most of the methods involved can throw a java.io.IOException. We've omitted the try and catch blocks from the example for clarity.

That's all there is to it. You can now connect your MIDlets to the world. Network access is subject to security policies on the device. We'll talk more about this near the end of this chapter, in the section "Permissions for Network Connections."

Passing Parameters

With HTTP GET, all parameters are passed to the server in the body of the URL. This makes it easy to send parameters to the server. The following code fragment shows how two parameters can be passed:

```
String url = "http://localhost/midp/simple?pOne=one+bit&pTwo=two";
InputConnection ic = (InputConnection)Connector.open(url);
InputStream in = ic.openInputStream();
```

The first parameter is named "pOne" and has "one bit" as a value; the second parameter is named "pTwo" and has "two" as a value.

A Simple Example

HTTP isn't all about exchanging HTML pages. It's actually a generic file-exchange protocol. In this section, we'll look at an example that loads an image from the network and displays it. Listing 10-1 shows the source code for ImageLoader, a MIDlet that retrieves an image from the Internet and displays it on the screen.

Listing 10-1. *Retrieving an Image from the Internet*

```
import java.io.*;

import javax.microedition.io.*;
import javax.microedition.lcdui.*;
import javax.microedition.midlet.*;

public class ImageLoader
    extends MIDlet
    implements CommandListener, Runnable {
  private Display mDisplay;
  private Form mForm;

  public ImageLoader() {
    mForm = new Form("Connecting...");
    mForm.addCommand(new Command("Exit", Command.EXIT, 0));
    mForm.setCommandListener(this);
  }

  public void startApp() {
    if (mDisplay == null) mDisplay = Display.getDisplay(this);
    mDisplay.setCurrent(mForm);

    // Do network loading in a separate thread.
    Thread t = new Thread(this);
    t.start();
  }

  public void pauseApp() {}

  public void destroyApp(boolean unconditional) {}

  public void commandAction(Command c, Displayable s) {
    if (c.getCommandType() == Command.EXIT)
      notifyDestroyed();
  }
```

```java
public void run() {
  HttpConnection hc = null;
  DataInputStream in = null;

  try {
    String url = getAppProperty("ImageLoader-URL");
    hc = (HttpConnection)Connector.open(url);
    int length = (int)hc.getLength();
    byte[] data = null;
    if (length != -1) {
      data = new byte[length];
      in = new DataInputStream(hc.openInputStream());
      in.readFully(data);
    }
    else {
      // If content length is not given, read in chunks.
      int chunkSize = 512;
      int index = 0;
      int readLength = 0;
      in = new DataInputStream(hc.openInputStream());
      data = new byte[chunkSize];
      do {
        if (data.length < index + chunkSize) {
          byte[] newData = new byte[index + chunkSize];
          System.arraycopy(data, 0, newData, 0, data.length);
          data = newData;
        }
        readLength = in.read(data, index, chunkSize);
        index += readLength;
      } while (readLength == chunkSize);
      length = index;
    }
    Image image = Image.createImage(data, 0, length);
    ImageItem imageItem = new ImageItem(null, image, 0, null);
    mForm.append(imageItem);
    mForm.setTitle("Done.");
  }
  catch (IOException ioe) {
    StringItem stringItem = new StringItem(null, ioe.toString());
    mForm.append(stringItem);
    mForm.setTitle("Done.");
  }
```

```
  finally {
    try {
      if (in != null) in.close();
      if (hc != null) hc.close();
    }
    catch (IOException ioe) {}
  }
}
}
```

The run() method contains all of the networking code. It's fairly simple; we pass the URL of an image (retrieved as an application property) to Connector's open() method and cast the result to HttpConnection. Then we retrieve the length of the image file, using the getLength() method. Given the length, we create a byte array and read data into it. Finally, having read the entire image file into a byte array, we can create an Image from the raw data.

If the content length is not specified, the image data is read in chunks, the size of which can be implementation dependent.

You'll need to specify the MIDlet property ImageLoader-URL in order for this example to work correctly. Note that you need to specify the URL of a PNG image, not of a JPEG or GIF. The URL http://65.215.221.148:8080/wj2/res/java2d_sm_ad.png produces the results shown in Figure 10-3.

Figure 10-3. *The ImageLoader example*

Posting a Form with HTTP POST

Posting a form is a little more complicated on the MIDlet side. In particular, there are request headers that need to be set in HttpConnection before the server is contacted. The process works like this:

1. Obtain an HttpConnection from Connector's open() method.

2. Modify the header fields of the request. In particular, you need to change the request method by calling setRequestMethod(), and you should set the "Content-Length" header by calling setRequestProperty(). This is the length of the parameters you will be sending.

3. Obtain the output stream for the HttpConnection by calling openOutputStream(). This sends the request headers to the server.

4. Send the request parameters on the output stream returned from the HttpConnection. Parameters should be encoded as described earlier (and in the documentation for the J2SE class java.net.URLEncoder, see http://java.sun.com/j2se/1.4.2/docs/api/java/net/URLEncoder.html).

5. Read the response from the server from the input stream retrieved from HttpConnection's openInputStream() method.

The following example, Listing 10-2, demonstrates how to send a single parameter to a server using an HTTP POST. Multiple parameters can be assembled by joining them with an ampersand separator. Note that the parameter in this example has been encoded as described previously. In this example, the parameter value "Jonathan Knudsen!" has been encoded to "Jonathan+Knudsen%21". Listing 10-3 shows a very simple servlet that can communicate with PostMIDlet.

Listing 10-2. *A Simple MIDlet Performing an HTTP POST*

```
import java.io.*;

import javax.microedition.io.*;
import javax.microedition.lcdui.*;
import javax.microedition.midlet.*;

public class PostMIDlet
    extends MIDlet
    implements CommandListener, Runnable {
  private Display mDisplay;
  private Form mForm;

  public PostMIDlet() {
    mForm = new Form("Connecting...");
    mForm.addCommand(new Command("Exit", Command.EXIT, 0));
    mForm.setCommandListener(this);
  }

  public void startApp() {
    if (mDisplay == null) mDisplay = Display.getDisplay(this);
    mDisplay.setCurrent(mForm);
```

```
  // Do network loading in a separate thread.
  Thread t = new Thread(this);
  t.start();
}

public void pauseApp() {}

public void destroyApp(boolean unconditional) {}

public void commandAction(Command c, Displayable s) {
  if (c.getCommandType() == Command.EXIT)
    notifyDestroyed();
}

public void run() {
  HttpConnection hc = null;
  InputStream in = null;
  OutputStream out = null;

  try {
    String message = "name=Jonathan+Knudsen%21";
    String url = getAppProperty("PostMIDlet-URL");
    hc = (HttpConnection)Connector.open(url);
    hc.setRequestMethod(HttpConnection.POST);
    hc.setRequestProperty("Content-Type",
        "application/x-www-form-urlencoded");
    hc.setRequestProperty("Content-Length",
        Integer.toString(message.length()));
    out = hc.openOutputStream();
    out.write(message.getBytes());
    in = hc.openInputStream();
    int length = (int)hc.getLength();
    byte[] data = new byte[length];
    in.read(data);
    String response = new String(data);
    StringItem stringItem = new StringItem(null, response);
    mForm.append(stringItem);
    mForm.setTitle("Done.");
  }
  catch (IOException ioe) {
    StringItem stringItem = new StringItem(null, ioe.toString());
    mForm.append(stringItem);
    mForm.setTitle("Done.");
  }
```

```
    finally {
      try {
        if (out != null) out.close();
        if (in != null) in.close();
        if (hc != null) hc.close();
      }
      catch (IOException ioe) {}
    }
  }
}
```

Listing 10-3. *A Simple Servlet That Responds to PostServlet*

```
import javax.servlet.http.*;
import javax.servlet.*;
import java.io.*;

public class PostServlet extends HttpServlet {
  public void doPost(HttpServletRequest request,
      HttpServletResponse response)
      throws ServletException, IOException {
    String name = request.getParameter("name");

    String message = "Received name: '" + name + "'";
    response.setContentType("text/plain");
    response.setContentLength(message.length());
    PrintWriter out = response.getWriter();
    out.println(message);
  }
}
```

You'll need to specify the MIDlet property `PostMIDlet-URL` in order for this example to work correctly. The URL `http://65.215.221.148:8080/wj2/post` can be used for testing.

Using Cookies for Session Tracking

HTTP is a stateless protocol, which means that each request and response pair is a separate conversation. Sometimes, though, you want the server to remember who you are. This can be done with a *session*. On the server side, a session is just a collection of information. When the client sends an HTTP request to the server, it includes a session ID as part of the request. The server can then look up the corresponding session and have some idea of the identity (or at least the state) of the client.

The most common way to store a session ID on the client side is using HTTP *cookies*. A cookie is just a little piece of data that is passed from the server to the client in an HTTP response. Most web browsers automatically store cookies and will send them back to the appropriate server when a new request is made.

In the MIDP world, of course, there's no web browser taking care of cookies for you. You have to do it yourself. Fortunately, it's not very complicated.

Network code that maintains a server session ID needs to do two things:

1. When receiving a response from a server, check for a cookie. If there is a cookie present, save it away for later (perhaps in a member variable, record store, or file). A cookie is just another HTTP response header line. You can check for a cookie by calling getHeaderField() on an HttpConnection object after the request has been sent.

2. When sending a request to the server, send the session ID cookie if it has been previously received. Again, sending a cookie to the server is just a matter of putting it in the request headers, using HttpConnection's setRequestProperty() method.

Each time you send a request to the server, you will be sending a session ID as a request header. The server uses this session ID to look up a session object that can be used, server side, to do useful stuff like retrieve preferences or maintain a shopping cart.

It's not hard to implement this behavior in a MIDlet. If you have a session ID cookie handy, you should send it when you open up an HTTP connection to the same server, like this:

```
HttpConnection hc = (HttpConnection)Connector.open(url);
if (mSession != null)
    hc.setRequestProperty("cookie", mSession);
```

This code assumes you have a session ID cookie saved away in the mSession member variable. The first time you contact the server, of course, you won't have a session ID cookie.

■**Note** In production code, if you save cookie in persistent storage such as a record store or file, you should check the cookie to see if it has expired before sending it back.

Later, when you receive a response from an HTTP request, look for a cookie. If you find one, parse out the session ID and save it away, like this:

```
InputStream in = hc.openInputStream();

String cookie = hc.getHeaderField("Set-cookie");
if (cookie != null) {
  int semicolon = cookie.indexOf(';');
  mSession = cookie.substring(0, semicolon);
}
```

The cookie string needs to be parsed because it comes in two pieces. The first piece contains the cookie value: the session ID—that's the part we parse out and save. The second part contains a cookie attribute: a path that can be used to determine when the cookie should be sent back to the server.

For more information on the different parts of a cookie string and how they are used, see http://www.ietf.org/rfc/rfc2965.txt and http://www.ietf.org/rfc/rfc2109.txt.

■**Note** In some applications, a server may return multiple cookie values. RFC 2965 has provisions for this. In these cases, the cookie string parsing code can be considerably more complex than this example.

Listing 10-4 shows a class, CookieMIDlet, that uses this technique to maintain a session with a server. It has a very bland user interface—just an empty Form with two commands. If you invoke the Send command, the MIDlet sends an HTTP request and receives a response using the cookie handling described earlier.

Listing 10-4. *Saving a Server Session ID Cookie*

```java
import java.io.*;

import javax.microedition.io.*;
import javax.microedition.midlet.*;
import javax.microedition.lcdui.*;

public class CookieMIDlet
    extends MIDlet
    implements CommandListener, Runnable {
  private Display mDisplay;
  private Form mForm;

  private String mSession;

  public void startApp() {
    mDisplay = Display.getDisplay(this);

    if (mForm == null) {
      mForm = new Form("CookieMIDlet");

      mForm.addCommand(new Command("Exit", Command.EXIT, 0));
      mForm.addCommand(new Command("Send", Command.SCREEN, 0));
      mForm.setCommandListener(this);
    }

    mDisplay.setCurrent(mForm);
  }

  public void pauseApp() {}

  public void destroyApp(boolean unconditional) {}
```

```java
public void commandAction(Command c, Displayable s) {
  if (c.getCommandType() == Command.EXIT) notifyDestroyed();
  else {
    Form waitForm = new Form("Connecting...");
    mDisplay.setCurrent(waitForm);
    Thread t = new Thread(this);
    t.start();
  }
}

public void run() {
  String url = getAppProperty("CookieMIDlet-URL");

  try {
    // Query the server and retrieve the response.
    HttpConnection hc = (HttpConnection)Connector.open(url);
    if (mSession != null)
      hc.setRequestProperty("cookie", mSession);
    InputStream in = hc.openInputStream();

    String cookie = hc.getHeaderField("Set-cookie");
    if (cookie != null) {
      int semicolon = cookie.indexOf(';');
      mSession = cookie.substring(0, semicolon);
    }

    int length = (int)hc.getLength();
    byte[] raw = new byte[length];
    in.read(raw);

    String s = new String(raw);
    Alert a = new Alert("Response", s, null, null);
    a.setTimeout(Alert.FOREVER);
    mDisplay.setCurrent(a, mForm);

    in.close();
    hc.close();
  }
  catch (IOException ioe) {
    Alert a = new Alert("Exception", ioe.toString(), null, null);
    a.setTimeout(Alert.FOREVER);
    mDisplay.setCurrent(a, mForm);
  }
}
}
```

On the server side, things are much simpler, as you'll see in Listing 10-5. If you're writing Java servlets, you don't even have to worry about cookies. Instead, you just deal with an HttpSession object. The code that follows shows a servlet that interacts with CookieMIDlet; it implements a session-based hit counter. It's been tested on Tomcat 5.5 but should work fine on other servers. Note that you will have to map the URL used by the MIDlet to this servlet class; for details, see an introductory book on servlets or your server's documentation.

Listing 10-5. *A Simple Session Handling Servlet*

```
import javax.servlet.http.*;
import javax.servlet.*;
import java.io.*;
import java.util.*;

public class CookieServlet extends HttpServlet {
  private Map mHitMap = new HashMap();

  public void doGet(HttpServletRequest request,
      HttpServletResponse response)
      throws ServletException, IOException {
    HttpSession session = request.getSession();

    String id = session.getId();

    int hits = -1;

    // Try to retrieve the hits from the map.
    Integer hitsInteger = (Integer)mHitMap.get(id);
    if (hitsInteger != null)
      hits = hitsInteger.intValue();

    // Increment and store.
    hits++;
    mHitMap.put(id, new Integer(hits));

    String message = "Hits for this session: " + hits + ".";

    response.setContentType("text/plain");
    response.setContentLength(message.length());
    PrintWriter out = response.getWriter();
    out.println(message);
  }
}
```

The servlet retrieves the HttpSession object. Then it pulls out the session ID and uses it as a key into a map of hit counts. After retrieving and incrementing the hit count for the session, the servlet sends it as the response back to the MIDlet. You can start up multiple copies of the emulator and run them simultaneously to see how the hit counts are independent of each other and associated with each session.

To test the MIDlet on a server without setting up your own, you can set the MIDlet property CookieMIDlet-URL to the URL http://65.215.221.148:8080/wj2/cookie.

Design Tips

This section contains some suggestions about creating networked MIDlets.

1. Use GET rather than POST. It's simpler, and you won't have to worry about fiddling around with the request headers.

2. Don't hard-code URLs. Put them in a MIDlet property in the application descriptor. This will make it possible to change the URL without recompiling your code.

3. Put network access in a separate thread. Network access always takes time; it shouldn't hold up the user interface. Furthermore, you must let your users know what's going on. Put up a "loading progress" type of message or some kind of indication that your application is trying to access a network resource.

4. Make sure you handle exceptions gracefully. Network connections on wireless devices are not tremendously reliable, so you should make sure you're prepared for the worst. Catch all your exceptions and do something reasonable.

5. Clean up after yourself. On a small device, resources are scarce, so be sure to close connections when you are done with them. try - finally blocks are especially useful for ensuring that unused streams and connections are closed.[1] The code in Jargoneer (Chapter 2) demonstrates this technique.

Using HTTPS

HTTP is not a secure protocol. It operates on top of TCP/IP sockets. Information exchanged using HTTP is highly susceptible to eavesdroppers. A more secure alternative, HTTPS, runs atop Transport Layer Security (TLS), Secure Sockets Layer (SSL), or a similar protocol. TLS and SSL provide a layer of authentication and encryption between sockets and higher-level protocols like HTTP, POP3, SMTP, and NNTP.

TLS 1.0 is really just an updated version of SSLv3. For more information on these protocols, see http://wp.netscape.com/eng/ssl3/ and http://www.ietf.org/rfc/rfc2246.txt.

In typical TLS interactions, the server sends a certificate to the client to authenticate itself. The client must have Certificate Authority (CA) root certificates on hand to verify the server's certificate. (The J2ME Wireless Toolkit comes with a utility, MEKeyTool, that can be used to modify the set of CA root certificates used by the toolkit emulator. Real devices may have similar utilities, but in general, you'll have to make sure that your server certificate is signed by a CA that is widely recognized.) If the client can verify the certificate, the client will then send a secret value

---

1. You are probably familiar with the try - catch blocks that are used in Java for exception handling. The finally clause is not as well known, but it is very useful. Code in the finally block will be executed regardless of how control leaves the try block.

to the server, encrypted with the server's public key. The server and the client both derive a *session key* from this secret value, which is used to encrypt all subsequent traffic sent between the client and server.

The generic connection framework makes it very easy to obtain HTTPS connections. All you have to do is construct an HTTPS connection string. So instead of this:

```
HttpConnection hc = (HttpConnection)
    Connector.open("http://www.cert.org/");
```

you would do this:

```
HttpsConnection hc = (HttpsConnection)
    Connector.open("https://www.cert.org/");
```

It's really that simple. HttpsConnection represents HTTP carried over some secure transport.

HttpsConnection is an extension of HttpConnection; it adds a getPort() method so that you can find out the server's port number. The default port for HTTPS is 443. More importantly, HttpsConnection has a getSecurityInfo() method that returns information about the secure connection. The new SecurityInfo interface encapsulates information about the cipher suite in use, the name and version of the secure protocol, and the server's certificate. The certificate is an implementation of javax.microedition.pki.Certificate and includes standard information like the subject, signer, signature algorithm, and validity dates of the certificate.

The following example shows how you can retrieve the subject of a server certificate from an HTTPS connection:

```
String url = "https://www.cert.org/";
HttpsConnection hc = (HttpsConnection)Connector.open(url);
SecurityInfo si = hc.getSecurityInfo();
Certificate c = si.getServerCertificate();
String subject = c.getSubject();
```

Using Datagram Connections

In this section, we'll briefly describe datagram connections. Although support for datagrams is not mandated by the MIDP specification, certain device implementations may choose to support datagram connections. Unlike stream-oriented connections, datagram connections are *connectionless*. This means that you can fire packets of data around the network, but you have no guarantee that they will reach their destination in the right order, or that they will even arrive at all.

Datagram communications is based on two interfaces in the javax.microedition.io package, DatagramConnection and Datagram. Figure 10-4 shows the methods in DatagramConnection.

The first step is to use the generic connection framework to obtain a DatagramConnection— something like this:

```
String url = "datagram://jonathanknudsen.com:7999";
DatagramConnection dc = (DatagramConnection)Connector.open(url);
```

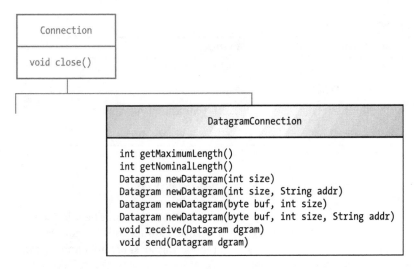

Figure 10-4. *The DatagramConnection interface*

The URL string passed to Connector's open() method contains both the host name and port of the opposite end of the datagram connection. If datagram connections are not supported by a MIDP implementation, an exception will be thrown from the open() method.

All data is exchanged using Datagrams. To send a datagram, first ask the DatagramConnection to create one for you using one of the newDatagram() methods. Then write some data into it and pass it into the send() method of DatagramConnection. Receiving a datagram is almost as easy. You just call receive(), which blocks until a datagram is received.

In essence, Datagram is a wrapper for an array of bytes that are the payload of the datagram. You can retrieve a reference to this byte array by calling getData(). Keep in mind, however, that the data for the Datagram may be only a subset of the data in the array. You can find the array offset and length of the actual data by calling getOffset() and getLength().

Interestingly, Datagram is an extension of both the DataInput and DataOutput interfaces, so it's possible to read and write data within a single Datagram as though it were a stream.

Datagram connections are represented by the UDPDatagramConnection interface, an extension of the DatagramConnection interface. UDPDatagramConnection adds two new methods, getLocalAddress() and getLocalPort(). You can use these methods to find out the originating point of datagrams sent using the connection.

Other Connection Types

Although the MIDP 2.0 specification requires only HTTP and HTTPS connections, it suggests that implementations support socket, server socket, and secure socket connections. The API provides appropriate interfaces for these connections. Devices may also choose to implement access to serial ports through the generic connection framework. Table 10-1 details the additional connection types, their supporting connection interfaces, and example connection strings. For more detailed information, see the API documentation for the corresponding interface.

Table 10-1. *Optional Connection Types*

Type	Interface	Example
Socket	SocketConnection	socket://jonathanknudsen.com:79
Server socket	ServerSocketConnection	socket://:129
TLS or SSL socket	SecureConnection	ssl://jonathanknudsen.com:79
Serial port	CommConnection	comm:com0;baudrate=19200

Responding to Incoming Connections

You may be used to thinking of mobile phones as client devices, but they may be full-fledged networked citizens, with the ability to receive incoming network connections. Although ServerSocketConnection provides the ability to listen for incoming socket connections, it can only be active while a MIDlet is actually running.

A typical server loop, listening for incoming socket connections on port 80, looks something like this:

```
ServerSocketConnection ssc;
ssc = (ServerSocketConnection)Connector.open("socket://:80");
boolean trucking = true;
while (trucking) {
  SocketConnection sc = (SocketConnection)ssc.acceptAndOpen();
  // Handle the client connection sc.
}
```

MIDP allows MIDlets to be launched in response to incoming network connections. The name for this technique is *push*. You could, in theory, create a web server MIDlet, although in practice a mobile phone is probably a poor platform for a web server. A more likely example would be an SMS MIDlet, something built using JSR 120, the Wireless Messaging API. Assuming the MIDlet was configured correctly, incoming SMS messages would cause the MIDlet to be launched to handle the connection.

A MIDlet may register for push connections in two ways: it can register at runtime using static methods in javax.microedition.io.PushRegistry, or it can register at install time using special entries in the application descriptor (JAD file). The important thing to remember is that the push registry has a lifetime beyond your MIDlet (in fact, even beyond multiple device reboot cycles). It is part of the MIDlet management software that runs on the device. When a MIDlet registers for push notifications, the device software is obligated to listen for incoming network connections and launch your MIDlet if the appropriate connection is made.

Inside your MIDlet, you don't have to do anything different to catch the incoming connection. All you do is call Connector.open() with the appropriate network listening string.

Let's say, for example, that you had created a web server in a MIDlet and called it PatchyMIDlet. (The source code for this book, available from http://www.apress.com/, includes PatchyMIDlet; it sends a randomly selected text message in response to incoming requests.) This MIDlet responds to incoming socket connections on port 80 (the default HTTP port). If you wanted to register the MIDlet at runtime, you'd do this in the code somewhere:

```
PushRegistry.registerConnection("socket://:80", PatchyMIDlet, "*");
```

The first two parameters are pretty clear—any incoming socket connections on port 80 should launch `PatchyMIDlet`. The third parameter is a filter that will be applied to incoming connections. In this case, we accept all incoming connections with the * wildcard. Other possibilities would be to restrict incoming connections to a single IP address or a range of addresses.

Remember, the results of the call to `registerConnection()` persist beyond the lifetime of the MIDlet. Even after the MIDlet has been destroyed, the MIDlet management software on the device is watching out for incoming socket connections on port 80. If a connection is received, `PatchyMIDlet` will be launched. The push registry doesn't actually do anything with the incoming connection; it just detects it and launches a registered MIDlet to respond. It's the MIDlet's responsibility to accept the incoming connection. To find out whether it has been launched by the push registry or the user, the MIDlet can call `PushRegistry`'s `listConnections()` method, passing `true` for the `available` parameter. The method will then return a list of connections that have input available. If this list is empty, then the MIDlet must have been launched by the user, not by an incoming connection.

Instead of a MIDlet registering push connections at runtime, it's much more likely that the push registrations would be contained in the application description for the MIDlet suite containing `PatchyMIDlet`. Thus, the push registration would be performed at installation time so that the user would never need to run the MIDlet manually. In this case, the MIDlet descriptor would contain a line like this:

```
MIDlet-Push-1: socket://:80, PatchyMIDlet, *
```

The parameters are exactly the same. The push registration is made when the MIDlet suite is installed. If the MIDlet cannot be registered (for example, some other application might already be listening for incoming socket connections on port 80), then the MIDlet suite will not be installed. Multiple push registrations are listed in the descriptor using ascending numbers: `MIDlet-Push-1`, `MIDlet-Push-2`, and so on.

The J2ME Wireless Toolkit version 2.2 allows you to register and test push connections easily. Just click the Settings button, and then choose the Push Registry tab. If you downloaded the source code for this book, you'll see an entry for `PatchyMIDlet`. Figure 10-5 shows this entry.

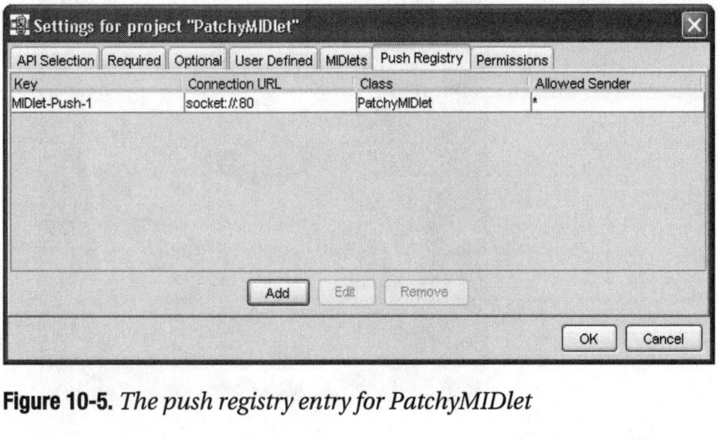

Figure 10-5. *The push registry entry for PatchyMIDlet*

To test the push notification, you'll have to package the application, and then deploy it on the WTK 2.2 emulator. First choose Project TRA Package ➤ Create Package to package the project into a MIDlet suite JAR. Then choose Project ➤ Run via OTA from the KToolbar menu. You'll see the emulator pop up, showing its Application Management Software (AMS). Select Install Application, and then accept the URL that is supplied. KToolbar contains a small OTA server; the URL is automatically preloaded when you select Run via OTA. You will see a series of other prompts about installing the application; just say yes to everything. Eventually the installation succeeds and you will see the MIDlet PatchyMIDlet listed in the emulator's menu. The emulator is now running, listening for incoming connections, even though no MIDlets are running.

Now test PatchyMIDlet by pointing your browser to http://localhost/. PatchyMIDlet will be launched and will send a response to the browser. (The emulator will ask if it's okay to send data back on the network; you'll have to say yes.) Figure 10-6 shows the emulator running PatchyMIDlet and a browser showing its output.

Figure 10-6. *PatchyMIDlet, a small web server*

Run via OTA is an excellent tool for testing your MIDlet's installation behavior rather than its runtime behavior. Just remember that you need to package the MIDlet first because the toolkit's small OTA distributes the MIDlet suite JAR file from the project's bin directory.

PushRegistry contains several other static methods that are related to network registrations. The getMIDlet() and getFilter() methods return the MIDlet name and filter for a given network connection string. The listConnections() method returns a string array containing all the registered network connection strings. Finally, to remove a connection-to-MIDlet mapping, use unregisterConnection().

Permissions for Network Connections

MIDP 2.0 includes a security framework that is designed to prevent MIDlets from running up your phone bill by making unauthorized network connections. As we discussed in Chapter 3, network access in MIDP is guarded by permissions and protection domains. Here are the permission names defined by MIDP:

- javax.microedition.io.Connector.http

- javax.microedition.io.Connector.https

- javax.microedition.io.Connector.datagram

- javax.microedition.io.Connector.datagramreceiver

- javax.microedition.io.Connector.socket

- javax.microedition.io.Connector.serversocket

- javax.microedition.io.Connector.ssl

- javax.microedition.io.Connector.comm

- javax.microedition.io.PushRegistry

These permissions have names corresponding to the API that they protect. All of these permissions, except one, protect connection types, which are accessed via the javax.microedition.io.Connector class, hence the prefix on those permission names. The very last permission refers to the push registry and shares its name with the PushRegistry class.

When you run a MIDlet suite in the toolkit, it runs in the untrusted domain by default. In the untrusted domain, HTTP and HTTPS connections are allowed if the user grants permission. You can see this when you run a MIDlet that attempts a network connection. Figure 10-7 shows how the emulator asks the user for permission and allows the user to make the decision stick for the remainder of the session.

You can indicate the necessary and optional permissions used by your MIDlet suite by using the MIDlet-Permissions and MIDlet-Permissions-Opt descriptor attributes. (In the J2ME Wireless Toolkit, you can set permissions in the descriptor by choosing Settings, and then clicking the Permissions tab.)

Figure 10-7. *The emulator asks for the user's permission for network connections.*

Summary

Networking on the MIDP platform is based on a generic connection framework. MIDP mandates the support of HTTP. You can perform GET, HEAD, or POST requests with just a few lines of code. HTTP session handling is also feasible. MIDP also requires support for HTTPS in addition to HTTP and formalizes the connection strings and APIs for handling additional connection types. Implementations are free to support additional connection types; datagrams, sockets, server sockets, and serial port communications are some of the possibilities. MIDP's security architecture protects users from unauthorized network use.

CHAPTER 11

Wireless Messaging API

Using the Internet on your cell phone is fun, but it can be quite costly. Connection time is billed per minute or per packet, and this can add up fast to a fat bill. In most cases, a lower cost alternative is readily available. Called Short Message Service (SMS), it is often offered by national carriers as text messaging.

The Wireless Messaging API, or WMA, is an optional API that enables MIDP applications to leverage the utility of SMS. In addition, the API can be used for receiving and processing Cell Broadcast Service (CBS) messages. WMA 2.0, recently finalized, adds the support for Multimedia Message Service (MMS) messages. It becomes easy for MIDP applications to send and receive images, video, and other multimedia content.

Ubiquitous SMS

Short Message Service, or SMS, is one of the most widely available and popular services for cell phone users. Often sold as text messaging service, it is the ability to send short messages between phone users.

SMS has its origin back in the day when cellular phones were expensive and operated over mostly analog-based technology. Even though the voice portion of a phone call is circuit switched over an analog network, the control network for the call is digital, and it has spare capacity to carry a small text message.

Since those early days, SMS has undergone some major technical changes under the hood. The user experience, however, remains the same.

The ubiquitous nature of SMS means that it is supported worldwide on cellular networks of (almost) any technology, including but not limited to TDMA, CDMA, WCDMA, GSM, GPRS, CDMA2000-1X, CDMA2000-MX, and EDGE.

SMS: The Killer App for Wireless

The ability to send short text messages (up to 160 characters in most cases) between cell phone users inexpensively is compelling enough. The possibility to send messages directly between J2ME applications running on cellular phones is even more exciting. Messages can now be sent and received between phones without

- Having Internet access from the phone (potentially additional cost service)

- Going through an intermediary server (potentially from the carrier at additional cost)

- Being restricted in terms of routing by the carrier's network

In most cases, if you can make a call to an endpoint (a cell phone), then you can also send an SMS message!

Unlike a cell phone call, however, a message is not lost if the receiving phone is not available when the message is sent. SMS messages are sent through a store-and-forward network, and messages will queue up until the receiving device is available. This can be used to great advantage for some applications. Through SMTP gateway services, it is even possible to send SMS messages using e-mail and receive SMS messages as e-mail.

The possible applications are unlimited. Chat-type applications are the obvious for SMS, but interactive gaming, event reminders, e-mail notification, mobile access to corporate resources, and informational service are a sample of other opportunities.

WMA makes SMS available to MIDP developers. In other words, WMA provides a generalized direct point-to-point communications mechanism for MIDP applications.

■**Note** SMS can also be used in conjunction with the push registry to launch MIDlets on your cell phone. See Chapter 10 for more details on push registry operations.

WMA and SMS

When a message is sent and received via WMA, there are two major benefits. First, the message can now be significantly larger in size than a single SMS message. Second, the content is no longer restricted to simple text messages. Under the hood, the WMA API will do the following:

- Encode a binary message and transmit it through SMS.

- Cut up a long message into segments, and send it via multiple (up to three) SMS messages.

Two current and finalized JSRs are relevant to WMA, and these are listed in Table 11-1.

Table 11-1. *The WMA JSRs*

JSR	Name	URL
120	Wireless Messaging API	http://jcp.org/jsr/detail/120.jsp
205	Wireless Messaging API 2.0	http://jcp.org/jsr/detail/205.jsp

JSR 120 actually describes WMA 1.1. Almost all devices that support WMA today have WMA 1.1 implementations.

With JSR 205, support of multimedia messaging is added. This is the crux of WMA 2.0. It is the ability to send large binary messages consisting of multiple parts. These messages are perfect for carrying images, sound, video, or multimedia presentations.

WMA API

WMA is built on top of CLDC (or CDC) and requires only the Generic Connection Framework (GCF) of CLDC 1.0. Therefore, WMA will work well on both CLDC 1.0 and CLDC 1.1 devices.

Like `SocketConnection` and `DatagramConnection` in the GCF, you get a `MessageConnection` by passing in an address to the `connect()` method. Unlike these other connections, however, you cannot open an input or output stream from it. `MessageConnections` are only used to send and receive messages. All the interfaces and classes in WMA are part of the `javax.wireless.messaging` package.

WMA's API is built around the GCF. Figure 11-1 shows the new APIs in WMA and how they relate to the GCF.

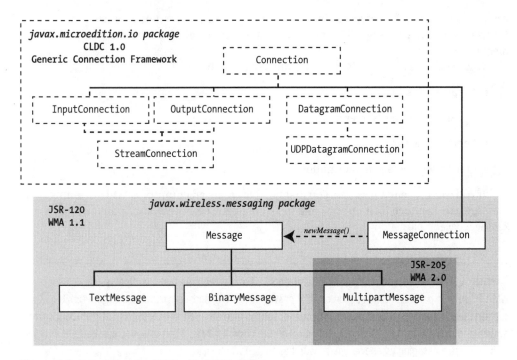

Figure 11-1. *Extending the GCF with WMA APIs*

A typical call to open a `MessageConnection` for sending or receiving message may be

```
MessageConnector msgConn = (MessageConnector) Connector.open("sms://5550001:1234");
```

This will create a client mode connection. A client mode connection can only be used to send messages. Messages sent through this connection will be destined for phone number 5550001, port 1234.

> **Note** WMA encompasses the concept of a port. It allows multiple applications to accept messages on the same device. It also enables the device to differentiate between SMS messages destined for a WMA application and standard text messages. The cost of this is a few bytes of data at the beginning of an SMS message, resulting in only 152 characters being available for text in most cases.

You can also create a server mode connection. Instead, if you were to open the connection using the following:

```
MessageConnector msgConn = (MessageConnector) Connector.open("sms:// :1234");
```

you would end up with a server mode connection. Typically, server mode connections are used to receive incoming messages. However, server mode connections can actually be used to send messages as well.

Once you have a `MessageConnection`, you can use it to

- Create messages.

- Receive messages (server mode only).

- Send messages.

- Obtain segmentation information on a message.

If you want to send messages, you first need to create an empty one. With an empty message, you can then fill it up and send it. To create the empty message, you must use a `MessageConnection`.

> **Note** JTWI is a godsend for WMA standardization. JTWI 1.0 requires that a compatible device support WMA 1.1 APIs. In particular, SMS support on GSM or WCDMA (UMTS) phones is mandated. MIDP `PushRegistry` support (see Chapter 10) for incoming SMS connections is also required. If access to GSM cell broadcast is available for Java APIs, it must be available through the WMA 1.1 APIs. Therefore, you can be right at home with wireless messaging whenever you're working on a JTWI phone.

Creating New Messages

A `MessageConnection` is the class factory for messages. There is no way to create a message other than using a `MessageConnection`. Figure 11-1 shows that a message is created using the `newMessage()` method, which actually has two variations:

```
Message newMessage(String messageType);
Message newMessage(String messageType, String address);
```

The second form is a code saver when you are using server mode connections. Since messages created with a server mode connection do not have a destination address, you can create a new message and set its destination address with one single call.

From Figure 11-1, you can see that there are three types of messages: TextMessage, BinaryMessage, and MultipartMessage. MultipartMessage will only be available if your MID implements WMA 2.0. To specify a message type for the newMessage() factory method, you can use the predefined constants MessageConnection.TEXT_MESSAGE, MessageConnection.BINARY_MESSAGE, and MessageConnection.MULTIPART_MESSAGE.

Sending Binary SMS Messages

SMS can be used to send text or binary messages. To send a binary message using WMA, first create an empty message using the newMessage() method of the open MessageConnection. You need to specify MessageConnection.BINARY_MESSAGE for its type.

Next, get the binary data into a byte array (possibly using one of the IO stream classes). Then set the payload of the BinaryMessage with the data in the byte array using

```
public void setPayloadData(byte [] data);
```

Binary messages are typically limited to 133 bytes per SMS message. For longer messages, WMA will take care of separating the message into segments for you (see the warning that follows).

You can use the following method of your MessageConnection instance to determine the number of SMS messages that a particular binary message may span:

```
int numberOfSegments(Message msg);
```

■Warning WMA requires an implementation to support messages spanning three segments. This means that you should not depend on WMA to send and receive any binary messages longer than 381 bytes (unless you know for sure that both the sender's and receiver's WMA implementation support longer messages).

After the payload and the receiving address has been set on the message, you are ready to send it using this MessageConnection method:

```
void send(Message msg) throws IOException, InterruptedIOException;
```

You will catch an IOException if there is a network problem or the MessageConnection is already closed. The InterruptedIOException will be thrown if the MessageConnection is closed during the sending operation or a timeout occurs.

As with any network operations, you should call send() on a separate non-GUI thread to avoid hanging the GUI.

■Tip   Remember that if you are using a server mode MessageConnection to send messages, you must set the recipient address explicitly on each new message that you create—before you call send(). If you are reusing an incoming message for replies, however, this is not necessary. You just need to set a new payload (the reply). The address of an incoming message is already filled in with the sender's address.

Sending Text SMS Messages

Sending a text message is similar to sending binary messages. First, create an empty message using MessageConnection's newMessage() method, specifying MessageConnection.TEXT_MESSAGE as its type.

Next, set the payload with the text string that you want to send:

```
public void setPayloadText(String data);
```

Finally, use the send() method of MessageConnection to send the message. Here is a code fragment that you may use to open a connection and send an SMS text message:

```
MessageConnection conn =
    (MessageConnection) Connector.open("sms://5550001:1234");
TextMessage txtmessage = (TextMessage) conn.newMessage(
MessageConnection.TEXT_MESSAGE);
txtmessage.setPayloadText(msgString);
conn.send(txtmessage);
```

Just like binary messages, you can also send large text messages that span multiple SMS messages. The WMA API will handle segmentation at the sending end and reassembly at the receiving end. However, some character encoding (namely UCS-2) limits the length of each SMS text message to only 72 characters (66 available due to the port information used by WMA). To accommodate this, the maximum sized text message that you can send safely is 189 characters (3 SMS segments). See JSR 205 for details of payload length calculation if you are interested.

Receiving SMS Messages

To receive messages using a MessageConnection, you have two choices:

- Use a blocking receive() method.
- Implement a listener callback to be notified when a message arrives.

When using the blocking receive() method, you typically will be managing your own threads. Using a listener allows you to code the logic in a callback method, without creating and managing additional threads. You can choose either approach.

Calling the Blocking receive() Method

The blocking receive() method is on the MessageConnection interface. This method will block the incoming call until an incoming message is available or until the connection is closed. The syntax for receive() is as follows:

```
public Message receive() throw IOException, InterruptedIOException
```

IOException will be thrown if an error is encountered during the receiving process, if the connection is closed, or if the method is called on a connection opened in the client mode (send only).

Since receive() is a blocking call, it should always be called on its own thread. A common approach is to create a "receiver thread" to receive messages in an application.

InterruptedIOException is thrown if the connection is closed while the call is still blocking. Closing a MessageConnection is a way to release a receiver thread that may be blocked waiting for incoming messages.

Typical message receive code when using the blocking receive() looks like this:

```
conn = (MessageConnection) Connector.open("sms://5550001:1234");
msg = conn.receive(); // Blocking here
mSenderAddress = msg.getAddress();   // Get info from message
if (msg instanceof TextMessage) {
String msgReceived = ((TextMessage)msg).getPayloadText();

// Do something with the message here

} else if (msg instanceof BinaryMessage) {
byte [] msgReceived = ((BinaryMessage)msg).getPlayloadData();
   // do something with the binary message here

}
 }
```

When working with the payload of incoming messages, the following method on the BinaryMessage interface is used to access the content of the binary message:

```
public byte [] getPayloadData();
```

On a TextMessage, the following method is used to access the content of the text message:

```
public String getPlayloadText();
```

A Nonblocking Approach to Receiving SMS Messages

MessageConnection supports a nonblocking, event listener–based way for receiving SMS messages. To use this, you will need to do the following:

1. Register a MessageListener with the MessageConnection.

2. Handle the callback on the notifyIncomingMessage() method of the MessageListener interface.

First, add a MessageListener using the setMessageListener() method on the MessageConnection:

```
public void setMessageListener(MessageListener lis) throws IOException;
```

The object that you register as a listener must implement the MessageListener interface. Only one listener can be registered at a time for a connection; any new registration will displace the old one. The MessageListener interface has a single callback method:

```
public notifyIncomingMessage(MessageConnection conn);
```

The callback is performed by WMA on a system thread, and the notifyIncomingMessage() method must return as soon as possible. This means that any work should be performed by another thread. In fact, WMA mandates that even the call to the receive() method (to pick up the incoming message) must be performed in another thread. This will require careful concurrent programming using Java's synchronization primitives. In addition, the WMA implementation may perform simultaneous callback on multiple threads if messages are arriving concurrently. This means that you need to be careful to synchronize access to any variables outside of your thread's run() method.

Even though this nonblocking approach is attractive conceptually, it is often simpler to use the blocking receive call alternative. The final example in this chapter (see Listing 11-3) shows some code using this nonblocking approach.

Examining Message Headers

In addition to the binary or text payload, other interesting information appears in the message header.

You can get access to the address information using the following methods on the Message interface:

```
public String getAddress();
public void setAddress(String addr);
```

The Message interface is the super interface of both TextMessage and BinaryMessage, and the preceding methods are available for both types of messages. The getAddress() method returns the recipient's address if it is an outgoing message, or the sender address if it is an incoming message. In fact, incoming messages can be reused for replies by just setting a new payload.

The setAddress() method can be used to set the destination address for an outgoing message. The destination address is set automatically when you're using a client mode MessageConnection to create new messages. You will only need to call setAddress() if you're using a server mode MessageConnection to create new messages.

Another method on the Message interface provides access to the timestamp on the message:

```
public Date getTimestamp();
```

This getTimestamp() method will return the timestamp on the message if it is available.

Receiving CBS Messages

Cell Broadcast Service, or CBS, is a carrier version of SMS. It enables a cell phone operator to broadcast messages to a group of cell phone users. A WMA application can only receive CBS messages.

There are no additional interfaces or classes for handling of CBS. You use the same mechanism as receiving SMS messages. However, the MessageConnection for CBS can only be opened in the server (receiver) mode, since it is not possible to send CBS messages. For example:

```
conn = (MessageConnection) Connector.open("cbs://:12345");
msg = conn.receive(); // Blocking for message
```

The digits 12345 in this case do not refer to a WMA-managed port as in SMS; instead, they serve as a message identifier. Message identifiers are a CBS-specific concept. They may represent different information channels that you can subscribe to. You need to consult your carrier for the available message identifiers if you are developing software to process CBS messages.

Do not call send() on a CBS MessageConnection. Only phone network operators can broadcast CBS messages. If you do call send(), you will get an IOException. Since CBS messages do not carry any timestamp, calling getTimeStamp() on the message always returns null.

Working with SMS APIs

Let's put some of this to work. SMSMIDlet is a MIDlet that can send and receive SMS messages. The GUI of SMSMIDlet is shown in Figure 11-2.

SMSMIDlet can be used to receive or send SMS messages. SMSMIDlet listens at port 1234. If the SMSMIDlet receives an SMS text message containing the word "red", an image with a red background will be displayed by the MIDlet. If the SMS text message received contains the string "blue", an image with a blue background will be displayed.

In Figure 11-2, you can enter the address that you want to send SMS messages to into the "Connect to:" text field. Using the menu, you can then send either a "red" or "blue" SMS message to the recipient.

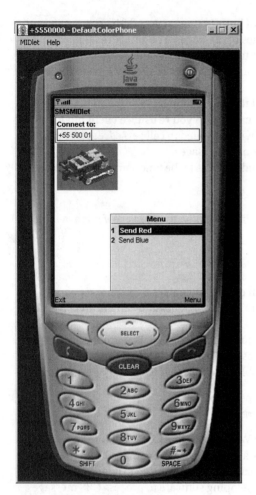

Figure 11-2. *GUI of SMSMIDlet*

The code for SMSMIDlet is shown in Listing 11-1.

Listing 11-1. *A MIDlet to Send and Receive SMS Messages—SMSMIDlet*

```
import javax.microedition.midlet.*;
import javax.microedition.io.*;
import javax.microedition.lcdui.*;
import javax.wireless.messaging.*;

import java.io.IOException;
```

```
public class SMSMIDlet
extends MIDlet
implements CommandListener, Runnable {
  private Sender mSender = null;
  private Thread mReceiver = null;
  private Command mExitCommand = new Command("Exit", Command.EXIT, 2);
  private Command mRedCommand = new Command("Send Red", Command.SCREEN, 1);
  private Command mBlueCommand = new Command("Send Blue", Command.SCREEN, 1);

  private Display mDisplay = null;
  protected ImageItem mColorSquare = null;
  protected Image [] mImages = new Image[2];
  protected Image waitImage = null;
  private String mPort = "1234";
  private TextField mNumberEntry= null;
  private Form mForm = null;

  private String mSenderAddress = null;
  public SMSMIDlet() {
      mSender = Sender.getInstance();
  }

  public void commandAction(javax.microedition.lcdui.Command c,
  javax.microedition.lcdui.Displayable d) {
      if (c == mExitCommand) {
      if (!mSender.isSending()) {
      destroyApp(true);
      notifyDestroyed();
      }
      } else if (c == mRedCommand) {
      String dest = mNumberEntry.getString();
      if (dest.length() > 0)
      mSender.sendMsg(dest, mPort, "red");

      } else if (c == mBlueCommand) {
      String dest = mNumberEntry.getString();
      if (dest.length() > 0)
       mSender.sendMsg(dest, mPort, "blue");
      }
   }
```

```
protected void destroyApp(boolean param) {
    try {
    mEndNow = true;
    conn.close();
    } catch (IOException ex) {
    System.out.println("destroyApp caught: ");
    ex.printStackTrace();

    }

}

protected void pauseApp() {
}

protected void startApp() {
    if (mForm == null) {
    mForm = new Form("SMSMIDlet");
    mNumberEntry = new TextField("Connect to:",
    null, 256, TextField.PHONENUMBER);
    try {
    mImages[0] = Image.createImage("/red.png");
    mImages[1] = Image.createImage("/blue.png");
    waitImage = Image.createImage("/wait.png");
    } catch (Exception ex) {
    System.out.println("startApp caught: ");
    ex.printStackTrace();
        }

    mColorSquare = new ImageItem(null, waitImage,ImageItem.
    LAYOUT_DEFAULT, "colored square");
    mForm.append(mNumberEntry);
    mForm.append(mColorSquare);
    mForm.addCommand(mExitCommand);
    mForm.addCommand(mRedCommand);
    mForm.addCommand(mBlueCommand);

    mForm.setCommandListener(this);
    }
    Display.getDisplay(this).setCurrent(mForm);
    startReceive();
}

private void startReceive() {
    if (mReceiver != null)
    return;
```

```java
        // Start receive thread
        mReceiver = new Thread(this);
        mReceiver.start();
}
private boolean mEndNow = false;
private MessageConnection conn = null;
public void run() {
        Message msg = null;
        String msgReceived = null;
        conn = null;
        mEndNow = false;
        /** Check for sms connection. */
        try {
        conn = (MessageConnection) Connector.open("sms://:" + mPort);
        msg = conn.receive();
        while ((msg != null) && (!mEndNow)) {

        if (msg instanceof TextMessage) {

        msgReceived = ((TextMessage)msg).getPayloadText();
        if (msgReceived.equals("red")) {
          Display.getDisplay(this).callSerially(new SetRed());
        } else if (msgReceived.equals("blue")) {
          Display.getDisplay(this).callSerially(new SetBlue());
        }
        }

        msg = conn.receive();
        }
        } catch (IOException e) {
        // Normal exit when connection is closed
        }

}
class SetRed implements Runnable {
        Display disp = null;

        public void run() {
        mColorSquare.setImage(mImages[0]);
        }
}
class SetBlue implements Runnable {
        public void run() {
        mColorSquare.setImage(mImages[1]);
        }
}
}
```

Creating an Independent Receive Thread

SMSMIDlet actually uses a separate receive thread to process incoming messages. This thread will also set the ImageItem of the GUI with a different Image depending on incoming SMS messages. The startReceive() method in Listing 11-1 contains the code that starts the receive thread. The run() method contains the logic of the receive thread. The blocking receive() call is used in this case. The mEndNow boolean flag stops the thread when the application is destroyed; see the destroyApp() implementation.

The receive thread opens a server mode MessageConnection on port 1234. When there are no incoming messages, the receive thread is blocked in one of the receive() methods. Upon receipt of a message, the text payload is extracted and compared to "red" or "blue". Then Display.callSerially() updates the image shown on the GUI. Two helper classes, SetRed and SetBlue, are used when calling this method.

Sending SMS Messages

Listing 11-2 shows the class, called Sender, that is used to send SMS messages. SMSMIDlet maintains an instance of this class called mSender. The instance is used to send SMS messages when the user selects either Send Red or Send Blue from the menu.

Listing 11-2. *Sending SMS Message with Sender*

```
import javax.microedition.io.*;
import javax.wireless.messaging.*;

import java.io.IOException;

public class Sender implements Runnable {
  private static Sender inst = new Sender();
  private Sender() {
  }
  public static Sender getInstance() {
      return inst;
  }
  private String mReceiver = null;
  private String mPort = null;

  private String msgString = null;
  private boolean mSending = false;
  public void sendMsg(String rcvr, String port, String msgText) {
    if (mSending) return;
    mReceiver = rcvr;
    mPort = port;
    msgString = msgText;
  Thread th = new Thread(this);
    th.start();
  }
```

```
public boolean isSending() {
  return mSending;
}
// Send the color message
public void run() {
  mSending = true;
  try {
    sendSMS();
  } catch (Exception ex) {
    System.out.println("run() caught: ");
    ex.printStackTrace();
  }
  mSending = false;
}


private void sendSMS() {

  String address = "sms://" + mReceiver + ":" + mPort;

  MessageConnection conn = null;
  try {
    /** Open the message connection. */
    conn = (MessageConnection) Connector.open(address);
    TextMessage txtmessage = (TextMessage) conn.newMessage(
    MessageConnection.TEXT_MESSAGE);
    txtmessage.setAddress(address);
    txtmessage.setPayloadText(msgString);
    conn.send(txtmessage);
  } catch (Throwable t) {
    System.out.println("Send caught: ");
    t.printStackTrace();
  }
  if (conn != null) {
    try {
    conn.close();
    } catch (IOException ioe) {
      System.out.println("Closing connection caught: ");
    ioe.printStackTrace();
    }
  }
}
}
```

In Listing 11-2, Sender is a singleton; the static getInstance() factory method is used to get the one and only instance. The sendMsg() method is used by SMSMIDlet to send the SMS message. It assigns the incoming arguments to member variables, and then starts a thread to send the message. The mSending boolean flag is used to avoid reentrant calls and to stop the MIDlet from shutting down if message sending is in progress. The actual work of sending SMS messages is performed in the sendSMS() method. The sendSMS() method is always called from a new thread. sendSMS() opens a new MessageConnection using a specified address and sends a text message to the destination.

Testing SMSMIDlet with WTK 2.x WMA Console

You can easily test SMSMIDlet, or any SMS application, using a utility called the WMA console in WTK 2.x. To access the WMA console, select File ➤ Utilities from KToolbar. Then click the Open Console button in the WMA box.

To test SMSMIDlet, first start an instance in an emulator. Answer yes to the security question when it starts up. Note on the title bar of the emulator that a phone number, beginning with a + (plus sign), has been assigned to the emulator. By default, it will be +5550000. This is the address of the emulator instance.

Now, start the WMA console. You will note that the WMA console is also assigned a phone number beginning with a + sign. Click the Send SMS button. Select the address of the emulator instance on the Text SMS tab, enter **1234** into the Port box, and then enter **red** for the message. Click the Send button. Note that the SMSMIDlet instance now displays an image with a red background. Try sending an SMS message containing "blue" and observe how the SMSMIDlet instance changes the graphics to a blue background.

Next, enter the address of the WMA console into the "Connect to:" text field of the SMSMIDlet instance. Then select Send Red from the menu of SMSMIDlet. Note that the console displays a message to indicate receipt of the SMS message. Figure 11-3 shows the WMA console interacting with SMSMIDlet.

Instead of using the WMA console, you can also start two emulator instances of SMSMIDlet and send SMS messages between them.

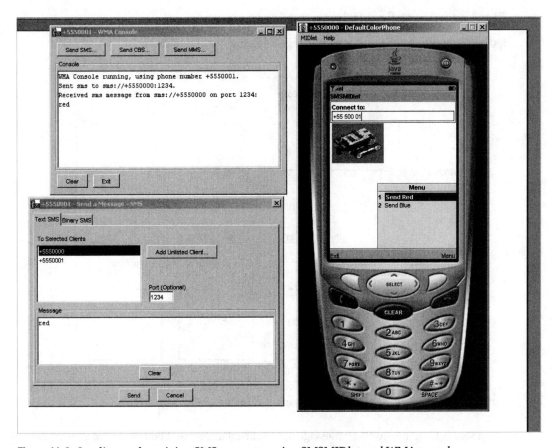

Figure 11-3. *Sending and receiving SMS messages using SMSMIDlet and WMA console*

Multimedia Messaging with WMA 2.0

The major addition in the WMA 2.0 API is the availability of multipart messages. Multipart messages are specially designed to support the new Multimedia Message Service. MMS is frequently found in 2.5G and 3G phone networks.

Essentially, MMS enables you to send and receive large binary messages in a manner similar to SMS. The messages supported can contain multiple message parts; each of the parts can contain text, an image, an audio clip, a video clip, or other multimedia content. For example, a complete multimedia presentation can be sent in a single MMS, containing a SMIL script and the individual media elements referenced by the presentation.

At the time of writing, there are very few phones supporting WMA 2.0. Since 2.5G and 3G networks are not yet in widespread deployment, the availability of MMS is still scarce.

The Anatomy of a Multipart Message

Figure 11-4 shows what a multipart message looks like conceptually.

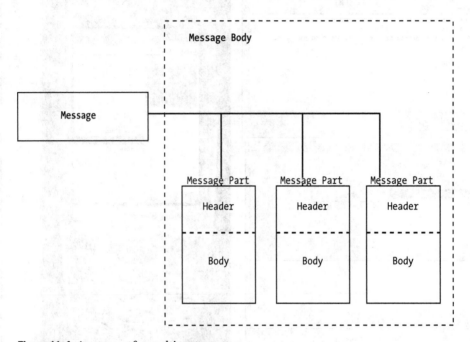

Figure 11-4. *Anatomy of a multipart message*

In Figure 11-4, the multipart message has the usual header and body found in all messages. However, the body itself contains many separate parts, called message parts. Each message part has its own header and content.

The type of each body part is specified in its header. Each body part can be of a MIME type that is supported by the communicating applications.

Working with Multipart Messages

A MultipartMessage is a subinterface of Message. The additional methods on the MultipartMessage interface deals with the additional features required by MMS messages.

First off, a multipart message differs from an SMS message in that it can have multiple recipients. Similar to e-mail, you can have multiple recipients for "to", "cc", and "bcc" fields. A message with multiple recipients can be sent to a Multimedia Message Service Center (MMSC) to be processed. The MMSC can then in turn send the message to all intended recipients.

Managing Addresses

The following methods are available for managing the addresses associated with a multipart message:

```
public String setAddress(String address);
public String getAddress();
public boolean addAddress(String type, String address);
public String [] getAddresses(String type);
```

The first two methods are inherited from the Message interface. setAddress() can be used to set the first "to" address for an outgoing message. Additional "to" addresses can be added using the addAddress() method. addAddress() can also be used to add "cc" and "bcc" recipients.

getAddress() will return the first "to" address on an outgoing message, and the "from" address from an incoming message. getAddresses() returns all the addresses associated with a address type, such as "cc", "bcc", "to", or "from".

You can remove all the addresses in an address type using this method:

```
public void removeAddresses(String type);
```

Remove all the addresses in the "to", "cc", and "bcc" fields of a message by using the following:

```
public void removeAddresses();
```

You can also be more selective and remove only a specific address:

```
public boolean removeAddress(String type, String address);
```

Content ID and Content Location

The content of each message part can have its own ID and location. This information is stored in the header of the message part. The content ID uniquely identifies a message part within the message, while the location can refer to the actual location where the content is stored (for example, a URL accessible over the Internet). The exact syntax of these two pieces of information and how they are used will depend on the application and/or the specific MMS implementation.

You can read the content ID and location using the following methods on the MessagePart interface:

```
public String getContentID();
public String getContentLocation();
```

The Start Content ID

For some applications, a particular message part in a message may contain the script or code to start a multimedia presentation. This is similar to the concept of a main class in Java programming. In order to signify that a particular message part can be used to start a presentation, its unique content ID can be designated as a start content ID. The following two methods help with this:

```
public String getStartContentId();
public void setStartContentId(String contentId);
```

Adding a Subject to the Message

MMS messages, like e-mail, can contain a subject header. There are two methods for working with subjects:

```
public String getSubject();
public void setSubject(String subject);
```

Working with Other Message Headers

Depending on the MMS implementation that you work on, there might be other header information that can be accessed. Consult JSR 205 for more details. The methods that access other headers are as follows:

```
public String getHeader(String headerField);
public void setHeader(String headerField, String headerValue);
```

Managing Message Parts

The payload of a multipart message is the collection of contained message parts. You can obtain any message part of a multipart message via its content ID:

```
public MessagePart getMessagePart(String contentID);
```

All the message parts of a multipart message can be obtained at once, as an array, using this code:

```
public MessagePart [] getMessageParts();
```

To delete a message part from a message, you can use any of the following:

```
public boolean removeMessagePart(MessagePart part);
public boolean removeMessagePartId(String contented);
public boolean removeMessagePartLocation(String contentLocation);
```

The first form is convenient if you already have a copy of the message part. Otherwise, if you have the content ID or the content location, you can use the other two variations to delete the message part.

Adding Message Parts to a Message

When sending messages, you must first use a MessageConnection to create a new multipart message. Next, you will follow these steps:

1. Create a new message part using the newMessage() class factory.

2. Set the message part's headers.

3. Populate the message part's content.

4. Add the part to the multipart message.

5. Repeat 1 to 4 for all the message parts.

Step 1 is identical to the SMS case. The next section shows you how to perform steps 2 and 3. Once you've created and populated a MessagePart and set the relevant headers, you can add it to a MultipartMessage using this method:

```
public void addMessagePart(MessagePart part);
```

Accessing Content of Message Parts

A message part consists of content (the payload) and header. The header contains MIME type information, the encoding used, the content ID, and the content location. The MessagePart class allows you to work with individual message parts. To create a new MessagePart, you can use one of its constructors:

```
public MessagePart(byte[] contents, int offset, int length, String mimeType,
    String contentId, String contentLocation, String encoding);
public MessagePart(byte[] contents, String mimeType, String contentId,
    String contentLocation, String encoding)
public MessagePart(InputStream is, String mimeType, String contentId,
    String contentLocation, String encoding);
```

The first two methods set the contents of the message part from a byte array, while the last one does so from an InputStream (for larger content such as audio or video). The first variant of the byte array methods allows you to specify an offset and length to extract part of the byte array as content. The second form uses the entire input byte array.

To access the content of a MessagePart, you can use the following:

```
public byte[] getContent();
public InputStream getContentAsStream();
```

For processing small-sized content, working with a byte array may be convenient. For very large multimedia content, especially audio and video, using getContentAsStream() can provide more usable access to the content.

MessagePart Header Information

You can use other methods of MessagePart to access header information:

```
public String getContentEncoding();
public String getMIMEType();
public String getContentID();
public String getContentLocation();
public int getLength();
```

The last method, getLength(), returns the length of the content in bytes.

A MIDlet to Send and Receive MMS

Putting the WMA 2.0 MMS API to work, the example presented in this section is a modification of the SMSMIDlet. The user interface is identical.

The major differences are as follows:

- The MIDlet is called MMSMIDlet and the sender class is called MMSSender.

- The MIDlet uses the nonblocking, event-driven notification mechanism to receive messages.

- Instead of just the text "red" or "blue" in an SMS message, the entire image to be displayed is sent as a MessagePart in a MultipartMessage.

First, Listing 11-3 shows the code for the MMSMIDlet.

Listing 11-3. *The MMSMIDlet for Sending and Receiving MMS*

```
import javax.microedition.midlet.*;
import javax.microedition.io.*;
import javax.microedition.lcdui.*;
import javax.wireless.messaging.*;

import java.io.IOException;

public class MMSMIDlet
extends MIDlet
implements CommandListener, MessageListener,Runnable {
  private MMSSender mSender = null;
  private Thread mReceiver = null;
  private Command mExitCommand = new Command("Exit", Command.EXIT, 2);
  private Command mRedCommand = new Command("Send Red", Command.SCREEN, 1);
  private Command mBlueCommand = new Command("Send Blue", Command.SCREEN, 1);
  protected static final String RED_IMAGE = "/red.png";
  protected static final String BLUE_IMAGE = "/blue.png";
  protected static final String DEFAULT_IMAGE = "/wait.png";

  private Display mDisplay = null;
  protected ImageItem mColorSquare = null;
  protected Image mInitialImage = null;
  private String mAppID = "MMSMIDlet";
  private TextField mNumberEntry= null;
  private Form mForm = null;
  private Integer mMonitor = new Integer(0);
  public MMSMIDlet() {
    mSender = MMSSender.getInstance();

  }
```

```java
public void commandAction(javax.microedition.lcdui.Command c,
javax.microedition.lcdui.Displayable d) {
  if (c == mExitCommand) {
    if (!mSender.isSending()) {
      destroyApp(true);
      notifyDestroyed();
    }
  } else if (c == mRedCommand) {
    String dest = mNumberEntry.getString();
    if (dest.length() > 0)
      mSender.sendMsg(dest, mAppID, RED_IMAGE);

  } else if (c == mBlueCommand) {
    String dest = mNumberEntry.getString();
    if (dest.length() > 0)
      mSender.sendMsg(dest, mAppID, BLUE_IMAGE);
  }
    }


protected void destroyApp(boolean param) {
  mEndNow = true;
  try {
    conn.close();
  } catch (IOException ex) {
  System.out.println("destroyApp caught: ");
    ex.printStackTrace();

  }
}
protected void pauseApp() {
  mEndNow = true;
  try {
    conn.setMessageListener(null);
    conn.close();
  } catch (IOException ex) {
   System.out.println("pausetApp caught: ");
  ex.printStackTrace();

  }
}
```

```
protected void startApp() {
  if (mForm == null) {
    mForm = new Form(mAppID);
    mNumberEntry = new TextField("Connect to:",
    null, 256, TextField.PHONENUMBER);
    try {
      mInitialImage = Image.createImage(DEFAULT_IMAGE);
    } catch (Exception ex) {
    System.out.println("starttApp caught: ");
     ex.printStackTrace();
    }

    mColorSquare = new ImageItem(null, mInitialImage,ImageItem.
    LAYOUT_DEFAULT, "waiting for image");
    mForm.append(mNumberEntry);
    mForm.append(mColorSquare);
    mForm.addCommand(mExitCommand);
    mForm.addCommand(mRedCommand);
    mForm.addCommand(mBlueCommand);
    mForm.setCommandListener(this);
  }
  Display.getDisplay(this).setCurrent(mForm);

  try {
    conn = (MessageConnection) Connector.open("mms://:" + mAppID);
    conn.setMessageListener(this);
    } catch (Exception e) {
    System.out.println("startApp caught: ");
    e.printStackTrace();
  }
  if (conn != null) {
    startReceive();
  }
}
private boolean mEndNow = false;
private void startReceive() {

  mEndNow = false;
  // Start receive thread
  mReceiver = new Thread(this);
  mReceiver.start();
  }

protected MessageConnection conn = null;
```

```
protected int mMsgAvail = 0;
public void run() {
Message msg = null;
String msgReceived = null;
Image receivedImage = null;

  mMsgAvail = 0;

  while (!mEndNow) {
    synchronized(mMonitor) { // Enter monitor
      if (mMsgAvail <= 0)
      try {
       mMonitor.wait();
        } catch (InterruptedException ex) {
      }
       mMsgAvail--;
       }
     try {
      msg = conn.receive();
      if (msg instanceof MultipartMessage) {
    MultipartMessage mpm = (MultipartMessage)msg;
    MessagePart[] parts = mpm.getMessageParts();
    if (parts != null) {
        for (int i = 0; i < parts.length; i++) {
    MessagePart mp = parts[i];
    byte[] ba = mp.getContent();
    receivedImage = Image.createImage(ba, 0, ba.length);
    Display.getDisplay(this).callSerially(
    new SetImage(receivedImage));
        } //of for
    }
     }
     } catch (IOException e) {
     System.out.println("Receive thread caught: ");
     e.printStackTrace();
   }
} // of while
 }
  private void getMessage() {
synchronized(mMonitor) {
    mMsgAvail++;
    mMonitor.notify();
  }
 }
```

```
public void notifyIncomingMessage(MessageConnection msgConn) {
  if (msgConn == conn)
 getMessage();
    }


 class SetImage implements Runnable {
   private Image img = null;
    public SetImage(Image inImg) {
   img = inImg;
     }
      public void run() {
    mColorSquare.setImage(img);
   }
 }
}
```

The `MessageConnection` is opened in server mode. Unlike SMS, MMS uses an application ID instead of a port to identify the message routing endpoint. Our application ID is stored as `mAppID` and is set to "MMSMIDlet". Once the `MessageConnection` is obtained from `Connector.open()`, `MMSMIDlet` is registered as the `MessageListener` for incoming messages.

The `startReceive()` method starts a receive thread that will pick up and process the incoming MMS messages. Initially, this thread will be blocked, waiting on a monitor called `mMonitor`. This thread will be notified whenever an incoming MMS message arrives, in the `getMessage()` method. In the `run()` method, you can see that `receive()` is used to pick up the pending MMS message. The `MessagePart` that has the image is then extracted, and the image is displayed on the GUI.

Sending MMS Messages with MMSSender

The `MMSSender` class is used by `MMSMIDlet` to send multipart messages. Each outgoing message is sent on a new thread. The source code of the `MMSSender` class is shown in Listing 11-4.

Listing 11-4. *Sending MMS Messages with MMSSender*

```
import javax.microedition.io.*;
import javax.microedition.lcdui.*;
import javax.wireless.messaging.*;
import java.io.*;

public class MMSSender implements Runnable {
  private static MMSSender inst = new MMSSender();
  private MMSSender() {
  }
  public static MMSSender getInstance() {
   return inst;
  }
  private String mReceiver = null;
  private String mAppID = null;
```

```
private String mImageToSend = null;
private boolean mSending = false;
public void sendMsg(String rcvr, String appid, String img) {
  if (mSending) return;
  mReceiver = rcvr;
  mAppID= appid;
  mImageToSend = img;
  Thread th = new Thread(this);
  th.start();
}
public boolean isSending() {
  return  mSending;
}
// Send the color image
public void run() {
  mSending = true;
  try {
  sendMMS();
  } catch (Exception ex) {
  }
   mSending = false;
}

public void sendMMS() {
  String address = "mms://" + mReceiver + ":" + mAppID;
  MessageConnection conn = null;
  try {
  /** Open the message connection. */
  conn = (MessageConnection) Connector.open(address);
  MultipartMessage mpMessage = (MultipartMessage) conn.newMessage(
  MessageConnection.MULTIPART_MESSAGE);
  mpMessage.setSubject("MMSMIDlet Image");
  InputStream is = getClass().getResourceAsStream(mImageToSend);
  byte[] bImage = new byte[is.available()];
  is.read(bImage);
  mpMessage.addMessagePart(new MessagePart(bImage, 0, bImage.length,
  "image/png", "id1",
  "location", null));
  conn.send(mpMessage);
  } catch (Throwable t) {
  System.out.println("Send caught: ");
  t.printStackTrace();
  } finally {
```

```
    if (conn != null) {
      try {
      conn.close();
      } catch (IOException ioe) {
    System.out.println("Closing connection caught: ");
        ioe.printStackTrace();
      }
    }
    }
    }
}
```

The basic structure is identical to the earlier SMS Sender class. However, the message created here for sending is a MultipartMesssage. The subject of the message is set to "MMSMIDlet Image". For the one and only MessagePart, the MIME type is "image/png", the content ID is "id1", and the content location is set to "location". The actual content of the message part is the image to be displayed on the destination device. The MessagePart is created, populated, and then added to the message. The message is then sent using the MessageConnector in the sendMMS() method, which is always called on a new thread.

Testing MMS Send and Receive

You can test out the MMSMIDlet using one of the following:

- The WMA console utility of WTK 2.x

- Two instances of the MMSMIDlet

Using the WMA Console

First, start the emulator running with an instance of the MMSMIDlet. From the KToolbar menu, select File ➤ Utilities. In the WMA box, click the Open Console button. This will start a console with its own phone number (address). Click the Send MMS button; a dialog box will be shown for entry of MMS header and message parts. Enter the information listed in Table 11-2 for the header.

Table 11-2. *Information for MMS Testing on WMA Console*

Field	Value
Subject:	MMSMIDlet Image
Application-ID:	MMSMIDlet
To:	mms://+5550000:MMSMIDlet

This "to" address assumes that you are running the WTK in its default configuration. Click the Parts tab, and add a part that includes the red.png image. Figure 11-5 shows the console with the message part added.

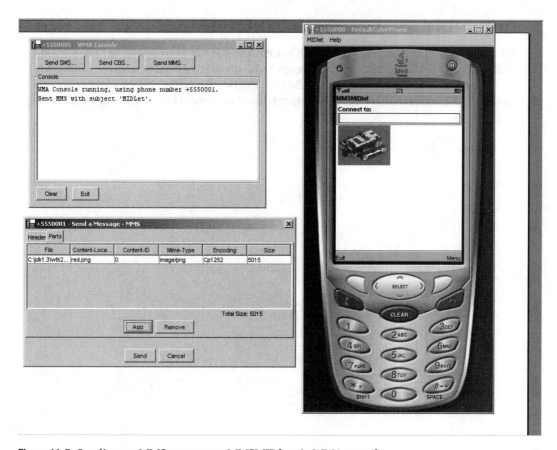

Figure 11-5. *Sending an MMS message to MMSMIDlet via WMA console*

Click the Send button. Take a look at the MMSMIDlet display—it should now show the car image with a red background. Figure 11-5 shows the result.

Using Two Emulator Instances

The second way of testing MMSMIDlet is to use two running instances of the emulator. Start one instance, and then the second one. In the "Connect to:" text field, enter the address of the first instance. By default, it will be +5550000. Then select Send Red from the menu of the second instance. You should see the red image displayed on the first instance.

■**Tip** The WTK environment is adequate for debugging and testing of standalone MIDP applications. When testing messaging applications using multiple instances, however, it can have quirks. The one and only solution is to make sure you fully test your messaging application on your target device and network before deployment.

Summary

Extending the CLDC's Generic Connection Framework, the Wireless Messaging APIs add the ability for J2ME applications to send and receive SMS messages as well as receive CBS broadcast messages. The latest JSR 205, specifying WMA 2.0, extends this further to take advantage of the content-rich Multimedia Message Service that is becoming available with 2.5G and 3G networks.

CHAPTER 12

■ ■ ■

Bluetooth and OBEX

Internet on cell phones is all about connecting to things that are a world apart wirelessly. Interestingly enough, frequently you may wish that you could somehow connect to things (devices, machines, or even people) that are right next to you. For example, you may be at a business associate's office, next to a printer that you wish you could use to print an urgent e-mail you've just received; or you may have walked past your dream house, which happens to be up for sale, and you want more information on it right away. While the Internet may help in some situations, it would be wonderful if there were a painless—and ideally airtime free—way for connecting to things that are next to you.

There is!

Bluetooth is a radio connectivity technology designed for creating Personal Area Networks (PANs). It is all about connecting to things that are next to you, wirelessly. Java APIs for Bluetooth is an optional API that adds radio PAN connectivity to MIDP applications.

Other than using radio, some devices can also communicate externally via an infrared beam. This is especially popular on phones that have built-in PDAs. OBEX, or Object Exchange Protocol, is a communication protocol that enables applications to talk to one another easily over infrared (OBEX can actually work over other transport/media as well, such as Bluetooth). The optional OBEX API contains utility classes that simplify programming using the protocol.

Bluetooth, CLDC, and MIDP

The Bluetooth radio hardware operates in the 2.45-gigahertz Industrial, Scientific, and Medical (ISM) frequency band, allowing for unlicensed operation worldwide. Bluetooth networks are formed ad hoc and dynamically, when Bluetooth-enabled devices come into proximity of one another. Technically, a Bluetooth network is a piconet, and it can consist of one master device and up to seven slave devices. The number of devices supported can be expanded beyond eight when a master device on one piconet acts as a slave in another, working as a bridge. However, all these hardware and radio protocol details are transparent to the application developer using the Java API for Bluetooth.

Java API for Bluetooth is not included as part of MIDP. It is also not a mandatory part of JTWI 1.0. Phones that have Bluetooth built in are in the minority, and vendors may expose proprietary APIs instead of the Java API for Bluetooth (or not expose Java API at all). At this time, the API is more prevalent with larger PDAs that support the CDC.

Relying only on CLDC 1.0, Java API for Bluetooth can be readily implemented on any modern devices supporting CLDC, MIDP, and/or JTWI 1.0. It is anticipated that the API will gain better vendor support in the near future.

Figure 12-1 illustrates the relationship between the optional Bluetooth API, CLDC, and MIDP.

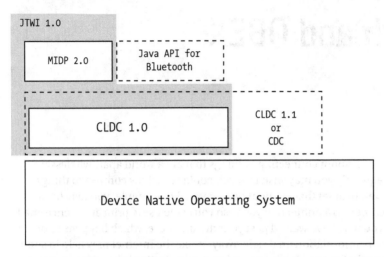

Figure 12-1. *Relationships between Java API for Bluetooth, CLDC, and MIDP*

The Bluetooth API leverages the Generic Connection Framework (GCF) built into CLDC in a similar manner to WMA and File Connection covered in earlier chapters.

JSR 82: The Bluetooth JSR

JSR 82 is called Java API for Bluetooth Wireless Technology, and the specification describes two complete and separate optional APIs:

- Java API for Bluetooth

- Java API for OBEX

While the first API covers exclusively communications via Bluetooth radio technology, the second one focuses on the OBEX protocol. The OBEX protocol can be implemented over a Bluetooth PAN, IP networks, and infrared communications links. You are most likely to find OBEX implemented over infrared links.

The first part of this chapter will focus on the Bluetooth APIs, the latter part on OBEX.

Networking with Devices Near You

Bluetooth is short-ranged radio technology that enables communications for devices physically located close to one another. A Bluetooth implementation contains both hardware and software components (and software in ROM, also known as firmware), as illustrated in Figure 12-2.

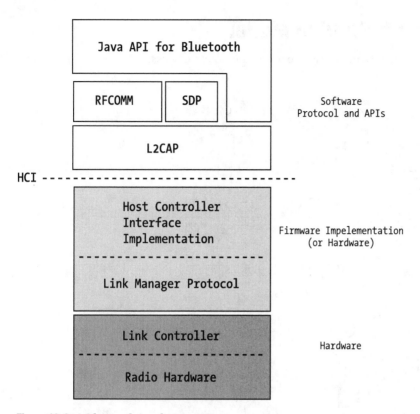

Figure 12-2. *A Bluetooth implementation*

A network consisting of devices connected via Bluetooth is often called a Personal Area Network (or PAN for short). The software portion of a Bluetooth "stack" enables data to be interchanged between locally connected devices in a variety of ways. The different interactions possible between devices in a PAN can be roughly classified as follows:

- *Discovery*: Find out what devices are connected, how they may be useful, and when a device is no longer available (for example, you may have traveled out of range).

- *Client activities*: Use services that other devices provide. For example, use a printer nearby to print your e-mail.

- *Server activities*: Provide services and/or information that other devices may use. For example, a Bluetooth-enabled storage server may accept data from mobile Bluetooth devices.

- *Peer activities*: Act as both client and server within an activity. For example, a business card exchange application may enable two phones to exchange business card information using Bluetooth.

The Bluetooth Service Model

Figure 12-3 illustrates typical interactions between Bluetooth devices.

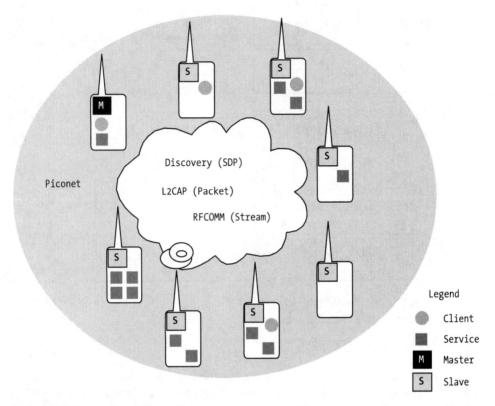

Figure 12-3. *Bluetooth device interactions*

In Figure 12-3, note that a single Bluetooth device can be offering multiple services at the same time. Bluetooth devices can also support both client and server functionality simultaneously. On a hardware level, a single master Bluetooth device can synchronize up to seven slave devices in a Bluetooth piconet.

Devices are the discoverable entities in a Bluetooth network. The discovery process is called an inquiry in Bluetooth lingo. You need to perform an inquiry to discover devices in your PAN before finding out what services the devices are offering.

Each service in a Bluetooth network is uniquely identified by a UUID. Any particular device in the Bluetooth network can be offering zero or more services. The same service may be offered by more than one device in the network. For example, one can easily imagine a printing service offered by a number of printers in the same room.

■**Note** A UUID is a Universally Unique identifier. This is usually a very large number, typically 128 bits. UUIDs are generated using a combination of unique items (such as the MAC address on an ethernet interface) and random elements (the clock ticks on the computer at time of number generation). The idea is that the probability of two numbers generated, anywhere in the world, at any time, is infinitesimally small. In Bluetooth, some UUIDs are "short" and are only 16 or 32 bits long. However, these short UUIDs are always converted to 128 bits before comparison. 128-bit UUIDs are frequently expressed in programs as hexidecimal strings ("BAE0D0C0B0A000955570605040302010", for example).

The Bluetooth specification describes a number of interoperability profiles, much like the role of the profiles in J2ME, for implementers of Bluetooth devices. These profiles specify interoperability standards between different implementations. The Service Application Discovery Profile (SADP) enables applications running on Bluetooth devices to discover services. The Java API for Bluetooth works over this profile to give you the high-level ability to discover services (with or without having to explicitly discover the devices).

At the lower level, the actual protocol used for service discovery between devices is called the Service Discovery Protocol (SDP).

Other than the SADP, JSR 82–compliant devices must also support the Generic Access Profile, or GAP (for access to device remotely), and the Serial Port Profile, or SPP (serial port emulation for sending and receiving streamed data between devices).

The Bluetooth API

The Java API for Bluetooth is delivered as the `javax.bluetooth` package. The following sections describe the most important classes and interfaces in this package.

Accessing Local Bluetooth Stack

You can talk to the software stack local to your device using the `LocalDevice` class. For example, you can get information on your stack by calling one of the following:

```
String getBluetoothAddress() ;
DeviceClass getDeviceClass();
DiscoveryAgent getDiscoveryAgent();
String getFriendlyName() ;
```

The first method returns the address, specific to Bluetooth, for the device. You don't really need to know how the address is formatted, since you will either store it or send it to somebody else "as is."

`getDeviceClass()` will return the major class of the device. `getDiscoverable()` will indicate whether the device can be discovered by other devices. The `getDiscoveryAgent()` method is a static factory method that can be used to obtain the singleton instance of the device's

DiscoveryAgent (covered in the next section, "Discovering Devices"). getFriendlyName() will return a string that contains a human readable (and understandable) name for your device.

You can determine if your device is discoverable by other Bluetooth devices with a call to the following:

```
int getDiscoverable() ;
```

To make your device discoverable, or disable its visibility in the network, call

```
boolean setDiscoverable(int mode)
```

Before you can call any of the information methods, you will need an instance of a LocalDevice. This singleton instance is often called the local Bluetooth manager. It can be obtained using this factory method:

```
 static LocalDevice getLocalDevice() ;
```

To obtain the singleton instance of your local Bluetooth manager, use code similar to the following:

```
LocalDevice myDevice = LocalDevice.getLocalDevice();
```

Each Bluetooth software stack must have a set of properties that you can query; use this static method on the LocalDevice:

```
 static String getProperty(String property) ;
```

Table 12-1 shows some properties for which you can query.

Table 12-1. *Properties That Must Be Available on a Bluetooth Device*

Property	Description
bluetooth.api.version	API version supported. Currently "1.0".
bluetooth.master.switch	Indicates whether a switch between master and slave Bluetooth role is allowed on this device. Not all devices support role switching between master and slave.
bluetooth.sd.attr.retrievable.max	The maximum number of service record attributes that can be retrieved. Service records and attributes are described later in this chapter.
bluetooth.connected.devices.max	The maximum number of connected devices in this implementation. Bluetooth supports the concept of a "parked connection," which can increase the maximum number of connected devices.
bluetooth.l2cap.receiveMTU.max	The maximum transmission unit size in bytes supported in the L2CAP low-level protocol. The L2CAP protocol is described later in this chapter.
bluetooth.sd.trans.max	The maximum number of concurrent service discovery transactions allowed.

Discovering Devices

The Bluetooth API has the concept of a discovery agent. You can think of it as a helper process that assists you in the discovery of other devices or services in a PAN.

It is called an agent because it works independently. Once you tell it what to do, it goes about its task merrily on your behalf. Sometime later, you can come back to the agent and request the status. Or you can tell the agent to call you back when it makes a new discovery.

To get an instance of a DiscoveryAgent, you need to go through the Bluetooth manager (the LocalDevice class). Basically, you need to make a call similar to the following:

```
DiscoveryAgent myDa = LocalDevice.getInstance().getDiscoveryAgent();
```

You can perform discovery on a device level or a service level. Device-level discovery allows for more control over the discovery process, but requires significantly more complex coding. When you perform discovery on a service level, the DiscoveryAgent handles the device-level manipulations for you.

Starting and Stopping Device Discovery

When you have a DiscoveryAgent instance, you can tell it explicitly to start discovery for devices via this method:

```
boolean startInquiry(int accessCode, DiscoveryListener listener) ;
```

The access code determines the type of inquiry and can be either DiscoveryAgent.GIAC (General Inquiry Access Code) or DiscoveryAgent.LIAC (Limited Inquiry Access Code). These codes are specified by the Bluetooth "Assigned Numbers" document (see http://www.bluetooth.org/assigned-numbers/). Almost all Bluetooth devices you encounter can be discovered using GIAC.

startInquiry() will start device discovery. For each device that is discovered, the listener that you register will receive a notification. This listener must implement the DiscoveryListener interface. The interface has four methods, but only two are important for device discovery:

```
void deviceDiscovered(RemoteDevice btDevice, DeviceClass cod) ;
void inquiryCompleted(int discType) ;
```

The deviceDiscovered() notification method is called when a device is discovered during the inquiry. The inquiryCompleted() method is called when the inquiry process is completed. This can be due to a timeout period (determined by the Bluetooth implementation) or when the DiscoveryAgent is being told to stop the discovery.

The inquiryCompleted() notification method is called when the discovery process completes. A discType value of DiscoveryListener.INQUIRY_COMPLETED indicates a normal completion, while a DiscoveryListener.INQUIRY_TERMINATED indicates a manual termination. Error-caused termination will have a discType value of DiscoveryListener.INQUIRY_ERROR.

You can tell the DiscoveryAgent to stop the discovery, before its natural termination, by calling its cancelInquiry() method:

```
public boolean cancelInquiry(DiscoveryListener listener);
```

Note that you must supply the same listener as the one that you've called startInquiry() with; otherwise, the discovery will not be stopped, and the method returns false.

A Simpler Way to Discover Devices

The DiscoveryListener callbacks are performed on a system notification thread, and the methods should complete their work as soon as possible. Any work that takes significant time should be performed on another thread. This requirement often makes device discovery code difficult to write and debug. An additional method on DiscoveryAgent can simplify discovery by eliminating the need to work with callback:

```
public RemoteDevice[] retrieveDevices(int option);
```

option can be either DiscoveryListener.CACHED or DiscoveryListener.PREKNOWN. This method will not start discovery; however, it will return RemoteDevices cached (discovered from a previous inquiry) or preknown. Preknown devices are Bluetooth devices that you can typically configure using a utility (called the Bluetooth Control Center, covered later) on your device.

Using code similar to the following, you can discover a list of nearby devices using relatively simple code:

```
myDiscoveryAgent.startInquiry(DiscoveryAgent.GIAC, myDoNothingListener);
Thread.sleep(10000l);
mDiscoveryAgent.cancelInquiry(myDoNothingListener);
RemoteDevice  [] remoteDevices = myDiscoveryAgent.retrieveDevices(CACHED);
```

The preceding code basically performs an explicit inquiry, waits 10 seconds (a reasonable delay for discovery), and then terminates it. After termination of inquiry, the retrieveDevices() method is used to obtain the discovered devices. The myDoNothingListener instance passed into startInquiry() implements DiscoveryListener, but does nothing within the four methods.

Caution There is a slight risk, when using the preceding simple code, that the discovery process will not have yet completed after the 10 second delay. To be absolutely sure, you need to use the listener-based callback, shown next. Another solution is to let the user set/modify the delay via a MIDlet property.

Discovering Services

Once you have a RemoteDevice, you can search through the services that it supports. You can use the searchServices() method on the DiscoveryAgent for this purpose:

```
public int searchServices(int[] attrSet,  UUID[] uuidSet,
        RemoteDevice btDev, DiscoveryListener discListener)
        throws BluetoothStateException
```

You specify the RemoteDevice via btDev. The uuidSet contains one UUID for each service you are interested in discovering. The attrSet contains the service record attributes you want to obtain with the search. discListener is a DiscoveryListener that you implement. You should save the returned transaction ID for the search. Your registered DiscoveryListener will be called with the results and this transaction ID. This transaction ID allows you to perform concurrent searches on multiple remote devices. Here are the two methods on DiscoveryListener that are used for service discovery callback:

```
void servicesDiscovered(int transID, ServiceRecord[] servRecord) ;
void serviceSearchCompleted(int transID, int respCode) ;
```

servicesDiscovered() is called when services are found during a search. The transID gives the transaction ID, while the servRecord array contains an entry for each matching service. serviceSearchCompleted() is called when the search is ending, either because of successful completion, forced termination, or error. You can terminate a search by calling the DiscoveryAgent method:

```
public boolean cancelServiceSearch(int transID);
```

A Simpler Way to Discover Services

Combining device discovery with service search, the pseudo-code to discover a Bluetooth service, given its UUID, may be as follows:

```
obtain the DiscoveryAgent
tell DiscoveryAgent to startInquiry()
save every discovered RemoteDevice discovered in a Vector
wait until device discovery finishes or terminate inquiry with cancelInquiry()
for each RemoteDevice discovered {
    tell DiscoveryAgent to searchServices() specifying the UUID seeked
    save every service record returned
}
```

The preceding pseudo-code translates to a lot of Java code. Because the discovery process is centered around asynchronous listener callbacks, the code will also necessarily involve multiple concurrent threads and tricky synchronization.

Unfortunately, no other way exists if you require fine control over service selection between devices. If you don't really care which device a service comes from, however, there is a simpler way to perform service discovery. The selectService() method on DiscoveryAgent can be used to find a service when you don't care which device it may come from:

```
String selectService(UUID uuid, int security, boolean master);
```

The returned value, if not null, is a connection string that you can use with GCF's Connector.open() to start talking to the service. security indicates whether authentication and encryption should be used; security can be one of the following:

- ServiceRecord.NOAUTHENTICATE_NOENCRYPT

- ServiceRecord.AUTHENTICATE_NOENCRYPT

- ServiceRecord.AUTHENTICATE_ENCRYPT

Bluetooth authentication, if implemented, is based on a PIN-generated challenge/response sequence. Encryption also requires this PIN; therefore it is not possible to perform encryption without first authenticating. Note that authentication and encryption may not be implemented by all Bluetooth implementations. The master flag indicates whether the client must be a master in the underlying Bluetooth connection.

When using the `selectService()` method, the code to obtain a connection to a desired service given its UUID is reduced to two lines:

```
String  dateConnect = mDiscoveryAgent.selectService(DATING_SERVICE_ID,
            ServiceRecord.NOAUTHENTICATE_NOENCRYPT, false);
StreamConnection  conn = (StreamConnection) Connector.open(dateConnect);
```

Access to Remote Devices

The previous section shows how to search for services on a `RemoteDevice`. If you are working with Bluetooth at a device level, the `RemoteDevice` instance also has security methods to authenticate and encrypt a connection:

```
boolean authenticate();
boolean authorize(Connection conn) ;
boolean encrypt(Connection conn, boolean on);
```

And a set of methods to test the security status of the connection:

```
boolean isAuthenticated() ;
boolean isAuthorized(javax.microedition.io.Connection conn) ;
boolean isEncrypted() ;
boolean isTrustedDevice();
```

Note When you create a server-side notifier using the GCF (shown later in the section entitled "Creating a Bluetooth Service"), you can specify an attribute on the connect string that indicates whether the service requires authentication, authorization, or encryption. If used, authentication must always be performed first before encryption or authorization.

The Bluetooth address and the user-understandable name of the device can be obtained via the following:

```
String getBluetoothAddress() ;
String getFriendlyName(boolean alwaysAsk) ;
```

If you have a GCF connection opened to a service, and you want to get the corresponding remote device, there is a static method that you can use:

```
static RemoteDevice getRemoteDevice(Connection conn) ;
```

The Bluetooth Control Center

The Bluetooth Control Center (BCC) is an external utility (not part of the API) that must exist in every JSR 82–compliant implementation. BCC allows the user to perform explicit configuration on the local Bluetooth stack. Some of the configuration that you may be able to specify include the following:

- The set of preknown Bluetooth devices (for example, printers that you know about)

- The text-based name used for your device during discovery

- The PIN for authentication and encryption

- The timeout period for device discovery

- Default security settings

- Turning on or off the discoverability of the device

- Turning the radio hardware on or off, essentially enabling and disabling Bluetooth

The exact user interface and configurability of a BCC is dependent on the implementation.

Within the Wireless Toolkit 2.x, you can access the BCC via the KToolbar menu by selecting Edit ➤ Preferences and then clicking the Bluetooth/OBEX tab.

ServiceRecord and Service Attributes

A ServiceRecord is an entry in the Service Discovery Database (SDDB), used by Bluetooth during service discovery. This database is maintained by the Bluetooth manager on each device. This is the database that will be searched when a client searches a RemoteDevice for service matches. Underneath the hood, transparent to the API, service discovery is performed via the Service Discovery Protocol.

The ServiceRecord entry is just a set of attributes. Each attributes has an ID and a value. The ID is a 16-bit unsigned integer. The value can be various data types and is represented in Java by a DataElement instance. Some frequently used attribute IDs are listed in Table 12-2.

Table 12-2. *Common ServiceRecord Attribute IDs*

ID	Description
0x0000	ServiceRecordHandle
0x0001	ServiceClassIDList
0x0002	ServiceRecordState
0x0003	ServiceID
0x0004	ProtocolDescriptorList

In Table 12-2, you can see that the UUID of the service corresponds to `ServiceRecord` attribute ID 0x0003. There are a very large number of possible attributes. For the entire list of attributes, their descriptions, and data types, see the Bluetooth "Assigned Numbers" document (http://www.bluetooth.org/assigned-numbers/sdp.htm).

Incidentally, the list of attributes in Table 12-2 is exactly the mandatory attributes that every `ServiceRecord` must have. They are also the default attributes that will be fetched during service discovery via a `searchServices()` method call.

The `ServiceRecord` class has the following methods for manipulation of attributes:

```
int[] getAttributeIDs(); .
DataElement getAttributeValue(int attrID);
boolean setAttributeValue(int attrID, DataElement attrValue);
```

The `getAttributeIDs()` method returns all the attributes that can be obtained via the `getAttributeValue()` call. Not all possible attributes are available; availability depends on the set of attributes specified during service discovery. If you want to update a `ServiceRecord`, use `setAttributeValue()`. You must call `updateRecord()` on the `LocalDevice` instance for the change to be reflected in the SDDB. See the next section for a description of how to place a `ServiceRecord` into the SDDB in the first place.

The GCF connection string associated with a `ServiceRecord` (that is, an available service) can be obtained via a call to the `getConnectionURL()` method:

```
String getConnectionURL(int requiredSecurity, boolean mustBeMaster);
```

If the `ServiceRecord` is result of discovery, you can also obtain a reference to the `RemoteDevice` by calling this method:

```
RemoteDevice getHostDevice();
```

Creating a Bluetooth Service

To offer a service over Bluetooth, your application first needs to register a `ServiceRecord` in the SDDB. The way you create and register a `ServiceRecord` is coupled with the GCF. First, you need to create a `StreamConnectionNotifier` (similar to a `ServerSocketConnection`). For example, the following call to `Connector.open()` will create a `StreamConnectionNotifier` and the corresponding `ServiceRecord`.

```
StreamConnectionNotifier myNotifier = (StreamConnectionNotifier)
Connector.open("btspp://localhost: BAE0D0C0B0A000955570605040302010;name=Dating
Service;authorize=false"
);
```

The protocol specification for the GCF connection string is "btspp://" for the Bluetooth Serial Port Profile. This is a Bluetooth profile that all JSR 82–compliant devices must implement, and it provides RS232 serial port emulation. Underneath the hood, a high-level stream-based protocol called RFCOMM is working on top of a lower-level packet-based protocol called L2CAP.

Note The Java API for Bluetooth also adds L2CAPConnection and L2CAPConnectionNotifier for working with the lower-level L2CAP protocol directly. Working with the lower-level L2CAP protocol is significantly more difficult because you must work with packet size limit, handle fragmentation, and reassembly of large messages yourself. L2CAP is often used directly by native applications that perform audio/video streaming. L2CAPConnection uses the protocol specification "btl2cap://" in the GCF connection string. The RFCOMM higher-level protocol simplifies application programming by providing a stream-based API and handling the packet assembly details for you.

Instead of a port number, as in IP-based connections, the UUID of the service is specified after the hostname, separated by a colon (:). A set of comma-separated connection parameters can follow the UUID in the GCF connection string. Some more useful parameters include authenticate, encrypt, authorize, and master.

You can obtain the ServiceRecord, if you have a notifier created by Connector.open(), using a method on the LocalDevice:

```
ServiceRecord getRecord(Connection notifier);
```

To register the ServiceRecord with the SDDB and wait for incoming connections, call the blocking acceptAndOpen() method on the StreamConnectionNotifier.

```
StreamConnection conn = myNotifier.acceptAndOpen();
```

You can update the registered ServiceRecord in the SDDB using the LocalDevice method:

```
void updateRecord(ServiceRecord srvRecord);
```

The ServiceRecord for a service is removed from the SDDB when the StreamConnectionNotifier is closed.

A Bluetooth Dating Service

The first example MIDlet creates a simple Bluetooth "dating service." It is odd how sometimes people in the same room who are attracted to each other are reluctant to start talking and "break the ice." This MIDlet may help.

You tell the MIDlet the type of date you're looking for, and the MIDlet will use Bluetooth to query anybody who comes near you for compatibility. Once compatibility is established, your potential date's e-mail address is displayed on your phone.

The MIDlet is called BTMIDlet. Create a new project called BTMIDlet and copy the two source files into the src directory of the WTK. Build the project.

Setting Your Dating Preferences

Next, you need to set five MIDlet properties using KToolbar: click the Settings button, click the User Defined tab, and add the MIDlet properties in Table 12-3.

Table 12-3. *MIDlet Properties for BTMIDlet Project*

Key	Value
BTMIDlet-mycontact	tallguy@yahoo.com
BTMIDlet-myheight	tall
BTMIDlet-mypref	male
BTMIDlet-seekheight	short
BTMIDlet-seekpref	female

To keep things simple, this example assumes you're a tall male, looking for a short female.

To test this MIDlet, you will need to start two instances of the emulator. The second instance must emulate the subject of your dating interest. To make this happen, create a new project called BT2, with the MIDlet name BTMIDlet. Copy the two source files into the src directory of the new BT2 project. Build the project. Next, enter the MIDlet properties in Table 12-4 for this project.

Table 12-4. *MIDlet Properties for BT2 Project*

Key	Value
BTMIDlet-mycontact	shortgal@yahoo.com
BTMIDlet-myheight	short
BTMIDlet-mypref	female
BTMIDlet-seekheight	tall
BTMIDlet-seekpref	male

Finally, run an instance of BT2. Without starting another KToolbar, open the BTMIDlet project, and run an instance of BTMIDlet. Now, launch both MIDlets. On initial startup, the security manager will ask for your permission to use Bluetooth. You need to approve it. Shortly after starting, you will see that the owners of the two devices have found each other, as shown in Figure 12-4.

Figure 12-4. *Bluetooth dating service running on WTK emulators*

You may want to start additional instances of BTMIDlet and BT2 to see how the MIDlet behaves in a group situation.

Coding the Bluetooth Client

The DateClient class contains the code for the Bluetooth client (see Listing 12-1). This client connects to nearby dating service(s) and writes its own height, sex, and e-mail. This is a singleton instance, obtained via the static getInstance() method. The startClient() method starts a thread and runs the client. The stopClient() method terminates the client thread gracefully. The setMyInfo() method is used to set the information that will be written to nearby dating service(s).

Listing 12-1. *Bluetooth Dating Client Code—DateClient.java*

```java
import java.io.*;
import javax.microedition.io.*;
import javax.bluetooth.*;

public final class DateClient implements Runnable {
    private Thread mClientThread = null;
    private static DateClient inst = new DateClient();
    private  DateClient() {
    }
    public static DateClient getInstance() {
        return inst;
    }
    private boolean mEndNow = false;

    private static final UUID DATING_SERVICE_ID =
        new UUID("BAE0D0C0B0A0009555706050403020l0", false);
    private String mDateConnect = null;
    private DiscoveryAgent mDiscoveryAgent = null;

    private String mPref = null;
    private String mHeight = null;
    private String mContact = null;

    public void setMyInfo(String inPref, String inHeight, String inContact) {
        mPref = inPref;
        mHeight = inHeight;
        mContact = inContact;
    }
    public void startClient() {
        if (mClientThread != null)
            return;
        mEndNow = false;
        // Start receive thread
        mClientThread = new Thread(this);
        mClientThread.start();
    }
    public void stopClient() {
        mEndNow = true;
        try {
            mClientThread.join();
        } catch (Exception ex) {}
        mClientThread = null;
    }
```

```
public void run() {
    // This is the BT client portion of the dating service
    try {
        mDiscoveryAgent = LocalDevice.getLocalDevice().getDiscoveryAgent();
    } catch (Exception ex) {
    }

    StreamConnection conn  = null;
    DataOutputStream dos  = null;
    while( !mEndNow)  {
        try  {
             mDateConnect = mDiscoveryAgent.selectService(DATING_SERVICE_ID,
             ServiceRecord.NOAUTHENTICATE_NOENCRYPT, false);

            if (mDateConnect != null)  {
                conn = (StreamConnection) Connector.open(mDateConnect);
                dos = conn.openDataOutputStream();
                dos.writeUTF(mPref);
                dos.writeUTF(mHeight);
                dos.writeUTF(mContact);
                dos.flush();
                dos.close();
            }

        } catch (Exception ex) {
        }
    }
}

}
```

In Listing 12-1, in the run() method, note the use of the selectService() method of DiscoveryAgent to greatly simplify Bluetooth client coding. This client will discover and use the dating service identified by the DATING_SERVICE_ID, a UUID. If there are multiple nearby dating services, however, the Bluetooth implementation will have control over the actual service that will be used.

Coding the Bluetooth Service

The BTMIDlet.java file contains both the GUI and the dating service code. The logic for the Bluetooth service is in the run() method. A thread called mServer is started in the startApp() method of the MIDlet for running the service. Listing 12-2 contains the code.

Listing 12-2. *Bluetooth Dating Service—BTMIDlet.java*

```java
import java.io.*;
import javax.microedition.midlet.*;
import javax.microedition.io.*;
import javax.microedition.lcdui.*;
import javax.bluetooth.*;

import java.io.IOException;

public class BTMIDlet
extends MIDlet
implements CommandListener, Runnable {
    private DateClient mClient = null;
    private Thread mServer = null;

    private Command mExitCommand  = new Command("Exit", Command.EXIT, 2);

    private Display mDisplay = null;
    private StringItem mDateContact = null;
    private Form mForm = null;
    private boolean mEndNow = false;

    private String mLastContact = "";
    private LocalDevice mLocalBT;
    private StreamConnectionNotifier mServerNotifier;
    private static final UUID DATING_SERVICE_ID =
    new UUID("BAE0D0C0B0A0009555570605040302010", false);


    private String myPref = null;
    private String myHeight = null;
    private String myContact = null;

    private String seekPref = null;
    private String seekHeight = null;
    private String seekContact = null;

    public BTMIDlet() {
        mClient = DateClient.getInstance();
        myPref = getAppProperty("BTMIDlet-mypref");
        myHeight = getAppProperty("BTMIDlet-myheight");
        myContact = getAppProperty("BTMIDlet-mycontact");
        seekPref = getAppProperty("BTMIDlet-seekpref");
        seekHeight = getAppProperty("BTMIDlet-seekheight");

    }
```

```java
public void commandAction(javax.microedition.lcdui.Command c,
javax.microedition.lcdui.Displayable d) {
    if (c == mExitCommand) {
        destroyApp(true);
        notifyDestroyed();

    }
}


protected void destroyApp(boolean param) {
    mEndNow = true;

    // Finalize notifier work
    if (mServerNotifier != null) {
        try {
            mServerNotifier.close();
        } catch (IOException e) {} // ignore
    }

    // Wait until acceptor thread is done
    try {
        mServer.join();
    } catch (InterruptedException e) {} // Ignore
    try {
        mClient.stopClient();
    } catch (Exception e) {} // Ignore
}

protected void pauseApp() {
}

protected void startApp() {
    if (mForm == null) {
        mForm = new Form("BTMIDlet");
        mDateContact = new StringItem("Potential date found at:",null);
        mForm.append(mDateContact);
        mForm.addCommand(mExitCommand);
        mForm.setCommandListener(this);
    }
    mDisplay = Display.getDisplay(this);
    mDisplay.setCurrent(mForm);
    mEndNow = false;
    startServer();
    mClient.setMyInfo(myPref, myHeight, myContact);
    mClient.startClient();
}
```

```java
private void startServer() {
    if (mServer != null)
        return;
    // Start receive thread
    mServer = new Thread(this);
    mServer.start();

}

public void run() {



    try {
        // Get local BT manager
        mLocalBT = LocalDevice.getLocalDevice();

        // Set we are discoverable
        mLocalBT.setDiscoverable(DiscoveryAgent.GIAC);
        String url = "btspp://localhost:" + DATING_SERVICE_ID.toString() +
        ";name=Dating Service;authorize=false";

        // Create notifier now
        mServerNotifier = (StreamConnectionNotifier) Connector.open(
        url.toString());
    } catch (Exception e) {
        System.err.println("Can't initialize bluetooth: " + e);
    }
    StreamConnection conn = null;
    while (!mEndNow) {
        conn = null;
        try {
            conn = mServerNotifier.acceptAndOpen();
        } catch (IOException e) {
            continue;
        }

        if (conn != null)
            processRequest(conn);
    }

}
```

```
private void processRequest(StreamConnection conn) {
    DataInputStream dis = null;
    String pref = null;
    String height = null;
    String contact = null;
    try {
        dis = conn.openDataInputStream();
        pref = dis.readUTF();
        height = dis.readUTF( );
        contact = dis.readUTF();
        dis.close();
        conn.close();

    } catch (IOException e) {} // Ignore
    if (!mLastContact.equals(contact)) {
        mLastContact = contact;
        if (pref.equals(seekPref)  && height.equals(seekHeight))
            mDisplay.callSerially(new ShowCandidate(contact));
    }
}
class ShowCandidate implements Runnable {
    Display disp = null;
    String contact = null;
    public ShowCandidate(String cont) {
        contact = cont;
    }
    public void run() {
        mDateContact.setText(contact );
    }
}
}
```

In the server code (the run() method), the LocalDevice is first set to discoverable, then a StreamConnectionNotifier is created called mServerNotifier. The server thread then waits for incoming requests by calling acceptAndOpen(). The incoming connection is read for the sex, height, and e-mail address of the nearby dating candidate. If the items match those you are looking for, the GUI will be updated with the date's e-mail address.

Infrared Communications and OBEX

Unlike the Bluetooth radio-based technology, communications via infrared requires a line-of-sight connection between the senders and receivers. This is because infrared devices communicate via light beams that must be aimed (roughly) at one another. Similar to Bluetooth devices, however, infrared devices can discover one another when they are in range. Connections between infrared devices can be formed dynamically.

As with Bluetooth, low-level communications over infrared is packet based. With Bluetooth, the "btspp://" protocol provides a high-level stream interface, via the RFCOMM protocol, over the low-level L2CAP packet-based protocol. With infrared communications, the lower-level packet-based protocol is called the IrDA protocol, and OBEX serves as a means to provide a high-level object-based communications protocol on top of IrDA.

OBEX

OBEX, or Object Exchange, is a protocol designed to enable exchange of data such as contact and scheduling information in vCalendar and vCard formats. It is a request/response protocol, loosely modeled after the ubiquitous Hypertext Transfer Protocol (HTTP). OBEX is not exclusively tied to IrDA as its transport protocol. For example, OBEX can work over TCP/IP as well as RFCOMM (Bluetooth).

■Tip While OBEX over TCP/IP and OBEX over RFCOMM/Bluetooth represent possible stackings of software protocols, you are less likely to find many devices supporting them. This is because IrDA and OBEX have a very strong bond if you are creating firmware and/or new devices. Furthermore, Bluetooth and IP networks have high-level protocol solutions that are similar to OBEX, rendering it significantly less important outside of the infrared arena. If you want to experiment, the Wireless Technology Kit 2.x supports these stacks on the emulator.

OBEX Requests

All of the Java APIs for OBEX are in the `javax.obex` package. JSR 82 fully specifies the content of this package.

As a request/response protocol, an OBEX session consists of a series of client requests and the corresponding server responses. Like HTTP, each request and response can contain a set of headers and a body. The `ClientSession` interface in the OBEX API has methods that facilitate the sending of client requests. The available OBEX requests, and their corresponding methods in `ClientSession`, are tabulated in Table 12-5. The GET and PUT operations, spanning multiple requests, are most frequently used to transfer large binary objects from and to the server.

When you're in a session (when `connect()` returns successful), you can get the current connection ID using the following:

```
public long getConnectionID();
```

Depending on your application's requirement, there are at least two ways to communicate using the OBEX APIs:

- Via OBEX request headers

- Via the `Operation` object with a PUT or GET

Table 12-5. *OBEX Requests*

OBEX Request	API Method	Description
CONNECT	HeaderSet connect(HeaderSet hdrs);	Connects and creates a session with the OBEX server. Must be called successfully before sending other requests. Returns a HeaderSet. Uses getResponseCode() on the HeaderSet to retrieve the server return code.
PUT	Operation put(HeaderSet hdrs);	Starts an OBEX PUT operation. Returns an Operation object. Use this to obtain an output stream that can be used to send arbitrarily large objects.
GET	Operation get(HeaderSet hdrs);	Starts an OBEX GET operation. Returns an Operation object. Use this to obtain an input stream that can be used to receive arbitrarily large objects.
DELETE	HeaderSet delete(HeaderSet hdrs);	Performs an OBEX DELETE request, typically used to delete an object on the server.
SETPATH	HeaderSet setpath(HeaderSet hdrs, boolean backup, boolean create);	Instructs the server to change working directory via an OBEX SETPATH request. backup indicates whether the server changes directory up one level before setting the path. create indicates whether the directory should be created if it does not yet exists. Returns a HeaderSet.
DISCONNECT	HeaderSet disconnect(HeaderSet hdrs);	Disconnects from the current session using an OBEX DISCONNECT request. Returns a HeaderSet.

Communications Using Headers

Other than standard OBEX headers that are predefined in the Javadocs of the javax.obex.HeaderSet interface (part of JSR 82), you can also create user-defined headers.

User-defined headers must have a header identifier value between 48 and 255. In fact, OBEX mandates that headers with a certain identifier must be of a certain type. Table 12-6 shows the range and corresponding type.

Table 12-6. *OBEX User-Defined Header Types*

Identifier Value	Java Type	Actual OBEX Type
48–63	String	Unicode string
112–127	byte[]	Byte sequence
176–191	Byte	Single 8-bit byte
240–255	Long (0 to $2^{32}-1$ only)	32-bits unsigned integer

Use the HeaderSet interface to set and get the values of user-defined headers. To add a user-defined header to a HeaderSet, use this method:

```
void setHeader(int headerID, java.lang.Object headerValue);
```

Check Table 12-6 to determine an identifier to use and the corresponding header type. For example, to add a user-defined string-typed header to a HeaderSet called OutHeader, use this:

```
String seekHeight = "tall";
OutHeader.setHeader(48, seekHeight);
```

From Table 12-6, you can see that the identifier value of 48 contains a user-defined header of Unicode string type.

To obtain the value of a particular header, use this method:

```
Object getHeader(int headerID);
```

For example, to retrieve the string-valued header set earlier using setHeader(), from a HeaderSet called InHeader, you can use

```
String seekHeight = (String) InHeader.getHeader(48);
```

You can get an array of int containing the identifiers of all the headers in a HeaderSet with this method:

```
int[] getHeaderList()
```

The array returned by getHeaderList() will only contain headers that have values set; you can call getHeader() on any of the returned indexes safely.

Every request that returns a HeaderSet has a response code from the OBEX server. However, since a Java method cannot return multiple values of different types, you must make an additional API call on the returned HeaderSet to obtain the OBEX response code for the request:

```
 int getResponseCode();
```

To interpret the response code from an OBEX server, consult the documentation for the ResponseCodes class. This class defines the static constants for all the possible OBEX response codes. Table 12-7 shows some of the most frequently used ones, and those used in the upcoming example.

Table 12-7 OBEX *Response Codes (Partial)*

Value	Description
ResponseCodes.OBEX_HTTP_OK	Successful request or operations
ResponseCodes.OBEX_HTTP_VERSION	Version of OBEX_HTTP not supported
ResponseCodes.OBEX_HTTP_UNAUTHORIZED	Unauthorized connection
ResponseCodes.OBEX_HTTP_FORBIDDEN	Forbidden access

The fact that OBEX is a request/response protocol modeled after HTTP is quite evident from Table 12-7.

Communications Using PUT or GET

User-defined headers are sufficient for communication tasks that are based on exchange of small messages. For communications that involve custom data types or large binary objects (files, images, etc.), you can use the PUT and GET requests. The put() method on ClientSession can be used to initiate a PUT request.

```
Operation put(HeaderSet headers) ;
```

Note that you can still include a HeaderSet for the request. For example, you may want to let the server application know the length and data type of the object that you will be sending— and you can set the appropriate headers.

To obtain a large data object from a server, use the get() method on ClientSession:

```
Operation get(HeaderSet headers);
```

Again, you can set the header of the request. Note that the headers from the response of the server are not directly accessible. Instead, you can use the following methods to obtain some pertinent header information (if they are set by the server):

- getLength() to obtain the value from the standard OBEX header: LENGTH

- getType() to obtain the value from the standard OBEX header: TYPE

Once you have an Operation instance from the get() method call, you can call one of the following:

- openInputStream() to obtain an InputStream

- openDataInputStream() to obtain a DataInputStream

Once you have an Operation instance from a put() method call, you can call one of these methods:

- openOutputStream() to obtain an OutputStream

- openDataOutputStream() to obtain a DataOutputStream

With the stream opened, you can use the read or write methods of the stream to process the incoming or outgoing data object. The OBEX implementation underneath will perform the necessary segmenting of packets, sending them, and reassembing them for you. This is one of the primary benefits of using the OBEX high-level API instead of lower-level packet-based APIs.

You can close the stream once you are finished reading/writing. Note that once you close the stream, the OBEX implementation underneath will be sending packets to the server that indicate the operation is completed. The server will send a response code; this response code can be obtained using the following:

```
int getResponseCode();
```

■**Caution** Do not call getResponseCode() unless you are finished with the stream you have obtained from the operation. Calling getResponseCode() will implicitly close the stream and signal to the server that the operation is completed. No further IO operations will be possible on the stream once getResponseCode() is called.

The abort() method may be used to abort a GET or PUT operation. It will close the operation's stream implicitly.

```
void abort();
```

Obtaining OBEX Client and Server Connections

When creating clients using OBEX over IrDA, the connection URL string provided to GCF's Connector.open() contains all the instructions necessary to work with the communications stack. The underlying implementation will parse the connection string for the instruction.

The general format is as shown here:

```
"irdaobex://{target};{parameters}"
```

If {target} begins with discover, the IrDA stack will perform discovery for accessible IrDA devices. The {target} of server connections always begins with localhost. A very useful parameter available for OBEX/IrDA is the ias parameter. The ias parameter is the string-based IAS class name used for server identification.

For example, a server application called DatingService can use the following connection string:

```
"irdaobex://localhost;ias=DatingService"
```

An OBEX client wishing to discover and connect to this service can simply use this connection string:

```
"irdaobex://discover;ias=DatingService"
```

The OBEX API extends the GCF with SessionNotifier for creating OBEX server connections. OBEX server code can wait for incoming client OBEX connections, blocking on an acceptAndOpen() call on a SessionNotifier.

See JSR 82 and documentation of your OBEX over IrDA implementation for more details on the available target and parameter values.

An OBEX Dating Service

Reusing the application logic from the Bluetooth dating service example earlier, this second example implements the same dating service using OBEX over infrared.

To try out this example, perform the following steps:

1. Using KToolbar, create a project called OBEXMIDlet.

2. Copy the source files to the src directory of OBEXMIDlet.

3. Build the project.

4. Set the MIDlet properties in Table 12-8.

5. Using KToolbar, create a project called OBEX2 with MIDlet name `OBEXMIDlet`.

6. Copy the source files to the `src` directory of OBEX2.

7. Build the project.

8. Set the MIDlet properties for OBEX2, with the values in Table 12-9.

9. Start an emulator instance of OBEX2 and launch the MIDlet.

10. Open the OBEXMIDlet project.

11. Start an emulator instance of OBEXMIDlet and launch the MIDlet.

Table 12-8. *MIDlet Properties for OBEXMIDlet Project*

Key	Value
OBEXMIDlet-mycontact	tallguy@yahoo.com
OBEXMIDlet-myheight	tall
OBEXMIDlet-mypref	male
OBEXMIDlet-seekheight	short
OBEXMIDlet-seekpref	female

Table 12-9. *MIDlet properties for OBEX2 Project*

Key	Value
OBEXMIDlet-mycontact	shortgal@yahoo.com
OBEXMIDlet-myheight	short
OBEXMIDlet-mypref	female
OBEXMIDlet-seekheight	tall
OBEXMIDlet-seekpref	male

Coding the OBEX Dating Service Client

Listing 12-3 shows `DateClient.java`, a singleton instance with the client logic in the `run()` method. The connector URL string used in `Connector.open()` is "irdaobex://discover;ias=DatingService". This provides the instruction for the underlying OBEX infrared transport to discover the associated dating service.

Listing 12-3. *An OBEX Dating Client—DateClient.java*

```java
Import java.io.*;
import javax.microedition.io.*;
import javax.obex.*;

public final class DateClient implements Runnable {
    private Thread mClientThread = null;
    private static DateClient inst = new DateClient();
    private  DateClient() {
    }
    public static DateClient getInstance() {
        return inst;
    }
    private boolean mEndNow = false;
    private String mPref = null;
    private String mHeight = null;
    private String mContact = null;

    private static final String url =
    "irdaobex://discover;ias=DatingService";
    public void setMyInfo(String inPref, String inHeight,
    String inContact) {
        mPref = inPref;
        mHeight = inHeight;
        mContact = inContact;
    }
    public void startClient() {
        if (mClientThread != null)
            return;
        mEndNow = false;

        // Start receive thread
        mClientThread = new Thread(this);
        mClientThread.start();
    }
    public void stopClient() {
        mEndNow = true;
        try {
            // Only on CLDC 1.1
            // mClientThread.interrupt();
            mClientThread.join();
        } catch (Exception ex) {
            System.out.println("in stop client");
            ex.printStackTrace();
        }
        mClientThread = null;
    }

}
```

```
public void run() {
    DataOutputStream dos  = null;
    Operation op = null;
    ClientSession ses = null;
    int code = 0;
    HeaderSet resp = null;
    HeaderSet hdrs = null;

    while( !mEndNow)  {
        ses = null;
        dos = null;
        op = null;
        try  {
            ses = (ClientSession) Connector.open(url);
        } catch (IOException ex) {
            // Discovery fails, sleep for a while and try again
            try {
                Thread.sleep(30001);
            } catch (Exception e) {}
            continue;
        }

        try {
            resp = ses.connect(null);
            code = resp.getResponseCode();

            if (code != ResponseCodes.OBEX_HTTP_OK) {
                throw new IOException("OBEX connect operation failed");
            }
            hdrs = ses.createHeaderSet();
            op = ses.put(hdrs);
            dos = null;
            dos = op.openDataOutputStream();


            if (dos != null)  {
                dos.writeUTF(mPref);
                dos.writeUTF(mHeight);
                dos.writeUTF(mContact);
                dos.flush();
                dos.close();

                code = op.getResponseCode();
                //   System.out.println("before os close");
                if (code != ResponseCodes.OBEX_HTTP_OK) {
                    throw new IOException("OBEX failure after put operations");
                }
```

```
            //   System.out.println("before op close");

            op.close();

        }

      } catch (Exception ex) {
          ex.printStackTrace();
      }
    } // while
  } // run
}
```

In Listing 12-3, it would have been possible to use a custom header to send our dating information. However, this example uses a PUT operation, showing the code required to handle the more complex OBEX PUT operation instead.

Coding an OBEX Service

The service code and the GUI MIDlet code are in OBEXMIDlet.java, shown in Listing 12-4. The service is started in its own mServer thread. Note the use of the connect string "irdaobex://localhost;ias=DatingService" to create the SessionNotifier required to accept incoming OBEX over IrDA connections.

Listing 12-4. *An OBEX Dating Service—OBEXMIDlet.java*

```java
import java.io.*;
import javax.microedition.midlet.*;
import javax.microedition.io.*;
import javax.microedition.lcdui.*;
import javax.obex.*;

import java.io.IOException;

public class OBEXMIDlet
extends MIDlet
implements CommandListener, Runnable {
    private DateClient mClient = null;
    private Thread mServer = null;
    private OperationHandler mOpHandler = null;

    private Command mExitCommand  = new Command("Exit", Command.EXIT, 2);
    private Display mDisplay = null;
    private StringItem mDateContact = null;
    private Form mForm = null;
```

```java
private boolean mEndNow = false;
private String mLastContact = "";



private String myPref = null;
private String myHeight = null;
private String myContact = null;

private String seekPref = null;
private String seekHeight = null;
private String seekContact = null;

private SessionNotifier mServerNotifier;
private static final String url =
    "irdaobex://localhost;ias=DatingService";
private Connection mConnection = null;


public OBEXMIDlet() {
    mClient = DateClient.getInstance();
    myPref = getAppProperty("OBEXMIDlet-mypref");
    myHeight = getAppProperty("OBEXMIDlet-myheight");
    myContact = getAppProperty("OBEXMIDlet-mycontact");
    seekPref = getAppProperty("OBEXMIDlet-seekpref");
    seekHeight = getAppProperty("OBEXMIDlet-seekheight");

}

public void commandAction(Command c, Displayable d) {
    if (c == mExitCommand) {
        destroyApp(true);
        notifyDestroyed();
    }
}


protected void destroyApp(boolean param) {
    mEndNow = true;
    if (mServerNotifier != null) {
        try {
            mServerNotifier.close();
        } catch (IOException e) {} // Ignore
    }
```

```
        // Wait until acceptor thread is done
        try {
            mServer.join();
        } catch (InterruptedException e) {} // Ignore
        try {
            mClient.stopClient();
        } catch (Exception e) {} // Ignore

    }

    protected void pauseApp() {

    }

    protected void startApp() {
        if (mForm == null) {
            mForm = new Form("OBEXMIDlet");
            mDateContact = new StringItem("Potential date found at:",null);
            mForm.append(mDateContact);
            mForm.addCommand(mExitCommand);
            mForm.setCommandListener(this);
        }
        mDisplay = Display.getDisplay(this);
        mDisplay.setCurrent(mForm);
        mEndNow = false;
        startServer();
        mClient.setMyInfo(myPref, myHeight, myContact);
        mClient.startClient();
        mOpHandler = new OperationHandler(this);
    }
    private void startServer() {
        if (mServer != null)
            return;
        // Start server thread
        mServer = new Thread(this);
        mServer.start();

    }

    public void run() {
        try {
            mServerNotifier = (SessionNotifier) Connector.open(url);
        } catch (Exception e) {
            System.err.println("Can't initialize OBEX server: " + e);
        }
```

```
    while (!mEndNow) {
        mConnection = null;

        try {
            mConnection = mServerNotifier.acceptAndOpen(mOpHandler);
        } catch (IOException e) {
            continue;
        }


        //          System.out.println(" got a connection!");
        try {
            // Bad bad API design, need to synchronize server thread
            synchronized(this) {
                this.wait();
            }

            //       System.out.println("svr: before conn close");
            mConnection.close();
        } catch (Exception ex) {
            // Log exception
        }

    } // of while
    try {
        mServerNotifier.close();
    } catch (Exception ex) {
        System.out.println("trying to close session...exception");
        ex.printStackTrace();
    }
}


private void processRequest(DataInputStream dis) {
    String pref = null;
    String height = null;
    String contact = null;
    try {
        pref = dis.readUTF();
        height = dis.readUTF( );
        contact = dis.readUTF();

                dis.close();
    } catch (IOException e) {
        System.out.println("in process request exception");
        e.printStackTrace();
    }
```

```
        if (! mLastContact.equals(contact)) {
            mLastContact = contact;
            if (pref.equals(seekPref)  && height.equals(seekHeight))
                mDisplay.callSerially(new ShowCandidate(contact));
        }
    }

    class OperationHandler extends ServerRequestHandler {
        DataInputStream dis = null;
        Object syncObject = null;
        public OperationHandler( Object inSync) {
            syncObject = inSync;
        }
        public int onPut(Operation op) {
            dis = null;
            try {
                dis = op.openDataInputStream();
            } catch (Exception ex) {
                // Okay for CREATE_EMPTY op
            }
            if (dis != null)   // Not a  CREATE_EMPTY op
            {
                processRequest(dis);
                try {
                    dis.close();
                    op.close();
                } catch (Exception ex) {
                }
                dis = null;
                synchronized(syncObject) {
                    syncObject.notify();
                }
            }
            return ResponseCodes.OBEX_HTTP_OK;
        }
    }
```

```
class ShowCandidate implements Runnable {
    Display disp = null;
    String contact = null;
    public ShowCandidate(String cont) {
        contact = cont;
    }
    public void run() {
        mDateContact.setText(contact );
    }
}
}
```

OBEX server handling uses a listener inherited from `ServerRequestHandler`. In Listing 12-4, the private `OperationHandler` is used for this purpose. Since the OBEX callback is performed on a system thread, the actual work of `processRequest()` is not performed there. Instead, thread synchronization is used to ensure that the work is performed on the `mServer` thread.

Summary

The Java API for Bluetooth is an optional API that provides MIDP applications with access to a device's support for radio connectivity with nearby devices. Using Bluetooth, devices can offer services to one another, or consume services provided by nearby network resources. You use the familiar CLDC GCF when working with Bluetooth connections.

JSR 82 specifies the Java API for Bluetooth, as well as an API for the OBEX protocol. The OBEX protocol provides a simple and standard way of creating communicating MIDP applications that utilizes the infrared link hardware available on some devices.

CHAPTER 13

■■■

Programming a Custom User Interface

Chapters 5, 6, and 7 were devoted to MIDP's generalized user-interface APIs. Clever as these APIs are, they are unsuitable for game development and other specialized user interfaces. Games are programmed "closer to the metal" than other applications. MIDP offers a class, javax.microedition.lcdui.Canvas, that provides low-level access to a device's screen and input facilities. You can find out exactly which keys a user is pressing and draw whatever you want on the screen.

The Game API, contained in the javax.microedition.lcdui.game package, includes a refinement of Canvas and classes for layer-based graphics and sprite animations. The Game API is fully discussed in Chapter 14. In this chapter, you'll learn the basics of Canvas and drawing with the Graphics class.

The Canvas Class

Canvas is the heart of MIDP's custom user-interface API. To use it, you must create a subclass of Canvas. This differs from the Screen subclasses, which are ready to use "out of the box."

Aside from that, however, Canvas fits in very nicely with the other subclasses of Displayable. A MIDlet can mix and match regular screens and Canvases. In a game, for instance, a high-score screen might be a Form, while the game itself would be played on a Canvas.

Canvas contains event-handling methods that are invoked by the MIDP implementation whenever something important happens. When the user presses a key, or when the screen needs to be painted, one of Canvas's methods will be called. Most of these methods have empty implementations in Canvas. To respond to an event, you need to override the appropriate method and provide an implementation.

The one exception to this rule is the paint() method, which is declared abstract and thus must be defined in subclasses.

Canvas Information

If you would like to draw your own user interface, you'll need some basic information about the Canvas. You can find out the size of the Canvas by calling getWidth() and getHeight(). As we'll discuss later, you can also find out the color capabilities of the device by calling methods in Display.

There is also a full-screen mode. Some Canvas implementations won't occupy all the available screen space, reserving areas of the screen for information about the state of the device or other purposes. If the device supports an alternate full screen mode for Canvas, you can use it by calling setFullScreenMode(true). Setting full screen mode on or off may result in calls to the sizeChanged() method Canvas inherits from Displayable.

Canvas also features event handler methods that will be called by the MIDP implementation as your Canvas is displayed and hidden. Each time your Canvas is shown, the showNotify() method will be called. If another Displayable is shown, or the application manager decides to run a different application, hideNotify() is called.

Painting and Repainting

The MIDP implementation calls a Canvas's paint() method when the contents of the Canvas need to be shown. This paint() method should look familiar to anyone who has ever implemented a custom Swing or AWT component.

The MIDP implementation passes a Graphics object to your paint() method. Graphics has methods for drawing shapes, text, and images on a Canvas. A typical Canvas implementation, then, looks something like this:

```
import javax.microedition.lcdui.*;

public class JonathanCanvas
    extends Canvas {
  public void paint(Graphics g) {
    // Draw stuff using g.
  }
}
```

What if you want to tell the Canvas to draw itself? You can't call paint() directly, because you don't have a suitable Graphics to pass to paint(). Instead, you need to tell the MIDP implementation that it's time to paint the Canvas. The way you do this is by calling repaint(). The first version of this method simply tells Canvas to paint everything.

```
public void repaint()
public void repaint(int x, int y, int width, int height)
```

The second version is a way of saying, "I only want you to paint this rectangular portion of the screen." If the drawing you're doing is very complicated, you can save some time by only painting the portion of the Canvas that has changed. This is implemented using a technique called clipping. A later section discusses clipping in more detail.

How exactly does repaint() work? When you call repaint(), paint() won't be called right away. The call to repaint() just signals to the MIDP implementation that you want the screen to be painted. Some time later, the implementation *services* the repaint request, which results in an actual call to the paint() method of the Canvas. The MIDP implementation may even combine several repaint requests, particularly if their repaint regions overlap.

■**Tip** Canvas does not automatically clear itself when you call repaint(). If you want to change what's on the screen, rather than adding to it, you should clear the screen in the paint() method. You'll see how to do this in the FontCanvas example later in this chapter.

An application can force the implementation to service all the repaint requests by calling serviceRepaints() on the Canvas object. This method does not return until all pending repaint requests have been serviced. If you are going to call serviceRepaints(), you should make sure that you aren't trying to acquire object locks in the paint() method that won't be released until serviceRepaints() returns. In general, you won't need to call serviceRepaints(); you can usually use Display's callSerially() method instead. (See the "Multithreading and Animation" section of this chapter for a discussion of callSerially().)

Drawing Shapes, Text, and Images

The Graphics class contains methods for drawing shapes, text, and images on a Canvas. It also maintains some state, like the current pen color and line style. MIDP's Graphics class is similar to the Graphics and Graphics2D classes in J2SE but much smaller.

Coordinate Space

All drawing on a Canvas takes place in a coordinate space based on the pixels of the device. By default, the origin of this coordinate space is located in the upper-left corner of the Canvas. X coordinates increase in the right-hand direction, while Y coordinates increase in the downward direction, as shown in Figure 13-1.

You can adjust the origin of this coordinate space by calling the translate() method of the Graphics class. This sets the origin to the given coordinates in the current coordinate system. To find out the location of the translated origin relative to the default origin, call getTranslateX() and getTranslateY().

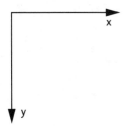

Figure 13-1. *Canvas coordinate axes*

Drawing and Filling Shapes

Graphics contains a collection of methods that draw and fill simple shapes. These are detailed in Table 13-1.

Table 13-1. *Drawing and Filling Shapes with Graphics*

Shape Outline	Filled Shape
drawLine(int x1, int y1, int x2, int y2)	
	fillTriangle(int x1, int y1, int x2, int y2, int x3, int y3)
drawRect(int x, int y, int width, int height)	fillRect(int x, int y, int width, int height)
drawRoundRect(int x, int y, int width, int height, int arcWidth, int arcHeight)	fillRoundRect(int x, int y, int width, int height, int arcWidth, int arcHeight)
drawArc(int x, int y, int width, int height, int startAngle, int arcAngle)	fillArc(int x, int y, int width, int height, int startAngle, int arcAngle)

These methods do basically what you'd expect. The following example demonstrates some simple drawing using Graphics. It consists of two pieces. First, PacerCanvas demonstrates some simple drawing and filling:

```
import javax.microedition.lcdui.*;

public class PacerCanvas
    extends Canvas {
  public void paint(Graphics g) {
    int w = getWidth();
    int h = getHeight();

    g.setColor(0xffffff);
    g.fillRect(0, 0, w, h);
    g.setColor(0x000000);

    for (int x = 0; x < w; x += 10)
      g.drawLine(0, w - x, x, 0);

    int z = 50;
    g.drawRect(z, z, 20, 20);
    z += 20;
    g.fillRoundRect(z, z, 20, 20, 5, 5);
    z += 20;
    g.drawArc(z, z, 20, 20, 0, 360);
  }
}
```

The next class is Pacer, a MIDlet that uses PacerCanvas.

```
import javax.microedition.lcdui.*;
import javax.microedition.midlet.*;
```

```
public class Pacer
    extends MIDlet{
  public void startApp() {
    Displayable d = new PacerCanvas();

    d.addCommand(new Command("Exit", Command.EXIT, 0));
    d.setCommandListener(new CommandListener() {
      public void commandAction(Command c, Displayable s) {
        notifyDestroyed();
      }
    } );

    Display.getDisplay(this).setCurrent(d);
  }

  public void pauseApp() { }

  public void destroyApp(boolean unconditional) { }
}
```

When you run Pacer in the Wireless Toolkit emulator, it looks like Figure 13-2.

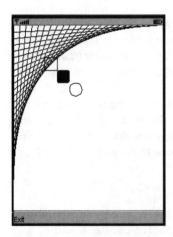

Figure 13-2. *Playing around with Graphics*

Working with Color

The Graphics class maintains a current drawing color that is used for drawing shape outlines, filling shapes, and drawing text. Colors are represented as combinations of red, green, and blue, with 8 bits for each color component. You can set the current drawing color using the following method:

```
public void setColor(int RGB)
```

This method expects the red, green, and blue values in a packed integer, as shown in Figure 13-3.

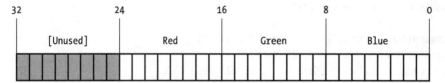

Figure 13-3. *Packing a color into an integer*

An alternate convenience method accepts red, green, and blue values as integers in the range from 0 to 255 inclusive:

```
public void setColor(int red, int green, int blue)
```

You can retrieve the current drawing color (as a packed integer) with getColor(). Alternatively, you can retrieve each component separately using getRedComponent(), getGreenComponent(), and getBlueComponent().

Of course, different devices will have different levels of color support, from black and white (affectionately known as "1-bit color") through full 24-bit color. As we mentioned in Chapter 5, the isColor() and numColors() methods in Display return useful information about the capabilities of the device.

For grayscale devices, Graphics provides setGrayScale() as a convenience method. You pass it a number from 0 (black) to 255 (white). You can find out the current grayscale value by calling getGrayScale(). If the current color of this Graphics is not a grayscale color (that is, if the red, green, and blue values of the current color are not the same), then this method returns its best guess as to the brightness of the current color.

Another handy method in the Graphics class is getDisplayColor(). This method can tell you at runtime exactly how a requested color will be displayed on the device. You feed it a color int, and it returns the color int that will actually be displayed on the device. For example, on the WTK's DefaultGrayPhone emulator, pure green (0x00ff00) maps to the gray level 0x959595.

Line Styles

Graphics also maintains a current line style, called a stroke style, that is used for drawing shape outlines and lines. There are two choices for line style, represented by constants in the Graphics class:

- SOLID is the default.

- DOTTED lines may also be drawn.

It's up to the implementation to decide exactly how dotted lines are implemented, so dotted lines on one device may look dashed on another. You can set or retrieve the current style using setStrokeStyle() and getStrokeStyle(). For example, the following code draws a square with a solid outline (the default) and another square with a dotted outline:

```
public void paint(Graphics g) {
  g.drawRect(20, 10, 35, 35);
  g.setStrokeStyle(Graphics.DOTTED);
  g.drawRect(20, 60, 35, 35);
}
```

Drawing Text

The Graphics class makes it easy to draw text anywhere on the screen. Text drawing is based around the idea of an anchor point. The anchor point determines exactly where the text will be drawn. Anchor points are described with a horizontal and vertical component. The Graphics class defines the horizontal and vertical anchor points as constants. Figure 13-4 illustrates the various anchor points for a string of text. Each anchor point is described as a combination of a horizontal and vertical anchor point.

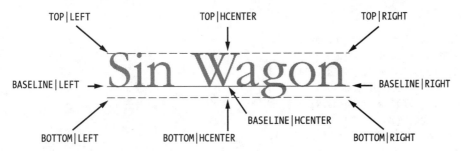

Figure 13-4. *Text anchor points*

To draw text, you just need to specify the text itself and the location and type of anchor point. You could, for example, place some text in the upper-left corner of the screen by using a TOP | LEFT anchor point located at 0, 0.

Text is specified as a String or an array of chars, which means you can draw text in many languages, provided that the fonts you're using have the corresponding glyphs.

Graphics provides four different methods for drawing text. You can draw characters or Strings, depending on what you have available:

```
public void drawChar(char character, int x, int y, int anchor)
public void drawChars(char[] data, int offset, int length,
    int x, int y, int anchor)
public void drawString(String str, int x, int y, int anchor)
public void drawSubstring(String str, int offset, int len,
    int x, int y, int anchor)
```

The following example shows how to place text at various places on a Canvas:

```
import javax.microedition.lcdui.*;

public class TextCanvas
    extends Canvas {
  public void paint(Graphics g) {
    int w = getWidth();
    int h = getHeight();

    g.setColor(0xffffff);
    g.fillRect(0, 0, w, h);
    g.setColor(0x000000);


    // First label the four corners.
    g.drawString("corner", 0, 0,
        Graphics.TOP | Graphics.LEFT);
    g.drawString("corner", w, 0,
        Graphics.TOP | Graphics.RIGHT);
    g.drawString("corner", 0, h,
        Graphics.BOTTOM | Graphics.LEFT);
    g.drawString("corner", w, h,
        Graphics.BOTTOM | Graphics.RIGHT);

// Now put something in the middle (more or less).
    g.drawString("Sin Wagon", w / 2, h / 2,
        Graphics.BASELINE | Graphics.HCENTER);
  }
}
```

To see this Canvas, you'll have to create a MIDlet that displays it. We suggest using Pacer; just edit the source file so it instantiates a TextCanvas instead of a PacerCanvas. The finished product is shown in Figure 13-5.

Note that Canvas denies us some real estate at the bottom of the screen. This is to allow space for commands. Canvas, like any other Displayable, can display commands and have a command listener.

Figure 13-5. *TextCanvas in the flesh*

Selecting a Font

MIDP fonts are represented by a font face, style, and size. You won't find a big selection of fonts, but there are a few choices. Three faces are available, as shown in Figure 13-6. These are represented by constants in the Font class: FACE_SYSTEM, FACE_MONOSPACE, and FACE_PROPORTIONAL.

Figure 13-6. *The three font faces in italics*

Once you've chosen a font face, you can also specify a style and a size. The styles are what you'd expect, and they are represented by constants in the Font class: STYLE_PLAIN, STYLE_BOLD, STYLE_ITALIC, and STYLE_UNDERLINE. You can combine styles, like bold and italic, by ORing the constants together. The size is simply SIZE_SMALL, SIZE_MEDIUM, or SIZE_LARGE.

You could create a small, italic, proportional font with the following call:

```
Font f = Font.getFont(
    Font.FACE_PROPORTIONAL,
    Font.STYLE_ITALIC,
    Font.SIZE_SMALL);
```

To tell Graphics to use a new font for subsequent text, call setFont(). You can get a reference to the current font by calling getFont(). You can also find out information about a Font with the getFace(), getStyle(), and getSize() methods. For convenience, Font also includes the isPlain(), isBold(), isItalic(), and isUnderlined() methods.

The MIDP implementation has a default font that you can retrieve from Font's static method getDefaultFont().

The following Canvas demonstrates the creation and use of fonts:

```
import javax.microedition.lcdui.*;

public class FontCanvas
    extends Canvas {
  private Font mSystemFont, mMonospaceFont, mProportionalFont;

  public FontCanvas() { this(Font.STYLE_PLAIN); }

  public FontCanvas(int style) { setStyle(style); }

  public void setStyle(int style) {
    mSystemFont = Font.getFont(Font.FACE_SYSTEM,
        style, Font.SIZE_MEDIUM);
    mMonospaceFont = Font.getFont(Font.FACE_MONOSPACE,
        style, Font.SIZE_MEDIUM);
    mProportionalFont = Font.getFont(Font.FACE_PROPORTIONAL,
        style, Font.SIZE_MEDIUM);
  }

  public boolean isBold() {
    return mSystemFont.isBold();
  }
  public boolean isItalic() {
    return mSystemFont.isItalic();
  }
  public boolean isUnderline() {
    return mSystemFont.isUnderlined();
  }

  public void paint(Graphics g) {
    int w = getWidth();
    int h = getHeight();
```

```
    // Clear the Canvas.
    g.setGrayScale(255);
    g.fillRect(0, 0, w - 1, h - 1);
    g.setGrayScale(0);
    g.drawRect(0, 0, w - 1, h - 1);

    int x = w / 2;
    int y = 20;

    y += showFont(g, "System", x, y, mSystemFont);
    y += showFont(g, "Monospace", x, y, mMonospaceFont);
    y += showFont(g, "Proportional", x, y, mProportionalFont);
  }

  private int showFont(Graphics g, String s, int x, int y, Font f) {
    g.setFont(f);
    g.drawString(s, x, y, Graphics.TOP | Graphics.HCENTER);
    return f.getHeight();
  }
}
```

To see this Canvas in action, you'll need a MIDlet that shows it. You could modify Pacer
again, if you wish, or use the following code:

```
import javax.microedition.lcdui.*;
import javax.microedition.midlet.*;

public class FontMIDlet
    extends MIDlet
    implements CommandListener {
  private FontCanvas mFontCanvas;
  private Command mBoldCommand, mItalicCommand, mUnderlineCommand;

  public FontMIDlet() {
    mFontCanvas = new FontCanvas();

    mBoldCommand = new Command("Bold", Command.SCREEN, 0);
    mItalicCommand = new Command("Italic", Command.SCREEN, 0);
    mUnderlineCommand = new Command("Underline", Command.SCREEN, 0);
    Command exitCommand = new Command("Exit", Command.EXIT, 0);

    mFontCanvas.addCommand(mBoldCommand);
    mFontCanvas.addCommand(mItalicCommand);
    mFontCanvas.addCommand(mUnderlineCommand);
    mFontCanvas.addCommand(exitCommand);
    mFontCanvas.setCommandListener(this);
  }
```

```
public void startApp() {
  Display.getDisplay(this).setCurrent(mFontCanvas);
}

public void pauseApp() {}

public void destroyApp(boolean unconditional) {}

public void commandAction(Command c, Displayable s) {
  if (c.getCommandType() == Command.EXIT) {
    notifyDestroyed();
    return;
  }


  boolean isBold = mFontCanvas.isBold() ^ (c == mBoldCommand);
  boolean isItalic = mFontCanvas.isItalic() ^ (c == mItalicCommand);
  boolean isUnderline = mFontCanvas.isUnderline() ^
      (c == mUnderlineCommand);

  int style =
      (isBold ? Font.STYLE_BOLD : 0) |
      (isItalic ? Font.STYLE_ITALIC : 0) |
      (isUnderline ? Font.STYLE_UNDERLINED : 0);

  mFontCanvas.setStyle(style);
  mFontCanvas.repaint();
  }
}
```

Measuring Text

The Font class can tell you useful information about the dimensions of text. If you read the previous example carefully, you'll notice we already used one of these methods, getHeight(). This method returns the height of an entire line of text and can be used to position multiple lines.

If you really need to know the location of the baseline, call getBaselinePosition(). This returns the distance from the top of a line of text to the baseline. However, given the flexibility offered by the anchor points in Graphics, you probably won't ever need to find the baseline yourself.

The rest of the methods in Font for measuring text measure the width of various pieces of text. The names and parameters of these methods are the same as text drawing methods in Graphics:

```
public int charWidth(char ch)
public int charsWidth(char ch, int offset, int length)
public int stringWidth(String str)
public int substringWidth(String str, int offset, int len)
```

You could draw a box around a string, for example:

```
import javax.microedition.lcdui.*;

public class BoxTextCanvas
    extends Canvas {
  private Font mFont;

public BoxTextCanvas() {
    mFont = Font.getFont(Font.FACE_PROPORTIONAL,
        Font.STYLE_PLAIN, Font.SIZE_LARGE);
  }

  public void paint(Graphics g) {
    int w = getWidth();
    int h = getHeight();

    g.setColor(0xffffff);
    g.fillRect(0, 0, w, h);
    g.setColor(0x000000);

    String s = "dolce";
    int stringWidth = mFont.stringWidth(s);
    int stringHeight = mFont.getHeight();
    int x = (w - stringWidth) / 2;
    int y = h / 2;

    g.setFont(mFont);
    g.drawString(s, x, y, Graphics.TOP | Graphics.LEFT);
    g.drawRect(x, y, stringWidth, stringHeight);
  }
}
```

Drawing Images

The Graphics class contains a single method for drawing an image:

```
public void drawImage(Image img, int x, int y, int anchor)
```

The drawImage() method uses an anchor point, just like the anchor point in the text drawing methods. The available anchor points are slightly different. BASELINE is no longer an option for the vertical anchor point of an image, as the concept of baseline is specific to text. Instead, VCENTER is an additional option for the vertical anchor point. Figure 13-7 shows the available combinations of anchor points.

Figure 13-7. *Image anchor points*

Advanced Image Rendering

The Graphics class also includes a drawRegion() method for rendering a region of an image and possibly manipulating it at the same time. The method looks like this:

```
public void drawRegion(Image src,
    int x_src, int y_src, int width, int height,
    int transform, int x_dest, int y_dest, int anchor)
```

The x_src, y_src, width, and height parameters describe a rectangular region of the image that will be rendered on the drawing surface of the Graphics. The region is drawn at x_dest and y_dest subject to the anchor, just as in the drawImage() method.

The transform parameter opens up a whole new world of possibilities. It may be any of the transformations described by constants in the Sprite class, listed here. (Sprite is part of the Game API and is described in the next chapter.)

- TRANS_NONE

- TRANS_ROT90

- TRANS_ROT180

- TRANS_ROT270

- TRANS_MIRROR

- TRANS_MIRROR_ROT90

- TRANS_MIRROR_ROT180

- TRANS_MIRROR_ROT270

The ROT transformations rotate the source image region by 90, 180, or 270 degrees. The MIRROR_ROT transformations first mirror the region around its vertical center, and then rotate the mirrored region.

The drawRegion() method allows easy manipulation and display of animation frames that are packed into a single image.

Images As Integer Arrays

You've already seen how a single color can be represented as an integer. By extension, an image can be represented as an array of integers, where each integer in the array contains the color for a single pixel in the image.

Rendering integer arrays as images is supported with the following method:

```
public void drawRGB(int[] rgbData, int offset, int scanlength,
    int x, int y, int width, int height,
    boolean processAlpha)
```

The image data is contained in the rgbData array, starting at offset. Consecutive rows of data are contained at offsets measured by multiples of scanlength. The image will be rendered at x and y with a size defined by width and height.

The relationship between width and scanlength is a little confusing at first. The following example should clear things up.

Consider the following code.

```
int[] rgbData = {
    0x123456, 0x123456, 0x123456,
    0x000000, 0xffffff, 0xffffff, 0x000000, 0x654321, 0x654321,
    0x000000, 0x000000, 0xffffff, 0x000000, 0x654321, 0x654321,
    0x000000, 0xffffff, 0x000000, 0x000000, 0x654321, 0x654321,
    0x000000, 0xffffff, 0xffffff, 0x000000, 0x654321, 0x654321
};

g.drawRGB(rgbData, 3, 6, 10, 10, 4, 4, false);
```

This code produces the very small image shown at great magnification in Figure 13-8. The first three elements of the array are ignored by passing an offset of 3. Although the image width is 4 pixels, each row of data is separated by 6 positions in the integer array. The image will be rendered at 10, 10, with a size of 4 by 4 pixels.

Figure 13-8. *A very small image*

The final parameter in the drawRGB() method, processAlpha, indicates whether the integer array is considered to contain an alpha (opacity) component. If the parameter is false, every pixel of the image is considered fully opaque. If processAlpha is true, the opacity of each pixel is determined by the high-order byte of the integer value, and the pixel's color will be blended with the drawing surface appropriately. An alpha value of 0 is fully transparent, while an alpha value of 255 is fully opaque.

Blitting

Blitting, the copying of one region of the screen to another location, is a crucial operation for some types of games. There is one method of the Graphics class that can be used for blitting:

```
public void copyArea(int x_src, int y_src, int width, int height,
    int x_dest, int y_dest, int anchor)
```

This method is pretty self-explanatory. It copies a portion of the screen, described by x_src, y_src, width, and height, to a destination described by x_dest, y_dest, and anchor. The anchor works the same as for the drawImage() method.

This method works only on a Graphics object that does not draw directly to the screen. A Graphics object that draws to an image is fine, as is a Graphics object that works on a double-buffered Canvas. A Graphics object from GameCanvas's getGraphics() method will also work. By contrast, a Graphics object for a non-double-buffered Canvas will throw an IllegalStateException if the copyArea() method is called. (See the upcoming section on double buffering for more information on the technique.)

Clipping

Graphics maintains a rectangular clipping shape. The clipping shape limits drawing, such that any drawing that takes place outside of the clipping shape will not be displayed. It's kind of like painting through a stencil, except you can only use a rectangular stencil. If you were writing a game that had some kind of border on the game board, you might set the clipping rectangle to be the inside of the game board, so that no drawing could overwrite the border.

You can find out the current clipping rectangle by calling getClipX(), getClipY(), getClipWidth(), and getClipHeight().

If you would like to modify the clipping rectangle, there are two methods that you can use. First, you can set the clipping rectangle directly by calling the following method:

```
public void setClip(int x, int y, int width, int height);
```

The other possibility is to limit the current clipping rectangle with another rectangle. The following method takes the intersection of the current clipping rectangle and the supplied rectangle and uses it to set the new clipping rectangle:

```
public void clipRect(int x, int y, int width, int height);
```

Key Events

Canvas handles events at a lower level than the other Displayable subclasses. Although you can add Commands and respond to them, Canvas also includes a set of methods that handle interaction with the individual keys of a device.

The following methods are called whenever the user presses and releases a key:

```
protected void keyPressed(int keyCode)
protected void keyReleased(int keyCode)
```

The key code that is passed to these methods will most likely be one of the constants defined in Graphics, from KEY_NUM0 through KEY_NUM9 and including KEY_STAR and KEY_POUND. Devices may have more keys than this, which will be returned as device-specific key codes. Assuming there's an obvious mapping between the key and some Unicode character, the rule of thumb is that a key should have a code equal to its Unicode character value. Keys that don't have a Unicode mapping should use negative values. This means that, given a positive key code, you can find out the corresponding Unicode character by casting the int key code to char.

Note that key presses and key releases are separate events, which allows you considerable flexibility in how you design your user interface. The time between the press and the release could determine how high a game character jumps or how powerful a laser blast will be.

Depending on the device and the MIDP implementation, a key that is held down may spit out repeated key events. You can find out if repeated keys are supported by calling hasRepeatEvents(). If repeated key events are supported, the keyRepeated() method will be called with these events.

Finally, you can find a text description of a given key code by calling getKeyName().

The Game API offers a mechanism to bypass the key event callback methods. You can poll the state of the device's keys directly using a method in GameCanvas. For more information, see the following chapter.

Game Actions

Key codes may be useful in certain situations, but they're fairly specific to a device. MIDP offers a simple abstraction called a *game action* that makes it easier to map user key events to events that will be useful for games and other applications with specialized user interfaces.

The concept is simple: supply a key code to getGameAction(), and you'll receive a game action—one of the following values: UP, DOWN, LEFT, RIGHT, FIRE, GAME_A, GAME_B, GAME_C, or GAME_D. Basically game actions are a way to map the physical keys on a device to a set of video game buttons such as you might find on game platforms like Sega Genesis or Nintendo Game Boy.

To understand how this maps to a physical device, think about how you might map the UP, DOWN, LEFT, and RIGHT game actions to keys. On the WTK emulator, there are navigation keys that have an obvious relationship to these game actions. Think about a simpler phone, however, one that has only a numeric keypad. In this case, you might want to map UP to the 2 key, DOWN to the 8 key, LEFT to the 4 key, and RIGHT to the 6 key.

Using game actions saves you from having to make these decisions yourself; the MIDP implementation simply provides a reasonable mapping for the device. To find the game action for a key code, pass the key code to getGameAction(). You can also find the key code for a game action by calling getKeyCode().

The following example listens for key presses in the keyPressed() method. It converts the key code to a game action and displays the game action on the screen.

```java
import javax.microedition.lcdui.*;

public class KeyCanvas
    extends Canvas {
  private Font mFont;
  private String mMessage = "[Press keys]";

  public KeyCanvas() {
    mFont = Font.getFont(Font.FACE_PROPORTIONAL,
        Font.STYLE_PLAIN, Font.SIZE_MEDIUM);
  }

  public void paint(Graphics g) {
    int w = getWidth();
    int h = getHeight();

    // Clear the Canvas.
    g.setGrayScale(255);
    g.fillRect(0, 0, w - 1, h - 1);
    g.setGrayScale(0);
    g.drawRect(0, 0, w - 1, h - 1);

    g.setFont(mFont);

    int x = w / 2;
    int y = h / 2;

    g.drawString(mMessage, x, y, Graphics.BASELINE | Graphics.HCENTER);
  }

  protected void keyPressed(int keyCode) {
    int gameAction = getGameAction(keyCode);
    switch(gameAction) {
      case UP:     mMessage = "UP";          break;
      case DOWN:   mMessage = "DOWN";        break;
      case LEFT:   mMessage = "LEFT";        break;
      case RIGHT:  mMessage = "RIGHT";       break;
      case FIRE:   mMessage = "FIRE";        break;
      case GAME_A: mMessage = "GAME_A";      break;
      case GAME_B: mMessage = "GAME_B";      break;
      case GAME_C: mMessage = "GAME_C";      break;
      case GAME_D: mMessage = "GAME_D";      break;
      default:     mMessage = ""; break;
    }
    repaint();
  }
}
```

To run this example, you'll need a corresponding MIDlet to display KeyCanvas. At this point, we think you should be able to do this by yourself.

Pointer Events

Some devices, particularly PDAs, may support a pointer. The popular Palm platform, for example, is based around the use of a stylus and a touch-sensitive screen. You can find out at runtime if your device supports pointer events by calling hasPointerEvents() and hasPointerMotionEvents(). If the device supports pointer events, the following methods get called when the pointer is pressed and released:

```
protected void pointerPressed(int x, int y)
protected void pointerReleased(int x, int y)
```

If the device supports pointer motion events, the following method will be called as the user drags the stylus around the screen:

```
protected void pointerDragged(int x, int y);
```

Double Buffering

Double buffering is a well-known technique for reducing flicker in drawing and animations. Imagine you are implementing an animation that clears and redraws the entire screen for each frame of the animation. Without double buffering, the animation will flicker badly as the screen is cleared and redrawn. With double buffering, the new frame is drawn into an off-screen image (the buffer). When the off-screen drawing is complete, the image is drawn on the screen in one smooth, quick move. You pay a price in the memory that's needed for the off-screen image, but the improvement in the quality of the animation is dramatic.

The MIDP implementation may provide double buffering by default. You can find out whether a Canvas is double buffered by calling the is DoubleBuffered() method.

If the implementation does not give you double buffering, you'll have to do it yourself. Fortunately, it's not terribly difficult. The process looks like this:

1. Create an off-screen image by calling the static Image.createImage(int width, int height) method.

2. Obtain a Graphics that draws *into the image* by calling getGraphics() on the Image.

3. Draw stuff into the off-screen image using the Graphics object.

4. In the paint() method of the Canvas, use drawImage() to put the off-screen image on the Canvas.

Here's a Canvas subclass that creates a simple off-screen image and displays it:

```
import javax.microedition.lcdui.*;

public class OffscreenCanvas
    extends Canvas {
  private Image mImage;


  public void paint(Graphics g) {
    if (mImage == null)
      initialize();
    g.drawImage(mImage, 0, 0, Graphics.TOP | Graphics.LEFT);
  }

  private void initialize() {
    int w = getWidth();
    int h = getHeight();

    mImage = Image.createImage(w, h);

    Graphics g = mImage.getGraphics();

    g.drawRect(0, 0, w - 1, h - 1);
    g.drawLine(0, 0, w - 1, h - 1);
    g.drawLine(w - 1, 0, 0, h - 1);
  }
}
```

Multithreading and Animation

As with any graphic-interface toolkit, threading with the MIDP user-interface classes is a little
tricky. The user-interface implementation has its own thread that handles both user-interface
methods and screen painting. For example, when the user presses a key on their device, the
implementation calls keyPressed() in your Canvas subclass. The thread that calls this method
belongs to the MIDP implementation. As such, it should be handled with some care. In MIDP
implementations, the same thread that calls event methods also calls paint().

■**Note** All event-driven user-interface toolkits have this idea of a system-owned user-interface thread.
In AWT and Swing, it's called the event dispatch thread. The same rule applies: if you're running inside
a thread that doesn't belong to you, don't take all day about it.

Methods that are called by a thread that doesn't belong to you are callbacks. The rule of
thumb for callbacks is that you shouldn't do anything that takes a long time. Since the thread
doesn't belong to you, you shouldn't hold it up a long time performing your work. Because this

thread is responsible for operating the user interface, holding it up with lengthy computations will make your application look lobotomized. Suppose, for example, that you had to retrieve some data from the network. In response to a command, you might do something like this:

```
public void commandAction(Command c, Displayable s) {
  if (c == mNetworkCommand) {
    // Create a progress screen, progressScreen.
    mDisplay.setCurrent(progressForm);
    // Now do the network stuff.
    // Oops! Users never see progressScreen.
  }
  // ...
}
```

The problem is that the progress screen won't be shown. The commandAction() method is called from the user-interface thread, the same thread that's responsible for painting the screen. If you tie up this thread with some lengthy processing of your own, the user-interface thread never has a chance to update the screen. If you need to do something that takes a long time, create a separate thread for it. In the Jargoneer example in Chapter 2, for example, network access was performed in a separate thread.

In certain situations, you will need to ask the user-interface thread to execute code on your behalf. If you are showing an animation, for example, you'll want to make sure that the frames of the animation are properly synchronized with the repainting cycle. Otherwise, you're likely to end up showing frames that are partially drawn.

Display has a mechanism for executing your code in the user-interface thread. It has a method, callSerially(), that accepts a Runnable. When the user-interface thread is ready, meaning when it has finished servicing all repaint requests, it will execute the run() method of the Runnable from the user-interface thread. A typical animation, then, looks like this:

```
public class AnimationCanvas
    extends Canvas
    implements Runnable {
  public start() {
    run();
  }

public void paint(Graphics g) {
    // Paint a frame of the animation.
  }

  public void run() {
    // Update our state.
    // Now request a paint of the new frame.
    repaint();
    Display.callSerially(this);
  }
}
```

You'd kick off the animation by calling start(), which in turn would simply call run(). Inside run(), you update your state and call repaint() to request the painting of a new frame. Then you use callSerially() to request that you get called again when the painting is done.

This technique results in an animation that runs as fast as the device allows. Many applications, however, need to provide a consistent experience across different devices. In these cases, it makes much more sense to use a separate animation thread with a consistent frame delay. The following example demonstrates this technique. It consists of two classes, Sweep and SweepCanvas. Sweep is a MIDlet that displays the class that actually implements the animation, SweepCanvas. The running SweepCanvas is shown in Figure 13-9.

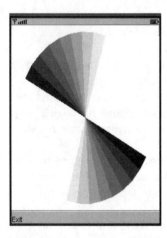

Figure 13-9. *SweepCanvas animation running on the WTK default emulator*

First, here's the source code for Sweep:

```
import javax.microedition.lcdui.*;
import javax.microedition.midlet.*;

public class Sweep
    extends MIDlet {
  public void startApp() {
    final SweepCanvas sweeper = new SweepCanvas();
    sweeper.start();

    sweeper.addCommand(new Command("Exit", Command.EXIT, 0));
    sweeper.setCommandListener(new CommandListener() {
      public void commandAction(Command c, Displayable s) {
        sweeper.stop();
        notifyDestroyed();
      }
    });
```

```
    Display.getDisplay(this).setCurrent(sweeper);
  }

  public void pauseApp() {}

  public void destroyApp(boolean unconditional) {}
}
```

And here's the code for SweepCanvas:

```
import javax.microedition.lcdui.*;

public class SweepCanvas
    extends Canvas
    implements Runnable {
  private boolean mTrucking;
  private int mTheta;
  private int mBorder;
  private int mDelay;

  public SweepCanvas() {
    mTheta = 0;
    mBorder = 10;
    mDelay = 50;
  }

  public void start() {
    mTrucking = true;
    Thread t = new Thread(this);
    t.start();
  }

  public void stop() {
    mTrucking = false;
  }

  public void paint(Graphics g) {
    int width = getWidth();
    int height = getHeight();

    // Clear the Canvas.
    g.setGrayScale(255);
    g.fillRect(0, 0, width - 1, height - 1);
```

```
    int x = mBorder;
    int y = mBorder;
    int w = width - mBorder * 2;
    int h = height - mBorder * 2;
    for (int i = 0; i < 8; i++) {
      g.setGrayScale((8 - i) * 32 - 16);
      g.fillArc(x, y, w, h, mTheta + i * 10, 10);
      g.fillArc(x, y, w, h, (mTheta + 180) % 360 + i * 10, 10);
    }
  }

  public void run() {
    while (mTrucking) {
      mTheta = (mTheta + 1) % 360;
      repaint();
      try { Thread.sleep(mDelay); }
      catch (InterruptedException ie) {}
    }
  }
}
```

The Game API offers another option for running an animation. In the next chapter, you'll see how Sweep's simple animation can be implemented using GameCanvas.

Summary

We've covered a lot of ground in this chapter. The Canvas class provides a low-level interface for games or other demanding applications. You can draw shapes, text, and images on a Canvas using the Graphics class. Furthermore, you can receive detailed input information about key and pointer events. Game actions are simple generalized input methods based on key events. Finally, you should understand the multithreading issues with repainting and event callbacks. Lengthy processing should be placed in a separate thread so that it doesn't bring the system-owned user-interface thread to a grinding halt. Animations can use Display's callSerially() method to synchronize with the user-interface thread, although more commonly they will be implemented using a separate animation thread. The next chapter details the Game API.

CHAPTER 14

■ ■ ■

The Game API

MIDP is an attractive platform for games, the leading edge of consumer J2ME software. In the next chapter, you'll read about the exciting new 3D graphics capabilities available, and in Chapter 16 you will read about MIDP's support for multimedia. This chapter describes the Game API, which simplifies writing 2D games.

Overview

The Game API builds on the Canvas and Graphics classes you read about in Chapter 13. The entire API is composed of five classes in the javax.microedition.lcdui.game package. One class, GameCanvas, provides methods for animation and key polling. The other four classes deal with layers, which can be used to compose scenes from several different elements.

GameCanvas offers two main advantages over Canvas. First, your application has control over exactly *when* the display is updated, instead of having to wait for the system software to call paint(). Second, you can control what region of the screen is updated. GameCanvas gives your application very specific control of display updates.

Driving Animation with GameCanvas

GameCanvas extends javax.microedition.lcdui.Canvas with methods for animation and key state polling. GameCanvas is used differently from Canvas:

- To use Canvas, you subclass it and define the paint() method. Inside paint(), you use Graphics to render graphics on the screen. When you change something and want to update the screen, you call repaint(), and the system calls paint() again for you.

- To use GameCanvas, you subclass it. To draw on the screen, you use the Graphics returned from getGraphics(). When you want updates to appear on the screen, call flushGraphics(), which does not return until the screen is updated. For more specific updates, use the method flushGraphics(int x, int y, int width, int height), which only updates a region of the screen.

```
public void flushGraphics(int x, int y, int width, int height)
```

GameCanvas's model of use makes it easy to use inside a game loop like this:

```
Graphics g = getGraphics();
while(true) {
  // Check for user input.
  // Update game state.
  // Draw stuff using g.
  flushGraphics();
}
```

To subclass GameCanvas, you need to call its protected constructor from your subclass's constructor. This constructor accepts a single boolean argument, which indicates whether the normal key event mechanism should be suppressed for the GameCanvas instance. The normal key event mechanism refers to the callback mechanism of keyPressed(), keyReleased(), and keyRepeated(). Suppressing the normal mechanism may result in better performance. GameCanvas provides an alternative method for responding to key events, which is detailed in the next section.

To show how GameCanvas works for drawing, we'll rewrite the SweepCanvas example from Chapter 13 using GameCanvas (see Listing 14-1). Note that the subclass no longer overrides paint(). All the action happens in run(), which is executed in a separate thread that drives the animation. The run() method calls render(), which does the actual drawing (and is identical to the old paint()).

Listing 14-1. *Using GameCanvas for Animation*

```
import javax.microedition.lcdui.*;
import javax.microedition.lcdui.game.*;

public class SweepGameCanvas
    extends GameCanvas
    implements Runnable {
  private boolean mTrucking;
  private int mTheta;
  private int mBorder;
  private int mDelay;

  public SweepGameCanvas() {
    super(true);
    mTheta = 0;
    mBorder = 10;
    mDelay = 50;
  }

  public void start() {
    mTrucking = true;
    Thread t = new Thread(this);
    t.start();
  }
```

```
public void stop() {
  mTrucking = false;
}

public void render(Graphics g) {
  int width = getWidth();
  int height = getHeight();

  // Clear the Canvas.
  g.setGrayScale(255);
  g.fillRect(0, 0, width - 1, height - 1);

  int x = mBorder;
  int y = mBorder;
  int w = width - mBorder * 2;
  int h = height - mBorder * 2;
  for (int i = 0; i < 8; i++) {
    g.setGrayScale((8 - i) * 32 - 16);
    g.fillArc(x, y, w, h, mTheta + i * 10, 10);
    g.fillArc(x, y, w, h, (mTheta + 180) % 360 + i * 10, 10);
  }
}

public void run() {
  Graphics g = getGraphics();
  while (mTrucking) {
    mTheta = (mTheta + 1) % 360;
    render(g);
    flushGraphics();
    try { Thread.sleep(mDelay); }
    catch (InterruptedException ie) {}
  }
}
}
```

We'll assume you can write your own MIDlet to display SweepGameCanvas. If you've downloaded the examples, SweepGame is a MIDlet that displays SweepGameCanvas.

Polling for Key States

GameCanvas offers an alternative method for responding to key presses, which are expected to be the way the user controls the game. Instead of passively waiting for the key event callbacks defined in Canvas, GameCanvas offers a method that returns the current state of the keys:

```
public int getKeyStates()
```

This is attractive for games because it gives your application more control. Instead of waiting for the system to invoke the key callback methods in Canvas, you can immediately find out the state of the device keys.

The returned integer uses one bit to represent each of the nine game actions. A one bit indicates a key press, while a zero bit indicates no key press. Each of the bits is represented by a constant in the GameCanvas class as shown in Table 14-1.

Table 14-1. *Game Action Bit Constants in GameCanvas*

GameCanvas Bit Constants	Corresponding GameCanvas Action Constants
UP_PRESSED	UP
DOWN_PRESSED	DOWN
LEFT_PRESSED	LEFT
RIGHT_PRESSED	RIGHT
FIRE_PRESSED	FIRE
GAME_A_PRESSED	GAME_A
GAME_B_PRESSED	GAME_B
GAME_C_PRESSED	GAME_C
GAME_D_PRESSED	GAME_D

By grabbing the current state of the keys (a technique called *polling*), you can respond to user actions within the game loop instead of relying on the event callback methods, which run in a different thread. You could expand the example GameCanvas loop presented earlier as follows to respond to key presses:

```
Graphics g = getGraphics();
while(true) {
  // Check for user input.
  int ks = getKeyStates();
  if ((ks & UP_PRESSED) != 0)
    moveUp();
  else if ((ks & DOWN_PRESSED) != 0)
    moveDown();
  // ...

  // Update game state.
  // Draw stuff using g.
  flushGraphics();
}
```

If you're still paying attention, you're probably wondering what happens when the user presses and releases a key between the times when your application calls getKeyStates(). The key states are *latched*, which means that a key press sets the corresponding bit and makes it stick until the next call to getKeyStates(). Every time you call getKeyStates(), the latched values are all cleared.

Understanding Layers

The rest of the Game API is devoted to *layers*. Layers are graphic elements that can be combined to create a complete scene. You might, for example, have a background of mountains, another background of city buildings, and several smaller items in the foreground: people, spaceships, cars, whatever.

The technique of combining layers resembles traditional hand-drawn animations. Background and foreground images are drawn on transparent cels, which are placed one on top of another and photographed to create the final scene.

In the Game API, an instance of the javax.microedition.lcdui.game.Layer class represents a layer. Layer is abstract, with two concrete subclasses. Layer itself is pretty straightforward. It has a location, a size, and can be visible or invisible. The location and size are accessed and modified with the following methods, which are self-explanatory:

```
public final int getX()
public final int getY()
public final int getWidth()
public final int getHeight()
public void setPosition(int x, int y)
```

Layer also offers a handy method for moving relative to the current position. Pass pixel offsets to the following method to adjust the position of the layer:

```
public void move(int dx, int dy)
```

The layer's visibility is accessed using getVisible() and setVisible().

The last method in Layer is paint(), which is declared abstract. Subclasses override this method to define their appearance.

Managing Layers

Before we tell you about Layer's concrete children, we'll explain how layers are put together to form a complete scene. You could do it yourself, maintaining a list of layers and drawing each of them using their paint() methods. Fortunately, the Game API includes LayerManager, a class that handles most of the details for you. To create a LayerManager, just call its no-argument constructor.

Most of LayerManager's job is keeping an ordered list of layers. Layers have an index, which indicates their position front to back. A position of 0 is on top, closest to the user, while larger indices are farther away, towards the bottom. (The order of layers is sometimes called the *z order*.)

Layers may be added to the bottom of the list using this method:

```
public void append(Layer l)
```

You can add a layer at a specific location using insert():

```
public void insert(Layer l, int index)
```

For example, you could add a layer to the top of the list by inserting a layer at index 0.

You can find the number of layers in the LayerManager by calling getSize(). If you'd like to retrieve the layer at a certain position, pass the index to the getLayerAt() method.

Finally, you can remove a layer by passing the Layer object to the remove() method.

LayerManager includes the concept of a *view window*, which is the rectangular portion of the scene that will be drawn. The assumption is that the overall scene is larger than the screen of the device, so only a portion will be drawn at any time. By default, the view window has its origin at 0, 0 and is as large as it can be (Integer.MAX_VALUE for both width and height). You can set the view window using the following method, where the x and y coordinates are relative to the origin of the LayerManager.

```
public void setViewWindow(int x, int y, int width, int height)
```

To actually draw the scene represented by the LayerManager's layers, call the paint() method:

```
public void paint(Graphics g, int x, int y)
```

The view window of the scene will be drawn using the given Graphics at the specified location, which is specified in the coordinate system of the Graphics.

If you're still fuzzy on the relationship between a layer manager, its layers, and its view window, see the API documentation for LayerManager, which contains two very helpful figures.

Using Tiled Layers

A tiled layer is made from a palette of tiles, just as you might assemble decorative tiles to create a pretty design next to your bathtub. The tiles come from a single image that is divided into equal-sized pieces.

A TiledLayer is drawn on a Graphics object using the paint() method inherited from Layer. Like any other Layer, a tiled layer renders itself at its current location in the coordinate system of the Graphics. Furthermore, like any other Layer, a tiled layer can be part of a LayerManager and can be rendered automatically when the LayerManager is rendered using *its* paint() method.

For example, Figure 14-1 is 240 pixels wide and 96 pixels high.

Figure 14-1. *A source image for a tiled layer*

The image can be divided into 10 square tiles, each with a width and height of 48 pixels. Tiles are numbered as shown in Figure 14-2.

1	2	3	4	5
6	7	8	9	10

Figure 14-2. *Tile numbering*

The image could have been laid out several different ways to achieve the same result. Two of the other possibilities are shown in Figure 14-3.

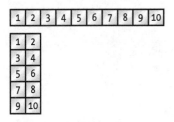

Figure 14-3. *Other tile image layouts*

Note that tile indices are numbered starting at one, while row and column numbers start at zero.

The tiled layer itself is a grid of *cells*, where each cell is occupied by one tile. You specify the number of rows and columns in the tiled layer at construction. The exact size of a tiled layer is as follows:

```
width = [number of columns] x [tile width]
height = [number of rows] x [tile height]
```

Creating and Initializing a TiledLayer

To create a TiledLayer, supply the number of columns and rows, the source image, and the tile dimensions to the constructor:

```
public TiledLayer(int columns, int rows,
    Image image, int tileWidth, int tileHeight)
```

The image and tile dimensions describe a *static tile set*. You can change the static tile set on an existing TiledLayer with the following method:

```
public void setStaticTileSet(Image image, int tileWidth, int tileHeight)
```

The number of columns and rows in a TiledLayer can be retrieved with getColumns() and getRows(). To retrieve the tile dimensions, use getCellWidth() and getCellHeight(). (Although the method naming isn't quite consistent, this works because the pixel size of each cell is the same as the pixel size of the tiles.)

A TiledLayer is empty when you first create it. To assign a tile to a cell, use this method:

```
public void setCell(int col, int row, int tileIndex)
```

All the cells in the TiledLayer are initially filled with tile index 0, which indicates a blank tile. You can retrieve the tile index of a particular cell by passing its column and row number to getCell(). If you would like to assign the same tile to a range of cells, use the fillCells() method:

```
public void fillCells(int col, int row, int numCols, int numRows,
    int tileIndex)
```

The col, row, numCols, and numRows parameters describe a rectangular region of cells that will be filled with the specified tile. For example, fillCells(2, 0, 1, 2, 6) would assign tile 6 to the cells in the first and second rows of the third column of the tiled layer.

The following excerpt (adapted from QuatschCanvas.java in the source code) demonstrates one way to create and initialize a TiledLayer:

```
Image backgroundImage = Image.createImage("/background_tiles.png");
TiledLayer background = new TiledLayer(8, 4, backgroundImage, 48, 48);
background.setPosition(12, 0);
int[] map = {
  1, 2, 0, 0, 0, 0, 0, 0,
  3, 3, 2, 0, 0, 0, 5, 0,
  3, 3, 3, 2, 4, 1, 3, 2,
  6, 6, 6, 6, 6, 6, 6, 6
};
for (int i = 0; i < map.length; i++) {
  int column = i % 8;
  int row = (i - column) / 8;
  background.setCell(column, row, map[i]);
}
```

Using the source image of Figure 14-1, this code produces the tiled layer shown in Figure 14-4.

Figure 14-4. *A tiled layer*

You now know almost everything there is to know about TiledLayer; it serves as a simple map between a palette of tiles and a fully assembled layer.

Using Animated Tiles

There is one additional twist: *animated* tiles. An animated tile is a virtual tile whose mapping can be changed at runtime. Although you could accomplish the same thing by calling setCell() on all the cells you wanted to change, using an animated tile allows you to make a single call that changes all the affected cells.

To use an animated tile, you create one by calling this method:

```
public int createAnimatedTile(int staticTileIndex)
```

You pass a regular tile index to the method, which is the initial tile that should be used for the animated tile. The method returns a special animated tile index. (There's no magic here; it's just a negative number.)

To assign an animated tile to a cell, pass the return value from `createAnimatedTile()` to `setCell()`. When you want to change the contents of an animated tile, use the following method:

```
public void setAnimatedTile(int animatedTileIndex, int staticTileIndex)
```

This assigns the supplied tile index to the animated tile. All cells that have the supplied animated tile will now display the given tile.

If you need to retrieve the current tile associated with an animated tile, just pass the animated tile index to `getAnimatedTile()`.

Using Sprites

While a `TiledLayer` uses a palette of tiles to fill a large area, a `Sprite` uses a palette of tiles to animate a layer that is the same size as a single tile. Usually a `Sprite` represents one of the protagonists in a game. In `Sprite` parlance, tiles are called *frames* instead. As with a `TiledLayer`, a `Sprite` is created from a source image that is divided into equally sized frames.

```
public Sprite(Image image, int frameWidth, int frameHeight)
```

There's also a special case—if the image contains just one frame, it will not be animated:

```
public Sprite(Image image)
```

Interestingly, a `Sprite` cannot be created from separate frame images; the frames must be packed into a single source image (this packing is better for compression).

If you want to change the source image after the `Sprite` is created, use `setImage()`:

```
public void setImage(Image img, int frameWidth, int frameHeight)
```

The total number of frames contained in the `Sprite` is returned from `getRawFrameCount()`.

Like any other `Layer`, Sprites are rendered when the `paint()` method is called. Usually the `Sprite` will belong to a `LayerManager`, in which case it is rendered automatically when the `LayerManager` is rendered.

Animating Sprites

Sprite animation is all about *frame sequences*. When a `Sprite` is created, it has a default frame sequence that includes every frame in the source image. For example, consider the source image for a fictional character named Dr. Quatsch, shown in Figure 14-5.

Figure 14-5. *A sprite source image*

This image is 192×48 pixels. If it is created with a 48×48-pixel frame size, there are four frames. The default frame sequence is { 0, 1, 2, 3 }. Note that frame indices are numbered starting at zero, while tile indices (in the TiledLayer class) are numbered starting at one.

In Figure 14-5, the first three frames represent Dr. Quatsch running, while the fourth is a frame that shows him standing still. The following method changes the current frame sequence:

```
public void setFrameSequence(int[] sequence)
```

For example, the following code shows how you could create a new Sprite and set its frame sequence to include only the running frames:

```
int[] runningSequence = { 0, 1, 2 };
Image quatschImage = Image.createImage("/quatsch.png");
Sprite quatsch = new Sprite(quatschImage, 48, 48);
quatsch.setFrameSequence(runningSequence);
```

Sprite provides several methods for navigating through the frame sequence. The animation doesn't happen automatically; your application needs to tell the Sprite when it's time to move to the next frame in the sequence. Usually this is accomplished in a separate thread, most likely as part of the animation thread. To move forward and backward in the sequence, use nextFrame() and prevFrame(). These methods do what you'd expect at the ends of the sequence, wrapping around to the next value. For example, using the frame sequence of { 0, 1, 2 }, if the Sprite's current frame is 2 and you call nextFrame(), the current frame will be set to 0.

You can jump directly to a particular frame using this method:

```
public void setFrame(int sequenceIndex)
```

Note that this method accepts a sequence index. If the Sprite's frame sequence is { 2, 3, 1, 9 }, then calling setFrame(1) would result in the Sprite's current frame being set to 3.

Nothing happens visually when you adjust the Sprite's current frame. Changes will only be visible the next time the Sprite is rendered using its paint() method. Typically, this will be at the end of your animation loop if you are using GameCanvas.

To find out the current frame sequence index, call getFrame(). Don't get confused here; the method does not return a frame index, but the current index in the current frame sequence. Interestingly, there is no getFrameSequence() method, so if you haven't saved the current frame sequence, there's no way to find out the current frame index. You can, however, retrieve the number of elements in the current frame sequence using getFrameSequenceLength().

Transforming Sprites

You may have noticed that the frames shown in Figure 14-5 only show Dr. Quatsch facing left. What if he's going to run to the right? Sprite includes support for *transformations* so that you can use the API to generate additional frames that are simple transformations of existing frames. This approach reduces the total number of stored images, effectively reducing resource (disk space, memory, etc.) usage. The following method applies a transformation to a Sprite:

```
public void setTransform(int transform)
```

The transform argument can be any of the constant values defined in the Sprite class:

```
TRANS_NONE
TRANS_ROT90
TRANS_ROT180
TRANS_ROT270
TRANS_MIRROR
TRANS_MIRROR_ROT90
TRANS_MIRROR_ROT180
TRANS_MIRROR_ROT270
```

To make Dr. Quatsch face right instead of left, you would apply a `TRANS_MIRROR` transformation. To understand all the transformations, see the `Sprite` API documentation, which contains a set of fighter plane images that are very helpful.

The only tricky part about transformations is the *reference pixel*. All `Sprite`s have a reference pixel, which is expressed in the `Sprite`'s own coordinate space; by default, the reference pixel is located at `0, 0`, the upper-left corner of the `Sprite`. When the `Sprite` is transformed, the reference pixel is also transformed.

When a transformation is applied, the `Sprite`'s position is changed so that the current location of the reference pixel does not change, even after it is transformed. For example, Figure 14-6 shows how the position of the `Sprite` changes when a simple `TRANS_MIRROR` transformation is applied.

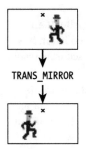

Figure 14-6. *The reference pixel doesn't move.*

Suppose, for example, that the original position of the `Sprite` was `100, 100` (in the coordinate system of the container), and the reference pixel position was `0, 0` (in the coordinate system of the `Sprite`). After applying a `TRANS_MIRROR` rotation, the `Sprite`'s position is adjusted so that the transformed reference pixel is in the same location as the original reference pixel. Because the frame width is 48 pixels, the `Sprite`'s position (its upper-left corner) changes from `100, 100` to `52, 100`.

To adjust the location of the reference point in the `Sprite`'s untransformed coordinate system, use this method:

```
public void defineReferencePixel(int x, int y)
```

In the case of Dr. Quatsch, we want to apply a mirror transformation without having the `Sprite` move, so we set the reference pixel to be at the center of the 48×48 frame:

```
// Sprite quatsch is defined as before.
quatsch.defineReferencePixel(24, 24);
```

To find the current location of the Sprite's reference pixel in its containing coordinate system, use getRefPixelX() and getRefPixelY(). Don't get confused: defineReferencePixel() accepts coordinates relative to the Sprite's origin, while getRefPixelX() and getRefPixelY() return values relative to the Sprite's container. It's also possible to set the position of the Sprite based on its reference point. You already know you can set the position of the Sprite's upper-left corner using the setPosition() method that is inherited from Layer, but the following method sets the current position of the Sprite's reference point:

```
public void setRefPointPosition(int x, int y)
```

This is more convenient than it might appear at first, as it allows you to place the reference point at a specific position, regardless of the current transformation.

Handling Collisions

Sprite provides methods to answer critical questions that come up in games—did the bullet hit the spaceship? Is Dr. Quatsch standing in front of the door?

The Game API supports two techniques for collision detection:

1. The implementation can compare rectangles representing a sprite and another sprite. A collision has occurred if the rectangles intersect. This is a quick way to test for collisions, but it may produce inaccurate results for nonrectangular shapes.

2. The implementation can compare each pixel of the sprite and another sprite. If an opaque pixel in the sprite overlaps an opaque pixel in the other sprite, a collision has occurred. This technique involves more computation but produces a more accurate result.

A Sprite has a *collision rectangle* that is used for collision detection. It is defined in the coordinate system of the Sprite itself, like the reference pixel. By default, the collision rectangle is located at 0, 0 and is the same width and height as the Sprite. You can change the collision rectangle using this method:

```
public void defineCollisionRectangle(int x, int y, int width, int height);
```

The collision rectangle serves two purposes. If pixel-level collision detection is not used, the collision rectangle is used to determine collisions. If pixel-level collision detection is used, then only pixels inside the collision rectangle are examined.

Sprite is capable of detecting collisions with other Sprites, TiledLayers, and Images.

```
public final boolean collidesWith(Sprite s, boolean pixelLevel)
public final boolean collidesWith(TiledLayer t, boolean pixelLevel)
public final boolean collidesWith(Image image,
    int x, int y, boolean pixelLevel)
```

The semantics of each method are subtly different, as described in Table 14-2.

Table 14-2. *Collision Detection with Sprite*

Target	Intersecting Rectangle	Pixel Level
Sprite	Compares collision rectangles	Compares pixels inside the collision rectangles
TiledLayer	Compares the Sprite's collision rectangle and tiles in the TiledLayer	Compares pixels inside the Sprite's collision rectangle with pixels in the TiledLayer
Image	Compares the Sprite's collision rectangle and the Image's bounds	Compares pixels inside the Sprite's collision rectangle with pixels in the Image

Copying Sprites

Sprite includes a copy constructor:

```
public Sprite(Sprite s)
```

This is more powerful than you might think. It creates a new Sprite with all of the attributes of the original, including

- Source image frames

- Frame sequence

- Current frame

- Current transformation

- Reference pixel

- Collision rectangle

Putting It All Together

QuatschCanvas, shown in Listing 14-2, is an example that showcases many of the features of the Game API. Although it looks long, it's broken into manageable methods and demonstrates quite a few features of the Game API:

- Using an animation loop in GameCanvas

- Polling for key state using GameCanvas

- Using a LayerManager to maintain multiple layers

- Creating a Sprite and TiledLayers

- Animating a Sprite, including changing frame sequences and transformations

- Using an animated tile in a TiledLayer

A corresponding MIDlet, QuatschMIDlet, is available in the code download but not presented here. It creates and displays a QuatschCanvas and provides commands for showing and hiding the layers.

Figure 14-7 shows QuatschMIDlet running in the emulator.

Figure 14-7. *The whole iguana: sprites and tiled layers*

Listing 14-2 contains the source code for QuatschCanvas.

Listing 14-2. *QuatschCanvas, a Game API Example*

```
import java.io.IOException;

import javax.microedition.lcdui.*;
import javax.microedition.lcdui.game.*;

public class QuatschCanvas
    extends GameCanvas
    implements Runnable {
  private boolean mTrucking;

  private LayerManager mLayerManager;

  private TiledLayer mAtmosphere;
  private TiledLayer mBackground;
  private int mAnimatedIndex;

  private Sprite mQuatsch;
  private int mState, mDirection;

  private static final int kStanding = 1;
  private static final int kRunning = 2;
```

```java
private static final int kLeft = 1;
private static final int kRight = 2;

private static final int[] kRunningSequence = { 0, 1, 2 };
private static final int[] kStandingSequence = { 3 };

public QuatschCanvas(String quatschImageName,
    String atmosphereImageName, String backgroundImageName)
    throws IOException {
  super(true);

  // Create a LayerManager.
  mLayerManager = new LayerManager();
  int w = getWidth();
  int h = getHeight();
  mLayerManager.setViewWindow(96, 0, w, h);

  createBackground(backgroundImageName);
  createAtmosphere(atmosphereImageName);
  createQuatsch(quatschImageName);
}

private void createBackground(String backgroundImageName)
    throws IOException {
  // Create the tiled layer.
  Image backgroundImage = Image.createImage(backgroundImageName);
  int[] map = {
    0, 0, 0, 0, 0, 0, 0, 0,
    0, 0, 0, 0, 0, 0, 0, 0,
    1, 2, 0, 0, 0, 0, 0, 0,
    3, 3, 2, 0, 0, 0, 5, 0,
    3, 3, 3, 2, 4, 1, 3, 2,
    6, 6, 6, 6, 6, 6, 6, 6
  };
  mBackground = new TiledLayer(8,6, backgroundImage, 48, 48);
  mBackground.setPosition(12, 0);
  for (int i = 0; i < map.length; i++) {
    int column = i % 8;
    int row = (i - column) / 8;
    mBackground.setCell(column, row, map[i]);
  }
  mAnimatedIndex = mBackground.createAnimatedTile(8);
  mBackground.setCell(3, 0, mAnimatedIndex);
  mBackground.setCell(5, 0, mAnimatedIndex);
  mLayerManager.append(mBackground);
}
```

```
private void createAtmosphere(String atmosphereImageName)
    throws IOException {
  // Create the atmosphere layer.
  Image atmosphereImage = Image.createImage(atmosphereImageName);
  mAtmosphere = new TiledLayer(8, 1, atmosphereImage,
      atmosphereImage.getWidth(), atmosphereImage.getHeight());
  mAtmosphere.fillCells(0, 0, 8, 1, 1);
  mAtmosphere.setPosition(0, 192);
  mLayerManager.insert(mAtmosphere, 0);
}

private void createQuatsch(String quatschImageName)
    throws IOException {

  // Create the sprite.
  Image quatschImage = Image.createImage(quatschImageName);
  mQuatsch = new Sprite(quatschImage, 48, 48);
  mQuatsch.setPosition(96 + (getWidth() - 48) / 2, 192);
  mQuatsch.defineReferencePixel(24, 24);
  setDirection(kLeft);
  setState(kStanding);
  mLayerManager.insert(mQuatsch, 1);
}

public void start() {
  mTrucking = true;
  Thread t = new Thread(this);
  t.start();
}

public void run() {
  int w = getWidth();
  int h = getHeight();
  Graphics g = getGraphics();
  int frameCount = 0;
  int factor = 2;
  int animatedDelta = 0;

  while (mTrucking) {
    if (isShown()) {
      int keyStates = getKeyStates();
      if ((keyStates & LEFT_PRESSED) != 0) {
        setDirection(kLeft);
        setState(kRunning);
        mBackground.move(3, 0);
        mAtmosphere.move(3, 0);
        mQuatsch.nextFrame();
      }
```

```
          else if ((keyStates & RIGHT_PRESSED) != 0) {
            setDirection(kRight);
            setState(kRunning);
            mBackground.move(-3, 0);
            mAtmosphere.move(-3, 0);
            mQuatsch.nextFrame();
          }
          else {
            setState(kStanding);
          }

          frameCount++;
          if (frameCount % factor == 0) {
            int delta = 1;
            if (frameCount / factor < 10) delta = -1;
            mAtmosphere.move(delta, 0);
            if (frameCount / factor == 20) frameCount = 0;

            mBackground.setAnimatedTile(mAnimatedIndex,
                8 + animatedDelta++);
            if (animatedDelta == 3) animatedDelta = 0;
          }

          g.setColor(0x5b1793);
          g.fillRect(0, 0, w, h);

          mLayerManager.paint(g, 0, 0);

          flushGraphics();
        }

        try { Thread.sleep(80); }
        catch (InterruptedException ie) {}
    }
  }

  public void stop() {
    mTrucking = false;
  }

  public void setVisible(int layerIndex, boolean show) {
    Layer layer = mLayerManager.getLayerAt(layerIndex);
    layer.setVisible(show);
  }
```

```
public boolean isVisible(int layerIndex) {
  Layer layer = mLayerManager.getLayerAt(layerIndex);
  return layer.isVisible();
}


private void setDirection(int newDirection) {
  if (newDirection == mDirection) return;
  if (mDirection == kLeft)
    mQuatsch.setTransform(Sprite.TRANS_MIRROR);
  else if (mDirection == kRight)
    mQuatsch.setTransform(Sprite.TRANS_NONE);
  mDirection = newDirection;
}

private void setState(int newState) {
  if (newState == mState) return;
  switch (newState) {
    case kStanding:
      mQuatsch.setFrameSequence(kStandingSequence);
      mQuatsch.setFrame(0);
      break;
    case kRunning:
      mQuatsch.setFrameSequence(kRunningSequence);
      break;
    default:
      break;
  }
  mState = newState;
}
}
```

Special Effects

Although they are not strictly contained in the Game API, two other methods in the Display class are closely related:

```
public boolean flashBacklight(int duration)
public boolean vibrate(int duration)
```

Both methods accept a duration in milliseconds that specifies how long the backlight should be turned on or how long the device should vibrate. Both methods return true to indicate success or false if the device does not support a backlight or vibration (or if your application is not running in the foreground).

Summary

This chapter described the Game API, a set of classes that simplify developing two-dimensional games. The GameCanvas class provides a drawing surface that can easily be rendered in a game thread. GameCanvas also provides key state polling, useful for detecting user input in a game thread. The remainder of the Game API is based on layers, which are elements that can be combined to create complex scenes. LayerManager makes it easy to maintain multiple layers. The Sprite class supports animation and collision detection. Large scenes or backgrounds can be constructed efficiently using TiledLayer. Finally, Display includes methods for controlling the backlight and vibration of a device. Game developers have a lot to be happy about. Read on to the next chapter and discover how to add 3D graphics to your MIDP applications and games.

CHAPTER 15

■ ■ ■

3D Graphics

The ability to use mobile communication devices to communicate via moving video images and interactive 3D graphics has long been a topic in science fiction and Hollywood movies. MIDP and MMAPI make video a reality. This chapter looks at JSR 184, the optional API for the rendering of 3D graphics.

Overview

A 3D graphics API is a prerequisite for easily developing 3D games. While 3D games are new to mobile devices such as cell phones, they are a staple and a growing market segment for desktop PCs. Many other applications for 3D graphics exist besides games, such as animated characters in user interfaces, architectural prototypes, and data visualization.

The Mobile 3D Graphics API, often called M3G, is an optional API that facilitates the display and manipulation of 3D graphics elements on mobile information devices. The M3G API 1.0 is fully specified in JSR 184; you can access this document here:

http://www.jcp.org/en/jsr/detail?id=184

Working with 3D graphics typically requires the computation of coordinates in floating point. Because of this, M3G can only be implemented on top of CLDC 1.1. CLDC 1.0 does not include floating-point support. To render 3D graphics onto the screen, M3G must be integrated with the user interface libraries on a device. This means that M3G will work well with familiar MIDP components such as Canvas, CustomItem, and GameCanvas.

Note Even though M3G requires CLDC 1.1's floating-point support, the API still attempts to use faster integer math wherever possible in order to work well on small devices that may not have floating-point hardware.

The actual M3G "3D engine" is usually implemented with the help of native libraries on the device. In many cases, it can be implemented on top of OpenGL ES. OpenGL has long been a robust and popular API for 3D rendering on workstations and PCs. OpenGL ES is the little cousin of OpenGL, a subset, and is becoming the de facto standard native 3D API for embedded devices. OpenGL ES is often found in game systems and other visual devices. Its popularity has made it a viable choice for mobile device vendors to include in their devices. The pairing of M3G with OpenGL ES is ideal since it greatly facilitates the implementation of M3G for mobile device vendors, allowing them to adopt 3D graphics with less effort (and cost). More information on OpenGL ES can be located at

```
http://www.khronos.org/opengles/
```

Figure 15-1 depicts the relationship between M3G, MIDP, OpenGL ES, and CLDC.

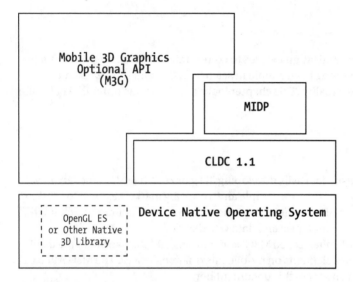

Figure 15-1. *M3G, MIDP, CLDC, and OpenGL ES relationship*

In Figure 15-1, you can see the dependence of M3G on CLDC, MIDP, and potentially a native 3D implementation such as Open GL ES.

Rendering 3D Graphics

The javax.microedition.m3g package contains all the 3D API classes.

Similar to the 2D Graphics context class that you get within the paint() method of a Canvas, you will need an instance of the Graphics3D class to render 3D graphics. Graphics3D is a singleton. You can obtain the one and only instance using this factory method:

```
static Graphics3D getInstance();
```

To render a single frame of 3D graphics, you need to follow these steps:

1. Obtain the Graphics3D instance.

2. Obtain a 2D Graphics instance (from Canvas, GameCanvas, etc.), which will be used to display the frame.

3. Bind the Graphics3D instance to the 2D Graphics instance; the frame of the 3D image will be drawn onto the 2D context.

4. Use the M3G API to set up and update the 3D scene.

5. Call one of the render() methods of Graphics3D to render a frame of the 3D scene.

6. Call the Graphics3D's releaseTarget() method to flush the rendered image to the 2D Graphics.

7. Call the 2D Graphic's flushGraphics() method to flush the drawing and update the visible component with the rendered frame.

The typical usage of M3G for 3D graphics rendering is very similar to a 2D game loop. When used in conjunction with a GameCanvas, it will look like the following:

```
Graphics g = getGraphics();
Graphics3D g3d = Graphics3D.getInstance();

while(true) {

        g3d.bindTarget(g);

        // ...
        // Perform setup of the 3D scene to render.
        // ...

        g3d.render(...);

        mGraphics3D.releaseTarget();
        flushGraphics();

}
```

If you compare the preceding rendering loop to the one used in the last chapter, in which we discussed the Game API, you will understand that it is essentially the same. The only exception is that now the M3G API is used to draw the graphics that will be displayed onto the 2D Canvas. In fact, this is the very essence of the M3G API: *it is used to draw graphics that represent a 3D scene onto a 2D display area.*

The M3G API encompasses many classes. Instead of covering all the details of every class in the confines of this chapter, only the foundations will be introduced. There will be three examples that allow you to see the API in action. These examples are designed for easy modification and experimentation with the full API.

To introduce some basic 3D graphics concepts and to cut through a bunch of frequently used M3G APIs, we'll start immediately with an example.

Getting Started with 3D

Many developers think that programming 3D graphics requires great mathematical skills. In reality, APIs such as M3G enable developers with little mathematical background to participate in the exciting world of 3D application programming.

Consider the TriangleMIDlet, shown in Figure 15-2. You can try it out from the source code download. This MIDlet simply rotates a triangle, which will appear red on your screen, in 2D when you start it. Watch it for a while.

Figure 15-2. *TriangleMIDlet rotating a 2D triangle*

You should be able to imagine how you'd create this animation program without using a single line of M3G code:

1. Create a subclass of Canvas.

2. In the paint() method of the Canvas (or the animation loop for a GameCanvas), you will draw the triangle, and then set a timer to repaint. In each successive repaint (frame), you will draw the triangle in a new position. The coordinates can be calculated using simple trigonometry.

3. Create a MIDlet to host the custom Canvas.

Figure 15-3 shows how you can animate the triangle in this MIDlet.

In Figure 15-3, initially the three vertices (0,0), (3,0), and (3,3) define the triangle. Subsequent frames of the animation rotate the triangle around the origin at (0,0).

Now that you are satisfied with your ability to create the same effect using MIDP's 2D graphics capability, we'll reveal to you that this animation is rendered using M3G. Yes, the M3G 3D API is used to rotate the triangle around the origin!

The geometry engine built into M3G understands the math of the rotation and recalculates the coordinates, plus redraws the triangle in each frame for you. All that you need to do is tell it the initial coordinates of the triangle and around what to rotate that triangle.

At this point, you are probably wondering what all of this has to do with 3D graphics. Here is the last secret that we have been keeping from you: the rotation you see in TriangleMIDlet is actually in 3D!

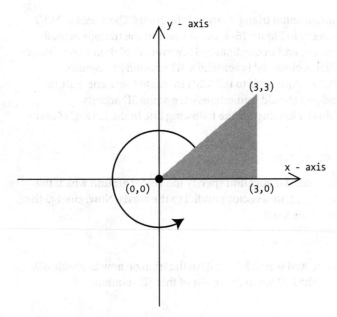

Figure 15-3. *Rotating a 2D triangle*

Rotating a Triangle in 3D

Take a quick look at Figure 15-4 to get an idea of what we mean.

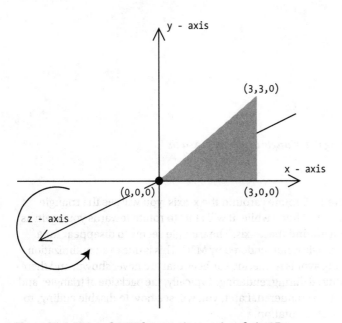

Figure 15-4. *TriangleMIDlet rotating a triangle in 3D*

M3G is actually rotating a 3-dimensional triangle around the z-axis. The z-axis in M3G points out towards you from the screen. In Figure 15-4, the vertices of the triangle actually point three dimensionally and have x, y, and z coordinates. However, all of their z coordinates have zero value. The 2D rotation that is observed is actually a 3D rotation in disguise.

If this is indeed the case, all that is required is to tell M3G to rotate the triangle around some axis other than the z-axis, and you should immediately see some 3D activity.

You can convince yourself of this by looking for the following line in the TriangleCanvas source code:

```
mTransform.postRotate(mAngle,  0, 0, 1.0f );
```

The last three numbers in this method invocation specify the vector around which the triangle will rotate—in this case (0, 0, 1), or a vector parallel to the z-axis. Now, change the vector to (1,0,0)—a vector parallel to the x-axis:

```
mTransform.postRotate(mAngle,  1.0f, 0, 0 );
```

Build the MIDlet and run it again, and watch M3G rotate the triangle now in visible 3D, around the x-axis! Figure 15-5 shows the MIDlet in the midst of this 3D rotation.

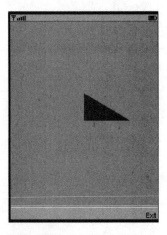

Figure 15-5. *TriangleMIDlet rotating the triangle around the x-axis*

The Effect of Culling

While the triangle shown in Figure 15-5 rotates around the x-axis, you will see the triangle disappear as it rotates away from you. After a while, it will start to rotate towards you again as it completes its clockwise rotation around the x-axis. The triangle seems to disappear for a moment because the back of the triangle is not rendered by M3G. This is due to an optimization technique known as *culling*. Culling avoids rendering surfaces that are never shown, and therefore saves on the computation required during rendering. Typically, the backside of triangles and polygons you define do not need to be rendered. Later, you will see how to disable culling, to make the triangle visible throughout its rotation.

Feeding M3G with Triangle Information

Examination of the code for TriangleCanvas will reveal how the triangle and rotation information is fed to M3G for rendering. The code for the TriangleCanvas is shown in Listing 15-1.

Listing 15-1. *The TriangleCanvas for Rotation of a Triangle in 3D*

```java
import javax.microedition.lcdui.Graphics;
import javax.microedition.lcdui.game.*;
import javax.microedition.m3g.*;

public class TriangleCanvas extends GameCanvas implements Runnable {
    private boolean mRunning = false;
    private Thread mPaintThrd = null;
    private Graphics3D mGraphics3D = Graphics3D.getInstance();
    private Camera mCamera = new Camera();;
    private Light mLight = new Light();
    private float          mAngle = 0.0f;
    private Transform      mTransform = new Transform();
    private Background     mBackground = new Background();
    private VertexBuffer   mVertexBuffer;
    private IndexBuffer    mIndexBuffer;
    private Appearance     mAppearance = new Appearance();
    private Material       mMaterial = new Material();
    public TriangleCanvas() {
        super(true);
    }

    public void init()  {

        short[] vertices = { 0, 0, 0,  3, 0, 0,   0, 3, 0 };
        VertexArray vertexArray = new VertexArray(vertices.length / 3, 3, 2);
        vertexArray.set(0, vertices.length/3, vertices);

        byte[] normals = { 0, 0, 127,    0, 0, 127,    0, 0, 127 };
        VertexArray normalsArray = new VertexArray(normals.length / 3, 3, 1);
        normalsArray.set(0, normals.length/3, normals);

        VertexBuffer verbuf = mVertexBuffer = new VertexBuffer();
        verbuf.setPositions(vertexArray, 1.0f, null);
        verbuf.setNormals(normalsArray);

        int[] stripLength = { 3 };
        mIndexBuffer = new TriangleStripArray( 0, stripLength );
```

```
            mMaterial.setColor(Material.DIFFUSE, 0xFF0000);
            mMaterial.setColor(Material.SPECULAR, 0xFF0000);
            mMaterial.setShininess(100.0f);
            mAppearance.setMaterial(mMaterial);

            mBackground.setColor(0x00ee88);

            mCamera.setPerspective( 60.0f,
            (float)getWidth()/ (float)getHeight(),
            1.0f,
            1000.0f );

            mLight.setColor(0xffffff);
            mLight.setIntensity(1.25f);

        }

        public void start() {
            mRunning = true;
            mPaintThrd = new Thread(this);
            mPaintThrd.start();
        }

        public void stop() {
            mRunning = false;
            try{
                mPaintThrd.join();}
            catch (InterruptedException ex){}
        }

        public void run() {
            Graphics g = getGraphics();

            while(mRunning) {

                if (isShown()) {

                    mGraphics3D.bindTarget(g);

                    mGraphics3D.clear(mBackground);

                    mTransform.setIdentity();
                    mTransform.postTranslate(0.0f, 0.0f, 10.0f);
                    mGraphics3D.setCamera(mCamera, mTransform);
```

```
            mGraphics3D.resetLights();
            mGraphics3D.addLight(mLight, mTransform);

            mAngle += 1.0f;
            mTransform.setIdentity();
            mTransform.postRotate(mAngle, 0, 0, 1.0f );
            mGraphics3D.render(mVertexBuffer, mIndexBuffer,
                                            mAppearance, mTransform);

            mGraphics3D.releaseTarget();
            flushGraphics();
            try {Thread.sleep(40); }
            catch(InterruptedException ie){
            }


        }
    } // of while
  } // of run()
}
```

You can probably write your own TriangleMIDlet to contain the TriangleCanvas. The one used for this example is reproduced in Listing 15-2.

Listing 15-2. *TriangleMIDlet to Contain the TriangleCanvas*

```java
import javax.microedition.midlet.*;
import javax.microedition.lcdui.*;
import java.util.*;

public class TriangleMIDlet extends MIDlet implements CommandListener {
    private Display mDisplay = null;
    private TriangleCanvas mCanvas = null;
    private Command exitCommand = new Command("Exit", Command.ITEM, 1);


    public TriangleMIDlet() {
        super();
        mDisplay = Display.getDisplay(this);
        mCanvas = new TriangleCanvas();
        mCanvas.setCommandListener(this);
        mCanvas.addCommand(exitCommand);
    }

    public void startApp() {
        mCanvas.init();
        mDisplay.setCurrent(mCanvas);
        mCanvas.start();
    }
```

```
public void pauseApp() {
}

public void destroyApp(boolean unconditional) {
 mCanvas.stop();
}

public void commandAction(Command cmd, Displayable disp) {
    if (cmd == exitCommand) {
        try {
            destroyApp(false);
            notifyDestroyed();
        }
        catch(Exception e) {
            e.printStackTrace();
        }
    }
}
}
```

Lights, Camera, Action!

Creating a 3D scene is like shooting a film on a movie set. You need to create the objects to render, orchestrate their movement, set up light(s), and set up camera(s). The M3G API comes with a full set of classes to support this staging.

You can manually create the objects that will be rendered. In Listing 15-1, this involves the definition of the triangle and the rotation. The M3G engine needs to be informed of where the triangle is and what sort of appearance it should take on.

Defining Triangle Vertices

In Listing 15-1, the position of the initial triangle is specified in a VertexArray by the following code:

```
short[] vertices = { 0, 0, 0,   3, 0, 0,    0, 3, 0 };
VertexArray vertexArray = new VertexArray(vertices.length / 3, 3, 2);
vertexArray.set(0, vertices.length/3, vertices);
```

A VertexArray is an M3G class that holds an array of triplets—(x,y,z). The elements of the array may represent vertex position, normals, texture, or color coordinates. Many methods in M3G take VertexArray as an input argument. In Listing 15-1, it holds the three vertices of the triangle.

There are two set() methods for VertexArray:

```
void set(int firstVertex, int numVertices, byte[] values);
void set(int firstVertex, int numVertices, short[] values);
```

The first version works with 8-bit byte values, while the second one works with 16-bit short values. In Listing 15-1, the 16 bit version is used to fill the vertexArray variable. The decision of which version to use will depend on what you will be using the resulting VertexArray for. In the next section, you will see that normals in M3G are defined in a VertexArray containing 8-bit values.

Defining Normals

During 3D rendering, a normal at a vertex tells the 3D engine which side of a triangle gets color and lighting effects. For example, consider Figure 15-6.

Normals are pointing out of the page, along positive z-axis.

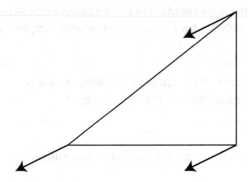

The side of the triangle that will be lighted and shaded is facing you.

Figure 15-6. *Using normals to indicate which side of a triangle gets lighting and effects*

The code from Listing 15-1 that defines the normals is shown here:

```
byte[] normals = { 0, 0, 127,    0, 0, 127,    0, 0, 127 };
VertexArray normalsArray = new VertexArray(normals.length / 3, 3, 1);
normalsArray.set(0, normals.length/3, normals);
```

The normal of a surface is always perpendicular (at 90 degrees) to the surface itself. In Figure 15-6, each of the normals specified corresponds to a vertex of the triangle, specified in vertexArray. For example, corresponding to the vertex (0,0,0), the normal is (0,0, 127); and corresponding to the vertex (0,3,0), the normal is (0,0,127). The set of normals for the triangle tells M3G that the side of the triangle facing you is the side to light and render.

Combining Vertex Information into a VertexBuffer

The M3G class VertexBuffer is used to combine the position of vertices, their normals, and other associated information into one single data structure. This allows the input of most of the information for the skeletal frame of a 3D object into one single data structure. In Listing 15-1, a VertexBuffer called verbuf is created using this code:

```
VertexBuffer verbuf = mVertexBuffer = new VertexBuffer();
verbuf.setPositions(vertexArray, 1.0f, null);
verbuf.setNormals(normalsArray);
```

The two methods used in VertexBuffer are as follows:

```
void setPositions(VertexArray position, float scale, float [] bias);
void setNormals(VertexArray normals);
```

The setPositions() method has a scale and bias that can be used to modify the position values. Since the input values are integer values (in the VertexArray), using a float scale and a float bias allow you to convert these values into floating point numbers. This is one example of a computation optimization used in M3G to cater for the limitations (that is, little or no hardware support for floating-point calculations) of mobile devices. If you do specify a scale and bias, the scale will be used to multiply each of the three coordinates by; the bias is a three-element array, whereby the element values will be added to the x, y, and z components, respectively.

■**Note** Specifying a float scale and bias can substantially slow down operations with a large VertexBuffer if the device in question does not have hardware floating-point support.

In Listing 15-1, no scaling or bias is used (by specifying a scale of 1 and null for bias).

Defining a Submesh with a TriangleStripArray

An object that can be rendered in M3G is contained in a submesh. In M3G 1.0, the only submesh available is a TriangleStripArray. The TriangleStripArray itself is a subclass of an IndexBuffer. An IndexBuffer, as its name implies, contain indices. An IndexBuffer is associated with a VertexBuffer; the indices contained in the IndexBuffer refer to the associated VertexBuffer. Specifically, the members of a TriangleStripArray tell M3G where the triangle strips are within the VertexBuffer. In Listing 15-1, the TriangleStripArray is defined with this code:

```
int[] stripLength = { 3 };
mIndexBuffer = new TriangleStripArray( 0, stripLength );
```

This tells M3G that only one single triangle is defined in the submesh, it starts at the index 0 in verbuf, and the number of indices occupied by this triangle is 3. In other words, M3G will use the first three indices in the verbuf VertexBuffer to render the object.

Giving Your Submesh an Appearance

In Listing 15-1, the code that associates an appearance with the triangle submesh is as follows:

```
Material mMaterial = new Material();
Appearance mAppearance = new Appearance();
Background mBackground = new Background();
....
```

```
mMaterial.setColor(Material.DIFFUSE, 0xFF0000);
mMaterial.setColor(Material.SPECULAR, 0xFF0000);
mMaterial.setShininess(100.0f);
mAppearance.setMaterial(mMaterial);

mBackground.setColor(0x00ee88);
```

An Appearance is an M3G class that groups together a set of objects that control how a submesh will appear when it is rendered. These objects are called *rendering attributes*. One of the rendering attributes is Material. As the name implies, the Material attribute controls the color and how light will reflect off the submesh being rendered. In the preceding code, the Material is set to be DIFFUSE and SPECULAR, with a red color (an RGB value of 0xFF0000). The possible values for the first parameter of the setColor() method of a Material are listed in Table 15-1.

Table 15-1. *Possible Values for Specifying the Reflective Quality of a Material's Color*

Value	Description
AMBIENT	The ambient color component, the color of the material that is revealed by ambient (evenly distributed) lighting
DIFFUSE	The diffuse color component, the color of the material that is revealed by a directional lighting
EMISSIVE	The emission color component, the color of the material that appears to be glowing
SPECULAR	The specular color component, the color displayed in the reflection highlights

The setShininess() method controls how shiny the material appears to be. It actually adjusts the concentration of the specular lighting component and can take on a value from 0 (dull) to 128 (very shiny).

The Background object is an M3G object that is used to render the background. You can specify either a color or an Image2D. These are the methods of Background to set color or image:

```
void setColor(int rgbColor);
void setImage(Image2D  image);
```

In the code in Listing 15-1, the Background of our rendering is set to a light green color (RGB value of 0x00ee88).

In summary, the code in the init() method of Listing 15-1 places a shiny red triangle against a light green background for the 3D rendering.

Setting Up Light and Camera

The last part of the init() method sets up the light and camera. Camera is an M3G class that controls what you see in the rendering. It has a position and an orientation. In addition, you can control other attributes such as the field of view, the aspect ratio, and clipping panes. These attributes tell M3G how much of the scene needs to be computed and rendered; anything outside of the field of view and clipping panes is not computed.

The following code from Listing 15-1 sets up the Camera to have a 60-degree field of view (controls how much of the scene you can see), an aspect ratio that is the same as the Canvas, and two clipping panes that allow you to see the entire triangle when it is rotated.

```
mCamera.setPerspective( 60.0f,  (float)getWidth()/ (float)getHeight(),
    1.0f, 1000.0f );

mLight.setColor(0xffffff);
mLight.setIntensity(1.25f);
```

Like a Camera, a Light is an M3G object that has a position and an orientation. It can also have other attributes such as a color, different modes (for example, spotlight versus diffused light), intensity, etc. Here, the color of our light is set to white (RGB 0xffffff), and its intensity is set to slightly brighter than default (default is a directional spotlight with an intensity of 1).

Transforms: Moving 3D Objects About

Each frame of a 3D animation is rendered through an iteration of the while loop within the run() method. A fragment of the code from this loop is reproduced here:

```
mGraphics3D.bindTarget(g);
mGraphics3D.clear(mBackground);

mTransform.setIdentity();
mTransform.postTranslate(0.0f, 0.0f, 10.0f);
mGraphics3D.setCamera(mCamera, mTransform);

mGraphics3D.resetLights();
mGraphics3D.addLight(mLight, mTransform);
```

Here is what is happening in the code:

- First, the Graphics3D instance is bound to the Canvas's Graphics context.

- Next, the Background is cleared out.

- Then the Camera and Light are moved around the scene.

Transform is an M3G object that can be used to move objects around the 3D world. To those familiar with 3D math, this type of object actually encapsulates a 4×4 matrix that will be multiplied with the coordinates of a 3D mesh to achieve scaling, translation, rotation, and orientation. However, it is not necessary to know the mathematical details to work with a Transform. A Transform has the following methods:

```
void setScale(float sx, float xy, float sz);
void setTranslation(float tx, float ty, float tz);
void preRotate(float angle, float ax, float ay, float az);
void postRotate(float angle, float ax, float ay, float az);
void setOrientation(float angle, float ax, float ay, float az);
```

The rotation and orientation methods take an angle and an axis of revolution as parameters. preRotate() is applied before the translation, and postRotate() is applied after the translation. Using these methods, you can manipulate the coefficients in the Transform matrix without knowing the math involved.

In the Listing 15-1 code, shown earlier in this section, the camera is moved to (0,0, 10). This is 10 units towards the viewer along the z-axis. When the camera is first created, it is located at (0,0,0) and pointing towards the z-axis (into the display).

The single light is also placed in the same position as the camera, giving the camera a "headlight" pointing at the direction of the view.

The final code in the rendering loop actually rotates the triangle submesh. The same Transform is reused here to save some memory. Calling setIdentity() on the Transform basically resets it to a Transform that performs no translation, scaling, or rotation. Then the postRotate() method is used to rotate the triangle one degree per frame around the axis of choice (z-axis in this case).

```
mAngle += 1.0f;
mTransform.setIdentity();
mTransform.postRotate(mAngle,          // Rotate 1 degree per frame
0, 0, 1.0f );
mGraphics3D.render(mVertexBuffer, mIndexBuffer,
                                      mAppearance, mTransform);
```

The call to render() will actually draw a 3D frame into the bound 2D Graphics instance. The Light and Camera have already been set up earlier using the Graphics3D instance. Notice how Graphic3D's render() method takes the VertexBuffer, the IndexBuffer (TriangleStripArray), the Appearance, and the Transform to perform its work.

Experimentation with Culling

TriangleCanvas is a great framework for experimenting with the M3G APIs. You can try moving the light, camera, and triangle around; or try working with different Material and Appearance attributes, etc. All you need is a copy of the Javadoc of the JSR 184 for reference.

As an example, we'll disable culling. Disabling culling will let you see the "back" of the triangle rendered. To add code to disable culling, look inside the init() method and insert the following highlighted code:

```
mAppearance.setMaterial(mMaterial);
PolygonMode tPoly = new PolygonMode();
tPoly.setCulling(PolygonMode.CULL_NONE);
mAppearance.setPolygonMode(tPoly);
mBackground.setColor(0x00ee88);
```

PolygonMode is an M3G class representing a rendering attribute. It is grouped by an Appearance instance and can be used to control culling. In this code, it is set to CULL_NONE, allowing the back of the triangle to be rendered. The default is CULL_BACK.

Assuming that you have modified TriangleCanvas to rotate the triangle around the x-axis, rebuild the MIDlet and run it. You should now see both sides of the triangle rendered during the rotation. Notice, however, that only the side with the vertex normals is rendered with light and color.

Understanding Triangle Strips

It is very important to understand what a triangle strip is and why it is used in M3G. As the name implies, a triangle strip is a strip of triangles. In TriangleCanvas, this strip contains just one single triangle. M3G allows for a strip with an arbitrary number of triangles.

Recall from basic geometry that any polygon can be decomposed into a number of triangles. This means that a triangle strip can be used to create any arbitrary polygon.

Because all triangles in a strip share common side(s) with others, TriangleStripArray in M3G can use a compact way of specifying vertices for multiple triangles. To specify one triangle, you will need three vertices; to specify two adjoining triangles, you will need only four vertices; to specify three, you need five vertices, and so on.

Take as an example a square composed of two triangles, as shown in Figure 15-7.

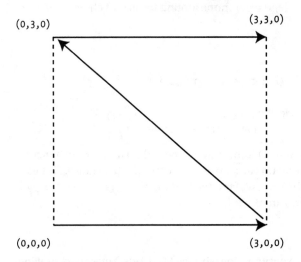

Figure 15-7. *Using four vertices to describe two triangles forming a square*

In Figure 15-7, you can see how four vertices—(0,0,0), (3,0,0), (0,3,0), and (3,3,0)—are sufficient to describe this strip of two triangles.

Modifying TriangleCanvas to Rotate a Square

We'll continue our experimentation with M3G APIs using TriangleCanvas by modifying it to display a rotating square instead of a triangle.

You will need to specify one more vertex for the triangle strip:

```
short[] vertices = { 0, 0, 0,  3, 0, 0,   0, 3, 0 ,  3,3,0 };
VertexArray vertexArray = new VertexArray(vertices.length / 3, 3, 2);
vertexArray.set(0, vertices.length/3, vertices);
```

One more vertex means an additional normal:

```
byte[] normals = { 0, 0, 127,   0, 0, 127,   0, 0, 127, 0,0, 127 };
VertexArray normalsArray = new VertexArray(normals.length / 3, 3, 1);
normalsArray.set(0, normals.length/3, normals);
```

The length of the `TriangleStripArray` instance also needs to be changed:

```
int[] stripLength = { 4};
mIndexBuffer = new TriangleStripArray( 0, stripLength );
```

Make the preceding modifications to the `TriangleCanvas` code, and rebuild and run it. You will see a red square rotating instead of a triangle. Using the same technique, you can create and rotate any abitrary polygon.

Rotating a 3D Corner Piece

The second example is actually an evolution of the `TriangleMIDlet`. It rotates a section of a cube in 3D. Try this out by running the `CornerMIDlet` example. When you copy over the source files, make sure you have included the `texture.png` file and placed it into the res directory of the WTK application. Figure 15-8 shows the `CornerMIDlet` running.

Figure 15-8. *CornerMIDlet rotating the corner of a cube*

In Figure 15-8, you see the corner of a cube that has a brick exterior being rotated in 3D. The code to perform this rotation is in the `CornerCanvas` class, which has the exact same general structure as `TriangleMIDlet`. The source code of `CornerCanvas` is shown in Listing 15-3.

Listing 15-3. *CornerCanvas—Rotating a Texture-Mapped Cube*

```
import javax.microedition.lcdui.*;
import javax.microedition.m3g.*;
import javax.microedition.lcdui.game.*;

public class CornerCanvas extends GameCanvas implements Runnable {
    private boolean mRunning = false;
    private Thread mPaintThrd = null;
```

```
private Graphics3D mGraphics3D = Graphics3D.getInstance();
private Camera mCamera = new Camera();;
private Light mLight = new Light();
private float          mAngle = 0.0f;
private Transform      mTransform = new Transform();
private Background     mBackground = new Background();
private VertexBuffer   mVertexBuffer;
private IndexBuffer    mIndexBuffer;
private Appearance     mAppearance = new Appearance();
private Material       mMaterial = new Material();
private Image          mImage;
public CornerCanvas() {
    super(true);
}

public void init()  {

    short[] vertices = {
        0, 0, 0,  3, 0, 0,  0, 3,  0,  3, 3,  0,
        3, 0, 0,  3, 3, 0,  3, 0, -3,  3, 3, -3,
        0, 0, 0,  3, 0, 0,  0, 0, -3,  3, 0, -3
    };

    VertexArray vertexArray = new VertexArray(vertices.length / 3, 3, 2);
    vertexArray.set(0, vertices.length/3, vertices);

    byte[] normals = {
        0,     0, 127,    0,    0, 127,    0, 0, 127,    0,    0, 127,
        127,    0,   0,  127,    0,   0,  127, 0,   0,  127,    0,   0,
        0,  -127,   0,    0, -127,   0,    0, -127, 0,    0, -127,   0
    };

    VertexArray normalsArray = new VertexArray(normals.length / 3, 3, 1);
    normalsArray.set(0, normals.length/3, normals);

    short[] texturecords = {
        0,1,    1,1,    0,  0,  1,  0,
        0,1,    0,0,    1,  1,  1,  0,
        0,0,    1,0,    0,  1,  1,  1 };

    VertexArray textureArray =
    new VertexArray(texturecords.length / 2, 2, 2);
    textureArray.set(0, texturecords.length/2, texturecords);
```

```
        VertexBuffer verbuf = mVertexBuffer = new VertexBuffer();
        verbuf.setPositions(vertexArray, 1.0f, null);
        verbuf.setNormals(normalsArray);
        verbuf.setTexCoords(0, textureArray, 1.0f, null);
        int[] stripLength = { 4, 4, 4};
        mIndexBuffer = new TriangleStripArray( 0, stripLength );
        try {
            mImage = Image.createImage( "/texture.png" );
        } catch (Exception ex) {
            ex.printStackTrace();
        }

        Image2D image2D = new Image2D( Image2D.RGB, mImage );
        Texture2D texture = new Texture2D( image2D );

        mAppearance.setTexture(0, texture);
        mAppearance.setMaterial(mMaterial);
        mMaterial.setColor(Material.DIFFUSE, 0xffffffff);
        mMaterial.setColor(Material.SPECULAR, 0xffffffff);
        mMaterial.setShininess(100.0f);

        PolygonMode tPoly = new PolygonMode();
        tPoly.setCulling(PolygonMode.CULL_NONE);
        mAppearance.setPolygonMode(tPoly);
        mBackground.setColor(0xffeecc);

        mCamera.setPerspective( 60.0f,
        (float)getWidth()/ (float)getHeight(),
        1.0f,
        100.0f );

        mLight.setColor(0xffffff);
        mLight.setIntensity(1.25f);


    }


public void start() {
    mRunning = true;
    mPaintThrd = new Thread(this);
    mPaintThrd.start();
}
```

```java
    public void stop() {
        mRunning = false;
        try{
            mPaintThrd.join();}
        catch (InterruptedException ex){}
    }

    public void run() {
        Graphics g = getGraphics();

        while(mRunning) {

            if (isShown()) {

                mGraphics3D.bindTarget(g, true,
                Graphics3D.DITHER |
                Graphics3D.TRUE_COLOR);

                mGraphics3D.clear(mBackground);

                mTransform.setIdentity();
                mTransform.postTranslate(0.0f, 0.0f, 10.0f);
                mGraphics3D.setCamera(mCamera, mTransform);

                mGraphics3D.resetLights();
                mGraphics3D.addLight(mLight, mTransform);

                mAngle += 1.0f;
                mTransform.setIdentity();
                mTransform.postRotate(mAngle,
                1.0f, 1.0f, 1.0f );
                mGraphics3D.render(mVertexBuffer, mIndexBuffer,
                mAppearance, mTransform);

                mGraphics3D.releaseTarget();

                flushGraphics();
                try {Thread.sleep(40); }
                catch(InterruptedException ie){
                }

            }
        }
    }

}
```

Defining Triangle Strips for the Corner Submesh

The corner of the cube is defined as three separate triangle strips. The vertices for these strips are specified in the same vertex buffer and loaded into the M3G rendering engine via an index buffer—the TriangleStripArray. The TriangleStripArray keeps track of where one strip ends and another starts.

The vertices for each of the strips are as follows:

- Strip 1 (square in the x-y plane): (0,0,0), (3,0,0), (0,3,0), (3,3,0)

- Strip 2 (square in the y-z plane): (3,0,0), (3,3,0), (3,0,-3), (3,3,-3)

- Strip 3 (square in the x-z plane): (0,0,0), (3,0,0), (0,0,-3), (3,0,-3)

The code to create the vertexArray in Listing 15-3 is shown here:

```
short[] vertices = {
    0, 0, 0,   3, 0, 0,   0, 3,  0,   3, 3,  0,
    3, 0, 0,   3, 3, 0,   3, 0, -3,   3, 3, -3,
    0, 0, 0,   3, 0, 0,   0, 0, -3,   3, 0, -3
};

VertexArray vertexArray = new VertexArray(vertices.length / 3, 3, 2);
vertexArray.set(0, vertices.length/3, vertices);
```

Corresponding to the vertices, the normals are defined as follows:

```
byte[] normals = {
    0,      0, 127,    0,    0, 127,    0,  0,  127,    0,    0, 127,
    127,    0,   0,  127,    0,   0,  127,  0,    0,  127,    0,   0,
    0,   -127,   0,    0, -127,   0,    0, -127,  0,    0, -127,   0
};

VertexArray normalsArray = new VertexArray(normals.length / 3, 3, 1);
normalsArray.set(0, normals.length/3, normals);
```

Texture Mapping the Cube Exterior

To make the exterior of the cube take on a brick-like appearance, texture mapping will be used. *Texture mapping* is the action of painting a texture (an image) over a 3D surface, like using wrapping paper to wrap a gift.

Obviously, you will first need an image that represents a texture. M3G has the Image3D class, which can be used in a texture. Here is one of the constructors for Image3D:

```
public Image2D(int format, Object image);
```

The format parameter to the constructor can be one of the following:

```
Image2D.RGB
Image2D.RGBA
Image2D.ALPHA
Image2D.LUMINANCE
Image2D.LUMINANCE_ALPHA
```

The first constant is used for the RGB pixel format, such as the data from an MIDP Image object. The alpha channel is typically used to indicate transparency on systems that support it. Luminance is an alternative way of encoding pixel data, typically used for monochrome images.

The second parameter can be an Image object from MIDP, allowing texture images to be easily loaded from resource with code similar to the following:

```
mImage = Image.createImage( "/texture.png" );
Image2D image2D = new Image2D( Image2D.RGB, mImage );
```

Applying Texture Image to Triangle Strips

Once you have an image, you need to tell M3G how to map it to the triangle strips. This is done through another vertex attribute called a *texture coordinate*. Figure 15-9 shows how the texture is mapped to a surface (square) using texture coordinates.

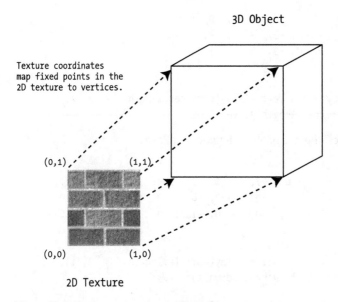

Figure 15-9. *Texture mapping a 3D surface*

In Figure 15-9, you can see that the texture coordinates essentially tell M3G how to place the texture on the surface by anchoring specific texture points to the vertices.

The code that performs the assignment of the texture coordinates to a VertexArray from Listing 15-3 is reproduced here:

```
short[] texturecords = {
    0,1,    1,1,    0,  0,  1,  0,
    0,1,    0,0,    1,  1,  1,  0,
    0,0,    1,0,    0,  1,  1,  1 };

VertexArray textureArray =
new VertexArray(texturecords.length / 2, 2, 2);
textureArray.set(0, texturecords.length/2, texturecords);
```

Since the texture is only in 2D, there is only an (x,y) coordinate associated with each vertex.

In TriangleCanvas, the vertices and normals are combined into a VertexBuffer for rendering. Here in CornerCanvas, the texture coordinate is added into the same VertexBuffer:

```
VertexBuffer verbuf = mVertexBuffer = new VertexBuffer();
verbuf.setPositions(vertexArray, 1.0f, null);
verbuf.setNormals(normalsArray);
verbuf.setTexCoords(0, textureArray, 1.0f, null);
```

A TriangleStripArray is then built to tell M3G where each of the four strips are within the VertexBuffer:

```
int[] stripLength = { 4, 4, 4};
mIndexBuffer = new TriangleStripArray( 0, stripLength );
```

Here, the first triangle strip starts at index 0 and has a length of 4. Subsequently, there are two more triangle strips of length 4.

The last piece of code that is required creates the texture from the Image2D and adds it to Appearance. Texture2D is a rendering attribute that is grouped by an Appearance object, just like Material and PolygonMode. The code from Listing 15-3 that is responsible for adding Texture2D to Appearance is shown here:

```
Texture2D texture = new Texture2D( image2D );
mAppearance.setTexture(0, texture);
```

That is all there is to the texture-mapping code. You should be able to see how you can build complex 3D scenes out of submeshes, applying texture and material to them, lighting them up, and then transforming them.

In reality, to create even a moderately complex 3D object—say, a jumping kangaroo—you may have to define hundreds of triangles. Even a simple 3D scene usually requires a few 3D objects, which means many vertices and a lot of M3G code! There must be a simpler solution.

Immediate Mode vs. Retained Mode

The simpler solution is to use the retained mode of the M3G API.

Thus far, all the examples have used the M3G API in immediate mode. Immediate mode provides low-level access to the rendering process, very close to the rendering engine. This level of access is similar to access provided by other industry-standard embedded 3D APIs such as OpenGL ES. Immediate mode works with the 3D scenes in terms of vertices, normals, transforms, appearance, etc.

Retained mode provides a significantly higher level of access to a 3D world (often called a *scene graph*).

High-Level Access to a Scene Graph via Retained Mode

A 3D world in retained mode can contain all the 3D objects in a scene prebuilt (all vertices, texture, normals, etc., specified) and in position; lights and cameras are predefined and in position, transformation can also be predefined, and animation can also be created beforehand.

The M3G application then simply activates or stages the animation and the transformation using high-level scene-graph control APIs.

The Elusive .m3g Serialized Scene Graph File Format

The 3D world used in retained mode is typically not painstakingly built using M3G APIs, but loaded from a file. In fact, JSR 184 specifies a file format, with the extension .m3g, that is used to store these serialized 3D worlds.

Using the retained mode in M3G literally involves the following steps:

1. Loading a complete serialized 3D world from a .m3g file

2. Rendering an animation using the newly loaded 3D world

What is not obvious, however, is how you would create the prefabricated 3D world (the .m3g file) in the first place. In fact, the M3G API cannot be used to create a .m3g file. There is no API call to serialize a 3D world.

Creating a .m3g File

The idea is to use a sophisticated 3D modeling package on a high-powered workstation (and not on your mobile device) to create your 3D world.

Once the world (all the objects, transformations, animations, etc.) are created, a .m3g file can then be generated. This .m3g file can then be moved to a mobile device and used within an application.

At the time of writing, however, very few sources exist for sophisticated 3D modeling packages that will generate .m3g worlds.

Superscape (http://www.superscape.com/) has a product called Swerve that can create these .m3g files. Unfortunately, Superscape has not yet made this tool available to the general public.

Autodesk's 3D Studio Max, Version 7 (http://usa.autodesk.com/) has the capability to export .m3g files. However, the exporter deals mainly with the creation of 3D objects, but does not have the ability to define and serialize animation.

HI Corporation (http://www.hicorp.co.jp/e_index.html) is also reported to have a .m3g exporter utility to export 3D models from Autodesk's 3D Studio Max and NewTek's LightWave.

So you see, it is not quite possible yet, unless you are up to creating your own 3D modeling tool, for you to easily make use of M3G's retained mode of operation.

Working with Retained Mode

Our last example will provide you with some hands-on experience with animating a retained mode 3D world.

Without the ability to create complete .m3g files, in this the example we'll use a prefabricated .m3g file from the Wireless Toolkit's 3D samples. This 3D world is created using Superscape's Swerve tool.

To try out this example, create a new project called RMMIDlet and copy the source code files into the src directory of the newly created application.

The .m3g file that you will need is called pogoroo.m3g. You can find it at the following path:

`<WTK 2.2 inst. dir.>/apps/Demo3D/res/com/superscape/m3g/wtksamples/pogoroo/content`

Copy this .m3g file to the res directory of the RMMIDlet project.

Now build and run the MIDlet. You will see a 3D kangaroo jumping up and down in front of you. Use the navigation keys on the phone emulator to move the camera around the kangaroo's world. Figure 15-10 shows the RMMIDlet in action.

Figure 15-10. *Interacting with a retained mode 3D world*

The custom GameCanvas subclass in this MIDlet is called RetainedCanvas. The source code for RetainedCanvas is shown in Listing 15-4.

Listing 15-4. *RetainedCanvas for Interacting with a Retained Mode 3D World*

```
import javax.microedition.lcdui.Graphics;
import javax.microedition.lcdui.game.*;
import javax.microedition.m3g.*;

class RetainedCanvas  extends GameCanvas implements Runnable {
    private boolean mRunning = false;
    private Thread mPaintThrd = null;

    private Graphics3D mGraphics3D = Graphics3D.getInstance();
    private World mWorld = null;
    private Camera mCam = null;
    private long mWorldStartTime = 0;

    public RetainedCanvas() {
        super(true);
    }
```

```java
public void init() {
    try {
        mWorld = (World) Loader.load("/pogoroo.m3g")[0];
        mCam = mWorld.getActiveCamera();
        mCam.translate(0, 0, -1.5f);
        mCam.setOrientation(180, 0, 1, 0);
    }
    catch(Exception e) {
        e.printStackTrace();
    }
    mWorldStartTime = System.currentTimeMillis();

}

public void start() {
    mRunning = true;
    mPaintThrd = new Thread(this);
    mPaintThrd.start();
}

public void stop() {
    mRunning = false;
    try{
        mPaintThrd.join();}
    catch (InterruptedException ex){}
}

public void run() {
    Graphics g = getGraphics();
    long startTime;

    while(mRunning) {

        if (isShown()) {
            int keyStates = getKeyStates();
            if ((keyStates & UP_PRESSED) != 0) {
                cameraForward();
            }
            else if ((keyStates & DOWN_PRESSED) != 0) {
                cameraBackward();
            }
            else if ((keyStates & LEFT_PRESSED) != 0) {
                cameraLeft();
            }
            else if ((keyStates & RIGHT_PRESSED) != 0) {
                cameraRight();
            }
```

```
            startTime = System.currentTimeMillis() - mWorldStartTime;
            mWorld.animate((int)startTime);
            mGraphics3D.bindTarget(g);
            mGraphics3D.render(mWorld);
            mGraphics3D.releaseTarget();
            flushGraphics();
            try {Thread.sleep(100); }
            catch(InterruptedException ie){
            }

        }
    } // of while
}


private void cameraForward() {
    mCam.translate(0f, 0f, 0.2f);
}
private void cameraBackward() {
    mCam.translate(0f, 0f, -0.2f);

}
private void cameraLeft() {
    mCam.translate(-0.2f, 0f, 0f);

}
private void cameraRight() {
    mCam.translate(0.2f, 0f, 0f);
}

}
```

You can write the MIDlet container class yourself, or download it from http://www.apress.com/.

Loading a Retained Mode 3D World

RetainedCanvas is a subclass of GameCanvas. This MIDlet takes advantage of GameCanvas's easy key polling and the simple rendering loop.

To load the retained mode world, an M3G Loader class is used. The sole purpose of a Loader is to load in and reconstitute an instance of an Object3D subclass. Object3D subclasses include many of the objects you've encountered, such as VertexBuffer, VertexArray, Material, PolygonMode, and so on. World is also an Object3D subclass.

A World is a complete serialized 3D world, including all the 3D objects, transformation, light, camera, animation, etc.

Also, a World is a specialized Group, another M3G class. A Group can contain multiple other Nodes. A Node can be a Camera, Mesh, Light, Group, or Sprite3D. This forms the data structure that allows a World to contain everything in a scene. The code from Listing 15-4 to load the .m3g file is as follows:

```
World mWorld;
...
mWorld = (World) Loader.load("/pogoroo.m3g")[0];
```

Once a World is created, you can use some of its methods to obtain familiar objects. The active Camera is obtained using this method:

```
Camera getActiveCamera();
```

The Background is obtained using this method:

```
Background getBackgroud();
```

In addition, the 3D modeling tool used to create the .m3g file will allow you to assign special integer IDs to any Object3D subclass that you create. You can then use the find() method to locate any object within the World:

```
Object3D find(int userID);
```

Retrieving the Active Camera in the Retained Mode World

In Listing 15-4, the Camera is retrieved from the World and moved to the front of the jumping kangaroo. The following code from the init() method illustrates this:

```
mCam = mWorld.getActiveCamera();
mCam.translate(0, 0, -1.5f);
mCam.setOrientation(180, 0, 1,  0);
```

It is necessary to change the orientation of the Camera. Initially, the Camera is facing the back of the kangaroo in the World defined within the .m3g file.

Rendering a Retained Mode World

Rendering a frame in retained mode is significantly simpler than in immediate mode. The code in the rendering loop that follow is from Listing 15-4:

```
startTime = System.currentTimeMillis() - mWorldStartTime;
mWorld.animate((int)startTime);
mGraphics3D.bindTarget(g);
mGraphics3D.render(mWorld);
mGraphics3D.releaseTarget();
flushGraphics();
```

The animate() method on the World is called to animate the hopping kangaroo (using predefined animation within the World). The entire World is rendered using the Graphic3D's retained mode rendering method:

```
void render(World world);
```

Also within the loop of the run() method is code to poll the keyboard and then move the Camera accordingly.

Summary

This chapter describes the Mobile 3D Graphics, or M3G, optional API specified by JSR 184. M3G, which brings powerful 3D rendering capability to mobile devices, has a high-level retained mode and a lower-level immediate mode of operation. Using the M3G API, you can render 3D graphics to a 2D MIDP component such as a Canvas by binding to the singleton Graphics3D instance.

In immediate mode, Graphics3D controls Lights for illuminating 3D scene and Camera to determine the portion of the scene that is displayed. You can create 3D meshes by specifying an array of triangle strips using the TriangleStripArray class. Each triangle strip contains vertices that describe a set of adjoining triangles. VertexArray is used to contain the vertices information, while a VertexBuffer holds associated normals as well as texture coordinates. An Appearance object can be associated with a triangle strip; it controls the material, culling, and texture map used during 3D rendering. A 3D object can be moved within the 3D scene by defining a Transform. A Transform provides scaling, translation, and rotation for a 3D object.

Retained mode allows a prefabricated 3D world to be loaded from a standard .m3g file. The entire world can be animated and rendered using the high-level retained mode API. In addition, the objects inside the world can be located and manipulated using immediate mode API calls.

CHAPTER 16

■ ■ ■

Sound, Music, and Video: MMAPI

MIDP includes basic audio capabilities. The media APIs are a strict subset of the Mobile Media API (MMAPI), a more general API for multimedia rendering. The full details on MMAPI are in JSR 135:

```
http://jcp.org/jsr/detail/135.jsp
```

The MMAPI itself is kind of a pint-sized version of the Java Media Framework (JMF), which is an optional package for J2SE. More information on the JMF is available here:

```
http://java.sun.com/products/java-media/jmf/
```

The subset of the MMAPI that is included is called the Audio Building Block (ABB). It includes the capability to play simple tones and sampled audio. The ABB is implemented in the javax.microedition.media and javax.microedition.media.control packages. This chapter covers all of MIDP's ABB support and the most commonly found features of MMAPI—including video handling. It begins with a rush of runnable code, and then backs off to explain some of the concepts and dig into the APIs more carefully.

Quick Start

You can play tones by calling this method in javax.microedition.media.Manager:

```
public static void playTone(int note, int duration, int volume)
```

In this method, note is specified just like a MIDI note, where each integer corresponds to a single key on a piano keyboard. Middle C is 60, and the A above middle C (a 440 Hz tone) is 69. The duration is in milliseconds, and volume can range from 0, silent, to 100, loudest.

Like most other methods in the ABB, playTone() may throw a MediaException. Although support for simple tones is required by the specification, the device may be temporarily unable to play tones. (For example, a mobile phone might be using the tone generation hardware to ring the phone.)

Figure 16-1 shows PianoCanvas, an example that displays a simple piano keyboard and allows the user to navigate through the keys to play different tones. PianoCanvas is presented in Listing 16-1. The code for playing the tones is very compact, consisting solely of a call to playTone() in the keyPressed() method. The rest of the code is devoted to the user interface.

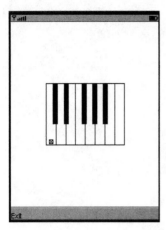

Figure 16-1. *An itty bitty piano*

Listing 16-1. *PianoCanvas Source Code*

```
import javax.microedition.lcdui.*;
import javax.microedition.media.*;

public class PianoCanvas
    extends Canvas {
  private static final int[] kNoteX = {
    0, 11, 16, 29, 32, 48, 59, 64, 76, 80, 93, 96
  };

  private static final int[] kNoteWidth = {
    16,  8, 16,  8, 16, 16,  8, 16,  8, 16,  8, 16
  };

  private static final int[] kNoteHeight = {
    96, 64, 96, 64, 96, 96, 64, 96, 64, 96, 64, 96
  };

  private static final boolean[] kBlack = {
    false, true, false, true, false,
        false, true, false, true, false, true, false
  };

  private int mMiddleCX, mMiddleCY;

  private int mCurrentNote;
```

```java
public PianoCanvas() {
  int w = getWidth();
  int h = getHeight();

  int fullWidth = kNoteWidth[0] * 8;
  mMiddleCX = (w - fullWidth) / 2;
  mMiddleCY = (h - kNoteHeight[0]) / 2;

  mCurrentNote = 60;
}

public void paint(Graphics g) {
  int w = getWidth();
  int h = getHeight();

  g.setColor(0xffffff);
  g.fillRect(0, 0, w, h);
  g.setColor(0x000000);

  for (int i = 60; i <= 72; i++)
    drawNote(g, i);

  drawSelection(g, mCurrentNote);
}

private void drawNote(Graphics g, int note) {
  int n = note % 12;
  int octaveOffset = ((note - n) / 12 - 5) * 7 * kNoteWidth[0];
  int x = mMiddleCX + octaveOffset + kNoteX[n];
  int y = mMiddleCY;
  int w = kNoteWidth[n];
  int h = kNoteHeight[n];

  if (isBlack(n))
    g.fillRect(x, y, w, h);
  else
    g.drawRect(x, y, w, h);
}

private void drawSelection(Graphics g, int note) {
  int n = note % 12;
  int octaveOffset = ((note - n) / 12 - 5) * 7 * kNoteWidth[0];
  int x = mMiddleCX + octaveOffset + kNoteX[n];
  int y = mMiddleCY;
  int w = kNoteWidth[n];
  int h = kNoteHeight[n];
```

```
    int sw = 6;
    int sx = x + (w - sw) / 2;
    int sy = y + h - 8;
    g.setColor(0xffffff);
    g.fillRect(sx, sy, sw, sw);
    g.setColor(0x000000);
    g.drawRect(sx, sy, sw, sw);
    g.drawLine(sx, sy, sx + sw, sy + sw);
    g.drawLine(sx, sy + sw, sx + sw, sy);
  }

  private boolean isBlack(int note) {
    return kBlack[note];
  }

  public void keyPressed(int keyCode) {
    int action = getGameAction(keyCode);
    switch (action) {
      case LEFT:
        mCurrentNote--;
        if (mCurrentNote < 60)
          mCurrentNote = 60;
        repaint();
        break;
      case RIGHT:
        mCurrentNote++;
        if (mCurrentNote > 72)
          mCurrentNote = 72;
        repaint();
        break;
      case FIRE:
        try { Manager.playTone(mCurrentNote, 1000, 100); }
        catch (MediaException me) {}
        break;
      default:
        break;
    }
  }
}
```

The ABB also offers support for playing sampled audio files, although the specification does not require support for this feature. To play sampled audio, you just need to get a Player for the data you wish to hear, and then start the Player running. You can get a Player by asking Manager for one. In its simplest form, playing sampled audio data looks like this:

```
URL url = "http://65.215.221.148:8080/wj2/res/relax.wav";
Player p = Manager.createPlayer(url);
p.start();
```

In this approach, the web server provides the content type of the data. Another approach is to obtain an InputStream to the audio data, and then create a Player by telling Manager the content type of the data. This is handy for reading audio files that are stored as resources in the MIDlet suite JAR. For example:

```
InputStream in = getClass().getResourceAsStream("/relax.wav");
Player player = Manager.createPlayer(in, "audio/x-wav");
player.start();
```

Listing 16-2 is a simple MIDlet that demonstrates both techniques.

Listing 16-2. *Playing Audio Files*

```
import java.io.*;

import javax.microedition.io.*;
import javax.microedition.lcdui.*;
import javax.microedition.midlet.*;
import javax.microedition.media.*;

public class AudioMIDlet
    extends MIDlet
    implements CommandListener, Runnable {
  private Display mDisplay;
  private List mMainScreen;

  public void startApp() {
    mDisplay = Display.getDisplay(this);

    if (mMainScreen == null) {
      mMainScreen = new List("AudioMIDlet", List.IMPLICIT);

      mMainScreen.append("Via HTTP", null);
      mMainScreen.append("From resource", null);
      mMainScreen.addCommand(new Command("Exit", Command.EXIT, 0));
      mMainScreen.addCommand(new Command("Play", Command.SCREEN, 0));
      mMainScreen.setCommandListener(this);
    }

    mDisplay.setCurrent(mMainScreen);
  }

  public void pauseApp() {}

  public void destroyApp(boolean unconditional) {}
```

```java
public void commandAction(Command c, Displayable s) {
  if (c.getCommandType() == Command.EXIT) notifyDestroyed();
  else {
    Form waitForm = new Form("Loading...");
    mDisplay.setCurrent(waitForm);
    Thread t = new Thread(this);
    t.start();
  }
}

public void run() {
  String selection = mMainScreen.getString(
      mMainScreen.getSelectedIndex());
  boolean viaHttp = selection.equals("Via HTTP");

  if (viaHttp)
    playViaHttp();
  else
    playFromResource();
}

private void playViaHttp() {
  try {
    String url = getAppProperty("AudioMIDlet-URL");
    Player player = Manager.createPlayer(url);
    player.start();
  }
  catch (Exception e) {
    showException(e);
    return;
  }
  mDisplay.setCurrent(mMainScreen);
}

private void playFromResource() {
  try {
    InputStream in = getClass().getResourceAsStream("/relax.wav");
    Player player = Manager.createPlayer(in, "audio/x-wav");
    player.start();
  }
  catch (Exception e) {
    showException(e);
    return;
  }
  mDisplay.setCurrent(mMainScreen);
}
```

```
  private void showException(Exception e) {
    Alert a = new Alert("Exception", e.toString(), null, null);
    a.setTimeout(Alert.FOREVER);
    mDisplay.setCurrent(a, mMainScreen);
  }
}
```

To play the audio file over the Internet, you will need to set up the MIDlet property AudioMIDlet-URL to have the following value:

```
http://65.215.221.148:8080/wj2/res/relax.wav
```

Playing MP3 Music

If your device supports the playback of MP3 music through MMAPI, the AudioMIDlet presented previously can be used to play MP3 music that is retrieved using HTTP by simply changing the AudioMIDlet-URL property to refer to an MP3 file. For example:

```
http://65.215.221.148:8080/wj2/res/mytrack.mp3
```

When you want to play an MP3 soundtrack from a resource file, you will need to change the following line in the playFromResource() method:

```
    InputStream in = getClass().getResourceAsStream("/mytrack.mp3");
    Player player = Manager.createPlayer(in, "audio/mpeg");
```

While the HTTP protocol enables the server to set the content, you must set the type explictly when playing back from a resource file. The content type string for MP3 is "audio/mpeg". (See http://www.iana.org/assignments/media-types/ for more types.) The next section explores content type further.

■**Note** Playback of MP3 files is not a mandatory requirement of MIDP or JTWI 1.0. In general, device manufacturers must pay additional licensing fees to implement MP3 playback. If your application or game needs to be usable across a variety of devices, it is wise not to have dependency on MP3 playback.

MMAPI Media Concepts

Audio data comes in a variety of *content types*. A content type is really just a file format, a specification that tells how each bit in the data contributes to the resulting sound. Common audio content types are MP3, AIFF, and WAV. In the MIDP 2.0 ABB, content types are specified using MIME types, which use a string to specify a primary and secondary type. For example, the MIME type for WAV audio is "audio/x-wav".

The content type tells how to translate bits into sound, but that's only half the battle. A *protocol* specifies how to get the data from its original location to the place where it will be rendered. You could use HTTP, for example, to transfer audio data from a server to a MIDP device.

In the ABB, a Player knows how to render audio data with a particular content type, while an associated *data source* handles transporting the data to the Player. In the Mobile Media API, the abstract DataSource class represents data sources. In the MIDP 2.0 ABB, data sources are not explicitly available, but implicitly associated with a Player. The path of the audio information is illustrated in Figure 16-2.

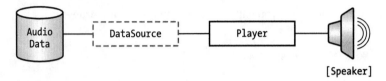

Figure 16-2. *Audio data path*

Manager doles out Players for content types and protocols requested via its createPlayer() methods. One or more *controls* may be associated with a Player to specify playback parameters like volume. In the ABB, javax.microedition.media.Control is an interface representing a control, while the javax.microedition.media.control package contains more specific subinterfaces. The relationship between the classes is shown in Figure 16-3.

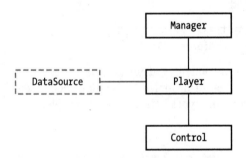

Figure 16-3. *Class relationships*

Supported Content Types and Protocols

One of the least understood aspects of the ABB is its supported content types. MIDP 2.0 is very flexible about the content types and protocols an implementation may support. All the specification says is that if sampled audio is supported at all, then 8-bit PCM WAV must be supported. Beyond that, the sky's the limit.

If you do ask Manager for data or a protocol that it can't handle, a MediaException will be thrown.

You can find out, at runtime, what content types and protocols are supported using two methods in the Manager class:

```
public static String [] getSupportedContentTypes(String protocol)
public static String [] getSupportedProtocols(String content_type)
```

You can find out the content types for a given protocol, or the protocols for a given content. If you supply null to either of these methods, you'll get a complete list of supported content types or protocols.

The MIDlet in Listing 16-3 finds all supported content types and prints out the corresponding protocols for each.

Listing 16-3. *Examining Content Types and Protocols at Runtime*

```java
import javax.microedition.lcdui.*;
import javax.microedition.midlet.*;
import javax.microedition.media.*;

public class MediaInformationMIDlet
    extends MIDlet
    implements CommandListener {
  private Form mInformationForm;

  public void startApp() {
    if (mInformationForm == null) {
      mInformationForm =
          new Form("Content types and protocols");
      String[] contentTypes =
          Manager.getSupportedContentTypes(null);
      for (int i = 0; i < contentTypes.length; i++) {
        String[] protocols =
            Manager.getSupportedProtocols(contentTypes[i]);
        for (int j = 0; j < protocols.length; j++) {
          StringItem si = new StringItem(contentTypes[i] + ": ",
              protocols[j]);
          si.setLayout(Item.LAYOUT_NEWLINE_AFTER);
          mInformationForm.append(si);
        }
      }
      Command exitCommand = new Command("Exit", Command.EXIT, 0);
      mInformationForm.addCommand(exitCommand);
      mInformationForm.setCommandListener(this);
    }

    Display.getDisplay(this).setCurrent(mInformationForm);
  }

  public void pauseApp() {}

  public void destroyApp(boolean unconditional) {}

  public void commandAction(Command c, Displayable s) {
    notifyDestroyed();
  }
}
```

Figure 16-4 shows the results if you run `MediaInformationMIDlet` on the J2ME Wireless Toolkit emulator (in the 2.0 beta 2 release). There are three things to understand about this list:

1. HTTP is a file transfer protocol, not a streaming media protocol. If you specify a media file with HTTP, the whole file will be downloaded before playback begins. By contrast, some devices may support real streaming protocols like RTP (see `http://www.ietf.org/rfc/rfc1889.txt`).

2. The "audio/x-tone-seq" content type is not really sampled audio; it's a special case for tone sequences, which we'll describe soon.

3. The list includes some features and content types (video, MIDI, audio capture) from the wireless toolkit's MMAPI implementation. If you want to see a bare-bones list of supported content types and protocols, turn off the MMAPI support as described later, in the section entitled "The Mobile Media API."

Figure 16-4. *MediaInformationMIDlet running on the toolkit's 2.0 beta2 emulator*

To find out the content type of an existing `Player`, just call `getContentType()`.

Player Life Cycle

Because playing audio may use scarce resources on a MIDP device, and because sampled audio files are relatively large, `Player` has a detailed life cycle that allows its behavior to be closely controlled. The life cycle is described in terms of *states*, represented by constants in the `Player` interface. The usual order of states in the `Player`'s life cycle is as follows:

A `Player` begins its life as `UNREALIZED`. This means that a `Player` implementation has been created, but it hasn't tried to find the audio data it's supposed to render, and it hasn't tried to acquire resources like the audio hardware.

A `Player` becomes `REALIZED` after it locates the media data, for example, by initiating a network connection and sending headers.

The next state, PREFETCHED, means the Player has done everything else it needed to do to get ready to start rendering audio. This might include obtaining control of the audio hardware, filling up buffers, or other operations.

When the Player has begun rendering audio data, it is in the STARTED state.

One final state, CLOSED, indicates that the Player has released all resources, shut down all network connections, and cannot be used again.

Player contains a corresponding set of methods that move from state to state:

```
public void prefetch()
public void realize()
public void start()
```

These methods work as you'd expect, for the most part. If you skip a step, the intervening states are implied. In the preceding example, we call start() on a freshly created Player, which implies calls to prefetch() and realize().

If anything goes wrong with locating the media data or acquiring system resources, these methods throw a MediaException.

Several other methods allow for backward state transitions, although their names are not as intuitive. The stop() method takes a STARTED Player back to PREFETCHED. The deallocate() method moves a PREFETCHED or STARTED Player back to the REALIZED state by releasing resources. The deallocate() method has one additional wrinkle; it will take an UNREALIZED Player that is stuck trying to locate its media (in the middle of realize()) back to the UNREALIZED state.

Finally, the close() method moves a Player in any state to CLOSED. All resources are released, all network connections are closed, and the Player cannot be used again.

You may retrieve the Player's current state by calling getState().

Now that you understand Player's life cycle, you can probably imagine ways to improve on the simple AudioMIDlet presented previously. You might, for example, call prefetch() on the newly created Player to ensure that playback could begin as soon as possible after the user selects the Play command. You might not have noticed much of delay, but a real device will perform much slower:

- Your desktop computer running the emulator has a lot more processing power and memory than a MIDP device.

- The emulator on your desktop probably has a much faster network connection than a real MIDP device.

- The file relax.wav that is used by AudioMIDlet is very small (1530 bytes). A larger media file would produce more noticeable delays.

As with network and persistent storage operations, any time-consuming operations with a Player should be performed in a thread that is separate from the user interface thread. Although the start() method does not block, both realize() and prefetch() will not return until they have finished their potentially slow work.

Controlling Players

A Player's *media time* is its current position in the audio playback. For example, a Player that is halfway through a 4-second audio clip would have a media time of 2,000,000 microseconds.

If you want to jump to a particular point in an audio clip, call setMediaTime(). You can find out the current media time using getMediaTime(). The total time represented by the audio clip is returned from getDuration(). For some types of streaming media, the duration cannot be determined, in which case the special value TIME_UNKNOWN will be returned.

Players can also loop, which means the audio clip is played over and over again. You can control this behavior by calling setLoopCount() before the Player is started. Pass a value of -1 to loop indefinitely.

Beyond the Player interface is a whole world of Controls. You can obtain a list of Controls for a Player by calling getControls() (a method Player inherits from the Controllable interface). This method returns an array of Controls that are appropriate for the Player. The ABB only defines a VolumeControl and a ToneControl, but implementations are free to provide other controls appropriate for the content types and protocols they support.

To obtain just one control, pass its name to Player's getControl() method (again inherited from Controllable). The name is the name of an interface in the javax.microedition.media.control package.

The Player must be in at least a REALIZED state to return its controls.

To use a VolumeControl to set playback volume to half its maximum, for example, you would do something like this:

```
// Player player = Manager.createPlayer(...);
player.prefetch();
VolumeControl vc = (VolumeControl)player.getControl("VolumeControl");
vc.setLevel(50);
```

Listening for Player Events

Player includes methods for adding and removing listeners that will be notified about various milestones in the Player's life:

```
public void addPlayerListener(PlayerListener playerListener)
public void removePlayerListener(PlayerListener playerListener)
```

PlayerListener defines a single method that is called with a variety of informational messages:

```
public void playerUpdate(Player player, String event, Object eventData)
```

The player parameter, of course, is the Player generating the event. The event is described by a string, event, and may include additional information, eventData. Constants in the PlayerListener interface describe common events: STARTED, END_OF_MEDIA, and VOLUME_CHANGED are a few. See the API documentation for the full list.

Tones and Tone Sequences

You've already seen how easy it is to play single tones using Manager. There's a somewhat more sophisticated tone sequence player lurking in the MIDP 2.0 media APIs. It's implemented within the Player and Control architecture, which is kind of a kluge, considering that tone sequences have little in common with sampled audio.

To obtain the tone sequence Player, just pass a special value (Manager's TONE_DEVICE_LOCATOR) to createPlayer(). If you examine TONE_DEVICE_LOCATOR, you'll see it is the value "device://tone", which kind of means a "device" protocol and an "audio/x-tone-seq" content type. You may remember seeing this in the output of MediaInformationMIDlet. As we said, it's kind of a kluge.

Once you've obtained the tone sequence Player, you can give it a tone sequence using its associated ToneControl object. To get this control, call getControl("ToneControl"). (Remember, the Player needs to be REALIZED first.)

ToneControl encapsulates a byte array whose syntax and construction is obtusely described in the API documentation. Master it and you'll be able to make any song into a monophonic masterpiece, Bobby McFerrin style. We'll describe the byte array format and present several examples.

The tones themselves are defined with note number and duration pairs. Note numbers are the same as for Manager's playTone() method, where 60 is middle C and 69 is the 440-Hz A above middle C. Duration is specified as multiples of the *resolution*. By default, the resolution of a tone sequence is 1/64 of one measure of 4/4 time (four beats). Therefore, a duration of 64 corresponds to a whole note (four beats), 16 corresponds to a quarter note (one beat), 8 is an eighth note, and so on.

All tone sequences must begin with a version. This is not the version of your data, but rather the version of the tone sequence format you're using. Currently the only accepted version is 1. A simple tone sequence looks like this:

```
byte[] sequence = new byte[] {
  ToneControl.VERSION, 1,
  67, 16, // The
  69, 16, // hills
  67,  8, // are
  65,  8, // a -
  64, 48, // live
  62,  8, // with
  60,  8, // the
  59, 16, // sound
  57, 16, // of
  59, 32, // mu -
  59, 32  // sic
};
```

This tone sequence relies on several default values. The default tempo is 120 beats per minute (bpm) and the default resolution is 1/64. The default volume is 100 (the loudest).

Other features are available in tone sequences. A reasonable amount of control is possible:

- Set the tempo by using the TEMPO constant and passing the tempo, in beats per minute, divided by four. For example, ToneControl.TEMPO, 15 sets the tempo to 60 bpm, or one beat per second. This may be done only once at the beginning of a sequence (following the VERSION).

- The resolution can be changed from its default of 1/64 using the RESOLUTION constant. The argument that is passed is the denominator, for example, using ToneControl.RESOLUTION, 64 will restore the default resolution of 1/64. This may be done only once at the beginning of a sequence (following the TEMPO).

- Reusable *blocks* of tones can be defined. To begin a block definition, use ToneControl.BLOCK_START and supply a block number. Then supply the notes and durations that go into the block. To end a block definition, use ToneControl.BLOCK_END and supply the same block number. To actually play a block, use ToneControl.PLAY_BLOCK and supply the number of the block you wish to play. Blocks must be defined following the VERSION, TEMPO, and RESOLUTION in a sequence.

- The volume can be set at any time during a sequence for dramatic dynamic effects. For example, ToneControl.SET_VOLUME, 25 sets the volume to one quarter of its maximum value.

- To indicate a rest of a certain duration, use the special note value ToneControl.SILENCE.

- You can repeat a single note multiple times. For example, ToneControl.REPEAT, 7, 60, 16 plays middle C (60) seven times with a duration of 16.

The MIDlet in Listing 16-4 contains several examples that will help you write your own tone sequences.

Listing 16-4. *Old Classics in Monophonic Glory*

```
import java.io.*;

import javax.microedition.io.*;
import javax.microedition.lcdui.*;
import javax.microedition.midlet.*;
import javax.microedition.media.*;
import javax.microedition.media.control.*;

public class ToneMIDlet
    extends MIDlet
    implements CommandListener {
  private final static String kSoundOfMusic = "Sound of Music";
  private final static String kQuandoMenVo = "Quando men vo";
  private final static String kTwinkle = "Twinkle number VII";

  private Display mDisplay;
  private List mMainScreen;

  public void startApp() {
    mDisplay = Display.getDisplay(this);

    if (mMainScreen == null) {
      mMainScreen = new List("AudioMIDlet", List.IMPLICIT);
```

```java
      mMainScreen.append(kSoundOfMusic, null);
      mMainScreen.append(kQuandoMenVo, null);
      mMainScreen.append(kTwinkle, null);
      mMainScreen.addCommand(new Command("Exit", Command.EXIT, 0));
      mMainScreen.addCommand(new Command("Play", Command.SCREEN, 0));
      mMainScreen.setCommandListener(this);
    }

    mDisplay.setCurrent(mMainScreen);
  }

  public void pauseApp() {}

  public void destroyApp(boolean unconditional) {}


  public void commandAction(Command c, Displayable s) {
    if (c.getCommandType() == Command.EXIT) notifyDestroyed();
    else run();
  }

  public void run() {
    String selection = mMainScreen.getString(
        mMainScreen.getSelectedIndex());

    byte[] sequence = null;
    if (selection.equals(kSoundOfMusic)) {
      sequence = new byte[] {
        ToneControl.VERSION, 1,
        67, 16, // The
        69, 16, // hills
        67,  8, // are
        65,  8, // a -
        64, 48, // live
        62,  8, // with
        60,  8, // the
        59, 16, // sound
        57, 16, // of
        59, 32, // mu -
        59, 32  // sic
      };
    }
```

```
  else if (selection.equals(kQuandoMenVo)) {
    sequence = new byte[] {
      ToneControl.VERSION, 1,
      ToneControl.TEMPO, 22,
      ToneControl.RESOLUTION, 96,
      64, 48, ToneControl.SILENCE, 8, 52, 4, 56, 4, 59, 4, 64, 4,
      63, 48, ToneControl.SILENCE, 8, 52, 4, 56, 4, 59, 4, 63, 4,
      61, 72,
      ToneControl.SILENCE, 12, 61, 12,
          63, 12, 66, 2, 64, 10, 63, 12, 61, 12,
      64, 12, 57, 12, 57, 48,
      ToneControl.SILENCE, 12, 59, 12,
          61, 12, 64, 2, 63, 10, 61, 12, 59, 12,
      63, 12, 56, 12, 56, 48,
    };
  }

  else if (selection.equals(kTwinkle)) {
    sequence = new byte[] {
      ToneControl.VERSION, 1,
      ToneControl.TEMPO, 22,
      ToneControl.BLOCK_START, 0,
      60, 8,          62, 4, 64, 4, 65, 4, 67, 4, 69, 4, 71, 4,
      72, 4, 74, 4, 76, 4, 77, 4, 79, 4, 81, 4, 83, 4, 84, 4,
      83, 4, 81, 4, 80, 4, 81, 4, 86, 4, 84, 4, 83, 4, 81, 4,
      81, 4, 79, 4, 78, 4, 79, 4, 60, 4, 79, 4, 88, 4, 79, 4,
      57, 4, 77, 4, 88, 4, 77, 4, 59, 4, 77, 4, 86, 4, 77, 4,
      56, 4, 76, 4, 86, 4, 76, 4, 57, 4, 76, 4, 84, 4, 76, 4,
      53, 4, 74, 4, 84, 4, 74, 4, 55, 4, 74, 4, 83, 4, 74, 4,
      84, 16, ToneControl.SILENCE, 16,
      ToneControl.BLOCK_END, 0,
      ToneControl.BLOCK_START, 1,
      79, 4, 84, 4, 88, 4, 86, 4, 84, 4, 83, 4, 81, 4, 79, 4,
      77, 4, 76, 4, 74, 4, 72, 4, 71, 4, 69, 4, 67, 4, 65, 4,
      64, 8,          76, 8,          77, 8,          78, 8,
      79, 12,                  76, 4, 74, 8, ToneControl.SILENCE, 8,
      ToneControl.BLOCK_END, 1,

      ToneControl.SET_VOLUME, 100, ToneControl.PLAY_BLOCK, 0,
      ToneControl.SET_VOLUME,  50, ToneControl.PLAY_BLOCK, 0,
      ToneControl.SET_VOLUME, 100, ToneControl.PLAY_BLOCK, 1,
      ToneControl.SET_VOLUME,  50, ToneControl.PLAY_BLOCK, 1,
      ToneControl.SET_VOLUME, 100, ToneControl.PLAY_BLOCK, 0,
    };
  }
```

```
  try {
    Player player = Manager.createPlayer(Manager.TONE_DEVICE_LOCATOR);
    player.realize();
    ToneControl tc = (ToneControl)player.getControl("ToneControl");
    tc.setSequence(sequence);
    player.start();
  }
  catch (Exception e) {
    Alert a = new Alert("Exception", e.toString(), null, null);
    a.setTimeout(Alert.FOREVER);
    mDisplay.setCurrent(a, mMainScreen);
  }
 }
}
```

Remember, Player's start() method does not block. If you want, you can start all three songs running simultaneously in the emulator. This works because the toolkit emulator is using a polyphonic device to play the tone sequences. On a real device, playing multiple sequences simultaneously is probably not possible. But you can set one sequence running, and assuming it doesn't suck up too much processor time, your MIDlet can go and do other tasks, like drawing a game display or connecting to a network.

The Mobile Media API

MIDP audio support is only a subset of the full power of the Mobile Media API. If you're using the J2ME Wireless Toolkit, its emulators support the full MMAPI by default. This means that you have other APIs available and several additional content types supported by the implementation.

If you'd like to remove MMAPI support, leaving only MIDP audio, click the *Settings* button from KToolbar; this will display the API Selection tab. You can uncheck the Mobile Media API (JSR 135) if you do not wish to use it.

Playing Video Using the MMAPI

You already know most of the concepts needed to play video on your phone. The great thing about the design of the MMAPI is that you can use the exact same approach to play video, as you have with audio.

You need to create a player, realize it, and then call start() on it to play video. These are the same steps as in the playback of audio. Only the content type and file extension change.

The VideoMIDlet code in Listing 16-5 is a modified version of the AudioMIDlet presented earlier. In this case, VideoMIDlet plays a MPEG1 video file, called fish.mpg, from the resource.

Look back at AudioMIDlet, compare the player creation code in the playFromResource() method of Listing 16-5:

```
          InputStream in = getClass().getResourceAsStream("/fish.mpg");
          mPlayer = Manager.createPlayer(in, "video/mpeg");
```

The only change is the content type, now "video/mpeg"; and the file name, now "/fish.mpg".

Displaying the Video

Unlike audio, which is played back through the speakers, video will take up some space on the user interface. MMAPI makes this quite simple. You have two choices:

- Display the video on a custom Canvas.

- Display the video as an Item within a Form.

In either case, you must first get hold of a VideoControl instance. You do this the same way you'd get a VolumeControl or ToneControl from an audio player:

```
(VideoControl) vidc = (VideoControl)  player.getControl("VideoControl");
```

Once you have this VideoControl instance, you can create either your custom Canvas class or a video Item for form-based display.

Video on Custom Canvas

If you want to display the video on a custom Canvas, you need to derive a class from Canvas. Say that your class is called VideoCanvas; the following code in the constructor will position and display the video:

```
public VideoCanvas(VideoControl videoControl) {

  videoControl.initDisplayMode(
      VideoControl.USE_DIRECT_VIDEO, this);

  try {
    videoControl.setDisplayLocation(5, 5);
    videoControl.setDisplaySize(getWidth()- 10, getHeight ()- 10);
  }
  catch (MediaException ex) {
    ....
  }
  videoControl.setVisible(true);
}
```

Note that you need to pass in the VideoControl instance during construction. The video display is created using the initDisplayMode() method, and the mode VideoControl.USE_DIRECT_VIDEO indicates to the VideoControl that you are working within a Canvas subclass. In this case, the video display takes up the entire VideoCanvas, with a 5-pixel border on all four sides.

Video on an Item Within a Form

Using an Item to display the video allows you to mix the video with other Items on a Form. The VideoMIDlet code in Listing 16-5 uses this approach. You can obtain an Item instance by calling the initDisplayMode() method using a mode of VideoControl.USE_GUI_PRIMITIVE:

```
(Item) mVideoItem = (Item)   mVideoControl.initDisplayMode(
          VideoControl.USE_GUI_PRIMITIVE, null);
mForm.append(mVideoItem);
```

The resulting Item can be immediately added to a form. Figure 16-5 shows VideoMIDlet running on the WTK emulator.

Figure 16-5. *Playing video with MMAPI*

■**Tip** The most common video content type supported by MMAPI is "video/mpeg" or MPEG-1 video. This is often called the VideoCD (VCD) format. It is the predecessor of MPEG-2, which is used in today's DVD products. While lower in resolution, MPEG-1 is more than adequate for the screen size found in today's mobile device. You can convert your video to MPEG-1 format easily using a variety of tools. An excellent free one can be found here: http://www.tmpgenc.net/.

Listing 16-5. *Playing Video Using MMAPI*

```
import java.io.*;
import javax.microedition.io.*;
import javax.microedition.lcdui.*;
import javax.microedition.midlet.*;
import javax.microedition.media.*;
import javax.microedition.media.control.*;
```

```java
public class VideoMIDlet
extends MIDlet
implements CommandListener, Runnable {
    private Display mDisplay;
    private Form mMainScreen;
    private Item mVideoItem;
    private VideoControl mVidc;
    private Command mPlayCommand;
    private Player mPlayer = null;


    public void startApp() {
        mDisplay = Display.getDisplay(this);

        if (mMainScreen == null) {
            mMainScreen = new Form("Video MIDlet");
            mMainScreen.addCommand(new Command("Exit", Command.EXIT, 0));
            mPlayCommand = new Command("Play", Command.SCREEN, 0);
            mMainScreen.addCommand(mPlayCommand);
            mMainScreen.setCommandListener(this);
        }

        mDisplay.setCurrent(mMainScreen);
    }

    public void pauseApp() {}

    public void destroyApp(boolean unconditional) {
        if (mPlayer != null)  {
                mPlayer.close();
        }

    }

    public void commandAction(Command c, Displayable s) {
        if (c.getCommandType() == Command.EXIT) {
            destroyApp(true);
            notifyDestroyed();
        }
        else {
            Form waitForm = new Form("Loading...");
            mDisplay.setCurrent(waitForm);
            Thread t = new Thread(this);
            t.start();
        }
    }
```

```
    public void run() {
        playFromResource();
    }


    private void playFromResource() {
        try {
            InputStream in = getClass().getResourceAsStream("/fish.mpg");
            mPlayer = Manager.createPlayer(in, "video/mpeg");

            mPlayer.realize();
            if ((mVidc = (VideoControl)
                            mPlayer.getControl("VideoControl")) != null) {
                mVideoItem = (Item)
                 mVidc.initDisplayMode(VideoControl.USE_GUI_PRIMITIVE, null);
                mMainScreen.append(mVideoItem);
            }

            mPlayer.start();
            mMainScreen.removeCommand(mPlayCommand);
            mDisplay.setCurrent(mMainScreen);
        }
        catch (Exception e) {
            showException(e);
            return;
        }
    }

    private void showException(Exception e) {
        Alert a = new Alert("Exception", e.toString(), null, null);
        a.setTimeout(Alert.FOREVER);
        mDisplay.setCurrent(a, mMainScreen);

    }

}
```

Snapping Pictures on a Camera Phone

An expensive executive toy in the past, cell phones with built-in cameras are now common-place and inexpensive. MMAPI offers your application access to the camera's picture taking ability.

The model is quite simple: the camera acts as a video player. The video displayed by this player will be the live action that the camera is viewing. At any time after the player starts, you can use the VideoControl to snap a still picture of the video.

If your camera phone has MMAPI support, you will be able to access it as a player using the URL "capture://video":

```
Player  mPlayer = Manager.createPlayer("capture://video");
```

You can then obtain a VideoControl instance from the player. This VideoControl can be used to show the live video on either a Canvas subclass or an Item within a form (shown in the previous section). At any time, you can capture a still picture by calling the getSnapshot() method of the VideoControl. You can specify a graphic format as a parameter (format supported depends on implementation), or use null to obtain the default (always supported) PNG format:

```
byte[] rawImg = mVidc.getSnapshot(null);
```

The returned byte array contains the raw image. This byte array can be converted to an Image using the call to Image's static factory method:

```
Image image = Image.createImage(rawImg, 0, rawImg.length);
```

WTK 2.x Camera Simulation

When using an emulator from the Wireless Toolkit, camera support in MMAPI is performed via simulated incoming video. The WTK does not support access to the underlying platform's video capture capability. This simplifies WTK maintenance and allows MMAPI snapshots to work over any platform, with or without camera support.

The simulated incoming video has a moving grid, with a seconds counter on the top left. This image ensures that every video frame is different from all the subsequent ones.

Listing 16-6 shows CameraMIDlet, which can be used to take snapshots using a camera phone. Figure 16-6 shows CameraMIDlet running on the emulator, with simulated camera video. The live video is displayed as an Item at the top of the form. You can click the Capture menu item, and a picture of the live video will be snapped and displayed below the video using an ImageItem.

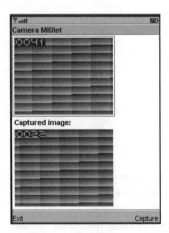

Figure 16-6. *Capturing images using simulated video on the WTK emulator*

Listing 16-6. *Capturing Images Using Your Camera Phone*

```java
import java.io.*;
import javax.microedition.io.*;
import javax.microedition.lcdui.*;
import javax.microedition.midlet.*;
import javax.microedition.media.*;
import javax.microedition.media.control.*;

public class CameraMIDlet
extends MIDlet
implements CommandListener, Runnable {
    private Display mDisplay;
    private Form mMainScreen;
    private Item mVideoItem;
    private VideoControl mVidc;
    private Command mCaptureCommand;
    Image mQMarkImg = null;
    private ImageItem mCapturedImgItem = null;
    private Player mPlayer = null;
    private boolean mEndNow = false;

    public void startApp() {
        mDisplay = Display.getDisplay(this);
        if (mQMarkImg == null)  {
            try {
               mQMarkImg = Image.createImage("/qmark.png");
              } catch (Exception ex) {
                 showException(ex);
            }
        }
        if (mMainScreen == null) {
            mMainScreen = new Form("Camera MIDlet");
            mMainScreen.addCommand(new Command("Exit", Command.EXIT, 0));
            mCaptureCommand = new Command("Capture", Command.SCREEN, 0);
            mMainScreen.addCommand(mCaptureCommand);
            mMainScreen.setCommandListener(this);
        }

        mDisplay.setCurrent(mMainScreen);
            Thread t = new Thread(this);
            t.start();
            mEndNow = false;
    }

    public void pauseApp() {}
```

```java
public void destroyApp(boolean unconditional) {

    if (mPlayer != null)  {
       mPlayer.close();
    }
    mEndNow = true;
    synchronized(this) {
      this.notify();
    }
}

public void commandAction(Command c, Displayable s) {
    if (c.getCommandType() == Command.EXIT) {
       destroyApp(true);
       notifyDestroyed();
    }
    else {
       // Capture
       synchronized(this) {
          this.notify();
       }
    }
}

public void run() {
    viewCamera();
    while(!mEndNow) {
       synchronized(this) {
          try {
          this.wait();
          } catch (InterruptedException ex) {
             // Ignore
          }
          if (!mEndNow)
          try {
          byte[] rawImg = mVidc.getSnapshot(null);
          Image image = Image.createImage(rawImg, 0, rawImg.length);
          mCapturedImgItem.setImage(image);
          } catch (MediaException ex) {
             continue;
          }

       }

    }
}
```

```
    private void viewCamera() {
        try {
            mPlayer = Manager.createPlayer("capture://video");
            mPlayer.realize();
            if ((mVidc = (VideoControl)
                            mPlayer.getControl("VideoControl")) != null) {
                mVideoItem = (Item)
                mVidc.initDisplayMode(VideoControl.USE_GUI_PRIMITIVE, null);
                int prefLayout = Item.LAYOUT_2 | Item.LAYOUT_LEFT |
                    Item.LAYOUT_NEWLINE_AFTER;
                mVideoItem.setLayout(prefLayout);
                mCapturedImgItem =
                new ImageItem("", mQMarkImg, prefLayout, "");
                StringItem lab = new StringItem("Captured image:", "");
                lab.setLayout(prefLayout);

                mMainScreen.append(mVideoItem);
                mMainScreen.append(lab);
                mMainScreen.append(mCapturedImgItem);
            }

            mPlayer.start();
            mDisplay.setCurrent(mMainScreen);
        }
        catch (Exception e) {
            showException(e);
            return;
        }
    }

    private void showException(Exception e) {
        Alert a = new Alert("Exception", e.toString(), null, null);
        a.setTimeout(Alert.FOREVER);
        mDisplay.setCurrent(a, mMainScreen);
    }
}
```

Summary

In this chapter, you learned about playing tones and sampled audio in MIDP. It utilized a subset of the Mobile Media API (MMAPI), the Audio Building Block (ABB). It is based on Players that know how to render audio data and implicit protocol objects that understand how to transport audio data to the Player. Aside from optional and flexible support for sampled audio, the ABB also includes a tone sequence player. In MMAPI, the same familiar Player and Control API model is used to display video and to snap pictures on a camera phone. Your MIDlets can now benefit from the excitement of music, sampled audio, and recorded video.

CHAPTER 17

■ ■ ■

Performance Tuning

MIDP is a small platform. The processor on a MIDP device will probably be much slower than a typical desktop computer processor, and the available memory will be much smaller also. Making your application run fast and lean is important. You'll need to use memory sparingly, make your application run fast enough to be easily usable, and structure it so that the code itself is as small as it can be.

This chapter describes simple methods for benchmarking your existing code. It then goes on to describe various optimizations that can make your code run faster or use less memory. Common sense will take you a long way, but this chapter is devoted to giving you the basic techniques for optimizing your application.

The important rule of thumb is this: only optimize where it's needed. Said another way: if it ain't broke, don't fix it. We suggest that your first pass at coding your application should concentrate on cleanliness and maintainability. If performance problems exist, identify them and begin optimizing. You shouldn't be optimizing code as you write it—that's just likely to result in hard-to-read, hard-to-maintain code. Write first, then test, then optimize.

Benchmarking

In the J2SE world, developers have many tools for examining the performance of code, the location of bottlenecks, and memory usage. Unfortunately, little of this is available in the J2ME world. For the most part, you'll have to perform benchmarking the old-fashioned way. For this, there are several methods in the MIDP API that will be useful. To test memory use, you can use the following methods in `java.lang.Runtime`:

```
public long freeMemory()
public long totalMemory()
```

The first method tells how much memory, in bytes, is currently available. The second method gives the total number of bytes in the current runtime environment, whether they are used for objects or not. Interestingly, this number can change because the host environment (device operating system) can give more memory to the Java runtime environment.

To find out how much memory an object uses, you can do something like this:

```
Runtime runtime = Runtime.getRuntime();
long before, after;
System.gc();
before = runtime.freeMemory();
Object newObject = new String();
after = runtime.freeMemory();
long size = before - after;
```

Aside from examining memory usage, you may also be concerned with the speed of your application. Again, you can test this the old-fashioned way—look at the clock before you start doing something, and then look at it again when you're finished. The relevant method comes from the `java.lang.System` class:

```
public static long currentTimeMillis()
```

You might calculate the execution time for a method like this:

```
long start, finish;
start = System.currentTimeMillis();
someMethod();
finish = System.currentTimeMillis();
long duration = finish - start;
```

For accurate timing, you should measure the duration multiple times and calculate an average.

Diagnostic Tools in the J2ME Wireless Toolkit

WTK 2.x contains three tools you can use to understand your application's performance characteristics.

The first tool is a memory monitor. You can see a graph of memory usage in your application over time or a detailed breakdown of every object in your application. Turn on the memory monitor by choosing Edit ➤ Preferences from the KToolbar menu. Click the Monitoring tab and check off Enable Memory Monitor. Next time you run the emulator, an additional window will pop up. You can examine the total memory used, which is useful when you're trying to make an application fit on a device with a limited heap size. (You can even set the heap size of the emulator in the Storage tab of the preferences window.) Figure 17-1 shows the memory monitor graph. You can click any column in the table to sort by that column. You can even search for specific items using View ➤ Find. Examining the memory monitor window will help you identify the places where memory is consumed most in your application.

Aside from the memory monitor, the toolkit also includes a *code profiler*—a tool that shows how much time is spent in every method in your application. To turn on the profiler, choose Edit ➤ Preferences from the KToolbar menu. Choose the Monitoring tab and check off Enable Profiling.

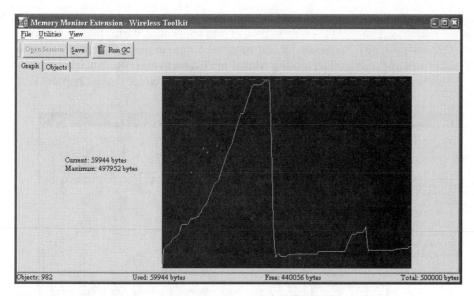

Figure 17-1. *Graph of memory use over time*

If you click the Objects tab in the memory monitor window, you'll see a detailed listing of the objects in your application. Figure 17-2 shows this view.

Name	Live	Total	Total Size	Average Size
java.util.TaskQueue	2	2	40	20
java.util.TimerTask[ ]	2	2	64	32
java.util.TimerThread	2	2	64	32
javax.microedition.lcdui.ImmutableImage	10	10	240	24
javax.microedition.lcdui.ImageItem	0	1	0	0
javax.microedition.lcdui.Display$DisplayManagerImpl	1	1	40	40
javax.microedition.lcdui.Display	3	4	144	48
javax.microedition.lcdui.Display$DisplayAccessor	3	4	72	24
com.sun.midp.lcdui.DisplayDeviceAccess	1	1	16	16
com.sun.midp.lcdui.EmulEventHandler	1	1	84	84
com.sun.midp.lcdui.DefaultEventHandler$QueuedEvent...	1	1	16	16
com.sun.midp.lcdui.DefaultEventHandler$EventQueue	1	1	68	68
com.sun.midp.lcdui.DefaultEventHandler$VMEventHan...	1	1	20	20
javax.microedition.lcdui.Graphics	1	1	92	92
short[ ]	2	2	48	24
java.lang.NullPointerException	0	1	0	0
com.sun.midp.dev.PersistentSelector	1	1	48	48
javax.microedition.midlet.MIDletStateMapImpl	1	1	12	12

Objects: 982   Used: 59944 bytes   Free: 440056 bytes   Total: 500000 bytes

Figure 17-2. *Objects and their memory*

You won't see the profiler until you exit the emulator. When you do, the profiler window pops up, summarizing time spent in every method in your application during the last emulator run. Note that what you do in the emulator will affect the output in the profiler; if you want to test the performance of your application as a whole, you'll have to exercise all of its options. Figure 17-3 shows the emulator after running the QuatschMIDlet example from Chapter 11.

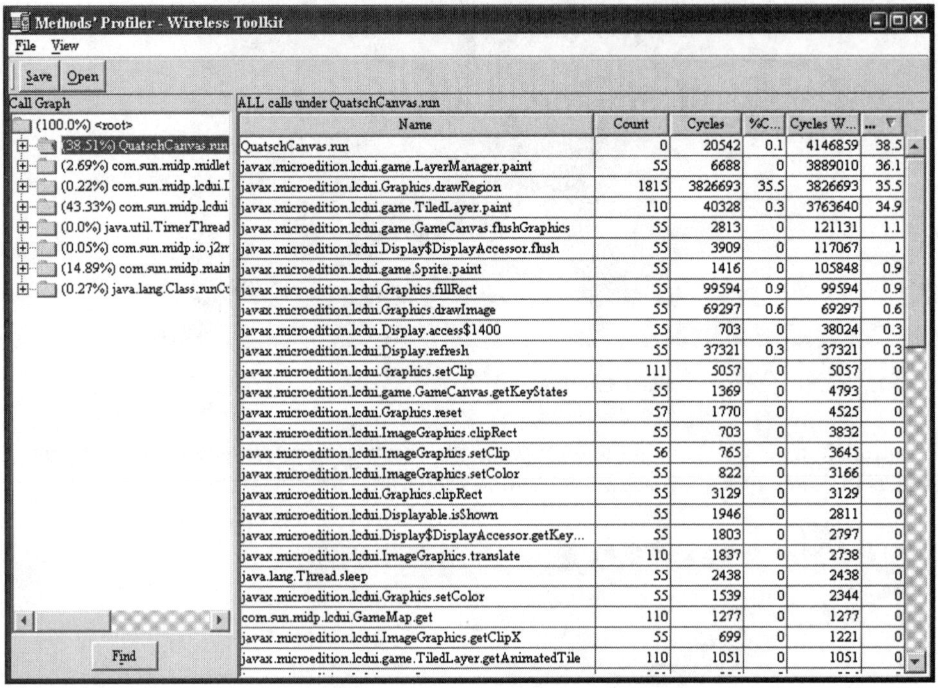

Figure 17-3. *The profiler times everything.*

Finally, the J2ME Wireless Toolkit also includes a network monitor. Although it's probably more useful for debugging network protocols than for optimization, it deserves mention here. To turn on the network monitor, choose Edit ➤ Preferences from the KToolbar menu. Choose the Monitoring tab and check off Enable Network Monitoring. Next time you run the emulator, a new window will pop up that tracks network usage. Figure 17-4 shows a few network interactions from the PeekAndPick application (http://developers.sun.com/techtopics/mobility/applications/peekandpick/2.0/index.html).

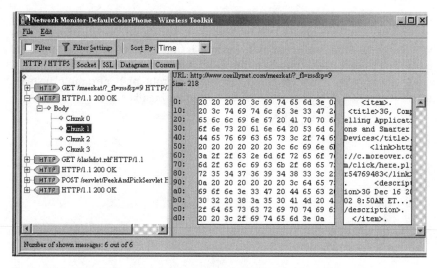

Figure 17-4. *Network activity from the PeekAndPick application*

Optimizing Memory Use

It's easy for J2SE programmers to be blasé about memory usage. After all, having a garbage collector means that you don't have to worry about explicitly freeing memory—objects that are no longer in use will be magically harvested by the garbage collector, running in a low-priority thread. In the J2ME universe, however, memory is scarce and should be treated with respect. Furthermore, both the allocation of memory and the work of the garbage collector can drag down the speed of your application. In this section, we'll look at techniques for efficient object use, particularly with `Strings` and `StringBuffers`. Finally, we'll talk about gracefully handling the situation when there really isn't any memory left.

Creating and Discarding Objects

If you're creating a new object inside a loop, it should be setting off alarm bells in your head. Every time you create an object (using `new`), memory is allocated. Allocating memory takes time. Worse, objects created at the beginning of a loop are likely to fall out of scope by the end of the loop, which means that each iteration through the loop pushes the runtime system closer to running the garbage collector. Here's an example:

```
// Set up the inputs and results arrays.
Object[] inputs = new Object[1000];
int[] results = new int[1000];
// Process each input to calculate a result.
int length = inputs.length;
for (int i = 0; i < length; i++) {
  Processor p = new Processor(inputs[i]);
  results[i] = p.calculateResult();
}
```

Creating objects in a loop imposes a double penalty in terms of performance. A new Processor is created every time through the loop; if these objects are large enough, then garbage collection may be forced one or more times before the loop is finished. You pay a price up front when the object is first created, then later when the object is garbage collected.

You can almost always restructure your code to avoid this problem. For example, instead of creating a new Processor for each input, you could do something like this:

```
// Set up the inputs and results arrays.
Object[] inputs = new Object[1000];
int[] results = new int[1000];
// Process each input to calculate a result.
int length = inputs.length;
Processor p = new Processor();
for (int i = 0; i < length; i++) {
  p.setInput(inputs[i]);
  results[i] = p.calculateResult();
}
```

Strings and StringBuffers

Strings have a special status in Java. They are the only objects for which the plus operator (+) is overloaded. Each time you concatenate strings using the plus operator, be wary—behind the scenes, new String and StringBuffer objects are being created for you.

String and StringBuffer share a curious relationship. When you can create and modify a StringBuffer, the actual work is performed on an internal character array. When you create a String from the StringBuffer, the String points to the same character array. Everything is fine so far, right? But if you further modify the StringBuffer, it cleverly creates a new character array, a copy of the old one. Thus, while StringBuffer is generally an efficient way to create Strings, it is not always obvious exactly when new objects are created.

The moral of the story is that every place you see string concatenation, there may be new objects being created. If you're assembling strings inside a loop, you should think about a different approach, possibly involving StringBuffer. Another possible optimization is to forego String and StringBuffer entirely and just use character arrays. While this may be a fast and efficient solution in your own code, keep in mind that many APIs require Strings as parameters and return Strings from methods, so you may end up doing a lot of conversion between character arrays and Strings.

Failing Gracefully

Given the paucity of memory in a typical MIDP device, your application should be prepared for disappointment each time it asks for memory. Each time objects are created, your code should catch java.lang.OutOfMemoryError. It is far better for you to catch OutOfMemoryErrors than for your host environment to catch them. You, at least, have a chance to do something reasonable— free up some memory and try again, or fail gracefully with a politely worded message to the user. The host environment is not likely to be so kind, and user perception of your application will be much worse. Bear in mind that you will probably need to free up memory by discarding large data structures before you will have enough space to create an Alert for your message to the user.

■Tip One possible strategy in production programming is an attempt to allocate all memory up front, when the application first starts.

Coding for Speed

Small devices have small, relatively slow processors. Part of your task as a developer is ensuring your application runs fast enough that users won't reject it.

Optimize Loops

One simple optimization has to do with looping. A typical loop through a Vector v might look like this:

```
for (int i = 0; i < v.size(); i++) {
  Object o = v.elementAt(i);
  // Process the Object o.
}
```

Each time through the loop, v's size() method is called. An optimized version would store the size of the vector first, like this:

```
int size = v.size();
for (int i = 0; i < size; i++) {
  Object o = v.elementAt(i);
  // Process the Object o.
}
```

This is a simple example, but it illustrates that loop conditions are one place you can look for speed optimizations.

Use Arrays Instead of Objects

Arrays are usually faster and leaner than collection classes. We touched on this theme earlier in our discussion of Strings and StringBuffers; if it's not too clumsy, using character arrays directly will probably be more efficient than dealing with String and StringBuffer objects. The same rule applies to the MIDP collection classes Vector and Hashtable. Although Vector and Hashtable are simple and convenient, they do impose some overhead that can be trimmed. Vector is basically just a wrapper for an array, so if you can work with an array directly, you'll save yourself some memory and processing time. Similarly, if you have a simple mapping of key objects to value objects, it might make sense to use object arrays instead of Hashtable.

If you do decide to use Hashtable or Vector, try to size them correctly when you create them. Both Vector and Hashtable grow larger as needed, but it is relatively expensive. Vector creates a new internal array and copies elements from the old array to the new array. Hashtable allocates new arrays and performs a computationally expensive operation called *rehashing*. Both Vector and Hashtable have constructors that allow you to specify the initial size of the collection. You should specify the initial size of these collections as accurately as possible.

If you are using the persistent storage APIs, you may be tempted to wrap stream classes around the record data. For example, you might read a record, then wrap a `ByteArrayInputStream` around the record's data, and then wrap a `DataInputStream` around the `ByteArrayInputStream` to read primitive types from the record. This is likely too heavy to be practical. If at all possible, work directly with the record's byte array.

Use Buffered I/O

Don't read bytes one at a time from a stream, and don't write them out one at a time. Although the stream classes provide methods that read and write a single byte, you should avoid them if at all possible. It will almost always be more efficient to read or write a whole array full of data. File and network access is usually quite slow.

J2SE includes `BufferedReader` and `BufferedWriter` classes that provide buffering functionality "for free." There is no such luxury in the MIDP universe, so if you want to use buffering, you'll have to do it yourself.

Be Clean

One simple piece of advice is to clean up after yourself. Releasing resources as soon as you are done with them can improve the performance of your application. If you have internal arrays or data structures, you should free them when you're not using them. One way to do this is to set your array reference to `null` so that the array can be garbage collected. You could even call the garbage collector explicitly with `System.gc()` if you're anxious to release memory back to the runtime system.

■**Caution** On most MIDP devices, continually acquiring and releasing resources can also degrade performance. This trade-off must be evaluated carefully.

Network connections should also be released as soon as you're done with them. One good way to do this is to use a `finally` clause. Consider the following code, which does not use a `finally` clause:

```
HttpConnection hc = null;
InputStream in = null;
try {
  hc = (HttpConnection)Connector.open(url);
  in = hc.openInputStream();
  // Read data from in.
  in.close();
  hc.close();
}
catch (IOException ioe) {
  // Handle the exception.
}
```

The problem occurs if an exception is thrown while you're trying to read data from the connection's input stream. In this case, execution jumps down to the exception handler, and the input stream and connection are never closed. In a J2SE environment, with memory to burn, this is probably not a big deal. But on a MIDP device, a hanging connection could be a disaster. When you absolutely, positively want to be sure to run some code, you should put it in a finally block like this:

```
HttpConnection hc = null;
InputStream in = null;
try {
  hc = (HttpConnection)Connector.open(url);
  in = hc.openInputStream();
  // Read data from in.
}
catch (IOException ioe) {
  // Handle the exception.
}
finally {
  try {
    if (in != null) in.close();
    if (hc != null) hc.close();
  }
  catch (IOException ioe) { }
}
```

This is starting to look a little ugly, particularly the try and catch inside our finally block. A cleaner solution would be to enclose this code in a method and declare that the method throws IOException. This cleans up the code considerably:

```
private void doNetworkStuff(String url) throws IOException {
  HttpConnection hc = null;
  InputStream in = null;
  try {
    hc = (HttpConnection)Connector.open(url);
    in = hc.openInputStream();
    // Read data from in.
  }
  finally {
    if (in != null) in.close();
    if (hc != null) hc.close();
  }
}
```

The deal with finally is that its code gets executed no matter how control leaves the try block. If an exception is thrown, or if somebody calls return, or even if control leaves the try block normally, our finally block still gets executed. Note that there is still a small amount of room for trouble here: if an exception is thrown when we try to close in, then hc will never be closed. You could enclose each close() call in its own try and catch block to handle this problem.

Being clean applies to any type of stream, record stores, and record enumerations. Anything that can be closed should be, preferably in a `finally` block.

Optimize the User Interface

It's important to remember that you are trying to optimize the *perceived* speed of your application, not the actual speed of the application. Users get fidgety if the application freezes up for a few seconds; adding some sort of progress indicator can go a long way toward making users happier. There's really nothing you can do to make the network run faster, but if you display a spinning clock or a moving progress bar, your application will at least look like it's still alive while it's waiting for the network.

Keep in mind that users of mobile phones and other small "consumer" devices will be much more demanding than typical desktop computer users. Through years of experience, bitter desktop computer users have fairly low expectations of their applications. They realize that most desktop applications have a learning curve and are frequently cantankerous. Consumer devices, on the other hand, are much more likely to work right the first time, requiring neither manuals nor advanced degrees to operate.

With this in mind, be sure that your MIDlet user interface is uncomplicated, fast, responsive, intuitive, and informative.

Optimizing Application Deployment

One last area of optimization has to do with the actual deployment of your application. As you may remember from Chapter 3, MIDlets are packaged in MIDlet suites, which are really just fancy JAR files. One way to optimize your application is to partition your classes so that only the ones you need are loaded into the runtime environment. If you are careful, you can reduce the size of your MIDlet suite JAR by eliminating classes you don't need. Finally, a code obfuscator may be used to further reduce the size of the MIDlet suite JAR.

■**Tip** In general, you should be careful not to use an excessive number of classes in your application. Each class you use has a fixed memory/storage overhead.

Partition Your Application

The MIDP runtime environment loads classes as they are needed. You can use this to your advantage to optimize the runtime footprint of your application. For example, suppose you write a datebook application that has the capability to send you reminder e-mails, or *ticklers*. You would probably realize that many people will not take advantage of the tickler feature. Why should tickler code take up space in a MIDP device if the user is not using ticklers? If you partition your code correctly, all of the tickler functionality can be encapsulated in a single class. If the rest of the application never calls the tickler code, the class will not be loaded, resulting in a slimmer runtime footprint.

Only Include Classes You Need

You may be using third-party packages in your MIDlet suite, like a cryptography package (see Chapter 18). For development, you might have simply dumped the whole package into your MIDlet suite. But come deployment time, you should prune out the excess packages to reduce the size of your MIDlet suite JAR. In some cases this will be fairly easy, like dumping out OBEX classes if you're only using the Bluetooth support. Other times it will not be so obvious which classes you need and which ones you can get rid of. However, if you really want to reduce your MIDlet suite JAR size, this is a crucial step. You don't need to do this by hand; an *obfuscator* will do the work for you.

Use an Obfuscator

Finally, a *bytecode obfuscator* can reduce the size of your class files. A bytecode obfuscator is a tool that is supposed to make it difficult to decompile class files. Decompilation is a process by which someone can re-create the source code that was used to make a particular class file. People who are worried about competitors stealing their code use obfuscators to make decompilation more difficult. However, obfuscation has the side effect of reducing class file size, mainly because the descriptive method and variable names you created are replaced with small machine-generated names. Some obfuscators will also remove unused code. If you're very serious about reducing the size of your MIDlet suite JAR, try obfuscating your code. We suggest running the obfuscator before preverifying the class files, but it's conceivable it would work the other way around, too. Here are two obfuscators to get you started:

```
http://proguard.sourceforge.net/
http://www.retrologic.com/retroguard-main.html
```

Summary

MIDP applications are targeted to run on a small platform, which means that using memory and processing power efficiently is important. Creating and destroying objects is expensive, so one way to optimize your code is to reduce the number of objects you create. One common source of new objects is code that creates Strings. Consider optimizing String manipulation using StringBuffer or character arrays. Similarly, you may be able to streamline code by using object arrays in place of Vectors or Hashtables. Remember that performance is as much about perception as anything else; provide a responsive, active user interface and handle failures gracefully. You can also optimize the delivery of your application in several ways. First, partitioning the functionality of your application intelligently can reduce the runtime footprint of your application. Next, trimming out excess classes can reduce the size of your MIDlet suite JAR. Finally, a bytecode obfuscator can further reduce the size of your MIDlet suite JAR.

CHAPTER 18

■ ■ ■

Protecting Network Data

MIDlets are undeniably cool—providing Java code that runs on a small device and HTTP network connectivity as well. But once you start thinking about the possibilities, you realize that a lot of applications just aren't possible without some form of data security. What if you were going to buy something? You shouldn't send credit card numbers over the Internet without some kind of protection, and you shouldn't send sensitive corporate information over the Internet to small devices. Many applications, then, need something else—something that keeps sensitive data from being stolen. The answer in the MIDP world is no different than the answer anywhere else: cryptography.

Cryptography Review

Cryptography is a branch of mathematics. It's based on the idea that certain kinds of mathematical problems are hard to solve. Using cryptography is a bit speculative; as research in mathematics continues, it's very possible that someone will discover a way to solve (or "break") most of the modern cryptographic algorithms. Nevertheless, for today at least, cryptography provides protection for sensitive data, and there aren't many acceptable alternatives in the everything-connects-to-everything modern world.

The Internet Is a Big Room

There are many aspects to the security of a system. We'll focus on the data your MIDlet sends and receives over the network. This data travels over some infrastructure most know nothing about (provided by your mobile carrier) and probably over the Internet, as well. The Internet is definitely not a secure network, and your carrier's mobile infrastructure probably isn't either. If you're passing sensitive data around, it's very possible that eavesdroppers at various points in the network can listen in on the data. They may even be able to change parts of it. If your MIDP application involves passing around credit card numbers or sensitive corporate data, you should be concerned.

Think of the Internet as a big room. You can talk to anyone else in the room, but everyone else can listen in on the conversation. Furthermore, you may be talking to someone on the other side of the room through intermediaries, like the children's game of "telephone." Any one of the intermediaries might be changing the conversation, and they can all hear what you're saying.

Data Security Needs and Cryptographic Solutions

Your applications will have some or all of the following data security needs:

- *Integrity*: At the simplest level, you'd like to be sure that the data you're sending is not getting changed or corrupted in any way. This is data integrity.

- *Authentication*: It's often important to verify the identity of the machine or person on the other end of your network connection. Authentication is the process of proving identity.

- *Confidentiality*: If you're sending sensitive data over the network, other people shouldn't be able to see that information. This is confidentiality.

Cryptography provides solutions for each of these needs:

- *Message digests*: A message digest smushes a large piece of data into a small piece of data. You might, for example, run an entire file through a message digest to end up with a 160-bit digest value. If you change even 1 bit of the file and run it through the message digest again, you'll get an entirely different digest value. A message digest value is sometimes called a *digital fingerprint*.

- *Digital signatures*: A digital signature is like a message digest except it is produced by a particular person, the *signer*. The signer must have a *private key* that is used to create the signature. A corresponding *public key* can be used by anyone to verify that the signature came from the signer. The private key and public key together are called a *key pair*. Keys are really just data—think of an array of bytes. *Certificates* are really just an extension of digital signatures. A certificate is a document, signed by some authority like the U.S. Postal Service, that proves your identity. It's like a driver's license, except it's based on digital signatures.

- *Ciphers*: Ciphers can either encrypt data or decrypt it. An encrypting cipher accepts your data, called *plaintext*, and produces an unreadable mess, called *ciphertext*. A decrypting cipher takes ciphertext and converts it back to plaintext. Ciphers use keys; if you encrypt the same plaintext with two different keys, you'll get two different sets of ciphertext. A *symmetric* cipher uses the same key for encryption and decryption. An *asymmetric* cipher operates with a key pair—one key is used for encrypting, while the matching key is used for decrypting. Ciphers operate in different *modes* that determine how plaintext is encrypted into ciphertext. This, in turn, affects the use and security of the cipher.

■**Note** For comprehensive coverage of cryptographic concepts and algorithms, see Bruce Schneier's *Applied Cryptography: Protocols, Algorithms, and Source Code in C* (John Wiley & Sons, 1995). To find out more about the JCA and JCE in J2SE, read Jonathan's *Java Cryptography* (O'Reilly, 1998). Sun's developer web site also contains Jonathan's excellent four-part series on security and cryptography in MIDP, located at http://developers.sun.com/techtopics/mobility/midp/articles/security1/.

HTTPS Is Almost Everything You Could Want

The Generic Connection Framework has always been flexible enough to allow MIDP implementations to include support for HTTPS, which is HTTP over a secure connection like TLS
or SSL. Support for HTTPS is built into the MIDP platform. (See Chapter 10 for the skinny on
HTTPS and its supporting APIs.)

TLS provides server authentication and an encrypted data connection between client and
server. The security provided by TLS is sufficient for most applications. There are only a handful of
reasons you might want to implement cryptographic solutions beyond what's available from
TLS, including the following:

- *Client authentication*: TLS provides server authentication, usually via an RSA certificate.
  But although TLS will support client authentication, the APIs in MIDP 2.0 don't allow
  you to take advantage of this feature. A technique for using password or passphrase
  authentication is presented later in this chapter (see the section "Protecting Passwords
  with a Message Digest"). If you're looking for something stronger, a scheme based on
  client certificates and signatures is described at `http://developers.sun.com/techtopics/`
  `mobility/midp/articles/security3/`.

- *Stronger encryption*: TLS usually results in encryption using 128-bit keys that are valid
  for a particular session. (Although you can't control which cipher suites are accepted
  on the client, you will probably have control of the server and will be able to configure
  acceptable cipher suites there.) For many applications, 128-bit session keys provide
  plenty of data security. However, if your application deals with especially sensitive or
  valuable data, you might want something stronger.

- *Message-driven applications*: HTTPS only provides encryption for channels. Some applications work by sending encrypted messages over insecure transport like HTTP or sockets.
  Here the MIDP APIs are insufficient and you'll need to do your own cryptography.

As we said, HTTPS support in MIDP is all you need for many applications. Read on if you
need something stronger, or if you're just curious.

More information about HTTPS and TLS in MIDP is at `http://wireless.java.sun.com/`
`midp/articles/security2/`.

The Bouncy Castle Cryptography Package

In the J2SE world, Sun provides support for cryptography through the Java Cryptography
Architecture (JCA) and the Java Cryptography Extension (JCE). The problem, of course, is that
the JCA and JCE are too heavy for the MIDP platform. MIDP's HTTPS support is very useful, but
it's definitely not a general-purpose cryptography toolkit.

If you're looking to move beyond HTTPS, your best bet is the Bouncy Castle cryptography
package, an open-source effort based in Australia. It's a wonderful piece of work, featuring a clean
API and a formidable toolbox of cryptographic algorithms. There are several other open source
cryptography packages around the world, but Bouncy Castle specifically offers a lightweight J2ME
distribution of their software. To download the package, go to `http://www.bouncycastle.org/`,
follow the link for latest releases, and choose the J2ME release of the lightweight API. As we write
this, the current version is 1.27.

Download the zip file into the location of your choice and unpack it. If you're using the J2ME Wireless Toolkit, just drop the `midp_classes.zip` file (extracted from your Bouncy Castle lightweight API for J2ME download) into the `lib` directory of your project. You can go ahead and write MIDlets that use the Bouncy Castle packages.

Protecting Passwords with a Message Digest

Having installed the Bouncy Castle cryptography package, try a simple example involving authentication. Computer systems often use passwords instead of digital signatures (or certificates) because they're so much easier. A password is a *shared secret*, which means that you know it and the server knows it, but nobody else should know it.

WHAT IF SOMEONE STEALS YOUR PHONE?

For convenience, an application will probably store your password in persistent storage. This is a conscious trade-off of security for usability. The user never enters a password, but the password is available in device storage, vulnerable to theft by other applications on the device. Furthermore, if someone steals the device itself, that person will be able to use the application without being challenged for a password.

JSR 177, Security and Trust Services for J2ME (`http://jcp.org/en/jsr/detail?id=177`), will address these concerns by providing an API to secure storage, among other things.

The Problem with Passwords

The problem with passwords is that you don't want to send them over an insecure network. Imagine, for example, that your MIDlet requires the user to sign on to a server using a user name and password. On the MIDP device, you key in your user name and password, and then click the button to send the information up to the server. Unfortunately, your data is sent as plaintext in some HTTP request. Anybody snooping on the network can easily lift your password.

Using a Message Digest

Message digests provide a way to solve this problem. Instead of sending a password as plaintext, you create a message digest value from the password and send that instead. An attacker could just steal the digest value, of course, so you add some other stuff to the digest as well so that only the server, knowing the password, can re-create the same digest value. Figure 18-1 shows the process.

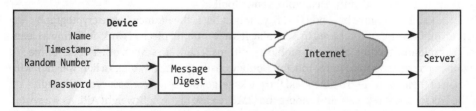

Figure 18-1. *Protecting a password with a message digest*

The MIDlet creates a timestamp and a random number, both of which are fed into the message digest along with the user name and the password. Then the MIDlet sends the user name, the timestamp, the random number, and the digest value up to the server. It does not send the password as cleartext, but the password is used to calculate the digest value.

The server takes the user name and looks up the corresponding password, which should be stored securely in a file or a database. Then it creates a digest value of the user name, password, timestamp, and random number. If the digest value created on the server matches the digest value sent by the client MIDlet, then the server knows that the user typed in the right password. The user has just logged in successfully.

The server needs some logic to prevent replay attacks. Specifically, the server should reject login attempts that use timestamps and random numbers that have been used before with that login. Although you could save the random numbers and timestamps of all user login attempts, it would be relatively expensive to compare each of these every time a user wanted to log in. An easier way to implement this is to save the timestamp of each user's last login attempt. For each subsequent login attempt, the server looks up the saved timestamp. If the timestamp on the current attempt is later than the saved timestamp, the attempt is allowed. The current attempt's timestamp replaces the saved timestamp for this user.

Using the Bouncy Castle Cryptography Package

In the Bouncy Castle package, message digests are generically represented by the `org.bouncycastle.crypto.Digest` interface. You can add data into the message digest using one of two `update()` methods. To calculate the message digest value, call `doFinal()`. Specific implementations of the `Digest` interface are contained in the `org.bouncycastle.crypto.digests` package. We'll be using one called `SHA1Digest`, which implements the SHA-1 digest algorithm. The following line shows how to create a SHA-1 message digest object:

```
Digest digest = new SHA1Digest();
```

The cryptography code is pretty simple. Most of the effort, in fact, is devoted to converting the timestamp and random number to bytes that can be pushed into the message digest object. Then it's just a matter of calling the `update()` method with each array of bytes.

To calculate the digest, call `Digest`'s `doFinal()` method. You'll need to pass in a byte array to hold the message digest value. To find out how long this array should be, call the `getDigestSize()` method.

```
byte[] digestValue = new byte[digest.getDigestSize()];
digest.dofinal(digestValue, 0);
```

Implementing a Protected Password Protocol

This section details an implementation of protected password login. On the client side, a MIDlet collects a user name and password, as shown in Figure 18-2.

When the `Login` command is invoked, the MIDlet sends data to a servlet, which determines whether or not the client is authenticated. The servlet sends back a message, which is displayed on the screen of the device, as shown in Figure 18-3.

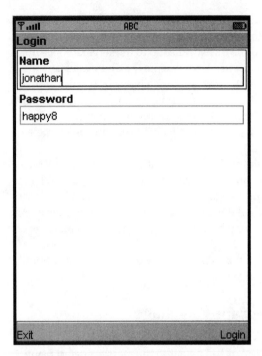

Figure 18-2. *A simple form collects a user name and password.*

Figure 18-3. *The server says whether you're logged in or not.*

The MIDlet and servlet exchange various byte arrays, such as the timestamp, the random number, and the message digest value. To make this work smoothly in the context of HTTP headers, which are plain text, the byte arrays are exchanged as hexadecimal strings. A helper class, HexCodec, handles the translation between hexadecimal strings and byte arrays. This same class is used by the MIDlet and the servlet.

Let's look at the MIDlet first. Its main screen is a form in which the user can enter a user name and a password. You might be tempted to use a PASSWORD TextField, but we chose not to. For one thing, it's hard to know exactly what text you're entering. For another thing, we're assuming that the screen of a small device is reasonably private—probably no one will be peeking over your shoulder as you enter your password.

When the user invokes the Login command, the MIDlet calculates a message digest value as described previously. It assembles various parameters into an HTTP request. It then reads the response from the server and displays the response in an Alert.

The meat of the protected password algorithm is in the login() method. We create a timestamp and a random number and convert these values to byte arrays using a helper method:

```
long timestamp = System.currentTimeMillis();
long randomNumber = mRandom.nextLong();
byte[] timestampBytes = getBytes(timestamp);
byte[] randomBytes = getBytes(randomNumber);
```

The user name and password strings, which come from the MIDlet's main form, are easily converted to byte arrays.

The entire source code for PasswordMIDlet is shown in Listing 18-1.

Listing 18-1. *PasswordMIDlet, a Protected Password Client*

```
import java.io.*;
import java.util.Random;

import javax.microedition.io.*;
import javax.microedition.midlet.*;
import javax.microedition.lcdui.*;

import org.bouncycastle.crypto.Digest;
import org.bouncycastle.crypto.digests.SHA1Digest;

public class PasswordMIDlet
    extends MIDlet
    implements CommandListener, Runnable {
  private Display mDisplay;
  private Form mForm;
  private TextField mUserField, mPasswordField;
  private Random mRandom;

  public void startApp() {
    mDisplay = Display.getDisplay(this);
    mRandom = new Random(System.currentTimeMillis());
```

```
  if (mForm == null) {
    mForm = new Form("Login");
    mUserField = new TextField("Name", "jonathan", 32, 0);
    mPasswordField = new TextField("Password", "happy8", 32, 0);
    mForm.append(mUserField);
    mForm.append(mPasswordField);

    mForm.addCommand(new Command("Exit", Command.EXIT, 0));
    mForm.addCommand(new Command("Login", Command.SCREEN, 0));
    mForm.setCommandListener(this);
  }

  mDisplay.setCurrent(mForm);
}

public void commandAction(Command c, Displayable s) {
  if (c.getCommandType() == Command.EXIT) notifyDestroyed();
  else {
    Form waitForm = new Form("Connecting...");
    mDisplay.setCurrent(waitForm);
    Thread t = new Thread(this);
    t.start();
  }
}

public void run() {
  // Gather the values we'll need.
  long timestamp = System.currentTimeMillis();
  long randomNumber = mRandom.nextLong();
  String user = mUserField.getString();
  byte[] userBytes = user.getBytes();
  byte[] timestampBytes = getBytes(timestamp);
  byte[] randomBytes = getBytes(randomNumber);
  String password = mPasswordField.getString();
  byte[] passwordBytes = password.getBytes();

  // Create the message digest.
  Digest digest = new SHA1Digest();
  // Calculate the digest value.
  digest.update(userBytes, 0, userBytes.length);
  digest.update(timestampBytes, 0, timestampBytes.length);
  digest.update(randomBytes, 0, randomBytes.length);
  digest.update(passwordBytes, 0, passwordBytes.length);
  byte[] digestValue = new byte[digest.getDigestSize()];
  digest.doFinal(digestValue, 0);
```

```
    // Create the GET URL. The hex encoded message digest value is
    //    included as a parameter.
    URLBuilder ub = new URLBuilder(getAppProperty("PasswordMIDlet-URL"));
    ub.addParameter("user", user);
    ub.addParameter("timestamp",
        new String(HexCodec.bytesToHex(timestampBytes)));
    ub.addParameter("random",
        new String(HexCodec.bytesToHex(randomBytes)));
    ub.addParameter("digest",
        new String(HexCodec.bytesToHex(digestValue)));
    String url = ub.toString();

    try {
      // Query the server and retrieve the response.
      HttpConnection hc = (HttpConnection)Connector.open(url);
      InputStream in = hc.openInputStream();

      int length = (int)hc.getLength();
      byte[] raw = new byte[length];
      in.read(raw);
      String response = new String(raw);
      Alert a = new Alert("Response", response, null, null);
      a.setTimeout(Alert.FOREVER);
      mDisplay.setCurrent(a, mForm);
      in.close();
      hc.close();
    }
    catch (IOException ioe) {
      Alert a = new Alert("Exception", ioe.toString(), null, null);
      a.setTimeout(Alert.FOREVER);
      mDisplay.setCurrent(a, mForm);
    }
  }

  private byte[] getBytes(long x) {
    byte[] bytes = new byte[8];
    for (int i = 0; i < 8; i++)
      bytes[i] = (byte)(x >> ((7 - i) * 8));
    return bytes;
  }

  public void pauseApp() { }

  public void destroyApp(boolean unconditional) { }
}
```

The HexCodec class contains a few static methods for converting between byte arrays and hex encoded strings. The complete class is shown in Listing 18-2.

Listing 18-2. *The HexCodec Helper Class*

```
public class HexCodec {
  private static final char[] kDigits = {
    '0', '1', '2', '3', '4', '5', '6', '7', '8', '9',
    'a', 'b', 'c', 'd', 'e', 'f'
  } ;

  public static char[] bytesToHex(byte[] raw) {
    int length = raw.length;
    char[] hex = new char[length * 2];
    for (int i = 0; i < length; i++) {
      int value = (raw[i] + 256) % 256;
      int highIndex = value >> 4;
      int lowIndex = value & 0x0f;
      hex[i * 2 + 0] = kDigits[highIndex];
      hex[i * 2 + 1] = kDigits[lowIndex];
    }
    return hex;
  }

  public static byte[] hexToBytes(char[] hex) {
    int length = hex.length / 2;
    byte[] raw = new byte[length];
    for (int i = 0; i < length; i++) {
      int high = Character.digit(hex[i * 2], 16);
      int low = Character.digit(hex[i * 2 + 1], 16);
      int value = (high << 4) | low;
      if (value > 127) value -= 256;
      raw[i] = (byte)value;
    }
    return raw;
  }

  public static byte[] hexToBytes(String hex) {
    return hexToBytes(hex.toCharArray());
  }
}
```

PasswordMIDlet also uses the URLBuilder class, which provides a simple interface for assembling GET URLs. The URLBuilder class is shown in Listing 18-3.

Listing 18-3. *The URLBuilder Helper Class*

```
public class URLBuilder {
  private StringBuffer mBuffer;
  private boolean mHasParameters;

  public URLBuilder(String base) {
    mBuffer = new StringBuffer(base);
    mHasParameters = false;
  }

  public void addParameter(String name, String value) {
    // Append a separator.
    if (mHasParameters == false) {
      mBuffer.append('?');
      mHasParameters = true;
    }
    else
      mBuffer.append('&');
    // Now tack on the name and value pair. These should
    //    really be URL encoded (see java.net.URLEncoder in
    //    J2SE) but this class appends the name and value
    //    as is, for simplicity. Names or values with spaces
    //    or other special characters will not work correctly.
    mBuffer.append(name);
    mBuffer.append('=');
    mBuffer.append(value);
  }

  public String toString() {
    return mBuffer.toString();

  }
}
```

You will need to set the MIDlet property `PasswordMIDlet-URL` to point to the location of the running `PasswordServlet`.

A simple implementation of a protected password servlet is shown in Listing 18-4.

Listing 18-4. *The PasswordServlet Class*

```
import javax.servlet.http.*;
import javax.servlet.*;
import java.io.*;
import java.util.*;
```

```java
import org.bouncycastle.crypto.Digest;
import org.bouncycastle.crypto.digests.SHA1Digest;

public class PasswordServlet extends HttpServlet {
  public void doGet(HttpServletRequest request,
      HttpServletResponse response)
      throws ServletException, IOException {
    System.out.println("user = " + request.getParameter("user"));
    System.out.println("timestamp = " + request.getParameter("timestamp"));
    System.out.println("random = " + request.getParameter("random"));
    System.out.println("digest = " + request.getParameter("digest"));

    // Retrieve the user name.
    String user = request.getParameter("user");
    // Look up the password for this user.
    String password = lookupPassword(user);
    // Pull the timestamp and random number (hex encoded) out
    //    of the request.
    String timestamp = request.getParameter("timestamp");
    String randomNumber = request.getParameter("random");

    // Compare the timestamp with the last saved
    //    timestamp for this user. Accept only timestamps
    //    that are greater than the last saved timestamp for this user.
    // [not implemented]

    // Gather values for the message digest.
    byte[] userBytes = user.getBytes();
    byte[] timestampBytes = HexCodec.hexToBytes(timestamp);
    byte[] randomBytes = HexCodec.hexToBytes(randomNumber);
    byte[] passwordBytes = password.getBytes();
    // Create the message digest.
    Digest digest = new SHA1Digest();
    // Calculate the digest value.
    digest.update(userBytes, 0, userBytes.length);
    digest.update(timestampBytes, 0, timestampBytes.length);
    digest.update(randomBytes, 0, randomBytes.length);
    digest.update(passwordBytes, 0, passwordBytes.length);
    byte[] digestValue = new byte[digest.getDigestSize()];
    digest.doFinal(digestValue, 0);

    // Now compare the digest values.
    String message = "";
    String clientDigest = request.getParameter("digest");
    if (isEqual(digestValue, HexCodec.hexToBytes(clientDigest)))
      message = "User " + user + " logged in.";
    else
      message = "Login was unsuccessful.";
```

```java
      // Send a response to the client.
      response.setContentType("text/plain");
      response.setContentLength(message.length());
      PrintWriter out = response.getWriter();
      out.println(message);
  }

  private String lookupPassword(String user) {
      // Here you could do a real lookup based on the user name.
      //    You might look in a text file or a database. Here, we
      //    just use a hard-coded value.
      return "happy8";
  }

  private boolean isEqual(byte[] one, byte[] two) {
      if (one.length != two.length) return false;
      for (int i = 0; i < one.length; i++)
        if (one[i] != two[i]) return false;
      return true;
  }
}
```

The basic procedure is to pull the parameters out of the request from the MIDlet, and then independently calculate the message digest value. The servlet looks up the user's password in the lookupPassword() method. In a more serious implementation, the servlet would probably look up the password in a database of some sort.

Once the servlet figures out the user's password, it pumps the user name, password, time-stamp, and random number into a message digest. Then it calculates the message digest value and compares this result with the digest value that was sent from the MIDlet. If the digest values match, the MIDlet client is authenticated.

Suggested Enhancements

One obvious enhancement to this system is to actually retrieve passwords (on the server side) from a database or password repository of some sort.

Furthermore, the servlet needs to validate the timestamp it receives from the client. Every time a user tries to log in, the servlet should make sure that the user's timestamp is greater than the timestamp from the user's previous login attempt.

One possible enhancement on the client side is to store the user's name and password in a record store so that they can be automatically sent with each login attempt. Normally this might seem like a bad idea. But small devices are generally kept physically secure by their owners—you try to keep your mobile phone in your possession at all times, or you lock it up somewhere. It's a trade-off between convenience and security. But just considering how diffi-cult it is to enter text on a mobile phone keypad, you might want to give your users the convenience of using a stored name and password.

Note that the authentication performed in this scheme is *per request*. Each time the client sends an HTTP request to the server, it is an entirely separate conversation. Therefore, each time the client needs to authenticate itself to the server to perform some work, it must go through the whole process again—creating a timestamp and random number, calculating a message digest, and sending the whole mess up to the server. In this system, then, you would probably add parameters to the HTTP request that specify an action or command that should be performed on behalf of the authenticated user.

Securing Network Data

Let's look at something a little more complicated. Suppose you wish to conceal the data you are sending over the network. The protected password example showed one way for a client to authenticate itself to the server, but we've still got the problem of eavesdroppers picking up credit card numbers or other sensitive information off the network.

This example consists of a matched MIDlet and servlet. The MIDlet, StealthMIDlet, has a simple user interface that allows you to enter a message. This message is encrypted using an RC4 stream cipher and sent to the servlet. On the server side, StealthServlet receives the encrypted message, decrypts it, and sends back its own encrypted message. Both messages pass over the insecure Internet as ciphertext, which is difficult for attackers to read without the proper keys.

RC4 is a symmetric encryption algorithm, which means that the same key is used to encrypt and decrypt data. StealthMIDlet and StealthServlet use two keys, one for each direction of data travel. One key is used to encrypt data in the MIDlet and decrypt it in the servlet; the other key encrypts data in the servlet and decrypts it in the MIDlet.

The servlet services multiple client MIDlets, each with their own encrypting and decrypting keys. Therefore, the servlet must keep track of two keys per client without getting them mixed up. It uses an HTTP session object to do this. Every time a client request is received, the servlet finds the corresponding ciphers in the session object. If the ciphers don't exist, they are created and initialized using client-specific keys.

This system provides both data confidentiality and authentication. The client and server are authenticated to each other because they must possess the correct keys to exchange data.

Figure 18-4 shows the main user interface of StealthMIDlet. It allows you to enter a message you want to encrypt and send to the server. When you're ready, hit the Send command to kick things off.

The servlet decrypts your message and sends back an encrypted response, which is displayed by the MIDlet as shown in Figure 18-5.

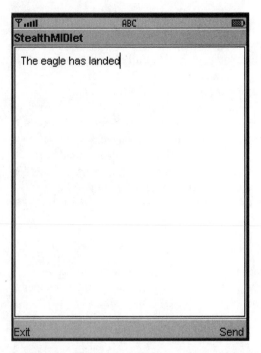

Figure 18-4. *Enter your secret message in StealthMIDlet's main screen.*

Figure 18-5. *The servlet sends back its own secret message.*

Using Bouncy Castle Ciphers

In the Bouncy Castle cryptography package, stream ciphers are represented by the org.bouncycastle.crypto.StreamCipher interface. You just need to initialize the cipher, using init(), and then you can encrypt or decrypt data using processBytes().

The Bouncy Castle package only provides one direct stream cipher implementation, org.bouncycastle.crypto.engines.RC4. If you'd prefer to use a different algorithm, you can use a block cipher instead. You can treat block ciphers like stream ciphers using Cipher Feedback (CFB) mode. In the Bouncy Castle package, this is implemented in the org.bouncycastle.crypto➥ .StreamBlockCipher class. This technique gives you access to Bouncy Castle's considerable arsenal of block cipher implementations, from the wizened DES through AES, Blowfish, Rijndael, and more. For more information on cipher modes, see Chapter 7 of *Java Cryptography*.

Our simple implementation instantiates a pair of RC4 objects, something like this:

```
StreamCipher inCipher = new RC4Engine();
StreamCipher outCipher = new RC4Engine();
```

The ciphers need to be initialized before they can be used. The first parameter to init() should be true if the cipher will be encrypting data, false for decryption. The second parameter is essentially the key, wrapped up in a KeyParameter object.

```
// Assume we have retrieved inKey and outKey, both byte arrays.
inCipher.init(false, new KeyParameter(inKey));
outCipher.init(true, new KeyParameter(outKey));
```

To encrypt data, we just need to create an array to hold the ciphertext. Then call the stream cipher's processBytes() method to perform the encryption. The processBytes() method accepts the plaintext array, an index into the plaintext, the number of bytes that should be processed, the ciphertext array, and the index at which the ciphertext should be written.

```
// Assume we have a byte array called plaintext.
byte[] ciphertext = new byte[plaintext.length];
outCipher.processBytes(plaintext, 0, plaintext.length, ciphertext, 0);
```

Decryption is identical, except you would use a cipher that has been initialized for decryption.

Implementation

The source code for StealthMIDlet is shown in Listing 18-5. This MIDlet has a simple user interface, initialized in the startApp() method. The MIDlet's ciphers are also created and initialized in startApp().

Listing 18-5. *StealthMIDlet, a Data Encryption MIDlet*

```java
import java.io.*;

import javax.microedition.io.*;
import javax.microedition.midlet.*;
import javax.microedition.lcdui.*;

import org.bouncycastle.crypto.StreamCipher;
import org.bouncycastle.crypto.engines.RC4Engine;
import org.bouncycastle.crypto.params.KeyParameter;

public class StealthMIDlet
    extends MIDlet
    implements CommandListener, Runnable {
  private Display mDisplay;
  private TextBox mTextBox;

  private String mSession;
  private StreamCipher mOutCipher, mInCipher;

  public StealthMIDlet() {
    mOutCipher = new RC4Engine();
    mInCipher = new RC4Engine();
  }

  public void startApp() {
    if (mSession == null) {
      // Load the keys from resource files.
      byte[] inKey = getInKey();
      byte[] outKey = getOutKey();

      // Initialize the ciphers.
      mOutCipher.init(true, new KeyParameter(outKey));
      mInCipher.init(false, new KeyParameter(inKey));
    }

    mDisplay = Display.getDisplay(this);

    if (mTextBox == null) {
      mTextBox = new TextBox("StealthMIDlet",
          "The eagle has landed", 256, 0);
```

```
      mTextBox.addCommand(new Command("Exit", Command.EXIT, 0));
      mTextBox.addCommand(new Command("Send", Command.SCREEN, 0));
      mTextBox.setCommandListener(this);
    }

    mDisplay.setCurrent(mTextBox);
  }

  public void commandAction(Command c, Displayable s) {
    if (c.getCommandType() == Command.EXIT) notifyDestroyed();
    else {
      Form waitForm = new Form("Connecting...");
      mDisplay.setCurrent(waitForm);
      Thread t = new Thread(this);
      t.start();
    }
  }

  public void run() {
    // Encrypt our message.
    byte[] plaintext = mTextBox.getString().getBytes();
    byte[] ciphertext = new byte[plaintext.length];
    mOutCipher.processBytes(plaintext, 0, plaintext.length, ciphertext, 0);
    char[] hexCiphertext = HexCodec.bytesToHex(ciphertext);

    // Create the GET URL. Our user name and the encrypted, hex
    //   encoded message are included as parameters. The user name
    //   and base URL are retrieved as application properties.
    String baseURL = getAppProperty("StealthMIDlet-URL");
    URLBuilder ub = new URLBuilder(baseURL);
    ub.addParameter("user", getAppProperty("StealthMIDlet.user"));
    ub.addParameter("message", new String(hexCiphertext));
    String url = ub.toString();

    try {
      // Query the server and retrieve the response.
      HttpConnection hc = (HttpConnection)Connector.open(url);
      if (mSession != null)
        hc.setRequestProperty("cookie", mSession);
      InputStream in = hc.openInputStream();

      String cookie = hc.getHeaderField("Set-cookie");
      if (cookie != null) {
        int semicolon = cookie.indexOf(';');
        mSession = cookie.substring(0, semicolon);
      }
```

```
      int length = (int)hc.getLength();
      ciphertext = new byte[length];
      in.read(ciphertext);
      in.close();
      hc.close();
    }
    catch (IOException ioe) {
      Alert a = new Alert("Exception", ioe.toString(), null, null);
      a.setTimeout(Alert.FOREVER);
      mDisplay.setCurrent(a, mTextBox);
    }


    // Decrypt the server response.
    String hex = new String(ciphertext);
    byte[] dehexed = HexCodec.hexToBytes(hex.toCharArray());
    byte[] deciphered = new byte[dehexed.length];
    mInCipher.processBytes(dehexed, 0, dehexed.length, deciphered, 0);

    String decipheredString = new String(deciphered);
    Alert a = new Alert("Response", decipheredString, null, null);
    a.setTimeout(Alert.FOREVER);
    mDisplay.setCurrent(a, mTextBox);
  }

  // Normally you would probably read keys from resource files
  //    in the MIDlet suite JAR, using the getResourceAsStream()
  //    method in Class. Here we just use hard-coded values that match
  //    the hard-coded values in StealthServlet.
  private byte[] getInKey() {
    return "Incoming MIDlet key".getBytes();
  }

  private byte[] getOutKey() {
    return "Outgoing MIDlet key".getBytes();
  }

  public void pauseApp() { }

  public void destroyApp(boolean unconditional) { }
}
```

When the user invokes the Send command, StealthMIDlet encrypts the user's message with its outgoing cipher. It then encodes the ciphertext as hexadecimal text in preparation for sending it to the servlet. The user's name and the ciphertext are packaged into a GET URL and sent to the server. Additionally, StealthMIDlet keeps track of a cookie that is used for session tracking. If the server sends back a session ID cookie, it is saved in StealthMIDlet's mSession member variable. The saved cookie is sent with each subsequent request. This allows the server to retrieve session information for this client. Without this session information, each HTTP request from client to server would need to reinitialize the ciphers so that they didn't get unsynchronized.

StealthMIDlet retrieves the response from the server as hexadecimal ciphertext. It converts the string to a byte array, and then decrypts the byte array using the MIDlet's incoming cipher. The decrypted message is displayed in an Alert.

StealthMIDlet makes use of the same HexCodec and URLBuilder classes that were presented earlier in this chapter. You will need to set the MIDlet property StealthMIDlet-URL to point to the location of the running StealthServlet.

On the server side, things are a little more complicated. StealthServlet should be capable of handling multiple clients, which means it should maintain a pair of ciphers for each user that connects. This is done using HTTP sessions, one session per user. When a client request comes in, StealthServlet attempts to find two ciphers in the user's session. If they don't exist, as will be the case the first time a user connects to the servlet, new ciphers are created. The ciphers are initialized using keys that are unique to each user. Exactly how these keys are located is left up to you. In this simple implementation, the getInKey() and getOutKey() methods are hard-coded.

You should notice that the keys on the servlet side appear to be reversed from the MIDlet. This is because the servlet's incoming cipher should decrypt using the same key as the MIDlet's outgoing cipher.

Once StealthServlet has located or created the ciphers that correspond to a particular user, it decrypts the incoming message and prints it out to the server console. Then it encrypts a response message (also hard-coded) and sends the response back to the MIDlet.

The entire StealthServlet class is shown in Listing 18-6.

Listing 18-6. *The Source Code for StealthServlet*

```
import javax.servlet.http.*;
import javax.servlet.*;
import java.io.*;
import java.util.*;

import org.bouncycastle.crypto.StreamCipher;
import org.bouncycastle.crypto.engines.RC4Engine;
import org.bouncycastle.crypto.params.KeyParameter;

public class StealthServlet extends HttpServlet {
  public void doGet(HttpServletRequest request,
      HttpServletResponse response)
      throws ServletException, IOException {
    String user = request.getParameter("user");

    // Try to find the user's cipher pair.
    HttpSession session = request.getSession();
    StreamCipher inCipher = (StreamCipher)session.getAttribute("inCipher");
    StreamCipher outCipher = (StreamCipher)session.getAttribute("outCipher");
```

```
    // If the ciphers aren't found, create and initialize a new pair.
    if (inCipher == null && outCipher == null) {
      // Retrieve the client's keys.
      byte[] inKey = getInKey(user);
      byte[] outKey = getOutKey(user);
      // Create and initialize the ciphers.
      inCipher = new RC4Engine();
      outCipher = new RC4Engine();
      inCipher.init(true, new KeyParameter(inKey));
      outCipher.init(false, new KeyParameter(outKey));
      // Now put them in the session object.
      session.setAttribute("inCipher", inCipher);
      session.setAttribute("outCipher", outCipher);
    }

    // Retrieve the client's message.
    String clientHex = request.getParameter("message");
    byte[] clientCiphertext = HexCodec.hexToBytes(clientHex);
    byte[] clientDecrypted = new byte[clientCiphertext.length];
    inCipher.processBytes(clientCiphertext, 0, clientCiphertext.length,
        clientDecrypted, 0);
    System.out.println("message = " + new String(clientDecrypted));

    // Create the response message.
    String message = "Hello, this is StealthServlet.";

    // Encrypt the message.
    byte[] plaintext = message.getBytes();
    byte[] ciphertext = new byte[plaintext.length];
    outCipher.processBytes(plaintext, 0, plaintext.length, ciphertext, 0);
    char[] hexCiphertext = HexCodec.bytesToHex(ciphertext);

    response.setContentType("text/plain");
    response.setContentLength(hexCiphertext.length);
    PrintWriter out = response.getWriter();
    out.println(hexCiphertext);
  }

  private byte[] getInKey(String user) {
    return "Outgoing MIDlet key".getBytes();
  }

private byte[] getOutKey(String user) {
    return "Incoming MIDlet key".getBytes();
  }
}
```

Suggested Enhancements

A few relatively minor enhancements would make this a serious application. The first area to tackle is key handling. StealthMIDlet should load its keys from resource files in the MIDlet suite JAR rather than using hard-coded values. This is possible using the getResourceAsStream() method in Class. The keys would probably be placed there at deployment time, which means the MIDlet would need to be deployed carefully, probably using HTTPS.

Likewise, StealthServlet should locate and load keys from a database or some kind of file repository. Something as simple as a standard naming scheme based on user names might be sufficient.

The keys themselves should be larger than the hard-coded samples here—how large is up to you. As long ago as 1996, the U.S. government was fairly sanguine about allowing the export of 40-bit RC4 technology, so you can rest assured that 40 bits is way too short. As the key length increases, of course, you may start to have memory or performance problems, particularly in a constrained environment like MIDP. Try to find a good balance between performance and security.

Furthermore, you might want to consider using a different algorithm, like Blowfish or Rijndael. The Bouncy Castle cryptography package has plenty of options in the org.bouncycastle.crypto.engines package. As we mentioned, you can treat a block cipher like a stream cipher using CFB mode.

Finally, the communication between the servlet and the MIDlet could be improved. It would be nice, for example, if the servlet had some way to tell the MIDlet it couldn't find a session. It's possible that the MIDlet will send up a cookie for a session that has expired on the server side. In the current implementation, the servlet will create a new set of ciphers, ones that are not synchronized with the MIDlet's ciphers. One way to solve this problem would be to have the servlet pass a response code to the MIDlet. One response code might mean, "I lost your session. Please reinitialize your ciphers and try again."

Deployment Issues

Suppose you dressed up this example and incorporated it into a product. What are the issues with distribution? For each copy of your software, you need to generate a pair of keys. These keys are stored as resource files inside the MIDlet suite JAR, which means that for each copy of your software, you'll need to generate a unique MIDlet suite JAR. At the same time, you need to save the keys on the server side somewhere. When the client MIDlet makes a connection, you need to be able to find the corresponding keys. None of this is particularly difficult, and it can be automated.

The MIDlet suite JAR contains keys that should be secret. Therefore, it is a security risk to transmit the JAR to a customer over the Internet. You might transfer it via HTTPS to a customer's browser, and then rely on that customer to install the MIDlet suite on a mobile telephone or other small device via a serial cable.

Trimming Bouncy Castle Down to Size

With both of the examples in this chapter, we're only using a small subset of the Bouncy Castle cryptography package. We use an obfuscator to trim out the pieces we don't need. A good obfuscator will find the methods, instance variables, and even entire classes that are not used in an application and simply remove them. This is important with third-party libraries, with which you may only be using a fraction of the available functionality. Bouncy Castle includes all sorts of stuff that isn't used in PasswordMIDlet and StealthMIDlet.

There is another reason an obfuscator is necessary when using Bouncy Castle and some other third-party APIs. Bouncy Castle includes implementations of classes in the core java.* namespace, like java.math.BigInteger. MIDP implementations will fail to load classes from this namespace in an application. An obfuscator can be used to rename these classes out of the forbidden namespace.

The sample code from this chapter (available from the Downloads section of the Apress web site [http:// www.apress.com]) contains an Ant build file that invokes the ProGuard 3.2 obfuscator. ProGuard is an excellent piece of software. It is written entirely in Java and may be used freely. For more information, see http://proguard.sourceforge.net/.

The Ant target that runs ProGuard looks something like this:

```
<target name="obfuscate_proguard" depends="compile, copylib">
  <mkdir dir="build/proguard"/>
  <jar basedir="build/classes"
      jarfile="build/proguard/$wj2-crypto-input.jar"/>

  <java fork="yes" classname="proguard.ProGuard"
      classpath="${proguard}">
    <arg line="-libraryjars ${midp_lib}"/>
    <arg line="-injars build/proguard/${project}-input.jar"/>
    <arg line="-outjar build/proguard/${project}-output.jar"/>
    <arg line="-keep
        'public class * extends javax.microedition.midlet.MIDlet'"/>
    <arg line="-defaultpackage"/>
    <arg line="-dontusemixedcaseclassnames"/>
  </java>

  <mkdir dir="build/obfuscated"/>
  <unjar src="build/proguard/${project}-output.jar"
      dest="build/obfuscated"/>
</target>
```

ProGuard expects its input classes to be packaged in a JAR, so the first thing to do is create a JAR based on the package name, wj2-crypto-input.jar. Note that this JAR includes the Bouncy Castle classes.

Next, ProGuard is run by forking a Java process. The first argument, -libraryjars, tells ProGuard where to find the MIDP classes. The next argument, -injars, points ProGuard to the JAR of input files. The output file name is specified using -outjar. Next come three important options. It's important that the MIDlet classes themselves retain their names so that MIDlet management software on a device can load and run the classes. The –keep argument makes this happen for all subclasses of MIDlet. The package renaming (moving things out of java.*) is accomplished using the -defaultpackage argument. Finally, -dontusemixedcaseclassnames works around asinine behavior in Windows where obfuscated class files like *a.class* and *A.class* cannot exist in the same directory.

For more information on ProGuard and its options, consult the documentation, which is quite good. For another example of its use, see `http://developers.sun.com/techtopics/mobility/midp/articles/security3/`.

The results are impressive. Without the obfuscator, the MIDlet JAR containing `StealthMIDlet` is 699KB. After running ProGuard, the MIDlet JAR is 32KB and the offending `java.*` classes have been renamed to something innocuous.

Summary

Data security is crucial for some types of applications. Data security is feasible in the MIDP world using the Bouncy Castle cryptography package, which provides sophisticated, accessible, industrial-strength cryptography for the MIDP platform. This example presented two possible applications—one using a message digest for secure password authentication, and the other using ciphers to encrypt data sent between a MIDlet and a servlet.

Keep in mind that adding cryptography to an application or system won't necessarily make it more secure. You need to take a comprehensive system-level approach to security. Cryptography is just one of the tools in your box.

MIDP API Reference

This appendix is a reference for the classes and interfaces of the MIDP API. This reference is designed to help you quickly find the signature of a method in the MIDP API. Exceptions and errors are not included. Optional APIs are not included.

For a full description of any class, interface, or method, consult the API documentation, either in HTML (usually distributed with a MIDP toolkit) or in the MIDP specification itself.

The API listings are alphabetical, grouped by package.

This reference covers MIDP 2.0, CLDC 1.0, and CLDC 1.1. Methods that are new in CLDC 1.1 are marked with a plus sign (+). You will find implementations of MIDP 2.0 paired with either CLDC 1.0 or CLDC 1.1 on currently available devices; keep this in mind as you browse the reference.

Package java.io

Class java.io.ByteArrayInputStream

```
public class ByteArrayInputStream
    extends java.io.InputStream {
  // Constructors
  public ByteArrayInputStream(byte[] buf);
  public ByteArrayInputStream(byte[] buf, int offset, int length);

  // Methods
  public synchronized int available();
  public synchronized void close();
  public void mark(int readAheadLimit);
  public boolean markSupported();
  public synchronized int read();
  public synchronized int read(byte[] b, int off, int len);
  public synchronized void reset();
  public synchronized long skip(long n);
}
```

Class java.io.ByteArrayOutputStream

```
public class ByteArrayOutputStream
    extends java.io.OutputStream {
  // Constructors
  public ByteArrayOutputStream();
  public ByteArrayOutputStream(int size);

  // Methods
  public synchronized void close();
  public synchronized void reset();
  public int size();
  public synchronized byte[] toByteArray();
  public String toString();
  public synchronized void write(int b);
  public synchronized void write(byte[] b, int off, int len);
}
```

Interface java.io.DataInput

```
  public interface DataInput {
    // Methods
    public boolean readBoolean();
    public byte readByte();
    public char readChar();
+   public double readDouble();
+   public float readFloat();
    public void readFully(byte[] b);
    public void readFully(byte[] b, int off, int len);
    public int readInt();
    public long readLong();
    public short readShort();
    public String readUTF();
    public int readUnsignedByte();
    public int readUnsignedShort();
    public int skipBytes(int n);
  }
```

Class java.io.DataInputStream

```
public class DataInputStream
    extends java.io.InputStream
    implements DataInput {
  // Static methods
  public static final String readUTF(DataInput in);
```

```
    // Constructors
    public DataInputStream(InputStream in);

    // Methods
    public int available();
    public void close();
    public synchronized void mark(int readlimit);
    public boolean markSupported();
    public int read();
    public final int read(byte[] b);
    public final int read(byte[] b, int off, int len);
    public final boolean readBoolean();
    public final byte readByte();
    public final char readChar();
+   public final double readDouble();
+   public final float readFloat();
    public final void readFully(byte[] b);
    public final void readFully(byte[] b, int off, int len);
    public final int readInt();
    public final long readLong();
    public final short readShort();
    public final String readUTF();
    public final int readUnsignedByte();
    public final int readUnsignedShort();
    public synchronized void reset();
    public long skip(long n);
    public final int skipBytes(int n);
}
```

Interface java.io.DataOutput

```
public interface DataOutput {
    // Methods
    public void write(int b);
    public void write(byte[] b);
    public void write(byte[] b, int off, int len);
    public void writeBoolean(boolean v);
    public void writeByte(int v);
    public void writeChar(int v);
    public void writeChars(String s);
+   public void writeDouble(double v);
+   public void writeFloat(float v);
    public void writeInt(int v);
    public void writeLong(long v);
    public void writeShort(int v);
    public void writeUTF(String str);
}
```

Class java.io.DataOutputStream

```
public class DataOutputStream
    extends java.io.OutputStream
    implements DataOutput {
// Constructors
public DataOutputStream(OutputStream out);

// Methods
public void close();
public void flush();
public void write(int b);
public void write(byte[] b, int off, int len);
public final void writeBoolean(boolean v);
public final void writeByte(int v);
public final void writeChar(int v);
public final void writeChars(String s);
```
+   `public final void writeDouble(double v);`
+   `public final void writeFloat(float v);`
```
public final void writeInt(int v);
public final void writeLong(long v);
public final void writeShort(int v);
public final void writeUTF(String str);
}
```

Class java.io.InputStream

```
public abstract class InputStream
    extends java.lang.Object {
// Constructors
public InputStream();

// Methods
public int available();
public void close();
public synchronized void mark(int readlimit);
public boolean markSupported();
public abstract int read();
public int read(byte[] b);
public int read(byte[] b, int off, int len);
public synchronized void reset();
public long skip(long n);
}
```

Class java.io.InputStreamReader

```
public class InputStreamReader
    extends java.io.Reader {
  // Constructors
  public InputStreamReader(InputStream is);
  public InputStreamReader(InputStream is, String enc);

  // Methods
  public void close();
  public void mark(int readAheadLimit);
  public boolean markSupported();
  public int read();
  public int read(char[] cbuf, int off, int len);
  public boolean ready();
  public void reset();
  public long skip(long n);
}
```

Class java.io.OutputStream

```
public abstract class OutputStream
    extends java.lang.Object {
  // Constructors
  public OutputStream();

  // Methods
  public void close();
  public void flush();
  public abstract void write(int b);
  public void write(byte[] b);
  public void write(byte[] b, int off, int len);
}
```

Class java.io.OutputStreamWriter

```
public class OutputStreamWriter
    extends java.io.Writer {
  // Constructors
  public OutputStreamWriter(OutputStream os);
  public OutputStreamWriter(OutputStream os, String enc);

  // Methods
  public void close();
  public void flush();
  public void write(int c);
  public void write(char[] cbuf, int off, int len);
  public void write(String str, int off, int len);
}
```

Class java.io.PrintStream

```
public class PrintStream
    extends java.io.OutputStream {
  // Constructors
  public PrintStream(OutputStream out);

  // Methods
  public boolean checkError();
  public void close();
  public void flush();
  public void print(boolean b);
  public void print(char c);
  public void print(int i);
  public void print(long l);
+ public void print(float f);
+ public void print(double d);
  public void print(char[] s);
  public void print(String s);
  public void print(Object obj);
  public void println();
  public void println(boolean x);
  public void println(char x);
  public void println(int x);
  public void println(long x);
+ public void println(float x);
+ public void println(double x);
  public void println(char[] x);
  public void println(String x);
  public void println(Object x);
  protected void setError();
  public void write(int b);
  public void write(byte[] buf, int off, int len);
}
```

Class java.io.Reader

```
public abstract class Reader
    extends java.lang.Object {
  // Constructors
  protected Reader();
  protected Reader(Object lock);

  // Methods
  public abstract void close();
  public void mark(int readAheadLimit);
  public boolean markSupported();
```

```
    public int read();
    public int read(char[] cbuf);
    public abstract int read(char[] cbuf, int off, int len);
    public boolean ready();
    public void reset();
    public long skip(long n);
  }
```

Class java.io.Writer

```
  public abstract class Writer
      extends java.lang.Object {
    // Constructors
    protected Writer();
    protected Writer(Object lock);

    // Methods
    public abstract void close();
    public abstract void flush();
    public void write(int c);
    public void write(char[] cbuf);
    public abstract void write(char[] cbuf, int off, int len);
    public void write(String str);
    public void write(String str, int off, int len);
  }
```

Package java.lang

Class java.lang.Boolean

```
   public final class Boolean
       extends java.lang.Object {
     // Constants
+    public static final Boolean FALSE;
+    public static final Boolean TRUE;

     // Constructors
     public Boolean(boolean value);

     // Methods
     public boolean booleanValue();
     public boolean equals(Object obj);
     public int hashCode();
     public String toString();
   }
```

Class java.lang.Byte

```
public final class Byte
    extends java.lang.Object {
  // Constants
  public static final byte MAX_VALUE;
  public static final byte MIN_VALUE;

  // Static methods
  public static byte parseByte(String s);
  public static byte parseByte(String s, int radix);

  // Constructors
  public Byte(byte value);

  // Methods
  public byte byteValue();
  public boolean equals(Object obj);
  public int hashCode();
  public String toString();
}
```

Class java.lang.Character

```
public final class Character
    extends java.lang.Object {
  // Constants
  public static final int MAX_RADIX;
  public static final char MAX_VALUE;
  public static final int MIN_RADIX;
  public static final char MIN_VALUE;

  // Static methods
  public static int digit(char ch, int radix);
  public static boolean isDigit(char ch);
  public static boolean isLowerCase(char ch);
  public static boolean isUpperCase(char ch);
  public static char toLowerCase(char ch);
  public static char toUpperCase(char ch);

  // Constructors
  public Character(char value);
```

```
    // Methods
    public char charValue();
    public boolean equals(Object obj);
    public int hashCode();
    public String toString();
}
```

Class java.lang.Class

```
public final class Class
    extends java.lang.Object {
    // Static methods
    public static native Class forName(String className);

    // Methods
    public native String getName();
    public InputStream getResourceAsStream(String name);
    public native boolean isArray();
    public native boolean isAssignableFrom(Class cls);
    public native boolean isInstance(Object obj);
    public native boolean isInterface();
    public native Object newInstance();
    public String toString();
}
```

Class java.lang.Double

```
+ public final class Double
    extends java.lang.Object {
    // Constants
+    public static final double MAX_VALUE;
+    public static final double MIN_VALUE;
+    public static final double NEGATIVE_INFINITY;
+    public static final double NaN;
+    public static final double POSITIVE_INFINITY;

    // Static methods
+    public static native long doubleToLongBits(double value);
+    public static boolean isInfinite(double v);
+    public static boolean isNaN(double v);
+    public static native double longBitsToDouble(long bits);
+    public static double parseDouble(String s);
+    public static String toString(double d);
+    public static Double valueOf(String s);
```

```
    // Constructors
+   public Double(double value);

    // Methods
+   public byte byteValue();
+   public double doubleValue();
+   public boolean equals(Object obj);
+   public float floatValue();
+   public int hashCode();
+   public int intValue();
+   public boolean isInfinite();
+   public boolean isNaN();
+   public long longValue();
+   public short shortValue();
+   public String toString();
  }
```

Class java.lang.Float

```
+ public final class Float
      extends java.lang.Object {
    // Constants
+   public static final float MAX_VALUE;
+   public static final float MIN_VALUE;
+   public static final float NEGATIVE_INFINITY;
+   public static final float NaN;
+   public static final float POSITIVE_INFINITY;

    // Static methods
+   public static native int floatToIntBits(float value);
+   public static native float intBitsToFloat(int bits);
+   public static boolean isInfinite(float v);
+   public static boolean isNaN(float v);
+   public static float parseFloat(String s);
+   public static String toString(float f);
+   public static Float valueOf(String s);

    // Constructors
+   public Float(float value);
+   public Float(double value);
```

```
    // Methods
+   public byte byteValue();
+   public double doubleValue();
+   public boolean equals(Object obj);
+   public float floatValue();
+   public int hashCode();
+   public int intValue();
+   public boolean isInfinite();
+   public boolean isNaN();
+   public long longValue();
+   public short shortValue();
+   public String toString();
  }
```

Class java.lang.Integer

```
  public final class Integer
      extends java.lang.Object {
    // Constants
    public static final int MAX_VALUE;
    public static final int MIN_VALUE;

    // Static methods
    public static int parseInt(String s, int radix);
    public static int parseInt(String s);
    public static String toBinaryString(int i);
    public static String toHexString(int i);
    public static String toOctalString(int i);
    public static String toString(int i, int radix);
    public static String toString(int i);
    public static Integer valueOf(String s, int radix);
    public static Integer valueOf(String s);

    // Constructors
    public Integer(int value);

    // Methods
    public byte byteValue();
+   public double doubleValue();
    public boolean equals(Object obj);
+   public float floatValue();
    public int hashCode();
    public int intValue();
    public long longValue();
    public short shortValue();
    public String toString();
  }
```

Class java.lang.Long

```
public final class Long
    extends java.lang.Object {
  // Constants
  public static final long MAX_VALUE;
  public static final long MIN_VALUE;

  // Static methods
  public static long parseLong(String s, int radix);
  public static long parseLong(String s);
  public static String toString(long i, int radix);
  public static String toString(long i);

  // Constructors
  public Long(long value);

  // Methods
+ public double doubleValue();
  public boolean equals(Object obj);
+ public float floatValue();
  public int hashCode();
  public long longValue();
  public String toString();
}
```

Class java.lang.Math

```
public final class Math
    extends java.lang.Object {
  // Constants
+ public static final double E;
+ public static final double PI;


  // Static methods
  public static int abs(int a);
  public static long abs(long a);
+ public static float abs(float a);
+ public static double abs(double a);
+ public static native double ceil(double a);
+ public static native double cos(double a);
+ public static native double floor(double a);
  public static int max(int a, int b);
  public static long max(long a, long b);
+ public static float max(float a, float b);
+ public static double max(double a, double b);
  public static int min(int a, int b);
```

```
    public static long min(long a, long b);
+   public static float min(float a, float b);
+   public static double min(double a, double b);
+   public static native double sin(double a);
+   public static native double sqrt(double a);
+   public static native double tan(double a);
+   public static double toDegrees(double angrad);
+   public static double toRadians(double angdeg);
  }
```

Class java.lang.Object

```
  public class Object {
    // Constructors
    public Object();

    // Methods
    public boolean equals(Object obj);
    public final native Class getClass();
    public native int hashCode();
    public final native void notify();
    public final native void notifyAll();
    public String toString();
    public final native void wait(long timeout);
    public final void wait(long timeout, int nanos);
    public final void wait();
  }
```

Interface java.lang.Runnable

```
  public interface Runnable {
    // Methods
    public void run();
  }
```

Class java.lang.Runtime

```
  public class Runtime
      extends java.lang.Object {
    // Static methods
    public static Runtime getRuntime();

    // Methods
    public void exit(int status);
    public native long freeMemory();
    public native void gc();
    public native long totalMemory();
  }
```

Class java.lang.Short

```
public final class Short
    extends java.lang.Object {
  // Constants
  public static final short MAX_VALUE;
  public static final short MIN_VALUE;

  // Static methods
  public static short parseShort(String s);
  public static short parseShort(String s, int radix);

  // Constructors
  public Short(short value);

  // Methods
  public boolean equals(Object obj);
  public int hashCode();
  public short shortValue();
  public String toString();
}
```

Class java.lang.String

```
  public final class String
      extends java.lang.Object {
    // Static methods
    public static String valueOf(Object obj);
    public static String valueOf(char[] data);
    public static String valueOf(char[] data, int offset, int count);
    public static String valueOf(boolean b);
    public static String valueOf(char c);
    public static String valueOf(int i);
    public static String valueOf(long l);
+   public static String valueOf(float f);
+   public static String valueOf(double d);

    // Constructors
    public String();
    public String(String value);
    public String(char[] value);
    public String(char[] value, int offset, int count);
    public String(byte[] bytes, int off, int len, String enc);
    public String(byte[] bytes, String enc);
    public String(byte[] bytes, int off, int len);
    public String(byte[] bytes);
    public String(StringBuffer buffer);
```

```
   // Methods
   public native char charAt(int index);
   public int compareTo(String anotherString);
   public String concat(String str);
   public boolean endsWith(String suffix);
   public native boolean equals(Object anObject);
+  public boolean equalsIgnoreCase(String anotherString);
   public byte[] getBytes(String enc);
   public byte[] getBytes();
   public void getChars(int srcBegin, int srcEnd, char[] dst, int dstBegin);
   public int hashCode();
   public native int indexOf(int ch);
   public native int indexOf(int ch, int fromIndex);
   public int indexOf(String str);
   public int indexOf(String str, int fromIndex);
+  public native String intern();
   public int lastIndexOf(int ch);
   public int lastIndexOf(int ch, int fromIndex);
   public int length();
   public boolean regionMatches(boolean ignoreCase, int toffset,
       String other, int ooffset, int len);
   public String replace(char oldChar, char newChar);
   public boolean startsWith(String prefix, int toffset);
   public boolean startsWith(String prefix);
   public String substring(int beginIndex);
   public String substring(int beginIndex, int endIndex);
   public char[] toCharArray();
   public String toLowerCase();
   public String toString();
   public String toUpperCase();
   public String trim();
 }
```

Class java.lang.StringBuffer

```
public final class StringBuffer
    extends java.lang.Object {
    // Constructors
    public StringBuffer();
    public StringBuffer(int length);
    public StringBuffer(String str);

    // Methods
    public synchronized StringBuffer append(Object obj);
    public native synchronized StringBuffer append(String str);
    public synchronized StringBuffer append(char[] str);
    public synchronized StringBuffer append(char[] str, int offset, int len);
```

```
      public StringBuffer append(boolean b);
      public synchronized StringBuffer append(char c);
      public native StringBuffer append(int i);
      public StringBuffer append(long l);
+     public StringBuffer append(float f);
+     public StringBuffer append(double d);
      public int capacity();
      public synchronized char charAt(int index);
      public synchronized StringBuffer delete(int start, int end);
      public synchronized StringBuffer deleteCharAt(int index);
      public synchronized void ensureCapacity(int minimumCapacity);
      public synchronized void getChars(int srcBegin, int srcEnd,
          char[] dst, int dstBegin);
      public synchronized StringBuffer insert(int offset, Object obj);
      public synchronized StringBuffer insert(int offset, String str);
      public synchronized StringBuffer insert(int offset, char[] str);
      public StringBuffer insert(int offset, boolean b);
      public synchronized StringBuffer insert(int offset, char c);
      public StringBuffer insert(int offset, int i);
      public StringBuffer insert(int offset, long l);
+     public StringBuffer insert(int offset, float f);
+     public StringBuffer insert(int offset, double d);
      public int length();
      public synchronized StringBuffer reverse();
      public synchronized void setCharAt(int index, char ch);
      public synchronized void setLength(int newLength);
      public native String toString();
  }
```

Class java.lang.System

```
  public final class System
      extends java.lang.Object {
    // Constants
    public static final PrintStream err;
    public static final PrintStream out;

    // Static methods
    public static native void arraycopy(Object src, int src_position,
        Object dst, int dst_position, int length);
    public static native long currentTimeMillis();
    public static void exit(int status);
    public static void gc();
    public static String getProperty(String key);
    public static native int identityHashCode(Object x);
  }
```

Class java.lang.Thread

```
public class Thread
    extends java.lang.Object
    implements Runnable {
  // Constants
  public static final int MAX_PRIORITY;
  public static final int MIN_PRIORITY;
  public static final int NORM_PRIORITY;

  // Static methods
  public static native int activeCount();
  public static native Thread currentThread();
  public static native void sleep(long millis);
  public static native void yield();

  // Constructors
  public Thread();
+ public Thread(String name);
  public Thread(Runnable target);
+ public Thread(Runnable target, String name);

  // Methods
+ public final String getName();
  public final int getPriority();
+ public void interrupt();
  public final native boolean isAlive();
  public final void join();
  public void run();
  public final void setPriority(int newPriority);
  public native synchronized void start();
  public String toString();
}
```

Class java.lang.Throwable

```
public class Throwable
    extends java.lang.Object {
  // Constructors
  public Throwable();
  public Throwable(String message);

  // Methods
  public String getMessage();
  public void printStackTrace();
  public String toString();
}
```

Package java.lang.ref

Class java.lang.ref.Reference

```
+ public abstract class Reference
      extends java.lang.Object {
    // Methods
+    public void clear();
+    public Object get();
  }
```

Class java.lang.ref.WeakReference

```
+ public class WeakReference
      extends java.lang.ref.Reference {
    // Constructors
+    public WeakReference(Object ref);
  }
```

Package java.util

Class java.util.Calendar

```
  public abstract class Calendar
      extends java.lang.Object {
    // Constants
    public static final int AM;
    public static final int AM_PM;
    public static final int APRIL;
    public static final int AUGUST;
    public static final int DATE;
    public static final int DAY_OF_MONTH;
    public static final int DAY_OF_WEEK;
    public static final int DECEMBER;
    public static final int FEBRUARY;
    public static final int FRIDAY;
    public static final int HOUR;
    public static final int HOUR_OF_DAY;
    public static final int JANUARY;
    public static final int JULY;
    public static final int JUNE;
    public static final int MARCH;
    public static final int MAY;
```

```
    public static final int MILLISECOND;
    public static final int MINUTE;
    public static final int MONDAY;
    public static final int MONTH;
    public static final int NOVEMBER;
    public static final int OCTOBER;
    public static final int PM;
    public static final int SATURDAY;
    public static final int SECOND;
    public static final int SEPTEMBER;
    public static final int SUNDAY;
    public static final int THURSDAY;
    public static final int TUESDAY;
    public static final int WEDNESDAY;
    public static final int YEAR;

    // Static methods
    public static synchronized Calendar getInstance();
    public static synchronized Calendar getInstance(TimeZone zone);

    // Constructors
    protected Calendar();

    // Methods
    public boolean after(Object when);
    public boolean before(Object when);
+   protected abstract void computeFields();
+   protected abstract void computeTime();
    public boolean equals(Object obj);
    public final int get(int field);
    public final Date getTime();
    protected long getTimeInMillis();
    public TimeZone getTimeZone();
    public final void set(int field, int value);
    public final void setTime(Date date);
    protected void setTimeInMillis(long millis);
    public void setTimeZone(TimeZone value);
  }
```

Class java.util.Date

```
  public class Date
      extends java.lang.Object {
    // Constructors
    public Date();
    public Date(long date);
```

```
  // Methods
  public boolean equals(Object obj);
  public long getTime();
  public int hashCode();
  public void setTime(long time);
}
```

Interface java.util.Enumeration

```
public interface Enumeration {
  // Methods
  public boolean hasMoreElements();
  public Object nextElement();
}
```

Class java.util.Hashtable

```
public class Hashtable
    extends java.lang.Object {
  // Constructors
  public Hashtable(int initialCapacity);
  public Hashtable();

  // Methods
  public synchronized void clear();
  public synchronized boolean contains(Object value);
  public synchronized boolean containsKey(Object key);
  public synchronized Enumeration elements();
  public synchronized Object get(Object key);
  public boolean isEmpty();
  public synchronized Enumeration keys();
  public synchronized Object put(Object key, Object value);

  protected void rehash();
  public synchronized Object remove(Object key);
  public int size();
  public synchronized String toString();
}
```

Class java.util.Random

```
public class Random
    extends java.lang.Object {
  // Constructors
  public Random();
  public Random(long seed);
```

```
    // Methods
    protected synchronized int next(int bits);
+   public double nextDouble();
+   public float nextFloat();
    public int nextInt();
+   public int nextInt(int n);
    public long nextLong();
    public synchronized void setSeed(long seed);
}
```

Class java.util.Stack

```
public class Stack
    extends java.util.Vector {
    // Constructors
    public Stack();

    // Methods
    public boolean empty();
    public synchronized Object peek();
    public synchronized Object pop();
    public Object push(Object item);
    public synchronized int search(Object o);
}
```

Class java.util.Timer

```
public class Timer
    extends java.lang.Object {
    // Constructors
    public Timer();

    // Methods
    public void cancel();
    public void schedule(TimerTask task, long delay);
    public void schedule(TimerTask task, Date time);
    public void schedule(TimerTask task, long delay, long period);
    public void schedule(TimerTask task, Date firstTime, long period);
    public void scheduleAtFixedRate(TimerTask task, long delay, long period);
    public void scheduleAtFixedRate(TimerTask task, Date firstTime,
        long period);
}
```

Class java.util.TimerTask

```
public abstract class TimerTask
    extends java.lang.Object
    implements Runnable {
  // Constructors
  protected TimerTask();

  // Methods
  public boolean cancel();
  public abstract void run();
  public long scheduledExecutionTime();
}
```

Class java.util.TimeZone

```
public abstract class TimeZone
    extends java.lang.Object {
  // Static methods
  public static String getAvailableIDs();
  public static synchronized TimeZone getDefault();
  public static synchronized TimeZone getTimeZone(String ID);

  // Constructors
  public TimeZone();

  // Methods
  public String getID();
  public abstract int getOffset(int era, int year, int month,
      int day, int dayOfWeek, int millis);
  public abstract int getRawOffset();
  public abstract boolean useDaylightTime();
}
```

Class java.util.Vector

```
public class Vector
    extends java.lang.Object {
  // Constructors
  public Vector(int initialCapacity, int capacityIncrement);
  public Vector(int initialCapacity);
  public Vector();
```

```
  // Methods
  public synchronized void addElement(Object obj);
  public int capacity();
  public boolean contains(Object elem);
  public synchronized void copyInto(Object[] anArray);
  public synchronized Object elementAt(int index);
  public synchronized Enumeration elements();
  public synchronized void ensureCapacity(int minCapacity);
  public synchronized Object firstElement();
  public int indexOf(Object elem);
  public synchronized int indexOf(Object elem, int index);
  public synchronized void insertElementAt(Object obj, int index);
  public boolean isEmpty();
  public synchronized Object lastElement();
  public int lastIndexOf(Object elem);
  public synchronized int lastIndexOf(Object elem, int index);
  public synchronized void removeAllElements();
  public synchronized boolean removeElement(Object obj);
  public synchronized void removeElementAt(int index);
  public synchronized void setElementAt(Object obj, int index);
  public synchronized void setSize(int newSize);
  public int size();
  public synchronized String toString();
  public synchronized void trimToSize();
}
```

Package javax.microedition.io

Interface javax.microedition.io.CommConnection

```
public interface CommConnection
     implements StreamConnection {
   // Methods
  public int getBaudRate();
  public int setBaudRate(int baudrate);
}
```

Class javax.microedition.io.Connector

```
public class Connector
     extends java.lang.Object {
   // Constants
   public static final int READ;
   public static final int READ_WRITE;
   public static final int WRITE;
```

```
  // Static methods
  public static Connection open(String name);
  public static Connection open(String name, int mode);
  public static Connection open(String name, int mode, boolean timeouts);
  public static DataInputStream openDataInputStream(String name);
  public static DataOutputStream openDataOutputStream(String name);
  public static InputStream openInputStream(String name);
  public static OutputStream openOutputStream(String name);
}
```

Interface javax.microedition.io.Connection

```
public interface Connection {
  // Methods
  public void close();
}
```

Interface javax.microedition.io.ContentConnection

```
public interface ContentConnection
    implements StreamConnection {
  // Methods
  public String getEncoding();
  public long getLength();
  public String getType();
}
```

Interface javax.microedition.io.Datagram

```
public interface Datagram
    implements DataInput, DataOutput {
  // Methods
  public String getAddress();
  public byte[] getData();
  public int getLength();
  public int getOffset();
  public void reset();
  public void setAddress(String addr);
  public void setAddress(Datagram reference);
  public void setData(byte[] buffer, int offset, int len);
  public void setLength(int len);
}
```

Interface javax.microedition.io.DatagramConnection

```
public interface DatagramConnection
    implements Connection {
```

```
    // Methods
    public int getMaximumLength();
    public int getNominalLength();
    public Datagram newDatagram(int size);
    public Datagram newDatagram(int size, String addr);
    public Datagram newDatagram(byte[] buf, int size);
    public Datagram newDatagram(byte[] buf, int size, String addr);
    public void receive(Datagram dgram);
    public void send(Datagram dgram);
}
```

Interface javax.microedition.io.HttpConnection

```
public interface HttpConnection
    implements ContentConnection {
    // Constants
    public static final String GET;
    public static final String HEAD;
    public static final int HTTP_ACCEPTED;
    public static final int HTTP_BAD_GATEWAY;
    public static final int HTTP_BAD_METHOD;
    public static final int HTTP_BAD_REQUEST;
    public static final int HTTP_CLIENT_TIMEOUT;
    public static final int HTTP_CONFLICT;
    public static final int HTTP_CREATED;
    public static final int HTTP_ENTITY_TOO_LARGE;
    public static final int HTTP_EXPECT_FAILED;
    public static final int HTTP_FORBIDDEN;
    public static final int HTTP_GATEWAY_TIMEOUT;
    public static final int HTTP_GONE;
    public static final int HTTP_INTERNAL_ERROR;
    public static final int HTTP_LENGTH_REQUIRED;
    public static final int HTTP_MOVED_PERM;
    public static final int HTTP_MOVED_TEMP;
    public static final int HTTP_MULT_CHOICE;
    public static final int HTTP_NOT_ACCEPTABLE;
    public static final int HTTP_NOT_AUTHORITATIVE;
    public static final int HTTP_NOT_FOUND;
    public static final int HTTP_NOT_IMPLEMENTED;
    public static final int HTTP_NOT_MODIFIED;
    public static final int HTTP_NO_CONTENT;
    public static final int HTTP_OK;
    public static final int HTTP_PARTIAL;
    public static final int HTTP_PAYMENT_REQUIRED;
    public static final int HTTP_PRECON_FAILED;
    public static final int HTTP_PROXY_AUTH;
    public static final int HTTP_REQ_TOO_LONG;
```

```
public static final int HTTP_RESET;
public static final int HTTP_SEE_OTHER;
public static final int HTTP_TEMP_REDIRECT;
public static final int HTTP_UNAUTHORIZED;
public static final int HTTP_UNAVAILABLE;
public static final int HTTP_UNSUPPORTED_RANGE;
public static final int HTTP_UNSUPPORTED_TYPE;
public static final int HTTP_USE_PROXY;
public static final int HTTP_VERSION;
public static final String POST;

// Methods
public long getDate();
public long getExpiration();
public String getFile();
public String getHeaderField(String name);
public String getHeaderField(int n);
public long getHeaderFieldDate(String name, long def);
public int getHeaderFieldInt(String name, int def);
public String getHeaderFieldKey(int n);
public String getHost();
public long getLastModified();
public int getPort();
public String getProtocol();
public String getQuery();
public String getRef();
public String getRequestMethod();
public String getRequestProperty(String key);
public int getResponseCode();
public String getResponseMessage();
public String getURL();
public void setRequestMethod(String method);
public void setRequestProperty(String key, String value);
}
```

Interface javax.microedition.io.HttpsConnection

```
public interface HttpsConnection
    implements HttpConnection {
  // Methods
 public int getPort();
 public SecurityInfo getSecurityInfo();
 }
```

Interface javax.microedition.io.InputConnection

```
public interface InputConnection
    implements Connection {
  // Methods
  public DataInputStream openDataInputStream();
  public InputStream openInputStream();
}
```

Interface javax.microedition.io.OutputConnection

```
public interface OutputConnection
    implements Connection {
  // Methods
  public DataOutputStream openDataOutputStream();
  public OutputStream openOutputStream();
}
```

Class javax.microedition.io.PushRegistry

```
public class PushRegistry
    extends java.lang.Object {
  // Static methods
  public static String getFilter(String connection);
  public static String getMIDlet(String connection);
  public static String listConnections(boolean available);
  public static long registerAlarm(String midlet, long time);
  public static void registerConnection(String connection,
      String midlet, String filter);
  public static boolean unregisterConnection(String connection);
}
```

Interface javax.microedition.io.SecureConnection

```
public interface SecureConnection
    implements SocketConnection {
  // Methods
  public SecurityInfo getSecurityInfo();
}
```

Interface javax.microedition.io.SecurityInfo

```
public interface SecurityInfo {
    // Methods
  public String getCipherSuite();
  public String getProtocolName();
  public String getProtocolVersion();
  public Certificate getServerCertificate();
}
```

Interface javax.microedition.io.ServerSocketConnection

```
public interface ServerSocketConnection
      implements StreamConnectionNotifier {
    // Methods
  public String getLocalAddress();
  public int getLocalPort();
}
```

Interface javax.microedition.io.SocketConnection

```
public interface SocketConnection
      implements StreamConnection {
    // Constants
  public static final byte DELAY;
  public static final byte KEEPALIVE;
  public static final byte LINGER;
  public static final byte RCVBUF;
  public static final byte SNDBUF;

    // Methods
  public String getAddress();
  public String getLocalAddress();
  public int getLocalPort();
  public int getPort();
  public int getSocketOption(byte option);
  public void setSocketOption(byte option, int value);
}
```

Interface javax.microedition.io.StreamConnection

```
public interface StreamConnection
      implements InputConnection, OutputConnection {
}
```

Interface javax.microedition.io.StreamConnectionNotifier

```
public interface StreamConnectionNotifier
    implements Connection {
  // Methods
  public StreamConnection acceptAndOpen();
}
```

Interface javax.microedition.io.UDPDatagramConnection

```
public interface UDPDatagramConnection
    implements DatagramConnection {
  // Methods
  public String getLocalAddress();
  public int getLocalPort();
}
```

Package javax.microedition.lcdui

Class javax.microedition.lcdui.Alert

```
public class Alert
    extends javax.microedition.lcdui.Screen {
  // Constants
  public static final Command DISMISS_COMMAND;
  public static final int FOREVER;

  // Constructors
  public Alert(String title);
  public Alert(String title, String alertText, Image alertImage,
      AlertType alertType);


  // Methods
  public void addCommand(Command cmd);
  public int getDefaultTimeout();
  public Image getImage();
  public Gauge getIndicator();
  public String getString();
  public int getTimeout();
  public AlertType getType();
  public void removeCommand(Command cmd);
```

```
    public void setCommandListener(CommandListener l);
    public void setImage(Image img);
    public void setIndicator(Gauge indicator);
    public void setString(String str);
    public void setTimeout(int time);
    public void setType(AlertType type);
}
```

Class javax.microedition.lcdui.AlertType

```
public class AlertType
    extends java.lang.Object {
    // Constants
    public static final AlertType ALARM;
    public static final AlertType CONFIRMATION;
    public static final AlertType ERROR;
    public static final AlertType INFO;
    public static final AlertType WARNING;

    // Constructors
    protected AlertType();

    // Methods
    public boolean playSound(Display display);
}
```

Class javax.microedition.lcdui.Canvas

```
public abstract class Canvas
    extends javax.microedition.lcdui.Displayable {
    // Constants
    public static final int DOWN;
    public static final int FIRE;
    public static final int GAME_A;
    public static final int GAME_B;
    public static final int GAME_C;
    public static final int GAME_D;
    public static final int KEY_NUM0;
    public static final int KEY_NUM1;
    public static final int KEY_NUM2;
    public static final int KEY_NUM3;
    public static final int KEY_NUM4;
    public static final int KEY_NUM5;
    public static final int KEY_NUM6;
    public static final int KEY_NUM7;
    public static final int KEY_NUM8;
    public static final int KEY_NUM9;
```

```
    public static final int KEY_POUND;
    public static final int KEY_STAR;
    public static final int LEFT;
    public static final int RIGHT;
    public static final int UP;

    // Constructors
    protected Canvas();

    // Methods
    public int getGameAction(int keyCode);

    public int getKeyCode(int gameAction);
    public String getKeyName(int keyCode);

    public boolean hasPointerEvents();
    public boolean hasPointerMotionEvents();
    public boolean hasRepeatEvents();
    protected void hideNotify();
    public boolean isDoubleBuffered();
    protected void keyPressed(int keyCode);
    protected void keyReleased(int keyCode);
    protected void keyRepeated(int keyCode);
    protected abstract void paint(Graphics g);
    protected void pointerDragged(int x, int y);
    protected void pointerPressed(int x, int y);
    protected void pointerReleased(int x, int y);
    public final void repaint(int x, int y, int width, int height);
    public final void repaint();
    public final void serviceRepaints();
    public void setFullScreenMode(boolean mode);
    protected void showNotify();
    protected void sizeChanged(int w, int h);
}
```

Interface javax.microedition.lcdui.Choice

```
public interface Choice {
    // Constants
    public static final int EXCLUSIVE;
    public static final int IMPLICIT;
    public static final int MULTIPLE;
    public static final int POPUP;
    public static final int TEXT_WRAP_DEFAULT;
    public static final int TEXT_WRAP_OFF;
    public static final int TEXT_WRAP_ON;
```

```
    // Methods
    public int append(String stringPart, Image imagePart);
    public void delete(int elementNum);
    public void deleteAll();
    public int getFitPolicy();
    public Font getFont(int elementNum);
    public Image getImage(int elementNum);
    public int getSelectedFlags(boolean[] selectedArray_return);
    public int getSelectedIndex();
    public String getString(int elementNum);
    public void insert(int elementNum, String stringPart, Image imagePart);
    public boolean isSelected(int elementNum);
    public void set(int elementNum, String stringPart, Image imagePart);
    public void setFitPolicy(int fitPolicy);
    public void setFont(int elementNum, Font font);
    public void setSelectedFlags(boolean[] selectedArray);
    public void setSelectedIndex(int elementNum, boolean selected);
    public int size();
}
```

Class javax.microedition.lcdui.ChoiceGroup

```
public class ChoiceGroup
    extends javax.microedition.lcdui.Item
    implements Choice {
    // Constructors
    public ChoiceGroup(String label, int choiceType);
    public ChoiceGroup(String label, int choiceType,
        String[] stringElements, Image[] imageElements);

    // Methods
    public int append(String stringPart, Image imagePart);
    public void delete(int elementNum);
    public void deleteAll();
    public int getFitPolicy();
    public Font getFont(int elementNum);
    public Image getImage(int elementNum);
    public int getSelectedFlags(boolean[] selectedArray_return);
    public int getSelectedIndex();
    public String getString(int elementNum);
    public void insert(int elementNum, String stringPart, Image imagePart);
    public boolean isSelected(int elementNum);
    public void set(int elementNum, String stringPart, Image imagePart);
    public void setFitPolicy(int fitPolicy);
    public void setFont(int elementNum, Font font);
    public void setSelectedFlags(boolean[] selectedArray);
    public void setSelectedIndex(int elementNum, boolean selected);
    public int size();
}
```

Class javax.microedition.lcdui.Command

```
public class Command
    extends java.lang.Object {
  // Constants
  public static final int BACK;
  public static final int CANCEL;
  public static final int EXIT;
  public static final int HELP;
  public static final int ITEM;
  public static final int OK;
  public static final int SCREEN;
  public static final int STOP;

  // Constructors
  public Command(String label, int commandType, int priority);
  public Command(String shortLabel, String longLabel,
      int commandType, int priority);

  // Methods
  public int getCommandType();
  public String getLabel();
  public String getLongLabel();
  public int getPriority();
}
```

Interface javax.microedition.lcdui.CommandListener

```
public interface CommandListener {
  // Methods
  public void commandAction(Command c, Displayable d);
}
```

Class javax.microedition.lcdui.CustomItem

```
public abstract class CustomItem
    extends javax.microedition.lcdui.Item {
  // Constants
  protected static final int KEY_PRESS;
  protected static final int KEY_RELEASE;
  protected static final int KEY_REPEAT;
  protected static final int NONE;
  protected static final int POINTER_DRAG;
  protected static final int POINTER_PRESS;
  protected static final int POINTER_RELEASE;
  protected static final int TRAVERSE_HORIZONTAL;
  protected static final int TRAVERSE_VERTICAL;
```

```
  // Constructors
  protected CustomItem(String label);

  // Methods
  public int getGameAction(int keyCode);
  protected final int getInteractionModes();
  protected abstract int getMinContentHeight();
  protected abstract int getMinContentWidth();
  protected abstract int getPrefContentHeight(int width);
  protected abstract int getPrefContentWidth(int height);
  protected void hideNotify();
  protected final void invalidate();
  protected void keyPressed(int keyCode);
  protected void keyReleased(int keyCode);
  protected void keyRepeated(int keyCode);
  protected abstract void paint(Graphics g, int w, int h);
  protected void pointerDragged(int x, int y);
  protected void pointerPressed(int x, int y);
  protected void pointerReleased(int x, int y);
  protected final void repaint();
  protected final void repaint(int x, int y, int w, int h);
  protected void showNotify();
  protected void sizeChanged(int w, int h);
  protected boolean traverse(int dir, int viewportWidth, int viewportHeight,
      int[] visRect_inout);
  protected void traverseOut();
}
```

Class javax.microedition.lcdui.DateField

```
public class DateField
    extends javax.microedition.lcdui.Item {
  // Constants
  public static final int DATE;
  public static final int DATE_TIME;
  public static final int TIME;

  // Constructors
  public DateField(String label, int mode);
  public DateField(String label, int mode, TimeZone timeZone);

  // Methods
  public Date getDate();
  public int getInputMode();
  public void setDate(Date date);
  public void setInputMode(int mode);
}
```

Class javax.microedition.lcdui.Display

```
public class Display
    extends java.lang.Object {
  // Constants
 public static final int ALERT;
 public static final int CHOICE_GROUP_ELEMENT;
 public static final int COLOR_BACKGROUND;
 public static final int COLOR_BORDER;
 public static final int COLOR_FOREGROUND;
 public static final int COLOR_HIGHLIGHTED_BACKGROUND;
 public static final int COLOR_HIGHLIGHTED_BORDER;
 public static final int COLOR_HIGHLIGHTED_FOREGROUND;
 public static final int LIST_ELEMENT;


  // Static methods
 public static Display getDisplay(MIDlet m);


  // Methods
 public void callSerially(Runnable r);
 public boolean flashBacklight(int duration);
 public int getBestImageHeight(int imageType);
 public int getBestImageWidth(int imageType);
 public int getBorderStyle(boolean highlighted);
 public int getColor(int colorSpecifier);
 public Displayable getCurrent();
 public boolean isColor();
 public int numAlphaLevels();
 public int numColors();
 public void setCurrent(Displayable nextDisplayable);
 public void setCurrent(Alert alert, Displayable nextDisplayable);
 public void setCurrentItem(Item item);
 public boolean vibrate(int duration);
}
```

Class javax.microedition.lcdui.Displayable

```
public abstract class Displayable
    extends java.lang.Object {
  // Methods
  public void addCommand(Command cmd);
  public int getHeight();
  public Ticker getTicker();
  public String getTitle();
  public int getWidth();
  public boolean isShown();
  public void removeCommand(Command cmd);
```

```
    public void setCommandListener(CommandListener l);
    public void setTicker(Ticker ticker);
    public void setTitle(String s);
    protected void sizeChanged(int w, int h);
  }
```

Class javax.microedition.lcdui.Font

```
public final class Font
    extends java.lang.Object {
  // Constants
  public static final int FACE_MONOSPACE;
  public static final int FACE_PROPORTIONAL;
  public static final int FACE_SYSTEM;
  public static final int FONT_INPUT_TEXT;
  public static final int FONT_STATIC_TEXT;
  public static final int SIZE_LARGE;
  public static final int SIZE_MEDIUM;
  public static final int SIZE_SMALL;
  public static final int STYLE_BOLD;
  public static final int STYLE_ITALIC;
  public static final int STYLE_PLAIN;
  public static final int STYLE_UNDERLINED;

  // Static methods
  public static Font getDefaultFont();
  public static Font getFont(int fontSpecifier);
  public static Font getFont(int face, int style, int size);

  // Methods
  public native int charWidth(char ch);
  public native int charsWidth(char[] ch, int offset, int length);
  public int getBaselinePosition();
  public int getFace();
  public int getHeight();
  public int getSize();
  public int getStyle();
  public boolean isBold();
  public boolean isItalic();
  public boolean isPlain();
  public boolean isUnderlined();
  public native int stringWidth(String str);
  public native int substringWidth(String str, int offset, int len);
  }
```

Class javax.microedition.lcdui.Form

```
public class Form
    extends javax.microedition.lcdui.Screen {
  // Constructors
  public Form(String title);
  public Form(String title, Item[] items);

  // Methods
  public int append(Item item);
  public int append(String str);
  public int append(Image img);
  public void delete(int itemNum);
  public void deleteAll();
  public Item get(int itemNum);
  public int getHeight();
  public int getWidth();
  public void insert(int itemNum, Item item);
  public void set(int itemNum, Item item);
  public void setItemStateListener(ItemStateListener iListener);
  public int size();
}
```

Class javax.microedition.lcdui.Gauge

```
public class Gauge
    extends javax.microedition.lcdui.Item {
  // Constants
  public static final int CONTINUOUS_IDLE;
  public static final int CONTINUOUS_RUNNING;
  public static final int INCREMENTAL_IDLE;
  public static final int INCREMENTAL_UPDATING;
  public static final int INDEFINITE;

  // Constructors
  public Gauge(String label, boolean interactive, int maxValue,
      int initialValue);

  // Methods
  public void addCommand(Command cmd);
  public int getMaxValue();
  public int getValue();
  public boolean isInteractive();
  public void setDefaultCommand(Command cmd);
  public void setItemCommandListener(ItemCommandListener l);
  public void setLabel(String label);
  public void setLayout(int layout);
  public void setMaxValue(int maxValue);
```

```
  public void setPreferredSize(int width, int height);
  public void setValue(int value);
}
```

Class javax.microedition.lcdui.Graphics

```java
public class Graphics
    extends java.lang.Object {
  // Constants
  public static final int BASELINE;
  public static final int BOTTOM;
  public static final int DOTTED;
  public static final int HCENTER;
  public static final int LEFT;
  public static final int RIGHT;
  public static final int SOLID;
  public static final int TOP;
  public static final int VCENTER;

  // Methods
  public void clipRect(int x, int y, int width, int height);
  public void copyArea(int x_src, int y_src, int width, int height,
      int x_dest, int y_dest, int anchor);
  public native void drawArc(int x, int y, int width, int height,
      int startAngle, int arcAngle);
  public native void drawChar(char character, int x, int y, int anchor);
  public native void drawChars(char[] data, int offset, int length,
      int x, int y, int anchor);
  public native void drawImage(Image img, int x, int y, int anchor);
  public native void drawLine(int x1, int y1, int x2, int y2);
  public native void drawRGB(int[] rgbData, int offset, int scanlength,
      int x, int y, int width, int height, boolean processAlpha);
  public native void drawRect(int x, int y, int width, int height);
  public native void drawRegion(Image src,
      int x_src, int y_src, int width, int height, int transform,
      int x_dest, int y_dest, int anchor);
  public native void drawRoundRect(int x, int y, int width, int height,
      int arcWidth, int arcHeight);
  public native void drawString(String str, int x, int y, int anchor);
  public native void drawSubstring(String str, int offset, int len,
      int x, int y, int anchor);
  public native void fillArc(int x, int y, int width, int height,
      int startAngle, int arcAngle);
  public native void fillRect(int x, int y, int width, int height);
  public native void fillRoundRect(int x, int y, int width, int height,
      int arcWidth, int arcHeight);
  public native void fillTriangle(int x1, int y1, int x2, int y2,
      int x3, int y3);
```

```
    public int getBlueComponent();
    public int getClipHeight();
    public int getClipWidth();
    public int getClipX();
    public int getClipY();
    public int getColor();
    public native int getDisplayColor(int color);
    public Font getFont();
    public int getGrayScale();
    public int getGreenComponent();
    public int getRedComponent();
    public int getStrokeStyle();
    public int getTranslateX();
    public int getTranslateY();
    public void setClip(int x, int y, int width, int height);
    public void setColor(int red, int green, int blue);
    public void setColor(int RGB);
    public void setFont(Font font);
    public void setGrayScale(int value);
    public void setStrokeStyle(int style);
    public void translate(int x, int y);
}
```

Class javax.microedition.lcdui.Image

```
public class Image
    extends java.lang.Object {
  // Static methods
  public static Image createImage(int width, int height);
  public static Image createImage(Image source);
  public static Image createImage(String name);
  public static Image createImage(byte[] imageData, int imageOffset,
      int imageLength);
  public static Image createImage(Image image, int x, int y,
      int width, int height, int transform);
  public static Image createImage(InputStream stream);
  public static Image createRGBImage(int[] rgb,
      int width, int height, boolean processAlpha);

  // Methods
  public Graphics getGraphics();
  public int getHeight();
  public native void getRGB(int[] rgbData, int offset, int scanlength,
      int x, int y, int width, int height);
  public int getWidth();
  public boolean isMutable();
}
```

Class javax.microedition.lcdui.ImageItem

```
public class ImageItem
    extends javax.microedition.lcdui.Item {
  // Constants
  public static final int LAYOUT_CENTER;
  public static final int LAYOUT_DEFAULT;
  public static final int LAYOUT_LEFT;
  public static final int LAYOUT_NEWLINE_AFTER;
  public static final int LAYOUT_NEWLINE_BEFORE;
  public static final int LAYOUT_RIGHT;

  // Constructors
  public ImageItem(String label, Image img, int layout, String altText);
  public ImageItem(String label, Image image, int layout, String altText,
      int appearanceMode);

  // Methods
  public String getAltText();
  public int getAppearanceMode();
  public Image getImage();
  public int getLayout();
  public void setAltText(String text);
  public void setImage(Image img);
  public void setLayout(int layout);
}
```

Class javax.microedition.lcdui.Item

```
public abstract class Item
    extends java.lang.Object {
  // Constants
  public static final int BUTTON;
  public static final int HYPERLINK;
  public static final int LAYOUT_2;
  public static final int LAYOUT_BOTTOM;
  public static final int LAYOUT_CENTER;
  public static final int LAYOUT_DEFAULT;
  public static final int LAYOUT_EXPAND;
  public static final int LAYOUT_LEFT;
  public static final int LAYOUT_NEWLINE_AFTER;
  public static final int LAYOUT_NEWLINE_BEFORE;
  public static final int LAYOUT_RIGHT;
  public static final int LAYOUT_SHRINK;
  public static final int LAYOUT_TOP;
  public static final int LAYOUT_VCENTER;
```

```
public static final int LAYOUT_VEXPAND;
public static final int LAYOUT_VSHRINK;
public static final int PLAIN;

 // Methods
public void addCommand(Command cmd);
public String getLabel();
public int getLayout();
public int getMinimumHeight();
public int getMinimumWidth();
public int getPreferredHeight();
public int getPreferredWidth();
public void notifyStateChanged();
public void removeCommand(Command cmd);
public void setDefaultCommand(Command cmd);
public void setItemCommandListener(ItemCommandListener l);
public void setLabel(String label);
public void setLayout(int layout);
public void setPreferredSize(int width, int height);
}
```

Interface javax.microedition.lcdui.ItemCommandListener

```
public interface ItemCommandListener {
  // Methods
  public void commandAction(Command c, Item item);
}
```

Interface javax.microedition.lcdui.ItemStateListener

```
public interface ItemStateListener {
  // Methods
  public void itemStateChanged(Item item);
}
```

Class javax.microedition.lcdui.List

```
public class List
    extends javax.microedition.lcdui.Screen
    implements Choice {
  // Constants
  public static final Command SELECT_COMMAND;

  // Constructors
  public List(String title, int listType);
  public List(String title, int listType, String[] stringElements,
      Image[] imageElements);
```

```
    // Methods
    public int append(String stringPart, Image imagePart);
    public void delete(int elementNum);
    public void deleteAll();
    public int getFitPolicy();
    public Font getFont(int elementNum);
    public Image getImage(int elementNum);
    public int getSelectedFlags(boolean[] selectedArray_return);
    public int getSelectedIndex();
    public String getString(int elementNum);
    public void insert(int elementNum, String stringPart, Image imagePart);
    public boolean isSelected(int elementNum);
    public void removeCommand(Command cmd);
    public void set(int elementNum, String stringPart, Image imagePart);
    public void setFitPolicy(int fitPolicy);
    public void setFont(int elementNum, Font font);
    public void setSelectCommand(Command command);
    public void setSelectedFlags(boolean[] selectedArray);
    public void setSelectedIndex(int elementNum, boolean selected);
    public void setTicker(Ticker ticker);
    public void setTitle(String s);
    public int size();
}
```

Class javax.microedition.lcdui.Screen

```
public abstract class Screen
    extends javax.microedition.lcdui.Displayable {
  // Methods
}
```

Class javax.microedition.lcdui.Spacer

```
public class Spacer
    extends javax.microedition.lcdui.Item {
  // Constructors
  public Spacer(int minWidth, int minHeight);

  // Methods
  public void addCommand(Command cmd);
  public void setDefaultCommand(Command cmd);
  public void setLabel(String label);
  public void setMinimumSize(int minWidth, int minHeight);
}
```

Class javax.microedition.lcdui.StringItem

```
public class StringItem
    extends javax.microedition.lcdui.Item {
  // Constructors
  public StringItem(String label, String text);
  public StringItem(String label, String text, int appearanceMode);

  // Methods
  public int getAppearanceMode();
  public Font getFont();
  public String getText();
  public void setFont(Font font);
  public void setPreferredSize(int width, int height);
  public void setText(String text);
}
```

Class javax.microedition.lcdui.TextBox

```
public class TextBox
    extends javax.microedition.lcdui.Screen {
  // Constructors
  public TextBox(String title, String text, int maxSize, int constraints);

  // Methods
  public void delete(int offset, int length);
  public int getCaretPosition();
  public int getChars(char[] data);
  public int getConstraints();
  public int getMaxSize();
  public String getString();
  public void insert(String src, int position);
  public void insert(char[] data, int offset, int length, int position);
  public void setChars(char[] data, int offset, int length);
  public void setConstraints(int constraints);
  public void setInitialInputMode(String characterSubset);
  public int setMaxSize(int maxSize);
  public void setString(String text);
  public void setTicker(Ticker ticker);
  public void setTitle(String s);
  public int size();
}
```

Class javax.microedition.lcdui.TextField

```
public class TextField
    extends javax.microedition.lcdui.Item {
  // Constants
  public static final int ANY;
  public static final int CONSTRAINT_MASK;
  public static final int DECIMAL;
  public static final int EMAILADDR;
  public static final int INITIAL_CAPS_SENTENCE;
  public static final int INITIAL_CAPS_WORD;
  public static final int NON_PREDICTIVE;
  public static final int NUMERIC;
  public static final int PASSWORD;
  public static final int PHONENUMBER;
  public static final int SENSITIVE;
  public static final int UNEDITABLE;
  public static final int URL;

  // Constructors
  public TextField(String label, String text, int maxSize, int constraints);

  // Methods
  public void delete(int offset, int length);
  public int getCaretPosition();
  public int getChars(char[] data);
  public int getConstraints();
  public int getMaxSize();
  public String getString();
  public void insert(String src, int position);
  public void insert(char[] data, int offset, int length, int position);
  public void setChars(char[] data, int offset, int length);
  public void setConstraints(int constraints);
  public void setInitialInputMode(String characterSubset);
  public int setMaxSize(int maxSize);
  public void setString(String text);
  public int size();
}
```

Class javax.microedition.lcdui.Ticker

```
public class Ticker
    extends java.lang.Object {
  // Constructors
  public Ticker(String str);
```

```
  // Methods
  public String getString();
  public void setString(String str);
}
```

Package javax.microedition.lcdui.game

Class javax.microedition.lcdui.game.GameCanvas

```
public abstract class GameCanvas
    extends javax.microedition.lcdui.Canvas {
  // Constants
  public static final int DOWN_PRESSED;
  public static final int FIRE_PRESSED;
  public static final int GAME_A_PRESSED;
  public static final int GAME_B_PRESSED;
  public static final int GAME_C_PRESSED;
  public static final int GAME_D_PRESSED;
  public static final int LEFT_PRESSED;
  public static final int RIGHT_PRESSED;
  public static final int UP_PRESSED;

  // Constructors
  protected GameCanvas(boolean suppressKeyEvents);

  // Methods
  public void flushGraphics(int x, int y, int width, int height);
  public void flushGraphics();
  protected Graphics getGraphics();
  public int getKeyStates();
  public void paint(Graphics g);
}
```

Class javax.microedition.lcdui.game.Layer

```
public abstract class Layer
    extends java.lang.Object {
  // Methods
  public final int getHeight();
  public final int getWidth();
  public final int getX();
  public final int getY();
  public final boolean isVisible();
  public void move(int dx, int dy);
```

```
    public abstract void paint(Graphics g);
    public void setPosition(int x, int y);
    public void setVisible(boolean visible);
    }
```

Class javax.microedition.lcdui.game.LayerManager

```
public class LayerManager
    extends java.lang.Object {
  // Constructors
  public LayerManager();

  // Methods
  public void append(Layer l);
  public Layer getLayerAt(int index);
  public int getSize();
  public void insert(Layer l, int index);
  public void paint(Graphics g, int x, int y);
  public void remove(Layer l);
  public void setViewWindow(int x, int y, int width, int height);
  }
```

Class javax.microedition.lcdui.game.Sprite

```
public class Sprite
    extends javax.microedition.lcdui.game.Layer {
  // Constants
  public static final int TRANS_MIRROR;
  public static final int TRANS_MIRROR_ROT180;
  public static final int TRANS_MIRROR_ROT270;
  public static final int TRANS_MIRROR_ROT90;
  public static final int TRANS_NONE;
  public static final int TRANS_ROT180;
  public static final int TRANS_ROT270;
  public static final int TRANS_ROT90;

  // Constructors
  public Sprite(Image image);
  public Sprite(Image image, int frameWidth, int frameHeight);
  public Sprite(Sprite s);
```

```
    // Methods
    public final boolean collidesWith(Sprite s, boolean pixelLevel);
    public final boolean collidesWith(TiledLayer t, boolean pixelLevel);
    public final boolean collidesWith(Image image, int x, int y,
        boolean pixelLevel);
    public void defineCollisionRectangle(int x, int y, int width, int height);
    public void defineReferencePixel(int x, int y);
    public final int getFrame();
    public int getFrameSequenceLength();
    public int getRawFrameCount();
    public int getRefPixelX();
    public int getRefPixelY();
    public void nextFrame();
    public final void paint(Graphics g);
    public void prevFrame();
    public void setFrame(int sequenceIndex);
    public void setFrameSequence(int[] sequence);
    public void setImage(Image img, int frameWidth, int frameHeight);
    public void setRefPixelPosition(int x, int y);
    public void setTransform(int transform);
}
```

Class javax.microedition.lcdui.game.TiledLayer

```
public class TiledLayer
    extends javax.microedition.lcdui.game.Layer {
  // Constructors
  public TiledLayer(int columns, int rows, Image image,
      int tileWidth, int tileHeight);

  // Methods
  public int createAnimatedTile(int staticTileIndex);
  public void fillCells(int col, int row, int numCols, int numRows,
      int tileIndex);
  public int getAnimatedTile(int animatedTileIndex);
  public int getCell(int col, int row);
  public final int getCellHeight();
  public final int getCellWidth();
  public final int getColumns();
  public final int getRows();
  public final void paint(Graphics g);
  public void setAnimatedTile(int animatedTileIndex, int staticTileIndex);
  public void setCell(int col, int row, int tileIndex);
  public void setStaticTileSet(Image image, int tileWidth, int tileHeight);
}
```

Package javax.microedition.media

Interface javax.microedition.media.Control

```
public interface Control {
  }
```

Interface javax.microedition.media.Controllable

```
 public interface Controllable {
    // Methods
   public Control getControl(String controlType);
   public Control[] getControls();
   }
```

Class javax.microedition.media.Manager

```
public final class Manager
     extends java.lang.Object {
   // Constants
   public static final String TONE_DEVICE_LOCATOR;

   // Static methods
   public static Player createPlayer(String locator);
   public static Player createPlayer(InputStream stream, String type);
   public static String getSupportedContentTypes(String protocol);
   public static String getSupportedProtocols(String content_type);
   public static void playTone(int note, int duration, int volume);
   }
```

Interface javax.microedition.media.Player

```
 public interface Player
     implements Controllable {
   // Constants
   public static final int CLOSED;
   public static final int PREFETCHED;
   public static final int REALIZED;
   public static final int STARTED;
   public static final long TIME_UNKNOWN;
   public static final int UNREALIZED;
```

```
  // Methods
  public void addPlayerListener(PlayerListener playerListener);
  public void close();
  public void deallocate();
  public String getContentType();
  public long getDuration();
  public long getMediaTime();
  public int getState();
  public void prefetch();
  public void realize();
  public void removePlayerListener(PlayerListener playerListener);
  public void setLoopCount(int count);
  public long setMediaTime(long now);
  public void start();
  public void stop();
}
```

Interface javax.microedition.media.PlayerListener

```
public interface PlayerListener {
  // Constants
  public static final String CLOSED;
  public static final String DEVICE_AVAILABLE;
  public static final String DEVICE_UNAVAILABLE;
  public static final String DURATION_UPDATED;
  public static final String END_OF_MEDIA;
  public static final String ERROR;
  public static final String STARTED;
  public static final String STOPPED;
  public static final String VOLUME_CHANGED;

  // Methods
  public void playerUpdate(Player player, String event, Object eventData);
}
```

Package javax.microedition.media.control

Interface javax.microedition.media.control.ToneControl

```
public interface ToneControl
    implements Control {
  // Constants
  public static final byte BLOCK_END;
  public static final byte BLOCK_START;
  public static final byte C4;
  public static final byte PLAY_BLOCK;
```

```
public static final byte REPEAT;
public static final byte RESOLUTION;
public static final byte SET_VOLUME;
public static final byte SILENCE;
public static final byte TEMPO;
public static final byte VERSION;

// Methods
public void setSequence(byte[] sequence);
}
```

Interface javax.microedition.media.control.VolumeControl

```
public interface VolumeControl
    implements Control {
  // Methods
  public int getLevel();
  public boolean isMuted();
  public int setLevel(int level);
  public void setMute(boolean mute);
}
```

Package javax.microedition.midlet

Class javax.microedition.midlet.MIDlet

```
public abstract class MIDlet
    extends java.lang.Object {
  // Constructors
  protected MIDlet();

  // Methods
  public final int checkPermission(String permission);
  protected abstract void destroyApp(boolean unconditional);
  public final String getAppProperty(String key);
  public final void notifyDestroyed();
  public final void notifyPaused();
  protected abstract void pauseApp();
  public final boolean platformRequest(String URL);
  public final void resumeRequest();
  protected abstract void startApp();
}
```

Package javax.microedition.pki

```
public interface Certificate {
    // Methods
  public String getIssuer();
  public long getNotAfter();
  public long getNotBefore();
  public String getSerialNumber();
  public String getSigAlgName();
  public String getSubject();
  public String getType();
  public String getVersion();
  }
```

Package javax.microedition.rms

Interface javax.microedition.rms.RecordComparator

```
public interface RecordComparator {
    // Constants
  public static final int EQUIVALENT;
  public static final int FOLLOWS;
  public static final int PRECEDES;

    // Methods
  public int compare(byte[] rec1, byte[] rec2);
  }
```

Interface javax.microedition.rms.RecordEnumeration

```
public interface RecordEnumeration {
    // Methods
  public void destroy();
  public boolean hasNextElement();
  public boolean hasPreviousElement();
  public boolean isKeptUpdated();
  public void keepUpdated(boolean keepUpdated);
  public byte[] nextRecord();
  public int nextRecordId();
  public int numRecords();
  public byte[] previousRecord();
  public int previousRecordId();
  public void rebuild();
  public void reset();
  }
```

Interface javax.microedition.rms.RecordFilter

```
public interface RecordFilter {
  // Methods
  public boolean matches(byte[] candidate);
}
```

Interface javax.microedition.rms.RecordListener

```
public interface RecordListener {
  // Methods
  public void recordAdded(RecordStore recordStore, int recordId);
  public void recordChanged(RecordStore recordStore, int recordId);
  public void recordDeleted(RecordStore recordStore, int recordId);
}
```

Class javax.microedition.rms.RecordStore

```
public class RecordStore
    extends java.lang.Object {
  // Constants
public static final int AUTHMODE_ANY;
public static final int AUTHMODE_PRIVATE;

  // Static methods
  public static void deleteRecordStore(String recordStoreName);
  public static String listRecordStores();
  public static RecordStore openRecordStore(String recordStoreName,
      boolean createIfNecessary);
  public static RecordStore openRecordStore(String recordStoreName,
      boolean createIfNecessary, int authmode, boolean writable);
  public static RecordStore openRecordStore(String recordStoreName,
      String vendorName, String suiteName);


  // Methods
  public int addRecord(byte[] data, int offset, int numBytes);
  public void addRecordListener(RecordListener listener);
  public void closeRecordStore();
  public void deleteRecord(int recordId);
  public RecordEnumeration enumerateRecords(RecordFilter filter,
      RecordComparator comparator, boolean keepUpdated);
  public long getLastModified();
  public String getName();
  public int getNextRecordID();
  public int getNumRecords();
  public int getRecord(int recordId, byte[] buffer, int offset);
```

```
    public byte[] getRecord(int recordId);
    public int getRecordSize(int recordId);
    public int getSize();
    public int getSizeAvailable();
    public int getVersion();
    public void removeRecordListener(RecordListener listener);
    public void setMode(int authmode, boolean writable);
    public void setRecord(int recordId, byte[] newData, int offset,
        int numBytes);
}
```

INDEX